Dorothy Hodgkin:
A Life

Dorothy Hodgkin:
A Life

Georgina Ferry

Granta Books
London

Granta Publications, 2/3 Hanover Yard, London, N1 8BE

First published in Great Britain by Granta Books 1998

A CIP catalogue record for this book is
available from the British Library.

1 3 5 7 9 10 8 6 4 2

ISBN 1 86207 167 5

Typeset in Palatino by M Rules
Printed and bound in Great Britain by Mackays of Chatham PLC

For David, Edward and William

Contents

Preface

Dorothy Crowfoot Hodgkin is so obvious a subject for a biography that I was astonished when I discovered, soon after her death in 1994, that none had been written. As Britain's only female Nobel laureate, she holds a unique place in the history of twentieth-century science. A quintessentially English woman whose humanity recognized no national boundaries, her memory is cherished from Buffalo to Beijing, from Bucharest to Bangalore. Family, friends and colleagues are only too happy to talk about her.

But Dorothy herself was wary of 'attempts on her life', and I suspect that were she still living this book would not now be in print. It came about as a result of an article about her that I wrote for the magazine *Oxford Today*, published only weeks before her death. Soon afterwards her daughter Elizabeth Hodgkin invited me to visit, and we talked about the fragment of autobiography Dorothy had left, which Elizabeth and her niece Kate Hodgkin were trying to prepare for publication. It was clear that there was scope for a much fuller account, and without further thought I said I would be very keen to take this on.

I was enormously touched by the trust the Hodgkin family placed in me when they agreed to my suggestion. I never met Dorothy; I am not a chemist by training, and certainly not a crystallographer; this is my first book. To do justice to the woman and her science is a formidable responsibility. Given her own mixed feelings about biography – she certainly did not like the idea of a 'life' appearing in her lifetime, unless she had written it herself – I have little hope that she herself would approve the result. But knowing something of the nature of her reservations, I hope I have been able to avoid the kind of writing that caused her most grief.

She became very fed up with being treated as *the* token woman scientist in endless newspaper interviews – 'It's very boring if you always ask the same people,' she told one surprised reporter. One of the most rewarding aspects of the research for this book was the number of other women who turned up as supporting characters – many of them scientists. In a similar vein, Dorothy had a horror of the term 'role model', and so I have not used it; however, she was glad that both men and women cited her example as a factor in the progress of their own careers, and any number of them feature in these pages. She vehemently rejected any suggestion that her gender was an obstacle to her progress. For the most part her life story bears this out, and I have tried to show what factors enabled her not only to achieve, but to be recognized for her achievements, at a time when women were not generally expected to have careers.

Today, even Dorothy's greatest admirers would have to admit that her name does not resonate in the minds of the public like that of Marie Curie, or those of other Nobelists such as Albert Einstein, or James Watson and Francis Crick. One reason perhaps is that the nature of her science, X-ray crystallography, is less easily accessible, and its practical consequences less discernible, than the work of these others. She was, in the words of Lord Phillips, a former colleague, not just a scientist's scientist but 'a crystallographer's crystallographer'. The structures she chose to work on – penicillin, Vitamin B_{12}, insulin – were all medically important; but she chose them first and foremost because they were interesting scientifically, and potentially soluble with the methods at her disposal. It was the quest for exact and beautiful solutions to difficult problems that motivated Dorothy to surmount indifferent facilities, experimental setbacks, the demands of marriage and motherhood, and persistent physical pain, to become one of the greatest scientists of the century.

At the same time she wore her fame lightly. Unlike her close friend the double Nobel laureate Linus Pauling, who died just a few weeks after Dorothy in 1994, self-promotion was not part of her nature. For example, unusually for a scientist of such distinction, she never wrote a book. She never demanded, nor did she seem to expect, to be placed at the head of a grand and well-equipped laboratory. With a list of honours including the Nobel prize, the Order of Merit, the Lenin Peace Prize – and the Freedom of Beccles – she always gave her name as plain Dorothy Hodgkin, and insisted that the most junior of her colleagues call her simply Dorothy (following this precept I have done so throughout this book).

There are many reasons why Dorothy deserves to be more widely known. Her distinction as a scientist should be enough. But to it she allied an active concern for international understanding that made her travel tirelessly in the cause of world peace, and promote scientific collaborations between East and West, North and South. At the same time she cared about people as individuals and showed it in great and small ways: giving money to Third World scientists to help them travel or train, sending letters of condolence or congratulation at every opportunity, asking after the children of colleagues and remembering their names. Modern science is often presented as the preserve of the coldly ambitious and ruthlessly competitive. If Dorothy's life has anything to teach us, it is that there is an alternative approach.

My task as a biographer has been made easier by the wealth of material available concerning Dorothy's life and work – she simply never threw anything away. (In the age of telephone and e-mail, today's scientists will leave barely a trace for the biographers of tomorrow.) My first thanks are due to Luke and Elizabeth Hodgkin who have given me full access to all Dorothy's surviving correspondence. This includes the almost daily letters she wrote to her husband Thomas during the many long periods when he lived elsewhere, letters that virtually constitute a diary of her everyday concerns. In the early days of my research Luke kindly allowed me to work on the letters at Crab Mill, the house in Warwickshire where Dorothy spent her last years; when this was no longer possible he allowed me to move them to the

Bodleian Library in Oxford. For letters written during the last years of her life I am grateful to Dorothy's neighbour and former secretary Irene Sabin, who allowed me to read her notebooks.

I owe an enormous debt to the work of Peter Harper and Paul Newman of the National Cataloguing Unit for the Archives of Contemporary Scientists at the University of Bath, who archived and catalogued Dorothy's scientific correspondence and other papers while she was still living. The archive now rests in Oxford University's Bodleian Library, where I have been grateful for the assistance of Stephen Tomlinson, and of Colin Harris and the staff in the Modern Papers Reading Room. Other institutions that have provided access to archives or photocopies include Oxford University, Somerville College, Lady Margaret Hall, Cambridge University Library, the Royal Society, the Royal Society of Chemistry, the Sir John Leman School in Beccles, the Rockefeller Archive Center in Tarrytown, New York, the Sophia Smith Collection at Smith College, Massachusetts, the National Archives and Records Administration at College Park, Maryland, and the Kerr Library, Oregon State University.

An invaluable reference was the collection of all Dorothy's scientific papers and lectures in three volumes, which also include historical articles by some of her closest colleagues. This massive task was the work of Guy Dodson, Jenny Glusker, Sivaraj Ramaseshan and K. Venkatesan, and it was published by the Indian Institute of Sciences in 1994. To have these volumes always at my elbow when I needed to check a fact or a date has saved me endless trips to the library.

Finally, the memories of those who knew Dorothy provide the colour and personal detail often missing from the written record. I should like to record my thanks to the following, all of whom it was a pleasure to talk to or correspond with: Sir Edward Abraham, Margaret Adams, Jean Banister, Frank Barnaby, the late Sir Isaiah Berlin, Bi Ruchang, Sir Tom Blundell, David Blow, Derek Bryan and the late Liao Hongying, Sir Julian Bullard, Sir Bryan Cartledge, Chang Wenrui, Sir Durward Cruickshank, John and Rita Cornforth, Barbara Craig, Elisabeth Crowfoot, John and Sue Cutfield, the late Lord Dainton, Nesta Dean, Guy and Eleanor Dodson, Dong Yicheng, Jack Dunitz, Fan Haifu, Mike Glazer, Jenny Glusker, Gu Xiaocheng, Maggi Hambling, Marjorie

Harding, Pauline Harrison, Mercy and Norman Heatley, Ruth van Heyningen, Christopher Hill, Edward Hodgkin, Elizabeth Hodgkin, Luke Hodgkin, Judith Howard, Louise Johnson, Olga Kennard, Sir Aaron Klug, Galen Lenhert, Liang Dongcai, Lin Zhengjiong, Barbara Low, Maureen Mackay, Jean Lady Medawar, Helen Megaw, the late Elisabeth Murray, Joan Payne, Max Perutz, Lord Phillips of Ellesmere, Flora Philpot, the late N. W. Pirie, Keith Prout, Sivaraj Ramaseshan, Sir Rex and Elsa Richards, John Robertson, Joseph Rotblat, Diana Rowley, Irene Sabin, Sir Fred Sanger, David and Anne Sayre, Tang Youqi, Baroness Thatcher, Ling Thompson, Ken and Jeannie Trueblood, Joan Turville-Petre, K. Venkatesan, M. Vijayan and Kalyani, M. A. Viswamitra, Wang Dachen, Bob Williams, Terry Willis, Wu Lingan.

I am particularly grateful to the Alfred P. Sloan Foundation whose generous grant enabled me to visit former colleagues of Dorothy's in Bangalore and Beijing. In both places I was overwhelmed by the warm hospitality of my hosts, Sivaraj Ramaseshan and his colleagues at the Raman Research Institute and the Indian Institute of Science in Bangalore, Tang Youqi at Beijing University, and Liang Doncai and his colleagues at the Institute of Biophysics in Beijing.

Finally I should like to thank Dorothy's son and daughter Luke and Elizabeth Hodgkin, her sisters Elisabeth Crowfoot, Joan Payne and Diana Rowley, her brother-in-law Edward Hodgkin and her colleagues Margaret Adams, Tom Blundell, Guy and Eleanor Dodson, Jenny Glusker, Barbara Low, David Phillips, Max Perutz and Ken Trueblood for reading sections of the manuscript in draft. The faults that remain are entirely my own responsibility.

Georgina Ferry
May 1998

1

'It was a rather rackety childhood in a way'

Cairo and Norfolk,
1910–1928

The house had four attics. The smallest one, at the back, was her private laboratory. It had a sloping roof, one small window, and a wooden cupboard in the corner which housed her collections – pieces of pot from her father's excavations, flints from the Sussex Downs, birds' eggs and fir cones. On the table stood a rack of test-tubes and other items of chemical hardware. There were bottles of crystals, powders and solutions for her experiments. Holding her breath, she turned the piece of platinum wire in the flame from the little spirit lamp, while a coloured bead gradually formed at its tip. Three little girls looked on in wonder, their eyes shining in the light of the lamp. She was eleven years old.

Dorothy Mary Crowfoot had begun her scientific career in a small private class for the children of parents of modest means and independent views. Miss Charlotte Mason of Ambleside had set up the Parents' National Educational Union (PNEU – motto: 'I am, I can, I ought, I will') as an alternative to the schools provided by local authorities. It trained young women as governesses to teach a set syllabus to groups of children up to the age of twelve years, often in rented rooms or private homes. The syllabus included one-term courses in physics and chemistry at a time when 'nature study' was the limit of most elementary teachers' scientific competence. At ten years old, Dorothy Crowfoot briefly attended a small class in the Rectory at Beccles, in Suffolk, taught by a Miss Fletcher who had been trained by the PNEU. Crucially, she was there for the term in which the class turned its attention to chemistry.

The progressive educators who designed the course had grasped the importance of practical demonstrations in catching the imagination of the young. Dorothy and her fellow students made solutions of alum and copper sulphate from which to grow crystals. Over the days that followed they watched as the solutions slowly evaporated. Gradually the crystals appeared, faceted like jewels, twinkling in the light. Dorothy was enchanted. 'I was captured for life,' she later wrote, 'by chemistry and by crystals.'

The year was 1920. Although Dorothy herself identified that experience as the spark that lit the fuse of her lifelong passion for crystals, the conditions that allowed the fuse to burn were already well established. Scientific research was a far from obvious choice for a girl of her generation and background. Her parents had come from conventional, well-to-do families. Yet both valued learning and intellectual enquiry above social position or convention. The examples set by her father and especially her mother imbued Dorothy with a fervent desire to find answers to questions through systematic investigation. Her first encounter with crystals was simply a signpost that set her out on one course among many others that she could have chosen.

There are many Crowfoots in East Anglia, possibly descended from Viking invaders. More or less continuously from the eighteenth century, elder sons of Dorothy's father's family practised as doctors in Beccles, a prosperous market town a few miles from the easternmost point of England's coastline. There was also a strong clerical tradition among the younger sons. Dorothy's grandfather, John Henchman Crowfoot, born in 1841, had studied classics at Oxford University before taking holy orders and travelling to India as a missionary. There he fell ill, and returned home to recuperate. During his convalescence in 1872 he met and married Mary Bayly, and recovered sufficiently to return to his ministry. A member of the Anglo-Catholic movement, he was Rector of the country parish of Wigginton in Oxfordshire when their first child, John Winter Crowfoot, was born in 1873; two daughters, Margaret and May, followed soon afterwards. The family later moved to Lincoln when their father was invited by

Bishop Edward King to join the centre of Anglo-Catholicism at Lincoln Cathedral as a Canon, with responsibility for the theological students. Canon Crowfoot later rose to become Chancellor of the cathedral, a position he held until his retirement.

Like his father, John Winter Crowfoot studied classics at Oxford. An outstanding student at Brasenose College, he was awarded a senior Hulme Scholarship on his graduation in 1896. This enabled him to spend several months visiting Greece, Cyprus and Asia Minor (now Turkey), where he worked with the art historian Josef Strygowski on excavations of early Christian churches. Having grown up with the austere grandeur of English Gothic church architecture, he found the intricate and vibrant designs of the Byzantine mosaics a revelation. He was also captivated by the sights, sounds and peoples of the Eastern Mediterranean, steeped in the culture of the receding Ottoman Empire. On his return to England he took up a temporary post as a lecturer in classics at Birmingham University. But he soon abandoned a formal academic career for the opportunity to return to the Middle East. In 1901 he joined the British administration of Egypt, as a civil servant in the Department of Education. Egypt's government at that time had recently passed from one colonial power, the Ottoman Empire, to a British Empire then in its most expansionist phase.

Although he had chosen to follow neither of the traditional family professions, John Crowfoot had inherited a strong sense of duty and service. After only two years in Cairo he was moved to Khartoum as Assistant Director of Education in the Sudan. Britain and Egypt had collectively moved to recover control of this vast country in January 1899, following General Kitchener's annihilation of the forces of the Khalifa Abdulla al-Ta'aisha at Omdurman the previous September. The Khalifa's downfall finally brought to an end a period of civil war between the peoples of the north and south of the country that had left it exhausted and economically bankrupt. The British dominated the Anglo-Egyptian 'condominium', and established a new administrative system in the northern part of the country that quickly acquired a prestige comparable with that of the Indian Civil Service.

Crowfoot's role was to inspect schools throughout the country, from the élite Gordon College in Khartoum to small village schools that owed their existence to the commitment of local community leaders. As a result he became involved in the beginnings of a movement for girls' education in the country. A remarkable teacher called Babikr Bedri, who had already established a school for boys in his home village, petitioned the Director of Education, James Currie, for funds to start one for girls, so that his eleven school-age daughters and nieces could be educated. Currie told him he 'must be mad' and thought no more of it. Two years later Bedri found John Crowfoot more sympathetic; the new Assistant Director promised to send him the princely sum of £10 to start the school. But Currie refused to honour the promise, and told Bedri if he wanted a school for girls he would have to fund it himself. He did just that, and within a year of its foundation the school received government recognition. The Bedri family and the Crowfoots were to become lifelong friends.

Before he left England, John Crowfoot had met Grace Mary Hood (known as Molly) at a ball in Lincoln. She fell for him at once, but the attraction on his side was less immediate. Molly was born in 1877, the eldest of six children of Sinclair Hood, squire of Nettleham Hall, a modest country estate in Lincolnshire. They were a striking family, all tall and athletic; Molly herself grew to 5 feet 9 inches. She had four brothers, who were handsome and talented; the eldest, Edward, became an officer in the regular Army, Ivo took holy orders, Alban was a gifted musician like his mother and the youngest, Martin, joined the Navy. Molly and her sister Dorothy (Dolly) were educated at home, and spent a year at a finishing school in Paris improving their French, music and drawing. Molly loved country pursuits, such as riding to hounds, as well as music and dancing. Her background had prepared her to be a good wife to a country gentleman – but she wanted more than this.[1]

Her mother, Grace, was friendly with Elizabeth Wordsworth, Principal of Oxford University's first college for women students. Lady Margaret Hall had opened its doors in 1878, and Dame Elizabeth urged her friend to send Molly there. But by then Grace Hood was a widow (Sinclair Hood died in 1897), her heart was bad, and she didn' t like the idea of her elder daughter going off to Oxford. The official reason for declining the suggestion was that Molly's short-sightedness would worsen with too much reading.

The first years of the new century must have been difficult for Molly Hood, disappointed in both her romantic and her academic ambitions. But she kept in touch with John Crowfoot, and her enquiring nature led her to broaden her education through her own efforts. Her horizons were already considerably wider than Nettleham's 1000 acres and the neighbourhood beyond. The house, originally a modest stone village house, had been extended during the nineteenth century to include a massive hall to display papyri and other antiquities collected by Molly's grandfather, William Frankland Hood. Frank Hood, as he was known, had travelled in Egypt in an attempt to relieve his tuberculosis, but he died young and his father mortgaged the property to build the hall as his memorial. Although she did not immediately see archaeology as a career she might follow herself, Molly acquired a more than common interest in ancient civilizations.

After Sinclair Hood died, the family commissioned the construction of a villa on the Italian Riviera, in the resort of San Remo near the border with France. They called it the Villa Lincolnia and there, like many other English families who could afford it, they would spend the winter months to escape the chill of draughty country houses. The girls accompanied their mother on the annual migration southward, where they joined enthusiastically in the activities of the expatriate community. Molly was a keen member of the Field Club, a natural history society run by a retired colonel.

In 1906 the club visited a cave some distance from San Remo in search of the blind beetles that were supposed to live there. But on hearing that it was also reputed to contain Neolithic remains, Molly decided to investigate further. 'The journey from San Remo to Badalucco, accomplished by a local omnibus, took two hours, and the climb up from Badalucco to the cave about one and a half hours,' she later recorded. The cave itself was long and low with a narrow, bottle-neck entrance that opened out on a near-vertical slope and had to be approached from above. Molly was not in the least daunted by the difficulties it presented. With the help of a local boy, Antonio Bianchi, she dug in the floor of the cave and found collections of human bones as well as worked flints and

bone pendants, points and beads. She visited the site in subsequent years, and corresponded about her finds with leading
specialists in prehistoric culture, concluding that the cave was
probably a Neolithic burial place.[2]

Molly's summers in England were divided between Nettleham
and London, where the family regularly rented a flat. In London
she was taken up by Augusta and Louisa Strode, suffragettes and
Christian Socialists who became close friends and inspired her to
join their cause. They were at the centre of an artistic and musical
circle deeply concerned with political and social reform.

In 1906 Molly finally managed to obtain some training. She
would have liked to study medicine, but her lack of formal education and continuing parental opposition made this difficult. So
she lowered her sights and went to the Clapham School of
Midwifery in south London. A devout young woman from a
High Anglican family, she had thought of becoming a missionary,
but disliked the idea of preaching. Her qualification in midwifery
gave her another idea. In 1909, writing to John Crowfoot, she
mentions 'Lady Dufferin's Medical Mission to the Women of
India'. She had already taken a personal vow to 'be ready if
called' to some form of service, probably overseas;[3] the idea of
taking medical care to women in countries where the purdah
restrictions meant that they could not see male doctors greatly
appealed to her, and she gave the clear impression that that was
what she was thinking of doing.

Finally her patience paid off. Having been posted back to the
headquarters of the Egyptian Education Service in Cairo, John
Crowfoot wrote to propose, in typically bluff style, almost ten
years after their first meeting.

> My dear Molly
> Will you marry me? I do believe that I could make you
> happy if you would let me try, and forget a good deal that
> has passed . . . I will tell you all you want to know when
> you have answered my question.[4]

Molly accepted him by return of post, before turning to John's
mother to find out a little more about her prospective bridegroom. The reply might have made a less determined woman

have second thoughts. Mary Crowfoot began by warning in a roundabout way that her son probably did not share Molly's strong religious convictions.

> His is a rather complex nature – he doesn't take anything
> for granted in a nice easy-going way, and on many points
> where you would have no difficulty he would still say he
> 'didn't know' – but it is a reverent nature, and he will
> always respect another's beliefs . . . I do believe him to be
> really a good and true man – and he is loving and tender,
> but not very demonstrative – rather a quick temper – and a
> little extra particular about little things – but that is all to
> the good . . . You will bring him a wealth of love and a
> stedfast heart – and real helpful gifts too.[5]

John and Molly, aged thirty-six and thirty-two, were married in fine style at Nettleham by the Bishop of Lincoln in July 1909 and immediately left for Cairo together.

Dorothy Mary Crowfoot was born on 12 May 1910. Her sister Joan followed in 1912, then Elisabeth Grace (Betty) in 1914. For the first four years of Dorothy's life the family enjoyed a life typical of the many English expatriates administering outposts of empire around the world. They lived comfortably in Cairo, 'within sight of the Pyramids'; the ready availability of domestic servants meant that there was plenty of leisure time for social visits and entertainment. It was a small community of civil and military officers and their wives, and guests at dinners and parties might include Lord Kitchener himself, who became British Agent and Consul-General in Egypt in 1911 (the title by which his predecessor Lord Cromer had effectively ruled the country from 1883 to 1907). The nature of John Crowfoot's work meant that he travelled widely around the country, and he found time to extend his archaeological interests to the civilization of Ancient Egypt.

Following the conventions of the time, Molly brought an English nurse, Nelly, out from Nettleham in time for Dorothy's birth; but shortly after Joan was born she took up another offer from an Egyptian family. Walking in the public gardens and wondering what to do, Molly came upon an English girl sitting in a state of despair. Katie Stevens turned out to be a children's nurse who had arrived from England to find that there was no job for her as her prospective employer had suffered a miscarriage. Molly engaged her on the spot, and she stayed with the family for nine years.

They all returned to England for three months of each year to escape the hot, dry Egyptian summers. But this orderly pattern of life ended with the outbreak of war in 1914. Believing Britain to be safer than any overseas dependency, Molly took Katie and the three girls (Elisabeth was then only a few months old) back to England. She rented a house for them in the south coast town of Worthing, where her husband's elderly parents had moved for their retirement. She herself 'wangled a flight on an Air Force plane'[6] to Cairo, and returned to be with her husband. In 1916 he was promoted to succeed Currie as Director of Education in the Sudan, and they moved to a new home in Khartoum.

For the rest of Dorothy's childhood, she and her sisters never lived under the same roof as both their parents for more than a few months at a time, with long gaps in between. Dorothy later saw the self-reliance engendered by this separation as 'the origin of her independent spirit'. It is worth remembering, however, that for the substantial number of families who were involved in civil, military or commercial activities throughout the Empire, such family dislocations were far from unusual. John and Molly Crowfoot were not neglectful parents: duty and economic necessity kept Crowfoot in the Sudan, love and duty kept his wife with him, they felt that the children's well-being was best served by their remaining in England.

Dorothy remembered the war as 'a quiet time'. Canon Crowfoot's memory was failing; their aunts May and Margie visited with their families from time to time. When the Crowfoot children were old enough they went to a small local school; they made expeditions to the South Downs to collect flints, and spent Sundays 'playing holy games with our grandparents'. But their day-to-day care was still in the hands of Katie Stevens, a warm and devoted young woman who was well aware that she had to substitute for their absent mother as best she could. She sent regular reports on their well-being to Molly, including some anxiety about seven-year-old Dorothy's tendency to exhaust herself: 'She was trying to do too much, even in her sleep she was at school.'[7]

There were frequent trips to the beach, within earshot of the trenches across the Channel, an early memory for Elisabeth Crowfoot.

> Almost the first thing I remember hearing is Katie on the beach at Worthing saying 'Don't worry Betty, it's only the Navy practising at Portsmouth.' It didn't occur to me until years later that all along the South coast you could hear the guns in France.[8]

In the entire four years of the war, the girls saw their mother only once, when she visited England for a few weeks 'to make sure we were all right'. Molly accompanied her husband on his tours of the Sudan, visiting schools; she impressed the Sudanese with her skill as a camel rider. But for much of the time she was left to her own resources, while John undertook wartime intelligence work, for example, or returned to headquarters in Cairo. She was an accomplished botanical illustrator, and occupied herself collecting and drawing flowers; she later published her work privately as *Flowering Plants of the Northern and Central Sudan*. She also became interested in traditional weaving techniques and taught herself to use the primitive looms used by the local women to weave cotton. Liking to have children around her, she taught embroidery and botanical drawing to the daughters of her Sudanese friends in Khartoum, sending her carriage to collect them every afternoon. It was a long way, in every sense, from the carnage of the trenches that was laying waste to a generation in Europe.

But even at this distance, Molly could not escape the tragedy of war. All four of her brothers died either in action or as a result of war injuries. Edward and Ivo were killed in France. Martin was invalided home to hospital in Lincoln after an attack on his ship. Severely shell-shocked, he discharged himself and set off on foot, possibly in an attempt to reach Nettleham; he was found dead of hypothermia. Alban, the musician, was badly gassed and survived in poor health until 1921.

The loss of her beloved brothers brought the senseless waste of war into sharp focus for Molly. But she did not give herself up to despair. She later told how, sitting in church soon after the war ended, she had been pondering the futility of their deaths, the failure of such a sacrifice to 'make the world a better place'. All at once, she thought she heard Ivo's voice saying, 'But that wasn't our job, that's *your* job.'[9] The experience confirmed Molly's already strong sense that she had a calling, that she could make a difference to people's lives: a sense that was perhaps her defining characteristic, and which she communicated to her eldest daughter.

The loss of the Hood uncles had another consequence for the Crowfoot girls; they were left in an extended family dominated by women. At Nettleham Hall and San Remo their grandmother presided, together with Aunt Dolly. John Crowfoot had no brothers, and his sisters Margie and May often deputized for the absent Crowfoot parents. Of their own parents, the girls saw a great deal more of their mother than of their father. Anxious to re-establish the bonds within her own family, Molly set out for England just before the armistice was signed. She arrived in Worthing and stepped off the train with a new baby (another girl, Diana) in her arms. Soon afterwards John Crowfoot joined her, and they rented a house for a holiday together at the foot of Cissbury Hill in Sussex. Only Dorothy remembered her parents well, Joan a little; Elisabeth's affections, by her own account, were entirely directed towards Katie. They needed time to re-establish themselves as a family.

In Cairo Katie had had a sweetheart called Jimmy Collins, who was a corporal in Kitchener's personal escort. He had been a regular visitor to the Crowfoot household, amusing Dorothy and Joan by leading them round the yard on the back of a pony. But he and Katie had lost touch when he left the Army with tuberculosis and went to Australia. He joined the Army again on the outbreak of war, was wounded at Gallipoli and sent to a London hospital for treatment. Aunt Dolly, who was a volunteer nurse, saw his name on a list and went to see him. Through her efforts Katie and Jimmy were reunited, and they married in Worthing before Jimmy returned to active service. (Dorothy and Joan came to the wedding, while Elisabeth was left outside the church in her pram, in the care of a policeman.) After the war was over, Jimmy went back to Australia to be demobbed. Once again Aunt Dolly took it upon herself to intervene. In 1919 she bought Katie a ticket and sent her off to Australia to join her husband. Katie later told Elisabeth Crowfoot that he had never expected to see her again; for her own part, she deeply regretted leaving the Crowfoot family.

After this Molly did without the services of a children's nurse for a time. Dorothy took the role of eldest daughter seriously, acquiring increasing levels of responsibility until her sisters were all grown up. Although at the time the younger ones slightly resented Dorothy's being 'so good' all the time – they did not always find it so easy to stay out of trouble – they grew extremely fond of 'Dossie', as she was always known. She showed them many little kindnesses. A few years later, when Betty was disappointed at being left behind while Dorothy and Joan went to visit their parents in Khartoum, Dorothy made her a little book, handwritten and illustrated, called *The Tale of the Sudanese Tree Fairies* ('To my sister Betty: This book was written in spare time on board ship when somebody else hadn't bagged the writing table . . .') Her mother in turn showed Dorothy special attention, for example taking her on a trip to Iona in the early 1920s.

Molly decided to stay with her daughters for a while, and life, in Dorothy's words, 'became much more memorable'. Before the war ended she had just started at a PNEU school in Burgess Hill in Sussex, but Molly had other plans for her daughters' education. After her husband returned to Khartoum she took them back to her childhood home at Nettleham in Lincolnshire. The house, at the top of a small hill, had views across open parkland to the spire of Lincoln Cathedral three miles away, and the grounds were an excellent children's playground. There were hazards, however; it was all too easy to slip in leather-soled shoes on the polished wood staircase in the imposing front hall. Rather than sending the girls to school, Molly chose to teach them herself, adding two cousins who lived in Lincoln, Evangeline and John Aston, to the group. Not having been formally educated herself, she devised her own methods, and taught all the subjects she knew.

For nature study they went for walks and collected specimens in the local fields. For geography they made relief maps out of mud on the floor of the greenhouse. They read adventure stories by Stevenson and Henty, and learned by heart the poems of

Tennyson and Longfellow. For history they made their own books covering different periods – the Roman and Saxon invasions, or the early kings of England. Those of Dorothy's books that still survive consist mostly of stirring poems with full-page pictures and decorative borders illustrating the clothes, artefacts and conditions of the period. They brim over with a sense of enjoyment in learning. Molly dressed the girls in loose tunics of Sudanese cotton with embroidered necklines, giving them a faintly medieval look. It was a blissful time – Dorothy's cousin Evangeline called it 'the happiest year of her life'.

This idyll came to an end as Dorothy approached the age of ten. Having considered, and rejected, the possibility of making Nettleham their permanent home, her parents put some serious thought into the future. John Crowfoot expected to retire from the Sudanese service within a few years, and felt the need to establish a permanent base in Britain for the family. He also recognized that his daughters' education to date had been somewhat hit-and-miss. Molly wished to spend at least part of the remaining years of his posting at his side, and to return to her friends and interests in the Sudan. They decided to put down roots near Beccles, where John's father had grown up and his cousin Amy's husband, Harry Wood-Hill, practised as a doctor. Apart from the family connection, the town possessed an excellent new, state-funded secondary school, the Sir John Leman School. The original Leman School had been founded in the seventeenth century by a successful fishmonger, to educate bright boys from humble families. On the suggestion of John's uncle William Crowfoot, the school newly built by the local council adopted the same name. John Crowfoot himself had been educated at a public (fee-paying) school, Marlborough College; but according to Dorothy, he felt that as a Director of a government education service, he ought to make use of the education provided by the government in his own country.

In 1920 they came to lodge at St Mary's, a pleasant house on the outskirts of Beccles, while they searched for a home. Within a year they had rented The Old House in the village of Geldeston, a few miles north on the other side of the border with Norfolk, but within cycling distance of the town. The large house of mellow red brick, dating from the seventeenth century, was surrounded by a walled garden, and a magnificent cedar stood on the front lawn. The garden stretched down to a small river, ideal for boating. Despite a rumour that it was haunted, the house, with its attics that gradually filled with the souvenirs of their parents' travels, became the Crowfoot girls' first and only real home. Molly, meanwhile, finding the village population without any real leadership, set about running everything.

It was during this settling-down period that Dorothy attended the little PNEU class at the Rectory in Beccles where she had her first taste of chemistry. As soon as they moved into The Old House, she commandeered one of the attics as a laboratory, and began to undertake her own experiments, using material bought from the local chemist with her pocket money. 'He didn't seem to have rules about what he would allow ten-year-old children to buy,' she later remembered. At the time it didn't occur to her to be surprised. Rules, apart from essential good manners, were not a dominant feature of the Crowfoots' upbringing. For example, when their parents were at home there were no set bedtimes; at ten and twelve years of age, Joan and Dorothy would sit up till nearly midnight 'while their father read Ibsen and Plato etc to them.'[10] The girls were free to mount expeditions on the river by boat, by themselves, or to make forays into the surrounding countryside to watch birds or pick flowers. The worst offence they could commit was to be unoccupied.

Molly Crowfoot stayed long enough to establish a comfortable home at The Old House, but within a year or two she took to spending half the year in Khartoum, leaving the girls to board with friends or relatives in Beccles while she was away. Her letters home are filled with details of her busy social round:

Last night we dined with the Sterrys and afterwards went on to a reception at the Palace . . . Last week I went to Buri, to the house of Sh[eik] Saleh Suwar ed Dahab, to see the beginning of Babikr's wedding . . . At night Mrs Hunt and I went out again to visit the bride. It really was amusing – the women who weren't quite sure where the house was and we wandered about Buri in the dark, falling into *gadwals* [ditches or small streams] – At last we found the place and the bride came and danced for the bridegroom,

and he waved his hand above her head and all the women
trilled – and then they veiled her up again – and home we
went to bed . . . Your *lovely* basket Dorothy came today – it
is a really fine piece of work – I am awfully pleased with it.
Love and kisses from both of us, yr loving Mum.[11]

In 1921 Dorothy entered the Leman School. It became another
fixed point while her parents continued to come and go at more
or less regular intervals. The school was housed in a substantial
brick building surrounded by playing fields. Today, with greatly
expanded premises, it flourishes as a local authority comprehensive school with more than 1300 children. When Dorothy joined
it had around 130 pupils, rather more girls than boys 'owing to
the tendency for parents to send boys away to more prestigious
schools'. Boys also had the option of the boys-only grammar
school in the next town, Bungay. Most of the children came from
the families of tradespeople in the town, or of farmers or fisher-
men in the surrounding area. To pass the School Leaving
Certificate was regarded as the height of ambition, and only a
dozen or so achieved that each year. But the school had a strong
sense of purpose, and some excellent teachers. Dorothy quickly
found that her knowledge of English, history, drawing and nature
study was more than adequate, but that she was very behind in
mathematics.

The science teaching was a disappointment at first. Chemistry
was not taught at all during the first year. The school also lost its
only physics teacher, as a result of funding cuts, within a year or
two of her arrival. Chemistry classes from the second year
onwards were, as Dorothy told listeners to a schools radio broad-
cast years later, 'the prerogative of the boys'. But after a struggle
to persuade her teachers that they would do themselves justice in
a 'boys' subject', she and her particular friend Norah Pusey were
allowed to join the boys' class 'since we both wanted to take up
science seriously and go to the University'. A photograph taken at
the time shows the two of them just visible in the back row of a
teaching laboratory otherwise filled with boys.

It was common in those days, and for a long while afterwards,
for girls in mixed schools to be actively steered away from
physical science and towards more 'suitable' subjects such as

physiology, languages or needlework. But it is surprising that this should have happened at the Leman School, for a simple reason: the chemistry teacher was a woman. Criss Deeley had graduated from Birmingham University with a first-class degree in chemistry in 1906. She taught chemistry and mathematics (and needlework!) at the Leman School from its opening in 1914 until 1939; Dorothy found her a 'marvellous teacher', and her love of the subject grew. Miss Deeley in turn found Dorothy a 'dear, loveable girl, a "good sweet maid" as well as being clever.'[12]

She was happy at school and despite her shy, quiet demeanour she soon made friends among the girls. The boys were a different matter. Although the school was mixed, mixing was discouraged. Boys and girls had separate entrances, separate playgrounds and separate dining halls, and although they sat in the same classes, they were kept to separate sides of the room. A classmate, Edmund Wurr, corresponded with Dorothy towards the end of her life. He had been known at school as 'Buzzer', but she confided: 'You were far too eminent, it seemed to me when I was at school, for me ever to know you by that name.' Soon her sister Joan joined her, and they would cycle the 3 miles together, crossing the bridge over the River Waveney with their schoolbags on the handlebars.

Dorothy worked hard to make up the gaps in her education, but her years at the Leman School were not entirely uninterrupted. A surviving diary shows that in 1923 she spent the entire spring term with her maternal grandmother at the villa in San Remo. Why she did this is not clear. Certainly when she was older her parents frequently expressed anxiety about her health, but the diary gives no indication of sickliness; perhaps they felt she was working too hard and needed a break. While in San Remo she intermittently attended a French convent school, but her grandmother's requests that she watch games of tennis or go to parties apparently took priority. The diary stops abruptly two days after Dorothy's return – two days for which the only entry was the subdued but refreshingly normal 'Went to school all day'.

Her parents took the view that school was just part of a much broader range of educational influences. At the end of the same year, Dorothy and Joan were summoned to spend Christmas and the whole of the following term with their parents in Khartoum, so that they could experience a different way of life before their father's expected retirement. The journey out proved to be an eventful one. First they almost missed their ship in Crete because Molly, who was travelling with them, took them to visit Sir Arthur Evans's excavations of the Minoan palace at Knossos during a brief stop at Heraklion. When they returned to the harbour the ship had left the quayside, and they had to pursue it in a small boat and be taken on board over the side. Then Dorothy became very unwell, and spent most of the train journey from Alexandria to Cairo being sick out of the window. It turned out that she had measles; Joan went down with it a week later, and they had to spend Christmas isolated in a little flat in Cairo rather than at their parents' home in Khartoum.

They resumed the journey three weeks later, and now Dorothy was well enough to appreciate the unforgettable landscapes unfolding outside the train window as they travelled southwards. 'I can still see Abu Simbel by night on the banks of the Nile, and the many mirages in the sand outside Khartoum,' she later wrote. They arrived to a lifestyle in complete contrast to that of the village community of Geldeston. Their parents' house on the banks of the Nile was large and cool, surrounded by gardens with green lawns, rose bushes and banana trees. It had a verandah floored in coconut matting, where the girls slept out on hot nights. John and Molly entertained frequently, and the guest list was long and eclectic. Dorothy remembered handing cakes to the country's three religious leaders, Sayed Abd al-Rahman al-Mahdi, Sayed Ali al-Mirghani and Sherif Yusuf al-Hindi. Others who came included the first intake of students at the new Medical School, established largely at John Crowfoot's instigation, and the formidable Wolff sisters. On her own initiative Molly, appalled at the traditional childbirth practices and female circumcision that she had witnessed, had invited two of her former classmates at Clapham to come and train local Sudanese women in midwifery. Mabel Wolff and her sister, known as 'Bee' and 'Gee', trained more than 200 midwives by 1933.[13]

The girls went with their mother when she returned social calls. They were with her when, visiting the tent outside Khartoum where Sherif Yusuf al-Hindi lived, she admired an intricately woven camel girth. With the traditional courtesy of his people, he immediately gave it to her. But Molly's interest was more than purely aesthetic. With Sherif Yusuf's help, she arranged to bring the woman who had made the girth into Khartoum. Sitt Zeinab, having travelled for days on the back of a camel, set up her loom in a courtyard and Molly, her daughters and their friends watched her at work in the weeks that followed, learning the technique themselves.[14]

Molly recognized that traditional weaving techniques could have very ancient origins and shed light on the textiles of the early Egyptian civilizations. Back in England she herself wove a replica of the complex girdle of Rameses III and in subsequent years became an international expert on ancient textiles. Towards the end of her life she would answer anyone surprised at her lack of academic training that 'if you spend 25 years working on anything you become the world expert'. It is perhaps no coincidence that despite very different educational histories, all four of her daughters became experts in different fields.

Formal education was not entirely forgotten amongst this whirl of social engagements. The wife of the Arabic scholar Dr S. Hillelson was a mathematics graduate, and she gave lessons to the Crowfoot girls so that they should not fall even further behind. They also learned to write the Arabic alphabet with reed pens. But the most important lesson for Dorothy came as a result of a social visit.

The pharmaceuticals magnate and philanthropist Sir Henry Wellcome, anxious to assist with the reconstruction of the country after the devastation of the war, had established a research laboratory for tropical medicine, agriculture and mineral resources in 1903, in a wing of Gordon College in Khartoum. The government chemist Dr A. F. Joseph, a close friend of John Crowfoot, worked in the soil science department of the Wellcome Laboratory and Molly took the two girls to visit him there. Just as they arrived a geological expedition returned with small nuggets of gold they had found in a stream. 'To amuse us children, they threw their gold into a basin of sand and water and then showed how the gold could be 'panned' by gently rocking the basin and gradually pouring the sand away.'

Dorothy was 'fired with an immediate desire to experiment' herself. There was a *gadwal* in their garden, and with a tin basin from the kitchen she and Joan set about panning it for gold. They didn't find any, but they did separate out grains of 'shining black-ish material'. Guessing from her 'primitive knowledge of chemistry' that it might be manganese dioxide, Dorothy rushed back to Dr Joseph's laboratory to ask if she might make some tests. 'As things turned out, he had to help me. The ore was ilmenite, a mixed oxide of iron and titanium; and titanium was not in my school chemistry book.'

Impressed with Dorothy's enthusiasm for his subject, 'Uncle' Joseph, as the girls came to know him, presented her when she left with a portable surveyor's box, containing everything needed to carry out simple chemical analyses. The box, with its spirit lamps, charcoal block and blowpipe, and 'forty-eight little tubes of minerals', was to become a valuable addition to the attic labo-ratory at home in England.

The Sudan trip opened the eyes of the impressionable teenager to more than the possibilities of scientific research. While their visit passed in peace and comfort, the girls' parents did not shield them from the more problematic aspects of British colonial rule. On a visit to the Nuba mountains, Molly had witnessed the after-math of a brutal suppression by British troops of a 'nationalist uprising' (one account said that it was simply a protest over the price of sugar). Villages had been destroyed and cattle slaugh-tered. Molly was shocked and distressed; she had seen the role of the British administration as a benevolent one, helping a proud people to rebuild its culture and society.

John Crowfoot also thought of the British rule as transitional. A year or two before, he had written that his ideal for the country would be 'a series of native states . . . the Sudan Government becoming a Union of Free States . . .[15] But as a government ser-vant he seems to have seen the occasional use of force as an unfortunate necessity. In December 1924, after outbursts of increasing unrest around the country, there was a mutiny among the 11th Sudanese Battalion in Khartoum. As he reported to Dorothy, John was one of the many English people, mainly women and children, who had to take shelter (Molly was safely at home near Gordon College).

I happened to be in a house near the Club when the first

shots were fired just after sunset . . . I couldn't go home
which would have been a very safe place because the
Argyll and Sutherland Highlanders are still in the College,
but had to go to the Palace where more than 200 people
gathered for protection. Of course we did not know at all
how many of the black troops had mutinied . . .The first
thing I did was help in preparing belts for machine guns . . .
I was given a rifle and stationed at the top of one of the side
staircases in the Palace with three other men to protect a
machine gun that had been set up on the balcony near us.[16]

As it turned out, he did not have to fire a shot. But he described
to Dorothy how he witnessed the shelling of a building, in which
the last few mutineers were holed up 'until no one could be left
alive'. Molly's own account of the incident was more muted, concluding, 'I hope nothing more will happen now – there are many
British troops here to protect us – the Egyptian troops have gone
away to Egypt now.'

Back home in Geldeston in the summers Molly found outlets
for her radical, idealistic spirit. Since the war she had been an
active member of the League of Nations Union, set up to support
the work of the League of Nations. The League was an international alliance for the preservation of peace, the forerunner of the
United Nations; its founding covenant was formulated as part of
the Treaty of Versailles in 1919. Molly Crowfoot enlisted all the
children of the village to put on a pageant in aid of the Union. It
made a great impression on Dorothy. 'We each represented a
nation and we acted scenes representing recent history – I for
example was Sweden and quarrelled with Finland over the
Åland Islands.'

In the play the League of Nations sent a 'wise counsellor' who
solved the problem by deciding that the Åland Islands must
belong to Finland for geographical reasons, but that the islanders
should continue to speak Swedish and have the links with
Sweden that they wanted. This event, one of few successful
peacekeeping initiatives undertaken by the League of Nations,
had taken place only recently, in 1921. Years later Dorothy
regretted that the same kind of solution had not been adopted in
the crisis over the Falklands.[17]

Plays and pageants became an important feature of the Geldeston scene, with the four Crowfoot girls in prominent roles. They made a striking family. Dorothy's cloud of long golden hair and large blue eyes were in sharp contrast to Joan's dark good looks. Betty was also dark, but small and mercurial. Diana was fair and had the sunny temperament of the indulged baby of the family. They all joined the pack of Brownies started by Molly with herself as Brown Owl; she later took on the village troop of Girl Guides. Under her leadership the Geldeston troop came to focus its fundraising efforts on alleviating suffering among victims of war and poverty. Dorothy was an enthusiastic member, even enlisting her absent father's help with the more challenging of the badges she sought to collect. In November 1924 he wrote from Khartoum:

> I hope you will be able to use my telescope to look at the stars . . . It is a pity that you were not working for your astronomer's badge last winter because the stars out here are so much brighter than at home . . . With much love and kisses to your three lazy little sisters, and more to yourself, from your loving Daddy[18]

Having seen so little of her in her early childhood, John Crowfoot conducted his relationship with his eldest daughter on a somewhat austere and intellectual plane. Effectively, he treated her as a fellow adult, and she tried hard to live up to his expectations. This was easier through correspondence than during his brief visits to Geldeston. After one such visit, when Dorothy was fourteen, Crowfoot wrote to his wife in a surprisingly critical tone.

> Dorothy is so wrapt up in her own thoughts, or so afraid of making any statement of which she is not quite sure, that she is likely to be considered rather a dull companion by anyone who looks for amusement. I have been for quite long walks with her without eliciting any spontaneous remark whatever.[19]

John Crowfoot was surely not the first or last father to underestimate the awe he inspired in his daughter, the dreadful fear of making a remark that might provoke disapproval or ridicule. Under other circumstances Dorothy could be less retiring. When no one else would stand as Labour candidate in the mock elections at school in 1924, Molly encouraged Dorothy to put herself forward and helped her to write her speech. The Labour Party, forged in an alliance between trade unionists and liberal intellectuals, had been in existence only since the turn of the century, and had never yet formed a government. Molly was an early member. (John Crowfoot had belonged to the Fabian Society while at school, but lately had described himself as a 'benevolent Whig, not a Socialist'.[20])

Spurred by a sense of duty to the cause, Dorothy overcame her natural shyness and addressed the entire school. It was not one of her more triumphant moments – family tradition has it that she polled as few as six votes. Meanwhile on the national stage the party achieved its first election victory, albeit a short-lived one. It was an early illustration that while Dorothy's own convictions were unshakeable, she could be less successful at converting others. But she acquired a taste for political debate, complaining to her mother the following winter that 'Mrs Pagan [with whom she lodged when Molly was in Khartoum] doesn't talk politics at suppertime like you used to.' Gleefully she reported that Mrs Pagan had made her present a bouquet to the wife of the local Tory MP, Gervais Rentoul. 'I wonder what Mrs R would have thought if she had known that among all that room full of Conservatives the one who presented the bouquet was Labour.'[21]

It was her mother, far more than her father, who was responsible for developing Dorothy's political sensibilities and encouraging her to lift her eyes beyond the cosy scene at Geldeston to the wider stage of world affairs. In September 1925 Molly took Dorothy with her to the Sixth Assembly of the League of Nations in Geneva. It was a historic meeting, and Dorothy remembered 'the atmosphere charged with emotion, of hope struggling against a sense of doom'.[22] The year before, the gathering of the Fifth Assembly had produced the 'Protocol for the Pacific Settlement of International Disputes', generally known as the Geneva Protocol. It established a series of procedures covering every kind of dispute and which in all cases would result in a definite decision. Arbitration would become compulsory. But early in the 1925 Assembly Austen Chamberlain, the British Foreign Secretary, argued that Britain could not accept the Protocol as it stood. On Friday, 11 September, Molly and Dorothy heard Joseph Paul-Boncour, the French Premier, make an impassioned speech in the hope of rescuing some of what had been achieved the previous year.

> The time has not yet come then for us to fling over the Protocol that gold and purple pall beneath which the dead gods sleep. The structure we once built on the shores of this lake is still there firm and unshaken. The passing wave may distort and dim its image, but its essential features form once again in the passing river. The fragmentary structure in which diplomacies must perforce put their faith can only be built upon the plan which we have drawn . . .[23]

The assembly ended on a more hopeful note, in particular calling for the general Disarmament Conference envisaged in the Geneva Protocol, which took place the following year. The image of the nations of the world sitting down to resolve their differences through discussion and debate made a powerful impression on Dorothy. And her mother's example taught her that to be a passive observer was not enough; she grew up with a strong sense that individuals could and should act for the betterment of mankind. This almost Puritan ideal of a duty of selflessness and service to humanity provided a spur to all Dorothy's later achievements.

Work in the attic laboratory continued. 'I was very cautious,' she assured an interviewer in 1983, 'I never did anything dangerous.' She did, however, use a special high-temperature wax burner, part of Uncle Joseph's chemistry kit, as well as a spirit lamp. Modern parents might question the wisdom of letting children play with naked flames in the attic of an old house. Dorothy amused her sisters by making borax beads, in different colours according to the minerals she added (although Elisabeth admits to having been disappointed that they could not be strung into a necklace). When the girls were all in quarantine for mumps, she took it upon herself to teach them chemistry; a notebook with several pages dutifully completed by Joan still survives. Molly actively encouraged the work in the attic lab, even on one occasion getting the girls to write poems about their experiments; these turned out, said Dorothy, to be 'more comic verse than poetical'.

Dorothy records only one 'shocking episode': when snatching a few moments in her lab between church and lunch one Sunday she spilt concentrated nitric acid on the hem of a new silk frock, staining it yellow. 'Madly I tried the effect of ammonia – the yellow stains turned brown. I dissolved into tears, knowing how wrong it was to do such experiments in one's best clothes on Sundays.' But Molly, who could be stern when she wanted, merely comforted her daughter and offered to cover the stain with a broad frill. A long time later, when Dorothy had begun to study organic chemistry, she recalled this incident and 'realized that I had carried out the Xantho test for proteins'. On another occasion, she recorded, 'I had a violent nosebleed and thought a pity all this good blood should go to waste so I collected it in a test-tube and used it to make haematoporphyrin.'

Perhaps because of her own frustrated desire to study medicine, Molly threw herself into supporting Dorothy's passion for chemistry. She bought her the published versions of two lecture series for children given at the Royal Institution by Sir William Bragg in 1923 and 1925, entitled *On the Nature of Things* and *Old Trades and New Knowledge*. With his son Lawrence, Bragg had pioneered the use of X-rays to study the atomic structure of materials. His elegant introduction to the subject excited the impressionable Dorothy beyond measure.

[L]et us realize that in the last twenty-five years or so we have been given, so to speak, new eyes. The discoveries of radioactivity and of X-rays have changed the whole situation . . . We can now understand so many things that were dim before; and we see a wonderful new world opening out before us, waiting to be explored . . . It is true that the new lines of advance now open lead the way to fresh difficulties: but therein lies the whole interest and spirit of research . . .

> The discovery of the X-rays has provided means by
> which we can look far down into the structure of solid
> bodies, and observe in detail the design of their composition.
> We have advanced a whole stage towards . . . the position
> from which we can see why a material composed of such
> and such atoms has such and such characteristics . . . How
> far our new powers will carry us, we do not yet know; but it
> is certain that they will take us far and give us a new insight
> into all the ways in which material things are handled . . .
> it may be in some industrial process, or it may be in some
> action of a living organism . . .
>   Broadly speaking, the discovery of X-rays has increased
> the keenness of our vision then a thousand times, and we
> can now 'see' the individual atoms and molecules.[24]

Mother and daughter found the books a revelation, though as
Dorothy recalled later, for different reasons.

> She was particularly fascinated by the discovery of the
> arrangement of the atoms in different materials, potsherds
> and cotton and linen fibres, in which she was interested for
> archaeological reasons. I was fascinated by the way this
> knowledge was acquired – by passing X-rays through
> crystals and studying the diffraction effects produced by
> the atoms on the X-rays. I began to see X-ray diffraction as
> a means to exploring many of the questions raised but left
> unanswered by school chemistry – the structure of solids
> and of biological materials.

Already her interests were turning towards the chemistry of
living things. A distant cousin, Charles Robert Harington, was in
the news at the time for his discovery of thyroxins, hormones
produced in the thyroid gland that play an important role in reg-
ulating the body's metabolism. Molly and Dorothy wrote to him
to ask him to recommend a book on biochemistry. His recommendation of Parsons's *Fundamentals of Biochemistry*[25] opened up
yet another world of possibilities (although it was also indirectly
responsible for the unfortunate episode with the silk dress). The
latest edition, which Molly bought for Dorothy, included a section

on the sensational discovery of insulin only a year or two before. The very first chapter of this unassuming little book was entitled 'The Nature of Living Matter: The Proteins', and began with a quotation from Shakespeare's *The Tempest*:

> *We are such stuff*
> *As dreams are made on, and our little life*
> *Is rounded with a sleep.*

Parsons went on:

> We cannot begin our study of the chemical changes occurring in the living organism more suitably than by considering the properties and behaviour of the most important and characteristic substances which enter into the composition of all its cells and tissues – to wit, the **proteins**.

It is tempting to suggest, given the many years Dorothy later spent struggling to understand more about proteins, that this sentence became lodged in her mind and acted as a powerful compass to direct her steps as a researcher.

Meanwhile Dorothy continued to make progress at school. By the time she was fifteen she was working in a class whose average age was a year and a half older. Her report for the summer of 1925 placed her first in the class in scripture, English literature, English composition, geography and drawing. She was second in algebra, third in geometry and fourth in trigonometry, but blundered badly in her arithmetic examination and came last out of eight. Criss Deeley found her 'good on the whole' in chemistry, but placed her only ninth in a class of fourteen. Miss Barton, her Form Mistress, commented that 'Dorothy has done a good year's work in a happy spirit and has given satisfaction in every respect. To do herself justice in examinations, however, she should try to work more quickly.'[26]

School Certificate, the passport to a university place, was only two years away. As the date of the examinations grew closer the strain began to tell, as Dorothy's sister Joan remembers. 'She worked very hard. She used to weep over her homework if it wasn't perfect, especially maths. She couldn't do anything without understanding why she was doing it, whereas most children do maths just by following the rules.' Elisabeth remembered Dorothy sitting with her feet in a bath of Rendel salts – she suffered terribly from chilblains – crying over her maths. When her mother said, 'Don't cry, I'm sure it's right,' Dorothy snapped back, 'Of course it's right, but I can't see why!'

In March 1927 Dorothy sat the School Leaving Certificate set by the Oxford Local Examinations Board in subjects including scripture, art, English and history as well as mathematics and chemistry. (It was oddly prophetic that her paper on Design and Decorative Composition required her to 'Design a repeating pattern based on the Persian style . . . the repeat is to be a regular hexagon with sides 3" long.') She was awarded distinctions in six subjects (which, however, did not include chemistry), giving her the highest overall mark of any girl candidate for Oxford Local examinations that year. The achievement brought her an award of the grand sum of £30.

John and Molly Crowfoot's disappointment at having no sons was an open secret. Even with their liberal sensibilities, it would have been hard to resist the prevailing sense of the importance of having a male heir to continue the name. But any disappointment her father might have felt at not having a son to follow in his footsteps was mitigated to a very great extent by Dorothy's outstanding academic ability. 'It was part of my father's plan for me,' she recorded, 'that I should be educated in the same way as a son, and therefore go to Oxford University.'

If this was his intention, then his choice of school had been a bold leap of faith. Good as it was, the Leman School had never entered a candidate for Oxford or Cambridge, although according to Dorothy it would get 'one or two boys to London' each year. But her outstanding result in School Certificate vindicated John Crowfoot's belief in the sound fundamental basis provided by the school for someone of her abilities and background. As for negotiating the complexities of Oxford entrance, the family took full responsibility.

In Cairo they had met Margery Fry, sister of the painter and art critic Roger Fry. She had been an undergraduate at

Somerville College (the second of Oxford's colleges for women, founded in 1882) and its first Librarian, before leaving to pursue her own interests in social and penal reform. She remained, however, an influential member of Somerville's Governing Council, and in 1926 she was elected Principal, a post she had accepted with some trepidation. This connection was enough to determine that Somerville was to be Dorothy's goal. The system for entrance to Oxford in those days was that candidates took an examination in March for entry the following October. After she had passed her School Certificate, Dorothy went with her mother to visit Somerville and find out if her education to date had prepared her sufficiently for the entrance exam the following year. They were in for a shock: all Oxford applicants had to be examined in Latin, which she had never studied; and Somerville required candidates for chemistry to take papers in more than one science, and to have covered more advanced mathematics.

But Dorothy had time – she was not yet seventeen – and her parents had learned friends. Aiming for entrance in 1928 gave them just a year to prepare. George Watson, headmaster of the Leman School, who 'could teach anything' undertook to introduce Dorothy to Latin. Her mother taught her botany as her second science, delegating to a neighbour who was the retired head of a Danish horticultural college when she was abroad. Dr Lumby of the Fisheries Research Institute at Lowestoft taught Dorothy mathematics, with the assistance of a Leman School old boy who had gone on to London University. She and a boy from her chemistry class who was also trying for university entrance spent a happy year doing experiments together on their own.

John Crowfoot's contribution included writing peremptorily from Khartoum to urge Dorothy to get a good haircut before the interview – 'Let Joan see to it!' If anything, Dorothy's mother was the more anxious of the two about her prospects of getting in. Molly had decided to enrol Betty and Diana in the Farmhouse School in Buckinghamshire run by Margery Fry's sister Isobel, a friend to whom she confided her fears about Dorothy's chances. 'Why, they'd practically pay her to go there,' was the reply, 'so few girls apply to read science.'

Dorothy's classmate Norah Pusey had already left school for a domestic science college. She had actually achieved a higher mark than Dorothy on the School Certificate chemistry paper, and as the Oxford examination date approached she wrote reassuringly and a touch enviously:

Don't go worrying about March as you are sure to get through for there are not many girls who have had your chances at home and the Leman School. You will just bless every lesson you did there when once you get away. Also very few girls stick at things as you do. After that you mustn't get a swollen head my dear although you have cause to have one . . . You are fortunate to be really going in for a degree. I don't think I shall stick this place for more than two years as at times I feel dreadfully out of things. I am considered an awful swot and I really don't work hard . . . I want to take applied chemistry instead of needlework but I don't think that it would be the use to me financially that the other would. Won't it seem strange to be actually earning one's living.[27]

Norah's letter illustrates the frustration of a bright girl brought up to have low expectations of her own abilities and opportunities. Her mother ran a small farm while her father was at sea most of the time, and it had long been agreed among them that Norah was to teach domestic science in elementary schools. Even an offer of a job on the staff of her London college did not deflect her from the path that had been chosen for her. Tragically, she died of tuberculosis while still in her twenties.

Dorothy sat the entrance examination in March 1928, and was interviewed at Somerville. The interviewer noted: 'Very shy and fragile-looking. Longs to do research – or social work.'[28] Dorothy was then ushered in to see Margery Fry, who asked her kindly if she had ever seen a bearded titmouse. Bemused, she replied that there were long-tailed tits in the garden at Geldeston, and then was overcome with embarrassment that Miss Fry might think she did not know the difference. (Towards the end of her life, Margery Fry declared that her two greatest ambitions were to see a bearded titmouse, and to see the end of capital punishment in Britain. She did not live to see the second; whether she ever saw a bearded titmouse is unrecorded.)

The years of hard work had paid off. Dorothy was accepted to read chemistry at Somerville from October 1928.

2

'Don't you understand, I've got to know!'

Somerville and Oxford, 1928–1932

Dorothy heard the news that she had been accepted at Somerville by telegram – 'Vacancy offered, wire reply' – at her grand-mother's house in San Remo. She was on her way, with her mother, to join an archaeological expedition codirected by her father in what was then the British mandate Trans-Jordan, now Jordan. It was the beginning of a wonderful summer in which she would at last be able to experience for herself the passion for exploration of the ancient world that so absorbed her parents.

John Crowfoot had retired from his post in Khartoum in 1926, at the age of fifty-three, the earliest date at which he could be awarded a full pension. It seems likely that he had every inten-tion of coming home to England permanently, although a characteristic letter from Molly makes it clear that they meant to make the most of the trip.

> My darling Dorothy and Joan
> You ought to have a letter each, when you have just sent
> me such nice long ones from Beccles, but I have so many to
> write this morning . . . You will be rather sorry to hear that
> there isn't any chance now of our getting back till the end
> of April – that is, till after the Easter holidays . . . I am
> writing to Mrs Pagan to find out whether you can possibly
> stay with her, which I think is what you would like to do

so as to be near Geldeston. It is a pity we don't know
anyone who could go out to Geldeston with you, as I
expect you would rather have your holiday there than
anywhere. Auntie May is *so* kind – perhaps she may be
able to have one of you again . . . Otherwise my poor
darlings, it looks as if your heartless mother would leave
you to camp in the wild woods! Of course I *could* come
back before Daddy, but I most desperately want to go
home with him, because he is going by Jerusalem and
Beyrout. *What* a chance! I just feel as if I must take it.[1]

But the chance was snatched away when John's father died suddenly just before they set out on their journey.

Just received your letter before leaving Khartum . . . we
have given up Beyrout and Jerusalem because Daddy wants
to get home to Granny . . . I don't expect we shall get to
Worthing til April 23rd. Poor Daddy! he was so awfully
sorry to hear of Grandpapa's death and he did so wish he
had been at home. Were you at Worthing darling? If so I
am sure you did your best to help and keep Betty happy.[2]

So their father's return home took place under less than joyful circumstances but still, Dorothy recalled, 'for a little time we hoped
that he might take a new appointment in England and come and
live with us'. That hope was short-lived, however. During the
journey home John had been offered his ideal job, as Director of
the British School of Archaeology in Jerusalem, and had immediately accepted. In the spring of 1927 he and Molly packed up
their belongings once more and set off for Palestine and a new
career. They arrived just before Easter, and Molly wrote home to
describe how they joined hundreds of Christian pilgrims in mark-
ing the festival.

My dearest Children
I must write a letter to you all, because there is so much to
see and do here . . . We are living above the museum, in a
suburb of the town. [On Good Friday] Daddy and I went
out at 6.45 am to the Via Dolorosa and walked up it with a

little party who were keeping the stations of the Cross.
People kept passing up and down while we were praying –
it felt most strange . . . A population most unlike that of
Cairo – not afraid of colour in their dress. At 3 we went to
the beautiful service of Tenebrae at the Church of the Holy
Sepulchre – then after kneeling at the Chapel of Calvary,
went home for a little rest . . . I wondered much what you
were all doing and do hope you had a happy time. Much
love to Auntie May . . .[3]

As soon as John Crowfoot arrived in Jerusalem he began to plan
a joint expedition with Yale University to excavate Byzantine
churches in the ancient city of Jerash, on the far side of the River
Jordan. The site included Greek temples and theatres as well as
the early Christian churches that were one of his main interests.
The first dig was to take place in the summer of 1928. With a few
months to relax between passing her entrance examination and
going up to Oxford, Dorothy was asked if she would like to
accompany her parents on the expedition. In her autobiography
she devoted an entire chapter to this trip, headed 'A blessed interlude'. Like her parents she arrived in Jerusalem at Easter, and
they retraced with her the solemn ceremonies they had followed
the previous year. Then they set off by car, crossing the Jordan
and heading up into the mountains. 'And then we came to a great
triumphal arch on the open hill side and looked down to Jerash.
It seemed to me one of the most beautiful places on earth.'

They slept in tents, with a roughly built hut for cooking, eating
and working. Including Dorothy, there were seven British and
American archaeologists in the group, with a team of experienced
Egyptians to carry out the digging. Dorothy's first job was to
clean the finds, especially coins. But as delicately patterned
mosaic pavements emerged from the excavations of fifth- and
sixth-century churches on the site, she assumed the task of
making an accurate recording of the designs. The intricacies of
the patterns, regular arrangements of pieces of coloured marble
about a centimetre square, enthralled her.

The pattern in the nave was of linked octagons, and there
were small panels, square or diamond-shaped, generally

with decorative motifs between them . . . I began to think
of the restraints imposed by two-dimensional order in a
plane.

It was an ideal preparation for the thinking she would later have
to do about the restraints imposed by three-dimensional order in
crystals.

The work continued for almost two months. On Sundays they
would rest and explore the 'flower-filled hills' around the ancient
city, on one occasion being entertained to coffee in a Bedouin
camp. 'My parents could talk Arabic freely and give all our
thanks for their ancient hospitality.' But Dorothy was not allowed
to forget entirely the years of study that lay ahead.

> A letter came for me from my Oxford tutor, pointing out
> that I had offered in my entrance examination Botany, not
> Physics, which I really needed to know for the study of
> Chemistry. I wrote back a casual, gay letter on the difficulties
> I might experience finding Physics books anywhere near
> Jerash. Not to be defeated, she sent me Hurst and Lattey's
> text book on Physics to help me with my first year
> examinations.

Dorothy dutifully studied the textbook in the evenings. When the
dig came to an end in early June, she and her parents returned to
Jerusalem, where she continued to work on her drawings of the
mosaics. She drew them carefully on a scale of one-tenth, then
coloured in enough of the area, dot by dot, to show the repeating
pattern of the tiles, or tesserae. But Père Vincent, a Dominican
monk and noted Jerusalem scholar who had excavated mosaics in
Constantinople, encouraged her to complete the whole floor in
colour. 'I did not finish the job in Jerusalem, but took it to Oxford
with me, and slowly in the course of my first two years at college
completed the two most important drawings.' Her work was
eventually published in her father's reports of the excavation,[4]
and the originals are now at Yale ('in a drawer where no one can
see them', she remarked with some regret in 1990[5]).

The 'blessed interlude' ended with a magical journey through
Lebanon with her parents, travelling on horseback and staying in

village rest houses in the mountains. '[The guides] lit a great fire in the courtyard and cooked meat and rice which we ate in the firelight, sitting round the blaze. Later, village notables would visit us over cups of coffee and pleasant conversation, in which I could take no part.' At the end of the holiday they took a cone from one of the legendary Cedars of Lebanon to plant in the garden at Geldeston, where it still grows.

Dorothy arrived at Somerville College, Oxford in October 1928 aged eighteen, but with a maturity beyond her years. As the eldest of the Crowfoot sisters, she took responsibility for the family in her parents' absence. In Jerash she had made a distinctive contribution to an archaeological expedition. Her parents had many friends in Oxford, such as the Regius Professor of Medicine, Sir Archibald Garrod, to whom they had taken care to introduce her before term began. The Principal of her college, Margery Fry, was also a family friend. Dorothy was already completely at ease with the tradition of independent study on which the Oxford system of undergraduate teaching was based. Unlike some of her contemporaries she had no immediate financial worries, her Aunt Dolly having made her an allowance of £200 a year. While some might have quailed a little at what Oxford represented, for Dorothy it opened up opportunities to know more, and to meet people with interesting ideas.

Opportunities for young women in Oxford at that time were still far from equal. Although there had been women students at the University for fifty years, they had been entitled to receive degrees only since 1920. There was still a widely held view that their presence had a 'demoralizing' influence on their male counterparts. Only the year before Dorothy arrived, a motion was passed in Congregation, the 'dons' parliament', preventing any further growth in the numbers of women students from the then total of 840. A fixed quota was introduced for each of the five women's colleges (there were twenty-two colleges for male undergraduates, with no restrictions on their intake), and a further clause in the statute prevented any new women's college being founded that would take the proportion of women undergraduates above one to every four men. This legislation made it impossible for the women's colleges, which lacked the generous historical endowments of many of their mullioned and gargoyle-encrusted counterparts, to increase their income by increasing the numbers of fee-paying students. Oxford was to remain, for another fifty years, 'a man's university with a certain number of women in it',[6] rather than a mixed university.

During Dorothy's time as a student there still existed individual lecturers who would evict any females from their audiences; others pointedly addressed the entire assembly as 'Gentlemen'. Many University societies, including the Oxford Union debating society and the equally prestigious Alembic Club for chemists, did not accept women students as members. A stringent disciplinary code was enforced by the University Proctors, more to prevent women from distracting men from their studies than to protect their own virtue. Students in the women's colleges had to obtain 'mixed party leave' if they wished to invite young men to tea, and mixed tea parties could not be held in the students' own rooms. They could not visit men in their college rooms unchaperoned, and never after evening Hall. Boating on the river in the summer also required special permission if men were involved, and Somervillians had to be back in college by 10 p.m. after such expeditions. These rules were a constant source of grievance to the women students, but by the end of the 1920s were to some extent honoured more in the breach than the observance.

There was a positive side to this partial segregation. The women's colleges had come into being through the passionate belief of their founders in the importance of women's education, and they remained havens of support and inspiration for their students. The women tutors, though few in number through lack of funds, were frequently outstanding scholars in their fields, and took a very personal interest in their charges. They knew that the future of women's education at Oxford depended on maintaining the highest possible standards of achievement and behaviour among their students. They expected hard work, but not overwork; afternoons and Sundays were meant for exercise and recreation, preferably out in the fresh air. Their reputation for seriousness of purpose ensured that most girls who applied were able and committed. Of the women's colleges, it was Somerville that had the highest reputation for earnest scholarship.

The College itself had grown rapidly since its foundation almost fifty years before. Its site on the Woodstock Road placed it nearer to the centre of the city, and to lecture rooms, libraries and laboratories, than any of the other women's colleges. Most of its red-brick buildings were set well back from the road behind a narrow gatehouse entrance, with trees and lawns between them. It had its own well-stocked library and panelled dining hall. Each student had her own room, some considerably more desirable than others, and a 'scout' or college servant would clean the rooms, polish shoes and bring coal for the fires.

It was an austere environment compared with some of the older (and richer) men's colleges. With the country's economy already in decline, few of the young women had much money to spend – there was little sign of the golden and dissolute youth of *Brideshead Revisited*. But Dorothy found it 'a gay sort of place'. She was allocated a room in 'House', the oldest part of the College. No one was left to find their way about alone – it was traditional for the second-years to scoop up nervous Freshers and bear them off to tea, coffee and introductions. It did not take long to settle into the rhythm of College life, with its set mealtimes and weekly tutorials. Under the forward-looking rule of 'the Fry', as the Principal was known by the students, more rigid social conventions such as changing into evening dresses for dinner had been quietly dropped. It was a close-knit community in which within a few weeks new students could expect to know all ten of the Fellows (two hapless victims being seized to dine on High Table each night), everyone in their own year, and many of the older students. The prevailing atmosphere among them was one of earnestness, innocence and occasional outbursts of girlish larkiness; but modern cynicism should not blind us to the real achievements involved in their being there at all.

The wider University was more of a challenge, but while students in the arts could spend most of their time in college if they so chose, scientists such as Dorothy might return only to eat and sleep. Women scientists, at any level, were in short supply. The numbers of women wishing to read science or mathematics had always been small compared with those of the historians, linguists and classicists. In chemistry, for example, there were typically three to five women students out of a total annual cohort of about sixty. The pool from which tutors in the sciences could be recruited was therefore also small; but more importantly, individual women's colleges simply did not have the resources to employ their own Fellows in the sciences to teach such small groups of students full-time. In Dorothy's year at Somerville, for example, among fifty Freshers there was one other chemist (Kathleen Beresford Knox), one botanist and one zoologist – an intake which Dorothy described as 'a rather large Science year for these times'.

The women's colleges solved the problem by sharing it. Dorothy formally came under the care of the zoologist Jane Willis Kirkaldy, Director of Studies and Moral Tutor for women studying the natural sciences at all five of the women's colleges. Miss Kirkaldy herself, as an undergraduate at Somerville, had been one of the first two women to study zoology at Oxford, in which she took a First in the Final Honour School in 1891 (although she could not at that time be awarded a degree). She was already close to retirement in 1928; when she died four years later another Oxford woman pioneer, the mineralogist Mary Winearls (Polly) Porter, said of her, 'My early education had been deficient, and I had no training in science, but by her determination and encouragement and by practical means she made it possible for me to pursue the subject in which I was interested.'[7]

Miss Kirkaldy, whom Dorothy found 'formidable' and 'remote', talked to her about life and work in Oxford and passed her on to Monica Farrow of St Hugh's for chemistry, and John Wolfendon of Exeter College for physics, to prepare her for the Preliminary Examinations at the end of the first year. She settled into the usual Oxford routine of reading in the Radcliffe Science Library for essays set during weekly one-to-one coaching sessions with her tutors, practical classes in the laboratories, and attendance at whatever lectures looked interesting.

It was decided my chemistry was nearly good enough already and I could also take part of the first year Honours lectures in chemistry if I could fit them in. I was free to organize my time to fit with the various lecture timetables and my own liking.

Scientific research and teaching had begun to be taken seriously in Oxford from the middle of the nineteenth century, although it was a long time before it achieved the same status as 'Greats' (classics), law or history. The need for laboratories meant that scientific subjects acquired an organization within the University quite different from that in the arts. Teaching in the arts was very much college-based. Students might go to other colleges to hear lectures or for tutorials in special subjects, but by and large individual tutors pursued their own interests and developed followings among their own students; the few holders of University professorships exerted little or no influence on the research of their colleagues.

In the sciences, by contrast, strong-willed professors with the contacts to generate outside funding gradually established purpose-built departments with strong research teams in the area around the University Museum. This wonderful Victorian gothic edifice, with its vaulted ceiling of wrought iron and glass, its marble pillars and its displays of stuffed animals, dinosaur skeletons and mineral specimens, had been constructed in 1860 in the belief that it would meet all the University's needs in science. By the time Dorothy arrived, chemistry, like most of the other sciences, had taken on more spacious quarters of its own. Inorganic chemistry was housed in the 'Old Chemistry Department', an extension to the University Museum built in 1863 and modelled on the Abbot's Kitchen of the medieval Glastonbury Abbey. Organic chemistry (the study of the carbon compounds that are the basis of all living things) was in the relatively new Dyson Perrins Laboratory (funded by a large grant from the heir to the Lea and Perrins Worcestershire Sauce fortune). Most of the research in physical chemistry went on in the few laboratories attached to men's colleges, such as those shared between Balliol and Trinity, and those at Jesus.

These extensive but dispersed facilities were combined, when Dorothy arrived, with a lack of coherent leadership. The Dr Lee's Professor of Chemistry was Sir Frederick Soddy, who had won the Nobel prize in 1921 for his discovery of radioactive isotopes, work he had carried out at Glasgow University. Unfortunately after his appointment to the newly created Oxford Chair in 1919 he had fallen out with many of his colleagues, and failed completely to master the political and diplomatic skills necessary to make the University's labyrinthine bureaucracy work to his advantage.

Although after nearly ten years in the post he managed to secure the funds to update his antiquated laboratories, a series of petty disagreements meant that he never became a member of the board of the Physical Sciences Faculty and therefore took no part in decisions on teaching or research. One such decision committed him to lecture only in inorganic chemistry, excluding him from physical chemistry – the field in which he had won his Nobel. His research efforts dried up completely as he became increasingly preoccupied with developing his own theories of monetary reform; at the same time he devoted considerable energy to opposing national policies intended to make university research more responsive to the needs of industry. Although Soddy remained in his post until his retirement in 1936, the running of the department was left to one of the lecturers, Freddy Brewer.[8]

The Professor of Organic Chemistry, William Perkin, who had established a flourishing research group, died a year after Dorothy's arrival. But individual scientists in his department, such as the physical organic chemist Nevil Sidgwick, maintained vigorous research programmes; and in 1930 Robert Robinson, a former student of Perkin's, arrived from London to take over the Organic Chemistry Chair with a team of twenty research assistants. He presided over a renaissance in the subject at Oxford, and later won the Nobel prize for his work on plant alkaloids. There was also a newly built and vigorous Department of Biochemistry under Rudolph Peters.

Sir Archibald Garrod, who had been instrumental in getting the new laboratory built, had shown Dorothy round when she visited Oxford with her parents the previous year, and she had been particularly struck by the inspiring inscription by the door:

For at first wisdom will walk with him by crooked ways
and bring fear and dread upon him and torment him with
her discipline until she may trust his soul and try him by
her laws; then she will return the straight way unto him
and comfort him and show him her secrets.*

* Ecclesiasticus 4, 17–21

However, at this time there was no BA degree in biochemistry – if there had been, Dorothy would have taken it – and no course in the subject for chemists.

Chemistry at Oxford was overwhelmingly an experimental discipline, and one that preferred clear boundaries between its various branches. There was little or no attempt to develop the theoretical underpinnings that would have provided some coherence to the whole. Since the mid-1920s Linus Pauling at the California Institute of Technology, inspired by the new quantum physics emerging in Europe, had been pouring out papers on the nature of the bonds that hold atoms together in molecules, a concept fundamental to the whole of chemistry. But Oxford was slow to take up these ideas, especially at undergraduate level. Students were required to memorize vast amounts of empirical information about atomic weights, reactions, pressures, temperatures and so on, and to carry out a series of prescribed syntheses and analyses in practical classes. No one sought to explain why one element might be more reactive than another, for example, or how the three-dimensional structure of a molecule might relate to its function. It was mostly chemistry as cooking: follow the recipe and observe the result.

This was not what Dorothy had come to Oxford for. But she applied herself with her customary diligence, and acquired an encyclopaedic knowledge of general chemistry that proved an invaluable resource for the rest of her working life. At the same time, she set about learning more about the study of crystals, the subject that had first inspired her interest. Disappointingly, there was no mention of it in her first-year course – it was not considered central to the discipline of chemistry. Crystal structure was largely the province of mineralogy, an optional subject for finalists in chemistry or geology.

Dorothy already knew from her schoolgirl reading that the flat faces and consistent angles of the outer surfaces of crystals reflected the regular, repeating arrangement of the atoms inside them. Just as a wallpaper pattern repeats endlessly in two dimensions, crystals consist of identical units repeated in three dimensions. This idea had been in circulation for at least 300 years: Robert Hooke, one of the founders of the Royal Society in 1660, suggested this explanation for crystal forms, illustrating his ideas with drawings of cannon balls stacked into pyramids. Early in the twentieth century an Oxford mineralogist, Thomas Vipond Barker, had embarked on the massive task of classifying all known crystals according to their external shape, with the idea that this would help with the identification of new crystals as they were discovered.

His principal collaborator in this task was Mary Porter, known as Polly, a young woman who, without any formal training in science, or ever holding a university post, became a key figure in classical crystallography. She had been 'discovered' in 1902 at the age of sixteen by Henry Miers, Waynflete Professor of Crystallography and Mineralogy at Oxford from 1896 until 1908, studying a collection of Italian marble specimens in the University Museum. She had made her own small collection the year before when in Rome with her parents, and was working on their classification. Miers, a classical crystallographer who was carrying out research into crystal formation and the measurement of crystal faces, offered her work in his research group. Although her parents would not allow her to enrol as a student at the University (she had never even been to school), they spent a succession of summers in Oxford and Polly worked with Miers for a few months at a time. Miers left Oxford to become Principal of the University of London in 1908, but by that time Polly's place in the laboratory was assured. During the First World War she worked on organic compounds for William Perkin in the Chemistry Department, as well as continuing her own work on the crystallography of a variety of compounds in the basement of the Museum.

In 1919 Polly Porter was elected to the Mary Carlisle Research Fellowship at Somerville College, which she told a friend excitedly was 'the best Fellowship in the country for women'.[9] It meant that at last she could work full-time on crystallography, and her research brought her first a BSc and later a DSc (the first for Somerville). During the 1920s she collaborated with Thomas Barker on his massive task of crystal classification, working on principles he had established for the choice of the key angles between crystal faces. The Fellowship came to an end in 1929, but Porter had a small private income and received occasional grants that enabled her to continue her work on the *Barker Index of*

Crystals and other research. She also assisted with teaching a practical class in crystallography for undergraduate chemists. Dorothy came to know her through these classes and her Somerville connection, and found her 'a great encouragement'.

Barker was still lecturing in 1929, and Dorothy went along at the end of her first year to hear him.

> He saw me – rather obvious, one girl and about eight
> men – and wrote a very nice letter, advising me to take the
> course later. (I think he was afraid of my ploughing
> prelims if I deviated from the prescribed course.) I agreed
> with him and stopped.

But she was never to hear the full course – Barker took an administrative position in the University, gave up lecturing and died two years later.

No one could dictate what Dorothy read in the library. Getting quickly through the reading set for her essays, she would turn to 'anything lying about'. One day she picked up the latest issue of the *Transactions of the Faraday Society*, dated March 1929, and found an entire discussion on crystal structure based on the use of X-ray diffraction.[10] She was first delighted, then appalled, then inspired.

> There was such a mass of material clearly already available
> on crystal structures that I had not known about – I
> wondered, for a moment, whether there was anything for
> me to find out – and gradually realized the limitations of
> the present which we could pass.

Dorothy saw immediately that the papers she was reading addressed a fundamental question. Everything is made of atoms. But how do those atoms combine together to make a drop of water, a diamond or a complex biological molecule such as haemoglobin? Diamond and graphite are both made of pure carbon – yet one is so soft you can write with it, while the other is one of the hardest substances known. The difference has to lie in the way the carbon atoms are connected. For Dorothy, it was even more exciting to contemplate the possibility that knowing the three-dimensional structure of more complex biological molecules might reveal the fundamental basis of life itself.

The tool that made it possible to ask this question was developed not by chemists, but by physicists. Wilhelm Röntgen in Wurzburg discovered X-rays in 1895. For some years physicists argued about what they were – were they highly energetic subatomic particles, or did they behave as waves of radiation, like light? When light passes through a very narrow slit or a pinhole, its waves spread out, or diffract, on the far side, like ripples in a pond. A grating of several slits produces a pattern of interference where the peaks and troughs of the waves combine. The more slits there are, the sharper the pattern. In 1912 the physicist Max von Laue in Munich reasoned that if X-rays behaved like waves their wavelengths would be very short indeed, too short to be diffracted by the gratings used in optical experiments. However, after discussion with his student Paul Ewald, he realized that the spacing of the atoms in a crystal, around a millionth of a millimetre apart, would make an effective diffraction grating for X-rays. So he suggested to his young colleagues Walter Friedrich and Paul Knipping that they try firing X-rays at a crystal of copper sulphate to see if it would diffract the beam.

To their delight it did, producing an ordered pattern of spots of different intensities on a photographic plate. They went on to produce even better photographs of another simple inorganic compound, zinc blende. The German physicists were satisfied that they had demonstrated that X-rays behaved as waves. But they did not immediately see the even greater implications of their discovery. The regularity of the pattern revealed that the atoms in the crystals were indeed arranged as an orderly lattice – and that in principle, it should be possible to work back from the diffraction pattern to discover this internal order.

It was not the Germans, but the British father-and-son team of William and Lawrence Bragg who immediately saw how this could be achieved when they looked at the first published photographs from Laue, Friedrich and Knipping. At the time William Bragg was Professor of Physics at Leeds University, his son a research student under J. J. Thompson at Cambridge. Ironically, Bragg *père* had been rather wedded to the particle theory of X-rays. His son set up experiments designed to demonstrate that diffraction effects could be the result of particles shooting through avenues in the crystal: but the results only convinced him that the wave theory was correct. Lawrence Bragg went on to construct a simple mathematical relationship between the intensity of the spots on the photographic plate, the wavelength of the X-rays and the positions of the atoms in the crystal.

He thought of the atoms in the crystal as a series of layers, like apples in a greengrocer's box. Each layer, or plane, could reflect the X-rays like a mirror, if they happened to hit an atom. Some X-rays would pass through one or more planes and be reflected from deeper ones. Bragg realized that the strongest spots in the diffraction patterns on his photographic plates would appear where reflections from two or more planes coincided *as long as they were in phase* – with peaks and troughs precisely aligned. Reflections that were out of phase would tend to cancel each other out. The reflections would be in phase only if the extra distance travelled by the X-rays between two planes was an exact multiple of their wavelength. And he could achieve this by adjusting the angle at which the incoming X-rays struck the planes.

His calculation, a simple mathematical relationship known as Bragg's Law, at last opened up the possibility of using X-rays to solve crystal structures. If you knew the position and intensity of the spots on the photographic plate, the angle at which the X-rays struck the planes and the wavelength of the X-rays, you could, in principle, deduce the positions of the planes of atoms.

Lawrence Bragg and his father were the first to do this with a very simple compound, sodium chloride or common salt. Salt contains equal numbers of sodium and chlorine atoms, and produces crystals shaped like simple cubes. The simplest possible way the atoms could combine in the crystal is to alternate, one sodium, one chlorine, from left to right, front to back and top to bottom throughout the crystal. This would leave each sodium surrounded by six chlorines, and each chlorine surrounded by six sodiums. It was a structure that some chemists had suggested in the nineteenth century, but others had demurred because it meant there was no individual sodium chloride molecule. Using X-ray diffraction, the Braggs proved that this structure was correct. The achievement won them the Nobel Prize for Physics in 1915; the younger Bragg heard of the award while on active service in France during the First World War.

Dorothy had been intrigued at the possibility of 'seeing' the internal atomic structure of crystals ever since she read of the Braggs' work in Sir William Bragg's Royal Institution lectures. At Oxford she began to read more widely. No one at the University was doing X-ray work during her first year, but British scientists, headed by the Braggs, were still in the forefront of the field. She learned about the work of J. D. Bernal, William Astbury and Kathleen Lonsdale at the Davy Faraday Laboratory of the Royal Institution in London, directed by William Bragg since 1923. They were beginning to extend the technique from inorganic compounds such as salt to the more complex organic (carbon-containing) compounds that are the basis of all living things. Dorothy's tutors found that her essays, far from parroting the textbooks, contained brand-new information about the structure of molecules. 'The benzene ring is flat,' she could assert with confidence, having read of Kathleen Lonsdale's important studies of the structure of this common constituent of organic compounds, six carbon and six hydrogen atoms arranged in a ring.

As well as reading, Dorothy made a point of going to hear the best lecturers. The local stars were Cyril Hinshelwood on physical chemistry and Robert Robinson on organic chemistry, both of whom later won Nobel prizes. Dorothy first attended Robinson's course at the beginning of her third year.

> We criticized him at first for telling us in a not very clear manner things that we knew already, but now he is moving far ahead . . . He is always drawing pictures of things and interpreting structures electronically, which is illuminating the dark recesses of organic chemistry.[11]

A slightly older student, Muriel Tomlinson, remembered that 'the asides and extras which [Robinson] interposed were often more rewarding than the main theme'.[12] Less inspired students complained that his style made it impossible to take notes but Dorothy, with her excellent memory, had no such problem. 'Some of his lectures I found myself remembering in detail long after,' she wrote, particularly that on the oxygen-carrying protein, haemoglobin. Robinson's main preoccupations were compounds with ring-like structures in their molecules, and the Electronic Theory, a development in physics that was having a huge impact on the way chemists thought about their subject.

To Dorothy's great excitement one of the fathers of the Electronic Theory, the Danish physicist Niels Bohr, was among the many illustrious visitors who came to speak in Oxford while she was a student. He spoke of his idea that electrons in atoms circled the nucleus in fixed orbits, and how a gain or loss of energy could make them jump from one orbit to another without passing through the space between – the origin of quantum theory, now the dominant theory of modern physics. He went on to describe how a galaxy of German theorists – Werner Heisenberg, Wolfgang Pauli, Max Born and Erwin Schrodinger – had found ways of using mathematics to predict what the consequences of this work of imagination would be when real atoms combined. The ideas were new and difficult, not only to Dorothy but to scientists everywhere, and she didn't understand all of what she heard. But she followed up the lecture by reading the paper he had written in the *Philosophical Magazine*, a paper that impressed her so much that she later encouraged all her pupils to read it.[13]

And there were many others. The Dutch physical chemist Peter Debye came to talk about conductivity and ionic solutions. J. D. Bernal, who had recently moved to Cambridge from the Royal Institution, lectured for the Alembic Club on how the unique properties of metals relate to the way their atoms combine. The 'young and shock-headed' lecturer she saw for the first time that evening made a powerful impression on Dorothy, making a subject in which she had previously had little interest seem fascinating. These lectures were not the dry, recycled material of undergraduate lecture courses. They were, said Dorothy, 'great occasions, on which the whole Chemistry School turned out, and serious science became the absorbing interest of us all'.

She liked best of all to be in the laboratory, and took to working there at all hours. In addition to her course work, she had undertaken to analyse some coloured glass tesserae, taken from mosaics on the walls of buildings, that her parents had found at Jerash during the 1929 season of excavation. Once again, this took her beyond what was required knowledge for a student at her stage in the course. 'Silicate analysis,' she remembered, 'was not usually attempted.' But she persuaded Ernald Hartley, University Demonstrator and 'a very charming elderly person' who gave practical classes in gravimetric analysis, to help her set up the experiment. He became an invaluable friend and ally.

He lent me his own platinum crucible, his own special Mekar burner, his own quartz crucible, his key of the laboratory, and we set up the necessary apparatus on the roof of the Old Chemistry Department with leads from the gas supply from one of the main labs through the windows, and I spent many happy hours analysing these things in the old fashioned, primitive way in which you had to weigh every constituent and hope that at the end you added them up to between 99.8 and 100.2 per cent.[14]

She wrote home to report on her progress.

My dearest Mummy and Daddy
    This letter is being written in the OCD [Old Chemistry Department] on Monday evening, with all my pots and pans boiling merrily all round me. I have been feeling so miserable this weekend but have quite cheered up now. This afternoon I found the slightest trace of my old friend Titanium in the blue glass – isn't that good news! Perhaps Mummy will remember the other time in my life I met titanium – in Khartum with Dr Joseph from the ilmenite Joan and I extracted from our gadwell. I carefully wrote down and kept the test he taught me and now after all these years I have used it again!
    But I'm afraid it's not really interesting from your point of view – the Gerasenes did not introduce it on purpose, it occurs in traces in so many rocks . . .
    I had a tragedy on Saturday and lost all the cobalt from the dark blue glass so I had to go to the Ashmolean on Monday and extract Mr Harden's last-but-one piece of it. So if you are prowling round Jerash and likely to find some more bits of it – you might bring them back.
    Next week I hope to send you a full analysis of the blue

glass and possibly too of some green!
    With very much love from Dorothy[15]

One day in the vacation Miss Kirkaldy came to the lab and discovered Dorothy hard at work. 'She scolded me for staying up in
vacations without consulting her . . . I explained that my parents
were abroad and I had nowhere to go. It sounded a bit pathetic
and though true, not the whole truth.' Miss Kirkaldy's concern
was not just that Dorothy was breaking University rules, but that
she was pushing herself too hard. It was a concern shared by the
group of young women from Somerville with whom she gradually became friendly. With her cloud of golden hair and deep
blue eyes she was an attractive if unworldly figure, often dressed
in handwoven or embroidered garments with little thought for
fashion. Somerville was a close-knit society, and many would
have welcomed her friendship. Her political idealism was widely
shared, Somervillians having something of a reputation as radi-
cals. She was a member of at least three University societies, the
Labour Club, the Archaeological Society and the Junior Scientific
Club. She also joined the Crime Club run in Somerville by
Margery Fry on Sunday evenings. This had nothing to do with
the popular detective stories written by a former Somervillian,
Dorothy L. Sayers; it was a serious discussion group held to raise
awareness of Miss Fry's principal concerns, the need for penal
reform and the abolition of capital punishment.

At first Dorothy attended very few meetings. Equally she took
little part in the conventional social round of tea parties, dances
and trips to the theatre and cinema. Throughout the first year,
her devotion to work was almost total. Not until well into the
second did she allow herself some relaxation and begin to open
up to her Somerville contemporaries. Elisabeth ('Betty') Murray
was an energetic, voluble and level-headed history student, the
grand-daughter of James Murray of *Oxford English Dictionary*
fame. She shared with Dorothy an enthusiasm for archaeology
and decidedly left-wing views. They became acquainted in the
first year, seeing each other at meetings of the Archaeological
Society and the Labour Club. But Betty knew almost nothing of
Dorothy's background until one day in December 1929. She had
gone to queue outside the Playhouse Theatre for tickets for

Journey's End, R. C. Sherriff's moving play about soldiers on the eve of battle during the First World War. 'Dorothy Crowfoot met me down there. I like her very much. She is very quiet and one just has to do all the talking but anything she says is usually worth while.'[16]

For the first time, she told her parents in a letter home, she learned of Dorothy's excavating parents and unusual childhood. But it was another two months before she found out why Dorothy never seemed to have time to join the others on Sunday walks in the surrounding countryside.

> It came out that what [Dorothy Crowfoot] has been so busy on (which we thought was work – since she has been busy every Sunday and weekdays too) is a marvellous painting of the tesselated pavement her father excavated at Jerash. She made a rough sketch of it two years ago when she was there and has been at work on it ever since. Alice [Burnet] saw it and said it is simply marvellous. The painting is to be photographed and is then being sent to Yale. She is an extraordinary person as she is so quiet and yet does all these things. If you can get her to talk she is very interesting too.[17]

And by the following week she had seen the painting herself.

> It was simply beautiful – both the painting and the actual mosaic – lovely soft colouring – and she had done it most exquisitely. I wonder she didn't go blind doing all the tiny squares. She got it finished and sent off to America.

After this Dorothy features much more frequently in the minutely detailed, closely typed and idiosyncratically spelled missives Betty wrote home every week. She began to join Betty, Alice Burnet and other friends on the hikes of several miles they habitually made on Sundays.

> We watched birds a lot – Dorothy knows as much about them as about everything else – and saw jays – and most THRILLING A GREAT SPOTTED WOODPECKER . . . I

had never seen one before nor had the others – though Dorothy knew at once what it was.[18]

She also became more active in the Archaeological Society, joining digs at weekends to excavate sites in local villages.

> They were pleasant, casual affairs. Usually some six or seven of us were taken out in a couple of cars to dig at sites in the neighbourhood . . . a bit of Roman road near the cement works at Water Perry, a Saxon village at Sutton Courtenay, bronze age burials near Horspath. We took along picks and spades and sandwiches and returned in time for tea.[19]

These expeditions were led by Mr Leeds, the Keeper of the Ashmolean Museum, and Dr Lattey, who had lectured to Dorothy in physics during the first year and was one of the authors of the textbook she had read under the stars in Jerash. Although Dorothy describes the digs as casual, they were carefully conducted and provided experience in practical archaeology that some members, particularly Betty Murray, later found extremely valuable. On a good day they would find bits of Saxon pottery, or a post hole from a wooden hut. The Society was relaxed and, for Oxford, untypically egalitarian: Betty Murray was elected Chairman in 1929, and on the excavations men and women, students and lecturers, all dug alongside one another.

By the end of the second year Betty had more or less taken Dorothy under her wing. Although Dorothy gave no indication that she thought she needed looking after, Betty seems to have succeeded, for a time, in getting her to enjoy Oxford for more than its laboratories. She also managed to get her to admit that having such busy, globe-trotting parents could be something of a strain.

> Last Sunday was a lovely morning and . . . Alice, Dorothy Crowfoot and I went on the river for breakfast getting up to just below Summertown . . . Dorothy still hasn't heard from her parents and has no idea whereabouts in Europe

or Asia they are so can't make any plans and doesn't know
if she will stay up here after term or go home or what.[20]

Betty was indignant when she discovered the extent to which
Dorothy was expected to look after her sisters. Before the end of
her first term at Somerville, her father had sent her a cheque for
£200 to open an account with Barclays Bank in Beccles. With this
she was to pay the fees for Elisabeth and Diana's education at
Isobel Fry's Farmhouse School, and manage the Geldeston household over Christmas, as her parents were not planning to return
that year. Someone came in to cook, and Dorothy reported that
the younger ones had been as good as gold – 'we had most glori-
ous fun'. This was a brave assessment given that Diana had had
to go into hospital to have her tonsils removed, and was not well
enough for Dorothy to leave her when term began in January. The
finances were an even worse headache.

> I have been doing accounts this evening. They are most
> awful. Bills seem to have been pouring in from all sides,
> and I don't know what to do with half of them! . . . I'm
> afraid I have not got enough money to pay for all.[21]

Later, when other cheques sent by her parents bore only scant
relation to the needs of the household, she solved the problem by
forwarding the unpaid bills to them. She also had to make sure
the younger girls had everything they needed for school, undertaking the thankless chore of sewing dozens of name-tapes on
their uniforms. On several occasions, when the Oxford term
started before the school term, she had to bring Elisabeth and
Diana to stay with her at Somerville for a few days. In the Easter
vacation before she was due to take her final examinations, when
most students would be planning four weeks' solid revision, she
had both Diana and Joan in bed with flu at Geldeston, and was
late back for the beginning of term again. Whatever Betty Murray
thought, there is no indication that Dorothy herself found this an
unreasonable imposition; Diana says she never minded having a
much younger sister 'tagging along'. Instead, she learned to cope
with having a lot of demands on her time by focusing intensely
on each task as it arose, and switching her attention rapidly and

completely between them. It was a skill that was to prove invaluable in the future.

Even when she did get away from Oxford and the family for vacations, Dorothy was never idle. Under the influence of Margery Fry, she joined a group of socially conscious Somerville students who went to London at the beginning of the Christmas vacation in 1929 for a Study Week on Social Legislation. The young women were to be accommodated in settlements for the destitute in some of the less salubrious parts of London and attend a series of lectures on provision for 'the Unfit, the Abnormal, the School child . . . prisons, mentally deficient, paupers etc etc.' According to Betty Murray's account, the organization was a bit haphazard.

> I heard yesterday in reply to my letter announcing my
> arrival that they hadn't heard I was coming but would be
> pleased to see me! . . . Dorothy Crowfoot who hadn't
> written heard that they couldn't have her and she is to go
> to Rotherhithe! So we are all scattered – which is a pity.
> Poor Kathleen Walker is alone in Millwall – Isle of Dogs –
> and is the only woman there! She is horrified and hopes
> she will be conducted to and from that lone region.[22]

Returning in mid-December from the stews of Depression-hit London to the rural tranquillity of Geldeston, Dorothy was immediately drawn into her mother's whirlwind of village activities. When the Crowfoot parents were at home, Christmas at Geldeston always involved community plays or pageants with a strong moral tone. Dorothy assisted her mother with these productions, which included J. M. Synge's last play, *Deirdre of the Sorrows*, for Christmas 1929, starring her sister Elisabeth who was planning to go on the stage. The following year there were three plays, involving all the village children. Even though she was away so much of the time Dorothy still showed interest in the Girl Guide troop. One year she planned to take a group of Guides from the village to see the Passion Play at Oberammergau in the summer, travelling by train third class. But this project never came off in the end, perhaps for lack of funds.

In her third year, with final examinations on the horizon, Dorothy again began to work obsessively. Pleas to join a party for the theatre or cinema were met with the cry 'Don't you understand, I've *got* to know, I've *got* to know!' Even her twenty-first birthday passed unmarked by any celebration. Betty Murray was disapproving, but Dorothy gave the explanation to her parents (she had only just managed to get her ailing sisters back to school and college): 'My birthday passed very quietly – practically all day in the labs, but it was my first day to myself for so long I wanted nothing more.'[23]

In addition to completing her work for the exams, Dorothy was preoccupied with the question of what to do next. Along with the rest of her year, she had discussed her future career with 'the Fry'. Margery Fry took a keen interest in the future direction of Somervillians, urging them to consider options wider than the 'eternal schoolmarming' which in practice many of them settled for. Teaching was not on Dorothy's agenda. She had stuck to the two possibilities mentioned at her interview: research or social work. After two years of chemistry she was desperate to do research, and to her great relief received Margery Fry's enthusiastic encouragement. She was also reassured that such a decision need not trouble her social conscience. So research it was to be. But research into what?

The BA Honours course in chemistry at Oxford includes a compulsory fourth year of original investigation, known as 'Part II'. Students have to find a member of the Chemistry Department willing to supervise them, and come up with a suitable topic for research. It is a measure of Dorothy's reputation, even as an undergraduate, that offers came to her from a number of quarters to carry out Part II research. With only sixty chemistry students per year, less than a third of the intake today, it was relatively easy for students and lecturers to get to know one another. But Dorothy clearly stood out, and not only because there were so few women students in her year.

The time she had spent in the labs in vacations gave her additional opportunities to meet and talk to those engaged in research. She had briefly worked for John Gulland in the Dyson Perrins Laboratory, making up chemical preparations, and he offered her a project in organic chemistry. The physical chemist

'Tommy' Thompson suggested she might like to do something with him in infrared spectroscopy. There seemed to be many possibilities, all of them interesting. But the inorganic chemist Freddy Brewer, who was at that time Dorothy's tutor, reminded her that she had always said she wanted to do X-ray crystallography. He told her that Professor Bowman in Mineralogy had bought an X-ray tube and camera, and had appointed a demonstrator (junior lecturer) to begin research. The demonstrator's name was Herbert Marcus Powell, but everyone called him Tiny because of his diminutive stature. It sounded too good to be true. 'Without more thought,' wrote Dorothy in her autobiography, 'I agreed to become Tiny Powell's first student.'

But there were still some uncertainties. If she were to begin research in X-ray crystallography, would she be able to continue after graduation – preferably somewhere else, and working with organic molecules? She had written to Uncle Joseph to ask his advice. Joseph replied after consulting his close friend the Cambridge Chemistry Professor T. Martin Lowry, who had been involved in appointing J. D. Bernal to a new lectureship in structural crystallography in 1927:

> X-ray work on organic compounds requires v. good
> crystallography. Bragg in London and Bernal in
> Cambridge are the best people. Lowry could possibly
> arrange a research in which the preparative work could be
> done in the Chem Dept and the X-rays in Mineralogy,
> where they have agreed to concentrate it.[24]

It was enough to make up Dorothy's mind, and she wrote to tell her parents that she had decided to work with Powell 'until [she] knew enough to face the greater men'.

> . . . All that sounded very nice – really excellent just then –
> since the X-ray work would be useful in absolutely
> anything I decided to do ever afterwards and yet if I did
> not do it now – I probably should not have the chance
> again.
>   But at the moment I'm feeling quite appalled at the
> prospect. There will be such a fearful lot of work – and

mathematics – involved. And I was just beginning to rejoice so much in the idea of a nice quiet organic research that would involve no brain whatever.

As it is, it will be practically pure brain work – and mosaics all over again. And I'm just shivering in my shoes – terribly afraid I really am trying to force too much on one poor little brain that is almost non-existent already. It is one thing to appreciate the structures that other people have worked out for crystals – and quite another to be able to work them out yourself. The first requires the same faculties I apply to mosaics – the second requires pure mathematics. It is quite dreadful to think about it . . .

Of course, if I really can do it it will be rather priceless.[25]

The same day, Sunday, 17 May 1931, Betty Murray sent her own parents a slightly different version of Dorothy's feelings. 'Dorothy Crowfoot is coming back to Oxford in early September to begin her research. She is going to research into crystals with X rays and is so thrilled wild horses won't keep her from it.'[26]

There was the small matter of Finals to get out of the way first, a gruelling series of theoretical and practical examinations in all aspects of chemistry. Among her friends at Somerville Dorothy was one of the last to finish, returning from her final paper to be revived with tea and cakes before climbing into a costume to join the chorus in the Going-Down Play. This Somerville tradition provided the finalists, most of whom were leaving, with an opportunity to poke gently satirical fun at the College and its idiosyncrasies. In Dorothy's year the target was the new Principal, Helen Darbishire.

To the anguish of the students, Margery Fry, who was enormously popular, had decided to leave Somerville after only five years in office. Her successor was a reserved, intellectual scholar of English literature, devoted to Wordsworth and Milton. 'The Darb' had immediately attempted to reverse many of the liberal reforms introduced more or less unofficially by Fry. For example, she arranged that coffee should be served in Hall after dinner rather than in the Junior Common Room, so that the students could not leave early. The central number trilled by Dorothy and her fellow-finalists in 1931 lampooned her watchwords:

My God, the whole damned place
Moves with Dignity and Grace
Ever since we all
Had our coffee served in Hall.[27]

With over two months of summer vacation to fill before she could begin her research, Dorothy arranged to go to Germany to gain some more laboratory experience while improving her German. At the time, the leading journal in which new crystal structures were published was *Zeitschrift für Krystallographie*, based in Stuttgart, while many of the international leaders in physics and chemistry also published their results in German. Polly Porter had worked in Heidelberg and offered to introduce Dorothy to the professor there, Victor Goldschmidt. (He was a cousin of the more famous V. M Goldschmidt, who had recently returned from Oslo to take up the professorship in crystallography at Göttingen.) It sounded just the thing, although Porter warned Dorothy 'not to talk about working on X-ray diffraction because [he] only likes the outside of crystals'. Dorothy found herself a warm-hearted and welcoming landlady, Frau Lili Valckenburg, and went off to meet the Professor, having equipped herself, as Porter advised, with a white lab coat.

He was, she found 'very old and small, practically a dwarf, also very wealthy and learned'. He was also devoted to his subject, and had inscribed the words 'Krystallographie ist die Königin des Wissenschaften' – 'Crystallography is the Queen of the Sciences' – above the laboratory that he had funded himself. Working alongside his junior colleagues, Dorothy gained more experience in the traditional techniques of the crystallographer. Goldschmidt had himself designed a new kind of goniometer – an instrument for measuring the external angles and faces of crystals – one of which Polly Porter had bought for the mineralogy lab in Oxford. He had also developed an improved method of drawing three-dimensional crystals accurately on a two-dimensional piece of paper, and one of his assistants set Dorothy to drawing a topaz crystal by this method. 'I did exactly as I was told, and made a very good impression,' she recorded. But her stay was cut short when her parents turned up one day, travelling back to England through Europe, and swept her off to look at the wonderful archaeological museums of Berlin – 'I never improved my German, bad luck.'

Nor did she have time to gain much idea of what was happening in the country, despite Uncle Joseph's parting request to 'let me know what you see when you turn your X-rays on Germany'. It was 1931: support for the Nazis was growing although they had not yet come to power. Professor Goldschmidt and his wife, a 'little gay grandmother' as Dorothy remembered her, were Jewish. The name of Herr Hitler certainly came up in discussion but 'my German hosts seemed unworried by his progress'. She was to see the Goldschmidts once more, a couple of years later when she was at Cambridge. They were by then refugees, about to start a new life in France. But after old Professor Goldschmidt died there his little wife, over eighty and gay no more, fled again to Prague. She killed herself in 1942 as she was about to be deported to a Polish concentration camp.

Dorothy returned to Oxford at the beginning of September 1931 to start her research. The X-ray crystallography laboratory was a large, hastily converted room on the first floor of the University Museum. A plaque outside proclaimed it to be the room in which Thomas Huxley had championed Charles Darwin's theory of evolution in a debate with Samuel Wilberforce, the Bishop of Oxford, at the first meeting of the British Association for the Advancement of Science in 1860. Its ceiling was so high that an extra room, suspended from above and reached by an open-tread staircase, had been installed as a darkroom for the goniometers. This ran the length of the room, against the blacked-out tops of the high, gothic windows. One corner of the main room was partitioned off as a photographic darkroom, and the table that held the X-ray tube was just outside it. Apart from Professor Bowman, who had rooms on the ground floor of the Museum, the entire Mineralogy and Crystallography Department worked at tables in this room: Tiny Powell, Polly Porter, Reginald Spiller (the Lecturer in Mineralogy) and the only research student, Dorothy Crowfoot. A screen divided them from the teaching area where the undergraduate crystallography classes were held.

The X-ray equipment was basic and somewhat temperamental. It consisted of a glass tube connected to a high-tension electricity supply of about 30,000 volts. When the current was switched on a stream of electrons struck a metal target, which emitted X-rays in response. The tube was hand-blown by Tiny Powell according to a design developed at the Royal Institution some ten years before. The air had to be pumped out of it using a mercury vapour lamp, and the vacuum maintained by means of sealing wax. The high-voltage source was an old rotary converter. The crystals to be photographed were mounted in front of the tube on a clockwork device that enabled them to be rotated about a single axis. The camera was an early model, without any of the refinements that had already been developed elsewhere. It was not an easy introduction to the subject. The tube was in principle capable of producing a strong beam of X-rays, but, Dorothy recalled, 'it was a full time job keeping it going sweetly'. Safety considerations were not at the forefront of anyone's mind, but this was nothing unusual: almost every personal reminiscence of the early days of X-ray crystallography features electric shocks, exploding glassware and similar hazards.

Tiny set Dorothy to help him find the structures of a group of compounds that were intermediate between the simple inorganic structures that had been solved to date, and the more complex organic compounds that still seemed out of reach. They were the thallium dialkyl halides, and the study would follow up some conclusions about the way atoms behaved in this class of compound already made by such well-known figures as Linus Pauling and J. D. Bernal. The molecules each contained one atom of the metal thallium, one of a halide (chlorine, bromine or iodine) and two alkyl groups, each consisting of a carbon atom with hydrogen atoms attached; Dorothy worked mainly with dimethyl compounds, which had three hydrogen atoms to each carbon. Finding their three-dimensional structure was to be the first serious project in X-ray crystallography undertaken at Oxford – although he had been appointed in 1929, Powell had spent the intervening years gaining further experience abroad. Dorothy began by synthesizing the compounds, then dissolved them in a variety of solvents which she cooled slowly, over several days, to produce the crystals she needed. Then she got to work, first using the techniques of classical crystallography to draw and measure the crystals, then taking X-ray photographs of the chloride, bromide and iodide. Having produced her photographs, she then had to measure the positions and intensities of the spots, grading them from 'very weak' to 'very strong'.

The principle of X-ray crystal structure analysis is that the pattern of spots, or reflections, generated by a crystal is related to the arrangement of atoms in a single unit of that crystal's repeating structure, or lattice. This unit is called the unit cell. The first task for a crystallographer is to establish the shape of the unit cell. A crystal lattice is made up of straight lines joining equivalent points – you would create a two-dimensional version by joining the centres of all the identical flowers on a wallpaper pattern horizontally and vertically. Each parallelogram thus created would contain all the elements of the pattern – its unit cell. In a three-dimensional crystal lattice the unit is box-shaped, but the box is not always a perfect cube (as it is in common salt). Variations in the lengths of its sides and the sizes of its angles give rise to seven possible basic shapes, known as crystal systems. These were established through purely geometrical considerations in the nineteenth century.

The crystal system to which a particular molecule belongs can make a considerable difference to how easy it is to solve. Dorothy had learned the technique of measuring the external angles of crystals to discover the crystal system in her third-year crystallography course, and perfected it during her brief stay in Heidelberg. Her X-ray photographs permitted her to go one stage further, finding the size as well as the shape of the unit cell. Geometrical rules also determine the possible ways in which a molecule in a crystal can be reflected, rotated, translated or otherwise transformed as it repeats itself throughout the crystal. These rules give rise to exactly 230 'space groups'. Dorothy also learned to identify the space group of a molecule, an essential prerequisite for finding the structure, by looking for spots that were missing from the regular array in an X-ray photograph.

With a simple structure this initial geometrical analysis could considerably narrow down the possible ways in which the atoms might be arranged. Crystallographers could then proceed by 'trial-and-error' – calculating what pattern of spots would be expected from a structure that seemed theoretically reasonable, and comparing it with the actual results. This was where the mathematics that Dorothy so dreaded came in.

Dorothy worked obsessively, compensating for the deficiencies of the equipment by simply putting in longer hours – despite the regular appearance of rats in the Museum after dark. But she found the work immensely satisfying, and cheerful letters to her parents began to expand on the detail of what the work involved.

> We've taken three photographs so far of which my first was better than my second . . . I felt so pleased because I developed and fixed the second one all alone while nobody else was at the lab . . . [she has drawn projections from the photographs] It really is a relief to have the chemical work mixed up with so much drawing.

> This week has been mostly exciting . . . We took a photograph on Thursday which was very good. I calculated it up on Friday morning while taking another and all our calculations fitted in beautifully. Scenes of rejoicing all round the lab . . .[28]

Somerville had only enough rooms to accommodate its students for three years; after that they had to rent digs from landladies approved by the College. The previous spring, Betty Murray had decided to stay on after her Finals in history and do research for a higher degree, the B.Litt. Dorothy had been delighted, and had immediately suggested that they share rooms. So they had gone round together inspecting possible lodgings, and although Betty complained that 'one simply cannot get Dorothy to express much opinion and it is so hard to find out what she wants', they eventually settled on two bedrooms and a sitting room in a house in Richmond Road, not far from college.

Betty came back to Oxford in early October, by which time Dorothy had already been working for several weeks. She was shocked at what she found.

> Until I came up she had been having nothing to eat except breakfast, a cup of coffee at lunchtime and the very light sort of cold sardine sort of supper provided here. Added to

this she has evidently had a very bad sort of cold . . . One day she made ether in the labs and owing to her cold didn't smell it and made herself almost sick with it. I think she looks very thin and not too well, but of course there is no stopping her working. . .[29]

Betty saw at once that more than ever Dorothy needed someone to look after her, and willingly reassumed the role. She made lemon and honey drinks to soothe Dorothy's cough and help her sleep, and once again began to tempt her out on social visits and country walks. They went together to Labour Club meetings, and commiserated with one another over the dissolution of the two-year-old Labour government and the formation of the National Coalition at the end of August. But the pull of the laboratory was always hard for Dorothy to resist, whether things were going well or badly. As well as technical setbacks, she had a more personal reason for working into the night: as she confessed to Betty, she was beginning to chafe under the supervision of Tiny Powell.

Dorothy began the week in extasies as they took a brilliant photo, then they took a bad one, and then for two and a half or three days she tried to adjust a second chrystal ready for a photo and just as she had done it, knocked the thing and upset and lost the chrystal for ever. Her one object is to stop up longer than her supervisor because she wants to work alone and is tired of being told exactly what to do and when.[30]

Herbert Marcus Powell was only a few years older than Dorothy, with a breadth of interests that should have made him an ideal collaborator. He was a considerable scholar who had learned several languages including Russian and Chinese. He was a skilled draughtsman who enjoyed sketching portraits. He was a good chemist, who later made important generalizations about the way atoms pack together in small molecules, and described for the first time a class of compounds called clathrates. He was also politically on the left. He tried to be kind, inviting Dorothy to his house to play table tennis.

But he was intellectually austere, and combined a finicky

attention to detail with a neglect of practical problems, such as getting better equipment for the laboratory. He saw it as his role to instruct Dorothy minutely about the course her research should take. Her chafing at this restriction on her independence – something she was experiencing almost for the first time – set the tone for their whole future relationship. They were to remain colleagues for decades, but though their relationship was always civil, they never became friends.

Between struggling with inadequate equipment and trying to avoid her supervisor, Dorothy's first year of research might have put her off for life. What mattered to her, however, was the work itself. And the work went well. Before the end of the first term she had already taken enough photographs to provide the raw material for her thesis. All three of the principal compounds she studied turned out to have a structure similar to that of common salt, with the thallium atoms alternating with the halogens (iodine, chlorine or bromine), but with the whole structure elongated by the intervening methyl groups. Not content with this, she went on to photograph a series of related compounds in an attempt to solve 'a small controversy in the literature' about whether or not the hydrocarbon chains were rotating. She concluded that they were not, but 'to find out what they were doing demanded more time than I had at my disposal'.

Despite the good progress she was making, Dorothy became downhearted by the end of the first term, convinced that her old bugbear, mathematics, was letting her down. She admitted to Betty Murray that she couldn't see any prospect of continuing with X-ray research, and so would have no subject to offer when applying for Fellowships or studentships the following year. But her despair only pushed her to greater efforts, much to Betty's concern.

> I am glad I am staying up a few days [at Oxford after the end of term] at any rate to keep an eye on her. When she heard I was staying up she was quite disappointed (altho' in her saner moments she is glad) as she was scheming all night sessions in the labs. It is quite absurd as she gets dead tired and owns that she would like a day in bed occasionally. On Tuesday and Thursday this week after

working all day long in the labs she would go back in the evening and didn't come in until nearly 11.30. I get rather worried when she doesn't come in as the machine she works on is a dangerous one. She did give herself a bad electric shock one day this week which if the current had been full on would have killed her. Her supervisor doesn't really like her playing about there alone.[31]

The Christmas holiday brought some moments of relaxation. One weekend in December 1931, Betty and Dorothy went up to London together to look at the Lindisfarne Gospels at the British Museum. Dorothy copied some of the exquisite Celtic illuminations, patterns of interwoven elements like intricate knots. They stayed with Dorothy's sisters who were sharing a flat. Joan had succumbed to a general family assumption that one of the girls would be a doctor, and was beginning her medical training at the Royal Free Hospital. Elisabeth, at her mother's suggestion, was training to be an actress at the Central School of Drama. (Her unworldly eldest sister was astonished that she wore makeup at seventeen.) That Christmas all the Crowfoots were to gather for a happy reunion in Rome, converging from East and West. At the last minute Dorothy had to sort out passports for her two youngest sisters, who had not travelled abroad since their return from Egypt. Betty Murray, who always had travel plans sorted out well in advance, was amused and exasperated at Dorothy's approach.

We are all relieved that Dorothy's Aunt has sent her the difference between 3rd and 2nd class fare to Rome . . . Dorothy of course who is a romantic is fearfully disappointed as she longed to travel 3rd but I should think it is really a good thing. Of course they are hopelessly unpractical – I said something about sleeping in the train and Dorothy said 'Oh we shan't sleep – you see it is Dill's and Lizzy's first long journey so they'll be looking out all the time! (2 nights on the way mind you!).[32]

There was a last-minute panic when Dorothy left her suitcase in the taxi on the way to Liverpool Street Station, so that she arrived in Italy with no clothes; but luckily it was recovered by

her Aunt Dolly and sent on afterwards. In Rome they stayed in a
pension, going out each day to visit churches and eating wonderful lunches in restaurants, and managed to fit in a whirlwind
tour of Florence on the way home. When the holiday was over,
however, Dorothy at once returned to her old habits. Even a visit
from Margery Fry, whom she admired enormously, could not
drag her back from the lab for more than an hour or so. She
caused Betty Murray and her other friends acute anxiety by failing to turn up for the dinner in honour of Miss Fry, who was
going to speak afterwards about her recent visit to the United
States.

> She arrived back however just before the lecture in one of
> her utterly irresponsible and delirious moods – leaping
> about on one foot and saying she had still two hours work
> to do that night – someone had lent her a thermostat for
> one day only. I do think the university might provide
> sufficient apparatus instead of making students work all
> day and night because there aren't enough to go round. Of
> course Dorothy had had nothing since lunch to eat and
> was obviously in a state of nervous excitement. There
> wasn't time to get the food from Janet's room which we
> had gathered – but Rosemary Hughes gave her some
> buisquits . . .
> I went home and put a hot bottle in her bed and
> prepared an orange for her and went to bed myself at
> about 12.25. She left the labs at 3 a.m . . . She was still in a
> state of excitement all [the next] day – though getting limp
> by evening and looked a rag for the rest of the week.[33]

By the following April Dorothy had regained some of her confidence, and was talking about trying to get a research post
overseas. She also applied for a junior teaching post at Bedford
College, a women's college that was part of the University of
London. The testimonials (typed by the long-suffering Betty) she
obtained to support her application give some indication of the
impact she had made in her time at Oxford.

> Miss Crowfoot has been a pupil of mine for a considerable

part of her time as a student for the Final Honour School of Natural Science (Chemistry) and her work at all times reached an extremely high standard. She has a very considerable knowledge of the subject . . . and her essays showed a keen penetration as well as a facility in expression which would I am sure be most valuable from a teaching standpoint . . . (*Freddy Brewer, Inorganic Chemistry*)

. . . It was obvious that she possessed exceptional ability to see the more far-reaching theoretical aspects of any problem which might be under discussion . . . I very strongly recommend Miss Crowfoot for the vacancy in the belief that she is fitted from every point of view for the position. (*S. G. P. Plant, Dyson Perrins Laboratory*)[34]

Margery Fry, meanwhile, departed from the dry formulae of testimonial writing for a warm and loving tribute:

Miss Crowfoot is one of the most interesting undergraduates who have been in the College whilst I have been Principal. Her mind is both mature and imaginative. Her interests are so varied that it is extraordinary that she should be able to keep her special work at so consistently high a level. She has a real passion for science, has studied crystallography and played at astronomy alongside her own subject. She spent a part of one vacation in analysing the colouring matter of early Palestinian mosaics, thus relating two of her main interests, chemistry and archaeology. To the latter subject she has already done valuable service by making exquisite drawings to be reproduced and published of early Christian mosaic floors. She is a most skilful draftsman, working with sensitive accuracy.

. . . Miss Crowfoot is also good at acting and much interested in the drama.

. . . I should do Miss Crowfoot less than justice if I did not add that she has a nature of great charm and sincerity, with a special flavour that is very much her own.

I believe that all my colleagues would agree with me in

thinking it waste of a rare personality if Miss Crowfoot
does not follow her strong natural bent for research
beyond the bounds of a degree examination.[35]

But in spite of all this, and the personal recommendation of
Margery Fry's successor Helen Darbishire, Dorothy did not get
the job. Almost certainly the Bedford authorities thought her too
inexperienced, which she was. They took their time over telling
her she was not being considered, time during which she had
finally to complete her Part II thesis. With a month to go she had
barely started writing, and was spending longer and longer in the
labs. On one occasion Betty Murray reported that she had worked
almost non-stop from 8.30 on a Wednesday morning until 11 p.m.
the following day.

> Naturally she looks like a ghost. She gets thinner and
> thinner. The awful part is that she has simply got to get the
> thesis in in the sixth week and she has so far written three
> pages of it only. We are so frightened that she won't leave
> long enough and that she hasn't got any reserve strength
> to fall back on.[36]

A week later she had a complete draft, but Tiny Powell rejected it
as being far too brief. Dorothy had assumed that 'as it wasn't the
examiners' subject they wouldn't be interested in details'. But
she expanded the draft, as requested, and delivered the conclusion to Powell at midday on 29 May, three days before the whole
thesis had to be delivered to the Examination Schools. He said it
had to be rewritten. There followed an episode of high comedy as
Dorothy, with the faithful Betty in attendance, rushed to rewrite
the conclusion and catch the midnight post to the typist so that it
would be back in time to meet the deadline. Betty related the
whole nightmarish story to her parents.

> At about 11.50 I heard groans from below and rushed
> down to find her nearly in tears – she had left the typist's
> address in College and wasn't sure of it.
>   So we got out cycles and dashed back to College – she
> had my bike as it goes better. Hers – on which I was – lost

its chain before we got to Little Clarendon Street and soon
jammed so it wouldn't wheel either, so I ran carrying it on
my back . . . Payne the porter goes to bed at 11.15.
Eventually he arrived in pyjamas and very cross. He let us
in though . . . [Dorothy found the address] We ran back to
the gate. Payne began to argue – I pushed D. out and said I
would stay and explain. D. took my bike and my lamp
which had ceased to work. She met a policeman but
exclaiming she must have forgotten to put it on she rushed
on . . . [she reached the Post Office with two minutes to
spare] She arrived [back at Richmond Road] in a very
hysterical and collapsed condition – but I had got her bath
ready and she went straight to bed. But what a Sunday!
Payne was quietened next day by 5/-.[37]

This escapade betrayed their landlady's obliging but highly ille-
gal habit of leaving a key for them in the letterbox. Without her
connivance, Dorothy's midnight sessions in the lab would have
been impossible.

The thesis, by some miracle, was finally submitted (five hours
after the midnight deadline, but fortunately the post-box was not
emptied until the morning). Dorothy was hugely relieved, not
because it meant she could have a break, but because she could
do some more experiments.

All these three or four weeks I have been simply aching to
get back to the labs and confirm and extend that work. I
kept on saying, 'If I get up to such and such a point by
such and such a day I'll let myself have a day off in the
labs.' But I never did. So now the fun begins.[38]

At the end of term Dorothy, with Betty Murray and three other
friends, celebrated with another flagrant breach of regulations:
they took a punt up river as night fell, 'running the risk of being
caught by the river Proctors'. They moored under a bank and
slept the night, Dorothy and Betty side by side in the narrow end
of the craft. As the exhausted Dorothy slept she curled up, leaving
Betty less and less space and in danger of falling in. But she
tenderly left her friend undisturbed until they rose for a picnic

breakfast the next day. Dorothy returned for a 9.30 interview with Miss Darbishire, to be told that she had been awarded half of the Vernon Harcourt Scholarship for 1932–3. She had £75 to put towards research the following year.

Dorothy was awarded a first-class degree, the third woman ever to achieve that distinction in chemistry at Oxford. A friendly note from Freddy Brewer makes it clear how seriously her scientific ambitions were taken by the older members of the Chemistry Department.

> My very warmest congratulations to you: you deserve all of it . . .
> You can tell Tiny from me that I think he has been a credit to you: I'm sure you have been an invaluable asset to him. And I hope dozens of good jobs materialize just when you want them.[39]

Dorothy's work for her thesis was published that year as a brief note in *Nature*,[40] the leading scientific journal, co-authored by Powell (later a fuller account appeared in *Zeitschrift für Kristallographie*).[41] It became more urgent than ever to find something to do the following year. To Dorothy's great delight she could be financially independent. Her Aunt Dolly, who had financed her entire university course, offered to make Somerville's £75 up to 'her usual £200'. Dorothy was determined to leave Oxford, where she could continue X-ray crystallographic work only under Powell. She thought of going to Göttingen to work with V. M. Goldschmidt. But he didn't answer her letters, having other problems on his mind: soon afterwards he had to flee back to Oslo to escape the Nazis, and he later moved to the United States.

She consulted Uncle Joseph again. He suggested working with one of the Braggs, but she felt 'rather shy of their eminence'. So he spoke again to T. Martin Lowry at Cambridge about the possibility of her working with Bernal. Since Dorothy had heard him lecture on metals, Bernal had moved on to become one of the first to use X-ray crystallography to tackle biological molecules. Most notably he had used the technique to resolve a dispute between organic chemists about the structure of sterols, which form the basis of a wide range of biological molecules, including some vitamins and sex hormones. It was exactly the kind of work she wanted to do. With Joseph and Lowry mentioning her name at the Cambridge end, she now enlisted the help of T. W. J. 'Tommy' Taylor, who had been one of her examiners, to effect an introduction. He wrote to Bernal on 10 July.

> I am writing about a women chemist of Somerville College, by name DOROTHY CROWFOOT, who got a first class in the Final Honour School of Chemistry here a week or so ago. I was one of the examiners and she thoroughly deserved her First . . . She has the chance of continuing to work at that kind of thing for one or two years more, having been elected a Senior Scholar of Somerville and, to reach the point of this letter, she has a great desire to go to Cambridge and work with you . . . She has ambitions to work in the more purely organic compounds and, if possible, natural products. She is quite a competent practical organic chemist . . . She is very keen on science and works very intelligently. She is of the rather shy type and very quiet, but a really nice person . . . Everyone is agreed that the best thing would be for her to work with you . . . I hope you will be able to take her.[42]

Bernal did not reply immediately, and for a while Dorothy was on tenterhooks. Towards the end of July Taylor wrote to her from Austria where he was on holiday to assure her he had done all he could. 'Sidgwick was going over to Cambridge just before I left England and I told him to make a point of seeing Bernal and of telling him that you were all right. I hope he did it.'[43]

It is unlikely that Bernal really had any doubts; according to Dorothy's later account, he was 'very short of research workers', and one who came not only with glowing testimonials but also with her own funding would be a godsend. That he took a couple of weeks to get round to replying indicates no more than pressure of other commitments. Once everything was agreed between her superiors, she finally wrote to Bernal herself for the first time on 4 August.

Dear Mr Bernal

I was very glad to hear yesterday from Mr Powell that Professor Bowman had received a letter from Professor Tilley [head of the Mineralogy Department at Cambridge] formally accepting me as a research student.[44]

Professor Bowman invited Bernal over to lunch to meet Dorothy. They walked across the University Parks together in the summer sunshine, 'too shy to talk about anything that I can remember' until they discovered a mutual interest in archaeology. After that 'all went well' and it was settled that she should join his lab at Cambridge in October.

3

'My years at Cambridge were rich with new discoveries'

J. D. Bernal and Cambridge, 1932–1934

John Desmond Bernal was a defiantly unconventional figure who dazzled almost everyone with whom he came into contact. His brilliant capacity to develop original perspectives on almost any topic – science, politics, aesthetics, morality – earned him the nickname 'Sage' when he was still an undergraduate. The name stuck. He was Desmond to his family, J. D. Bernal for posterity, but Sage to his closest friends and associates until the end of his life.

With his slightly stooping figure, pale skin and shock of reddish hair, he was not strictly handsome; but his combination of intellectual brilliance and radical reforming zeal proved irresistible to many. First as an undergraduate at Cambridge and then at the Royal Institution with Sir William Bragg, he had made a number of notable theoretical and practical contributions to the fledgling field of X-ray crystallography. A committed socialist, he joined the Communist Party in 1923 and made the first of numerous visits to the USSR in 1931. He believed passionately in the application of science to the betterment of mankind, and that only a socialist state would have the organizational capacity to implement scientifically based policies. His Utopian visions included free and unrestricted sexual relations between men and women; although he had married Eileen Sprague on graduation, he made no attempt to conceal or justify his numerous liaisons with other women. His character was perhaps summed up by his choice of four men as his greatest influences: Leonardo da Vinci, John Donne, V. I. Lenin and Sigmund Freud.[1]

Neither Bernal's politics nor his private life endeared him to the Cambridge authorities, and he fought constant battles over resources for his laboratory. But he had no difficulty finding kindred spirits in the University. When Dorothy arrived in October 1932 Bernal, then aged thirty-one, was one of a group of mainly left-wing scientists, men and women who vigorously debated topics in science, art and politics, and held liberal views on sexual relationships. Cambridge University, as an institution, was no more radically inclined than Oxford. Nor was it any more advanced in its treatment of women; it did not award full degrees to them until after the Second World War. But the convergence of a few individuals working in the overlapping areas between physics, chemistry and biology was enough to create an atmosphere startlingly different from anything Dorothy had known at Oxford.

The two laboratories principally concerned were Bernal's crystallography group, at this stage formally part of the Mineralogy Department, and Sir Frederick Gowland Hopkins's Dunn Biochemical Institute, with which Bernal's group had close and frequent contacts. Hopkins himself, known to all as 'Hoppy', was a benign and tolerant figure, widely respected as one of the leading biochemists of his day – he won a Nobel prize in 1929 for his work on vitamins – and not overtly political. But he took on and promoted such figures as J. B. S. Haldane, another brilliant and innovative thinker and left-winger whose private life also scandalized the Cambridge establishment; Joseph Needham, Conrad Waddington, N. W. 'Bill' Pirie and others closely identified at the time with left-wing politics; and increasingly during the 1930s, a steady stream of Jewish refugees including Hans Krebs and Ernst Chain, both future Nobel prizewinners.

Perhaps more significantly, both Bernal and Hopkins not only liked women but encouraged them to work in their laboratories. At Oxford women were very scarce in research laboratories, although they did exist: Polly Porter in Mineralogy, Robert Robinson's wife Gertrude in the Dyson Perrins Laboratory, where Muriel Tomlinson was also a research student. In Cambridge Bernal already had Nora Wooster (née Martin) and Helen Megaw working with him as research students. Hopkins, whose mother had been a suffragette, had recruited Marjorie Stephenson (who in 1945 became one of the first two women elected Fellows of the Royal Society), Dorothy Needham (née Moyles) and Antoinette Pirie (née Patey) among others. The number of marriages between research workers that resulted led to his lab being nicknamed 'Hopkins's Matrimonial Agency'; it was also known as 'Little Moscow' for the predominance of left-wingers.[2] A visiting Medical Research Council officer reported that the lab seemed to be full of 'talkative women and clever Jews'.[3]

It was a world in which scientific collaborations took place in a context of close and genuine friendships, where the boundaries between scientific, political and social life had almost dissolved. Hans Krebs, arriving in 1933 as a refugee from a Germany riven by class, race and religious distinctions, found it a revelation.

> For the first time I was living in a society virtually free from prejudice and permeated by a spirit of mutual respect and kindness . . . In the laboratory at Cambridge there was intense mutual interest in one another's research; ideas, difficulties and results were openly and frankly discussed. There was also much light-hearted gaiety, wit and humou . . . What struck me, in particular contrast to the German scene, was the strong 'social conscience' of Hopkins and his school, their deep concerns for the affairs of the world at large.[4]

The contrast with her experience of research at Oxford was almost as strong for Dorothy. Coming from the cloistered atmosphere of Somerville and the oppressive formality of Tiny Powell's laboratory, she seemed at first almost overwhelmed. She arrived unannounced a few days after the beginning of term, having been with her parents at the first International Congress of Christian Archaeology in Ravenna, Italy. Bernal was not there to show her round; no one else seemed to know she was coming that day, but W. A. 'Peter' Wooster, the junior lecturer in crystal physics, stepped in.

> I hadn't the slightest idea about Dorothy: I had no idea

about her background and she didn't help me at all –
she was very shy – and so I showed her round all the
Department and explained what all the things were for,
and I couldn't discover from my conversation with her
whether she understood what I was saying or whether
she was bored . . .[5]

Bernal soon returned, and took Dorothy to see Cambridge's principal tourist attraction, King's College Chapel. But she, 'soaked in
the problems of Byzantine decoration', after her trip to Ravenna,
told him it was very lovely but not her period.

There were some similarities in the way crystallography research
was organized at Oxford and at Cambridge. Hastily converted
and unsuitable laboratory space was the most obvious. Bernal's
lab was in the 'mineralogy hut' which was demolished a few
years later, and he had even less space than Powell. 'One entered
over a coffin-like structure covering pipes into an almost dark
room filled with X-ray apparatus,' remembered Dorothy.

The next room, where we students worked, was light, and
filled with tables. Beyond that there were two more rooms,
one small dark room and one larger room for Bernal. Our
working room had a bench along one side, for chemical
experiments, and a gas ring for heating coffee.

Much of the X-ray apparatus was more or less home-made, some
of it to Bernal's own designs. While he had been at the Royal
Institution he had developed a new kind of X-ray camera that
allowed the crystal to rotate or oscillate to different positions in
the X-ray beam. As it rotated, the different planes of atoms in the
crystal moved in and out of the positions required by Bragg's
Law, so that a complete set of reflections could be obtained for
one of the three crystal axes.

He had little aptitude as an instrument-maker, however, and
fortunately had the assistance of the extremely able Arthur
Lanham as laboratory technician. Bernal's practical ineptitude
had nearly killed both himself and Lanham when he first arrived.
Deciding to insert a milliammeter into the high-tension circuit

feeding the X-ray tube, he asked Lanham to cut the earth wire he was holding. The tube was still running. 'Sage gave a tremendous yell and went halfway across the room, and I went down on my backside about 6 yards away. We had got the full voltage straight through us.'[6]

By the time Dorothy arrived Bernal's rotation camera, whose prototype was made out of an alarm clock, a piece of drainpipe and some bicycle clips (or a stopwatch and a coffee tin – accounts vary), was being commercially manufactured near Cambridge. Bernal had also obtained the funds to buy one of the first Weissenberg cameras, which made it even easier to collect data from crystal samples. Yet the lab still had a Heath Robinson air to it, as Arthur Lanham recalled.

After a while we got some transformers . . . we used to
feed all the equipment all round the room with very fine
wire, because Sage stated at the time that you either had to
use for high tension very thin wire or a very thick one.
Well, we strung very fine wires around which was pretty
dangerous; in fact when you went into the room your hair
used to stand on end, literally.[7]

Lanham remembered Dorothy as 'very quiet, very ladylike and very able'. Bill Pirie recalled that her most striking quality was her unobtrusiveness; he also remembered that another colleague said Dorothy always looked 'as if she was just getting over a good cry' (she may have had good reason). Helen Megaw took responsibility for 'settling her in at a table with her own gas tube and generally showing her around'.[8] They soon discovered that she knew what she was doing. Anyone who had managed to produce an interesting crystal used to bring it to Bernal to examine. He always had far too much to do, and soon it became obvious that Dorothy would be the one who took most of the photographs. So gradually people began to bring their crystals to her directly. Quietly, effectively, she became Bernal's right hand. When the first commercially made sealed X-ray tube arrived in the lab, a vast improvement on the home-made variety, it was given to Dorothy, the most recent recruit.

Because his interests were so broad, Bernal had always tended to give away interesting problems rather than pursuing them for himself. He was already deeply involved in discussions about the international organization of crystallography, and was beginning to travel extensively. Almost as soon as Dorothy arrived he left Cambridge to spend some time as a visiting scientist at the Institute of Crystallography in Moscow. He left her three jobs to do, on the face of it rather menial ones. He asked her to sort out the stacks of reprints piled around his room, copies of papers by others covering the entire history of crystallography to that date, and arrange them on his bookshelves. He asked her to look at the numerous tubes of crystals he had been sent, arrange them tidily and choose three that he and she might work on when he returned. And he asked her to make a chart to simplify the business of indexing the reflections on photographs taken with the new Weissenberg camera, which moved the film one millimetre horizontally each time it rotated the crystal through one degree, so that the position of the spots on the film was directly related to the angle of rotation of the crystal. He himself had made a similar chart for the earlier rotation camera (such charts were called Bernal charts, and remained in use for years), and they would be needing the new one as soon as they got started.

She did all this, and moved on to tidy the holy of holies, his microscope table, where he made a first examination of crystals that arrived for analysis. Somehow her ancillary devotion became something of a talking point. The Leipzig-based chemical physicist and X-ray pioneer Peter Debye, visiting the lab later, teased her about it saying, 'You're the girl who has an international reputation for tidying Bernal's microscope table.' But Dorothy did not resent these tasks, which might have seemed an unpromising start to a research career. On the contrary, she found the opportunity to browse through Bernal's reprints 'good for my general crystallographic education' and saw the crystals as 'gold' just lying around waiting to be picked up.[9]

She soon became settled in Cambridge. She had not initially thought of registering for a degree, and did not expect to have a connection with a college. But the view in the lab was that she should sign up for a PhD. At that time the PhD was by no means a requirement for a research scientist. It had existed in Oxford only since 1920 (where perversely it was, and still is, known as

the DPhil) and was looked on as a new-fangled German introduction. Miss Kirkaldy had once told Dorothy that if she went in
for research, she hoped she would 'wait properly for a DSc'. But
Bernal thought she should take the opportunity (despite having
no doctorate himself); so with the help of her father's archaeologist friend Dorothy Garrod she became a postgraduate member
of Newnham College and registered as a PhD student. This also
had the advantage that, as a student of Cambridge University, she
had the right to attend any lectures she liked.

At first she lodged with Eric Dingwall and his wife Doris, also
friends of her parents. Dingwall enlivened her evenings with
accounts of his investigations into extra-sensory perception and
conjuring tricks – he was a member of the Magic Circle. But the
following Easter her two sisters, first Joan, then Elisabeth, came to
live in Cambridge. Elisabeth was trying to get work at the
Festival Theatre, while Joan had given up her medical training
because of a problem with her eyes, and had begun to work with
her parents on excavations in the Middle East, specializing in
flints. Through Dorothy Garrod, she had the opportunity to work
in the Archaeology Department at Cambridge. The sisters moved
into a flat in Scroope Terrace for three months while its tenant, an
entomologist, was on a field trip to the Amazon. Their next home,
an upstairs flat in Queen Edith's Way, some distance from the
town centre, was less successful. Between them they kept late
hours and received a lot of visitors, to the extent that these three
hard-working young women provoked complaints from the
neighbours. At one point Dorothy even received a solicitor's
letter.

> We are informed that late at night you cause noises in your
> flat which considerably affect the quietude of our client's
> other tenant who has gone so far as to state that unless you
> abate the nuisance at once he will be compelled to give up
> his flat . . .[10]

Fortunately Dorothy and Joan (Elisabeth had by this time lost
her job at the Festival Theatre and moved to the Maddermarket
Theatre in Norwich) were able to move to a far more pleasant flat
in Bateman Street, nearer to the town centre, just before Christmas

1933. After Joan went back to Jerusalem the following summer an old Oxford friend, Gwen Davies (later Koblenz), joined Dorothy for a few months. She was very happy there.

> The flat was delightful. It was on the third and fourth floor of a substantial town house. The living room windows looked over the garden at the back of the house, and the walls were dark brown hung with Japanese bird prints. The furniture had been borrowed from the Crowfoot house in Beccles, a dark wood refectory table and chairs and a dresser with Spode plates on the shelves . . . Dorothy gave Joan the credit for the furnishing of the room . . . Dorothy's own bedroom was austere by comparison.[11]

Koblenz remembered dinner parties, and picnics in the flat Cambridgeshire countryside, the 'vastness of the sky' so reminiscent of Dorothy's Norfolk childhood.

Bernal himself was often away, leaving the half-dozen or so members of his group to get on with work he had suggested to them. These absences were something of a relief to them, providing the opportunity for quiet and orderly progress. But when he returned he found them an avid audience for his ideas. Nora Wooster had started a tradition of lab lunches, getting her au pair girl to bring in fresh bread and cheese, and milk for the coffee. The big central table in the workroom would be cleared, and everyone would gather to discuss topics ranging from the origin of life to Romanesque architecture, or to hear Bernal enthuse about his latest visit to the Soviet Union. He led by inspiration rather than management – the demands on his time were such that his office was always chaotic. His own output was prodigious; he wrote fast and fluently, whether for a technical crystallographic journal or a political weekly.

By 1932 Bernal had become one of the pioneers in applying X-ray crystallography to biological molecules. While such molecules do not normally function as crystals in the body, very pure samples of them prepared in the laboratory can sometimes be persuaded to form crystals. The structure of any compound that does so can be studied by X-ray crystallography, and knowledge of the three-dimensional structure of a molecule is a vital step in knowing how it works in living creatures. Bernal's studies on sterols, begun in 1931, had demonstrated for the first time the power of the technique in deciding unequivocally between competing theories about a particular chemical structure. This group of compounds, which includes cholesterol and ergosterol, provides the basis of a variety of important biological molecules, including Vitamin D (calciferol) and the sex hormones. Encouraged by his friends Solly Zuckerman and J. B. S. Haldane, Bernal had obtained crystals of calciferol and the female sex hormone oestrin. Finding some similarities in his first photos, he had gone on to look at five more sterols, concluding that they all had a similar basic structure – long, flat molecules, put together in a way that could not possibly fit with the generally accepted formula for the steroid nucleus.

This formula had been published a few years before by two German organic chemists (both of them Nobel prizewinners), Heinrich Wieland and Adolf Windaus at Göttingen. But the British chemists O. Rosenheim and H. King in London, with whom Bernal was in close touch, were already beginning to have doubts. Bernal's findings provided the opportunity for a reassessment by all those involved, which led eventually (after a somewhat acrimonious dispute over priority) to the corrected formula being published more or less simultaneously by both the British and German groups.[12]

Compared with the small number of organic molecules whose structures had been fully solved, the sterols were relatively complex. Bernal's investigations stopped well short of fixing the exact positions of the atoms in three dimensions. But they did show that the X-ray technique could tell chemists a great deal about an unknown substance that was difficult to establish by the conventional techniques of degradation followed by attempts at synthesis: principally the size, shape and symmetry of the molecule, and its molecular weight. That was often enough to decide between rival formulae. His publications in 1932 attracted the attention of chemists all over the world. Crystals began to pour into the lab. When Dorothy arrived, there was a huge amount of work waiting to be done, much of it pursuing lines that had been suggested by Bernal's preliminary work on sterols. Within a few

months of her arrival she had moved on from tidying up after the
great man to immersing herself in new research. A letter home,
written a week before Christmas Day in 1932, gives the flavour of
her life at the time.

My dearest Mummy and Daddy
   I can't remember in the least when I wrote to you last . . .
I have been having a most wildly busy time.
   Last Thursday was the discussion meeting of the
Chemical Society [in London] on ergosterol, and Sage was
asked to give a paper on that, and also to speak to the
Biochemical Society on Friday. So about a week before that
we gave up all our other jobs and concentrated entirely on
the sterols. By about Monday we were beginning to get the
most interesting photographs . . . I had three X-ray tubes
going all the time. It was quite hectic . . . [Bernal] then had
to go up to London and left me to bring on the photographs
then taking next day. I had a lovely morning rushing
things through – drying all my films with methlyated
spirits – and then caught the 1.55 for King's Cross. I reached
Hampstead where Sage lives at about 4 p.m. We had a
rather hasty tea, and then started on the newly obtained
photographs. I just had time to get to know his wife
Eileen . . . At five o'clock Sage was due for a conference
with Dr Rosenheim at the National Medical Laboratory so
he took me with him and introduced me to everyone there.
It was all very exciting – comparing results all round and
planning what we should do next. We then collected our
papers and rushed off to the Chemical Society at Burlington
House. There was no time for supper. It was simply
marvellous. Sage was working out structures all the way
there – in the bus, in the tube and in the station waiting for
the next train – to say nothing of during the meeting while
everyone else was speaking. And then it all came out
beautifully arranged and ordered as though he had known
it all weeks ago!
   . . . [the next day] At about 4 p.m. I got to Hammersmith,
Lyons research labs, where the meeting of the Biochemical
Society was being held. It was lovely fun meeting again so

many of the people I'd got to know the day before, and
they all welcoming and congratulating. At that meeting
there were a whole series of papers – not only on sterols . . .
After that . . . we all retired into the anteroom and went on
discussing things – we being the band of workers from the
National Medical Lab., Robertson from the Royal
Institution, several other chemists, Sage and I.

Then I dashed back to [Joan and Elisabeth's] flat in the
hopes of catching a glimpse of Diana . . . We had a
celebratory supper before everyone dispersed again,
consisting mostly of cider, tomato soup and meringues.
Joan was going to a party at the Medical School so Lizzie
and I went to a play together before I dashed back to
Cambridge . . .[13]

When the time came to decide on the topic for her PhD thesis, it
was the sterols that Dorothy chose. Over the next year she photographed and characterized dozens of different molecules.

She had barely started work when she heard from Somerville,
in the middle of her second term in Cambridge, that the
Governing Body would like to discuss the possibility of her
coming back to Oxford. She went back for an interview, and
found that they were proposing to offer her a research Fellowship
at the College, with some teaching responsibilities, as a possible
first step towards a full Fellowship. At the time it was the last
thing she wanted (in a recent letter home she had exclaimed, 'I
want to stay in Cambridge for ages!'), and she made no secret of
the fact. It would mean taking on responsibility for students not
only of chemistry, but also of all the other sciences and medicine,
a teaching load that would seriously cut into her time for
research. Not only did she not have to teach in Cambridge, but
the facilities for research were far better, and the company more
congenial.

The Governing Body was rather taken aback. Ever cautious
about the expense, but conscious of their shortcomings in the
teaching of the sciences, they had formed a committee to consider
the question and come up with a recommendation: that 'in
making a permanent appointment . . . the question of research
should be taken into account, and an appointment made of

someone who is already distinguished in research or shews like-
lihood of becoming so'. The College historian notes that they
must have had a particular person in mind.[14]

While they considered the particular person's surprisingly negative attitude, Dorothy 'sat on the floor by the fire in the
Principal's sitting room, thinking how much [she] did not want to
leave Cambridge'. That day the issue was left undecided. The
Somerville authorities could have washed their hands of this
ungrateful woman – Fellowships were far from easy to come by,
especially for women – but instead they used a more subtle
approach. They wrote offering her a two-year Fellowship at £200
per year, of which she could spend the first year in Cambridge,
and devote most of the second to research rather than teaching
undergraduates.

It was a very shrewd move. While Dorothy was certain that she
did not want to leave Cambridge at once, she knew she would
eventually have to think about a more permanent future. She
consulted her Cambridge colleagues. Bernal was 'a little sad',
and revealed that he had already asked Cambridge for the money
to fund an assistant's post. But he and all the others said she
would be foolish to turn down the offer, as it would almost certainly lead to a permanent job. And permanent jobs in science
were very scarce. In the face of such emphatic advice from friends
she respected, Dorothy's resistance gave way. Expressing herself
amazed and delighted, she wrote to the Principal to accept the
terms offered. It was a decision that provided the foundation for
her whole future career.

She realized that if she was to continue with research when she
returned to Oxford, she would need laboratory space and her own
equipment. As an independent researcher, she could hardly return
to the frustrations of her undergraduate days, waiting for Tiny
Powell's permission to use an already inadequate supply of instruments. So six months before she was due to return, just before the
Easter vacation in 1934, she took a day off to go over to Oxford and
talk to Professor Bowman. It quickly became clear that there was
not much the gentle, elderly mineralogist could do to help. The
Department's annual grant from the University was only £200,
and that covered little more than the salary of the technician, Frank

Welch. Dorothy herself, as a College fellow with no associated University appointment, would not be on the University's payroll. However, Bowman agreed that she could have space in the Crystallography Laboratory to carry out her research, that she would have senior status and therefore pay no laboratory fees, and that she could install her own equipment if she could get someone else to pay for it. Having no experience of applying for research funds himself, he had little idea to whom she might turn.

This was a setback, but Dorothy did not give up. She went straight over from the Museum to the nearby Dyson Perrins Laboratory to find the Professor of Organic Chemistry, Robert Robinson. He ran a huge research group and must, she thought, know whom to ask for money. He was also beginning to be interested in using the results of X-ray studies for his own researches. By a stroke of luck she found him in his office and at leisure to speak to her – something even his own research assistants rarely achieved. She reported the outcome to her parents in another breathless letter home.

> I was scared stiff talking to Robinson, and he started awfully badly by saying 'Of course ICI have been financing a great deal of X-ray work lately . . . I've always thought it a great waste of money myself.' My heart sank like anything, and then he suddenly said 'But your work and Bernal's is quite different. I have wanted it to be done in my department for a long time. What kind of room to you need? And how much money?' . . . My breath was quite taken away.[15]

Robinson thought he might be able to get some money from the chemicals firm ICI, and told her to 'think about what you want and send the details to me'.

Rather uncharacteristically, Dorothy had arranged to go to Austria in the Easter vacation for a skiing holiday. She had never previously participated in sports of any kind, apart from compulsory school games, but friends including Helen Megaw had got together to book a chalet in the Tyrol near Innsbruck through the National Union of Students, and persuaded Dorothy to join them. Dorothy also took along her youngest sister Diana. Skiing proved to be a 'very exciting but often painful' experience for her (sixteen-year-old Diana turned out to be a natural; one of her daughters has skied for Canada). While nursing her bruises Dorothy looked through various catalogues of laboratory equipment and began to make a list for Robinson. She put down two X-ray tubes, a transformer set to power them, and two goniometers with rotation cameras of the type designed by Bernal and Peter Wooster. Later she added a Buerger Weissenberg goniometer to the list, the most up-to-date camera available. The tubes had to come from Holland, and the Weissenberg from Cambridge, Massachusetts. The total bill came to around £600. She sent the list off to Robinson and hoped for the best. He duly got the money out of ICI; as Dorothy herself said, a wonderfully easy way of getting research support. Without further intervention on her part, almost everything she asked for was waiting for her when she arrived in Oxford; the Weissenberg took a couple of years longer. But she was not to work under Robinson; to avoid bad feeling he had agreed that the equipment was to be installed in Mineralogy after all.

With her future settled, Dorothy continued her work on the sterols and an assortment of other crystals that came Bernal's way. She photographed hundreds, calculated the unit cell measurements and, from the most intense reflections, could gain some idea of the internal structure of the molecules. Bernal's style was to write up short reports on small groups of crystals, then move on to something else. He always put Dorothy's name on papers for which she had done some of the work, so that by the time she left Cambridge she already had an impressive list of publications. She appreciated his generosity – not all PhD supervisors were so scrupulous – but she regretted that they never 'settled down and worked things out properly'. For her, to do things properly meant going on to solve the complete structure, placing every atom in its correct three-dimensional relationship with every other. In fact, at the current state of knowledge and technology, probably only the simplest of the structures she worked on in Cambridge, Rochelle salt, could have been fully solved at the time. But Bernal gave the job to someone else, preferring Dorothy to keep working on the sterols and other biological crystals.

She complained mildly when she found her name attached to a paper on calciferol in which he supported a structure that was very uncertain and eventually turned out to be incorrect. He simply teased her 'for thinking he had destroyed my international reputation'. The truth was that even if Bernal was sometimes wrong, having her name attached to many of the papers that poured out of his lab in the early 1930s could only enhance Dorothy's reputation. She was a co-author of twelve of the papers published by Bernal between 1933 and 1936; only five of the papers he published in this period had any other co-authors at all. The most significant publication, although at the time its repercussions for chemistry were far less than those of the sterol work, came in her last term at Cambridge. Once again, her name is on the paper and so indelibly associated with the work in crystallographic folklore; but as she herself made clear at every opportunity, she was not even in the lab at the crucial moment.

The paper concerned the first successful X-ray photograph of a single crystal of a protein. Proteins are large molecules whose complex three-dimensional structures are directly related to the tasks they carry out in the body. Haemoglobin, which transports oxygen in red blood cells, is one example. There are thousands of others including structural materials such as keratin in hair or collagen in skin and bones; enzymes, a sub-group of proteins that act as biological catalysts, assembling and disassembling protein components to keep the machinery of the living body running smoothly; and hormones such as insulin. The structure of proteins was a complete mystery at the beginning of the 1930s, and a hot topic for debate. In addition to the many known roles of proteins in the body, many people thought genes were made of protein. Thirty years earlier the German chemist Emil Fischer had shown that proteins were made up of different combinations of around twenty simpler molecules called amino acids. He discovered that they could link end to end into chains known as polypeptides. But did proteins contain these chains, and if so, how did they form a three-dimensional molecule?

Crystallographers had been on the case for some time. Bill Astbury had moved from the Royal Institution to Leeds University, where he was using X-ray techniques to investigate the structure of the fibrous proteins in wool and hair. His pictures were nowhere near clear enough to solve these structures completely. But they suggested a regular, repeating structure that he interpreted as a chain constrained into zig-zag folds. Soluble or 'globular' proteins, such as haemoglobin or enzymes, were much more difficult. Although pure preparations did form crystals, no one had managed to produce an X-ray diffraction pattern from them. Cynics concluded that proteins had no internal order – but if that were the case, how could they form crystals? Others thought that even if you could get a clear X-ray picture, you could not possibly sort out the positions of the thousands of atoms in each molecule.

Bernal's reputation and international contacts put him in a position to try for an answer. In 1934 a young American friend of his, Glen Millikan (son of the Nobel-prizewinning physicist Robert Millikan) happened to be visiting the laboratory of the Swedish chemist, Arne Tiselius, in Uppsala. Tiselius and his colleague Theodor Svedberg were world leaders in the art of purifying proteins, using the ultracentrifuge to spin solutions until the molecules settled out in order of molecular weight. Among those who came to his lab to learn the technique was John Philpot, an Oxford biochemist. One of the proteins he purified while he was there was the digestive enzyme pepsin. Returning from a skiing holiday, he found that his pepsin samples, left in the fridge, had formed a mass of 'lovely shining crystals'. He showed them to Millikan, who reportedly said, 'I know a man in Cambridge who would give his eyes for those crystals.' Philpot at once gave him a couple of test-tubes full, which he took back to Cambridge in his pocket.

Bernal dropped everything when he saw the crystals and started work – but without Dorothy's assistance. After much pressure from her family, she had gone to London to see a Harley Street doctor about rheumatic pains in her hands. Bernal, meanwhile, took a crystal from the tube, and looked at it under the microscope. It immediately lost the brightness and transparency of the others still in the tube, and looked 'rather shrivelled'. Nevertheless he mounted it on the goniometer and took a photograph. But instead of the array of bright spots he hoped for, there was just a 'vague blackening' of the film. It meant there was no orderly arrangement of molecules in the crystal. Yet the perfect hexagonal bipyramids still in the test-tube must have had an internal order to produce those shapes.

Bernal realized that when the crystals dried in the air they lost water that was essential to maintain their structure. So for his next attempt, he drew a crystal into a fine glass tube with some of the 'mother liquor' from which it had crystallized. He then photographed the crystal while it was sealed in the tube, a technique he had used before in work with Helen Megaw on the structure of ice crystals. The results were spectacular – the photograph was covered with reflections. Bernal was able to calculate the size of the unit cell, and the molecular weight of the protein. His figure for molecular weight agreed exactly with that produced in Uppsala using the ultracentrifuge. He could also infer something about the size and shape of the molecules, and how they were arranged in relation to one another. Solving the detailed structure of such a large molecule was far beyond the capacity of any crystallographic laboratory at the time. This did not stop Bernal from suggesting, erroneously as it turned out, that in wet crystals the amino acids did not form chains. But the final paragraph of the letter he published in *Nature* a few weeks later, co-authored by Dorothy, made it clear that whether his conclusions were right or not, the experiment itself had significant long term implications.

[N]ow that a crystalline protein has been made to give X-ray photographs, it is clear that we have the means of checking [our ideas] and, by examining the structure of all crystalline proteins, arriving at far more detailed conclusions about protein structure than previous physical or chemical methods have been able to give.[16]

Dorothy had come back from her trip to London with no clear diagnosis and instructions to rest for a month. When she discovered what had been happening in her absence she decided that the rest could wait till the summer vacation. She immediately took over the pepsin photographs, confirming the measurements Bernal had made on that first day. When their brief report came out in *Nature* it made a huge impact. They had shown for the first time that it was possible to obtain good X-ray photographs of a protein; and they had discovered that the secret of photographing

protein crystals was to keep them wet. Most protein X-ray crystallographers, now a large and international community, date the
history of their field from that moment.

Working with Bernal placed Dorothy in the front rank of a new
breed of scientists who were breaking down the boundary
between chemistry and biology. At the same time she caught the
full force of his passionate commitment to the betterment of
mankind. Bernal was educated in England but born in Nenagh,
Ireland. He had spent his teens devising innovations in military
technology with which he hoped one day to advance the cause of
Irish nationalism. But as an undergraduate at Cambridge he
turned his attention to a more global cause, and a less violent
means of pursuing it. In the course of one long evening in 1919 his
friend H. D. Dickinson introduced him to the ideas of Karl Marx,
and to the 'great Russian experiment'. He found it 'all so clear, so
compelling, so universal . . . It was the people themselves that
would sweep away all the things that I hated . . . It would bring in
the Scientific World State.'[17] Shortly afterwards he rejected the
Catholic faith in which he had been brought up, seeing the Church
as 'an active agent of political reaction throughout the world'.

   He and his wife Eileen became members of the Communist
Party in 1923, when they moved to London. (Ten years later, by
his own account, he 'lost' his card and did not renew his membership.) Bernal was certainly politically active during this
period, supporting the workers during the General Strike of 1926,
for example. But it was some years before he began to work seriously on harnessing science to the cause of solving society's
problems. The catalyst was his meeting with the Russian delegation to the International Congress of the History of Science and
Technology at the Science Museum in London, on 4 July 1931.
The delegation was led by Nikolai Bukharin, who held the posts
of both head of the Academy of Science's History of Science
Division, and Director of Industrial Research for the Supreme
Economic Council. Under direct instructions from Joseph Stalin,
he and his fellow-delegates more or less hijacked what was to
have been a run-of-the-mill academic conference to present the
scientific and technological achievements of the USSR to a baffled
audience of mainly Western scientists and historians.

Bukharin himself, in an address entitled 'Theory and Practice from the Standpoint of Dialectical Materialism', told them that the three main social functions of science were: to increase our knowledge of the external world; to invent and perfect technical processes; and to overcome those forces opposed to human advancement. He argued that to meet these goals, theoretical scientists must remain in close touch with workers engaged in technological production. Only in a socialist state, he proclaimed, could this synthesis be achieved; and it was precisely such a synthesis that was responsible for the great achievements of the USSR.

Bernal's own thinking made him peculiarly open to these ideas, which were received in stony silence by most of the audience. A couple of years before, he had published an odd little book called *The World, The Flesh and The Devil: An Enquiry into the Future of the Three Enemies of the Rational Soul,*[18] in which he speculated (wildly in some cases) about how humanity, individually and collectively, might achieve perfect rationality through the application of science. To his ears, it sounded as though Russia was already putting such thinking into practice. The Soviet delegation had come to the meeting at short notice and with so many papers that not all could be delivered in the time available. But copies of all the papers were made available to the participants and published as a book, *Science at the Cross Roads*, which Bernal reviewed (rather surprisingly) for the right-wing *Spectator*. The impact on his own thinking was immediately apparent. 'Is it better,' he wrote, 'to be intellectually free but socially ineffective, or to become a component part of a system where knowledge and action are joined for one common social purpose?' He made his own first visit to the Soviet Union a few weeks later.

The enthusiasm of Bernal, as well as other left-wing scientists such as Needham, Haldane and Pirie, for the Soviet approach is easier to understand in the light of the prevailing position of science in British cultural life. Science had suffered from the economic decline of the 1920s, with jobs and research funds being increasingly scarce, and laboratories ill-equipped and in poor repair. There was very little in the way of central planning, and virtually no sense that a properly funded science could have an important role to play in solving practical problems such as housing, health and nutrition, or even industrial development. The threat to intellectual liberty of openly fascist movements in Italy and Germany was viewed with increasing alarm, as was the expansion of secret military research. Under these circumstances it was hardly surprising that, to Bernal and his fellow-left-wingers, the Soviet model of science should appear as the ideal for which they had been striving. They desperately needed something to be optimistic about, and the Soviet model of society seemed to fit the bill.

Dorothy arrived in Cambridge just at the point at which Bernal had '[thrown] himself into the business of creating what had not previously existed in Britain: namely organizational channels that helped to translate intellectual discontents into socialist grievances'.[19] Cambridge itself provided fertile ground. The organization most closely associated with Bernal was the Cambridge Scientists' Anti-War Group, founded in 1932 as a talking shop, but which later rose to prominence with a series of publications and demonstrations after the outbreak of the Spanish Civil War in 1936.

The urgent need to counter the Fascist threat softened antagonisms that had split the Left and helped Communists and liberals to join together in the Popular Front. This realignment strengthened the influence of left-wing intellectuals such as Bernal and his Cambridge friends. They were also instrumental in reviving the fortunes of the Association of Scientific Workers, a group whose numbers had previously been in terminal decline after it rejected association with the Trades Union Movement without putting in place any alternative reason for its existence. Bernal, Peter Wooster and Bill Pirie all joined the new ASW Steering Group in Cambridge, ensuring strong recruitment from the Dunn and Cavendish labs. Two years later Bernal was on the National Executive Committee, just one of the sixty or so committees of which he was reputed to be a member by the end of the decade.

Although Dorothy joined the ASW in Cambridge and once went to a meeting of CSAWG, she was unquestionably a supporter rather than an activist. She put her name, as one of seventy-nine signatories, to a letter published in the *Cambridge Review* in 1934 protesting against the militarization of research. And she took part in the Armistice Day protest in November

1933, in which a group led by Joseph Needham marched to the War Memorial bearing a wreath with the legend 'To the Victims of a War they Did Not Make, from Those Who Are Determined to Prevent all Similar Crimes of Imperialism'. Dorothy later said she became 'caught up in' the demonstration after going for Sunday afternoon tea with Sir Frederick and Lady Hopkins.

> Lady Hopkins was worried lest they should bring her husband's laboratory into disrepute, and said they should go in tidy clothes. It wasn't really good advice – there were toughs who threw eggs and rotten tomatoes. Luckily I put on a mackintosh myself.

The incident was reported in the London *Evening Standard* under the headline 'Hooligans at Cambridge'. Dorothy and her friends were incensed to discover that the headline referred to them, not to the members of the Cambridge University Conservative Association who threw the eggs.

Dorothy herself wrote no articles on political or social topics, nor did she hold office on any committee. Why should this be? All her later writings suggest that she was wholly sympathetic to the objectives of the organizations to which she belonged. It was certainly not a case of leaving it to the men – as Gary Werskey points out, Dorothy Needham, Tony Pirie, Reinet Fremlen and Nora Wooster were at least as politically active as their husbands, sometimes more so. Dorothy had a lifelong reluctance to speak on topics on which she did not feel fully informed; but a simpler explanation might be that she was not prepared to give up time that might otherwise be spent on science. She herself notes that although she had intended to use her time at Cambridge to broaden her education, she attended only two courses of lectures in two years: Joseph Needham on biochemistry and I. A. Richards on modern poetry.

Another potential source of distraction was harder to ignore. Dorothy was in love, certainly successively and possibly simultaneously, with two men.

Conrad Hal Waddington is identified by the rest of the family as Dorothy's first love. 'Wad' was perhaps an unlikely candidate in the role: although only a few years older than she, he was bald, thick-set and married with a child. But he was already a scientist of distinction, as well as having wide interests in the arts and in politics. He had made the crucial step in his career two years earlier. Having trained as a palaeontologist, he became interested in embryonic development and went to work at the Strangeways Laboratory outside Cambridge. Its Director, the pioneering cell biologist Honor Fell, taught him the culture techniques that had enabled her to see under the microscope the differentiation of cells in early chick embryos. He used her methods to demonstrate for the first time that tissue transplanted from the embryo of a warm-blooded species could induce developmental changes in other embryonic cells. When Dorothy arrived he was back in Hopkins's laboratory, pursuing the search for an 'organizer' that drove cells in the embryo to develop specialized roles. After the Second World War he went on to establish a major genetics laboratory at the University of Edinburgh.

Like Dorothy herself Waddington was cultured and widely read, and his artistic interests developed further under the influence of the older woman he had married on graduating, Cecil Elizabeth 'Lass' Lascelles. He discoursed regularly on modern art and modern poetry, as well as general scientific subjects, in the *Cambridge Review*; and he belonged to the inner circle of left-wing thinkers around Bernal. For light relief he was an enthusiastic member of The Round, a country dancing club, and was squire of the Cambridge Morris Men.

Dorothy began to mention him in her letters home in January 1933. First she reports that they had tea together. A few weeks later she feels he needs more of an introduction.

> I have got to know Wad rather well during the last week or two. He is 27. He married very young someone ten years older than himself and lately they've been rather miserable together and so have separated for the time. He's still rather miserable about it all, I think . . . I'm going to ask him home in the summer if you'll agree.[20]

In her autobiography she recalls that she and Wad took to accompanying Robin Hill, another biologist, up into the nearby Gog

Magog Hills on Sundays, when he went in search of views to paint with home-made plant pigments. 'But the two of us became very idle and often went walking and talking together instead of painting, returning to Robin at intervals. In the evening we would often meet after a spell in the lab and talk until late over cups of tea.'

But the relationship foundered after a couple of months, possibly because Dorothy did not feel ready to go further than walking and talking and late-night cups of tea. The decision to stop seeing Waddington was hers, but the split left her in a state of some anguish. It happened at an emotionally vulnerable moment, when she had just reluctantly agreed to return to Oxford the following year. She turned to Margery Fry for consolation and advice, and in May 1933 Margery replied in sympathetic but practical terms.

> I'm rather an old brute not to have answered your letter all this time – but I half think you'd rather feel you can let off steam whenever you like without feeling it's got to be answered. Besides – how *dare* I answer with anything like advice! I get more and more shy of trespassing where people's feelings for each other are concerned. Only, my poor darling, remember that love's a most powerful microscope – and that as a rule, if people really ought to get together after trying to separate they *do*. But rather a strong instinct makes me doubt whether it *is* love for good and always with you, and if it isn't half loaves are a very cruel kind of starvation diet, and probably friendship *must* wait if love's got to be with-held . . .[21]

Waddington meanwhile had left the scene, so Dorothy was not faced with the problem of trying to avoid him while they moved in the same social circle. He had gone to the Kaiser Wilhelm Institute for Biology in Berlin, to continue his experiments on embryology, and clearly hoped that they could part without hard feelings. 'Am I allowed to write to you? It would be nice if we could be friends and I don't think you need be afraid of me . . . I should like a letter from you sometime if you feel like it, but don't bother.'[22] She did write, though his reply suggests she still had misgivings.

You know, it is partly yours to say whether we can be
friends or not. I think it ought to be quite possible. We
have definitely entertained and rejected the possibility of a
quickly ripening, very intimate friendship. Now I feel
quite able to begin again with a more ordinary and gradual
thing. But if you find it too disturbing, let's leave it a bit
longer.[23]

Waddington returned to Cambridge in the autumn, having
been appointed to a Fellowship at Christ's College – a position for
which Bernal was rejected. Dorothy resumed a 'rather desultory'
connection with him, meeting every few weeks. The following
summer he met Justin Blanco-White, an architecture student and
a cousin of his wife's, at a party given by the photographer Lettice
Ramsay. Christmas 1934 found the two of them warmly
attached – and at Dorothy's invitation, spending the holiday with
her and Elisabeth at Geldeston. Soon afterwards Waddington's
wife divorced him, and he married Justin in 1936. But by this
time Dorothy had begun on a second emotional experiment, even
more complex in its ramifications. She was in love with Bernal.

In analysing what it was that attracted her it would be impossible to separate her admiration for his intellectual brilliance and
his political commitment from any purely physical or emotional
attachment. Much later, long after she was happily married, the
fleeting opportunities that arose to spend time talking with
Bernal always appeared as highlights in her life. But by all
accounts he also charmed women in a manner that few could
resist – and which, by all accounts, few did. His attraction seems
to have resided in the fact that he never patronized or humiliated
these women. He presented his sexuality as a natural expression
of friendly and mutually respectful human relations – a position
he maintained so successfully that jealousies between his numerous partners were kept to a minimum.

It is not clear at what point the close working relationship
between Bernal and Dorothy developed into something more
intimate. She was characteristically unobtrusive in this as in
everything, so that at least one close colleague in Cambridge at
the time was unaware of any relationship. Indeed, until
Dorothy's daughter Elizabeth casually mentioned that Bernal and

Dorothy had been lovers (at a memorial meeting after her death) many of her colleagues assumed that she was the exception that proves the rule, as far as Bernal and his female associates were concerned.

What correspondence remains – and what is available is clearly incomplete – suggests a gradually increasing involvement that did not reach its peak until some time after Dorothy had left Cambridge in 1934. They probably became lovers some time during 1935 or 1936. Even then, although her affection and admiration for Bernal were unalloyed, something held Dorothy back. She had known him long enough to realize that she could never hope for more than a partial share of his affections. He still lived with his wife Eileen and two children. He had also begun a long-term relationship with Margaret Gardiner, with whom he had set up a second home in London. The news in 1936 that Gardiner was expecting a child was likely to have been a factor in Dorothy's retreat from her affair with Bernal.

Belief in free love – or at least the appearance of such a belief – was more or less a requirement for any woman Bernal became close to. Dorothy ostensibly accepted this doctrine. But nothing in her own life suggests that unlimited sexual freedom was something she wanted for herself. A long-term, mutually loving partnership, complete with children, was her ideal – a marriage, in fact, on the model of her parents' – although she had no clear plan about how she was to achieve this for herself. Clearly it was never going to be an option with Bernal. So she appears to have decided that to have the beam of his brilliance turned in her direction from time to time was enough. This pragmatic approach ensured that their close friendship endured until his death.

It was hard for Dorothy to turn her back on such a rich period of scientific and self-discovery and return to Oxford to take up her fellowship at Somerville. In between she spent a short holiday at Geldeston with her mother, inviting Helen Megaw, a fellow-exile-to-be who had just finished her PhD, to spend a few days with her there before they went their separate ways. Helen was off to Vienna for a year's post-doctoral research. She recalls that they made a little overnight excursion to the Norfolk Broads in a small boat with an outboard motor.

The day we turned home we misjudged our timing, and
had the tide against us as we came back to Beccles – and
then the flow of the river on the last lap. But the motor
gave up at that stage, and we had to paddle. It was well
into the night, and I clearly remember the full moon
looking down mistily on us! Dorothy decided it would be
better to tow. So she got out and took the tow-line – as she
knew the towpath (which I did not) and I sat in the bows
and fended off the prow of the boat from the bank – and so
we arrived safely.[24]

A superficial reading of this story could conclude that it was an
example of the impracticality of the academic scientist. On the
other hand, as an instance of Dorothy's capacity to overcome
adverse circumstances through sheer personal determination,
and to remain calm in a crisis, it can hardly be bettered.

In the event, the return to Oxford almost certainly worked out for
the best. Had Dorothy remained as Bernal's assistant, it would
have been much harder for her to establish her own course of
research and make a name for herself. Bernal himself had little
room for manoeuvre in Cambridge, where he held the title of
Assistant Director of Research but no College Fellowship. He had
little in common with Ernest Rutherford, head of the Cavendish
Laboratory to which the Crystallographic Laboratory was nominally attached in 1934. His political activism and unconventional
personal style meant that he would never become one of the
Cambridge establishment. In 1937 he left to take up the
Professorship of Physics at Birkbeck College in London, a college
established principally so that working people could take part-
time degrees. Most of the lively group around him dispersed,
although the force of his personality and the strength of their
common interests ensured that they remained in regular contact.
Dorothy was to make Oxford one of the key points of exchange in
this network.

4

'It'll serve me absolutely right if the thing is all wrong'

Oxford, insulin and Thomas, 1934–1937

In the first year or two after Dorothy's return to Oxford in September 1934 she clearly did not anticipate that her position at Somerville would become permanent. She was well aware that Bernal and his friends in Cambridge dreamed of setting up an institute that would use the techniques of physics and chemistry to attack problems in biology – a far-sighted idea at the time – and that if he succeeded in raising the necessary support, she would be invited to work there. But Somerville made every effort to make Dorothy feel at home, and she found the environment sympathetic, if not quite the intellectual and social ferment she had left behind in Cambridge.

She was given a 'beautiful room in the front quad', one of two Fellows' rooms in a redevelopment of the College's Woodstock Road frontage that had been completed only the year before. The College selected it for her on the grounds that it would give her the shortest possible journey to her lab in the Museum. On opening the door for the first time, she found a bunch of red roses from Dorothy Wrinch, a mathematician from Lady Margaret Hall who lectured on behalf of all five of the women's colleges and taught some Somerville students. Wrinch had been an object of admiration to Dorothy and her fellow science students; she was the first woman to take an Oxford DSc, and was reputed to have conversed with Albert Einstein. She had recently begun work on a theoretical approach to protein structure, which had brought her into contact with Bernal and his associates when Dorothy was in Cambridge. Now, apparently, she hoped to make Dorothy her ally as she strove to establish herself in this new field.

The Principal, Helen Darbishire, was warm and supportive to Dorothy, even though she lacked the worldliness and ebullience of Margery Fry. Other recently appointed young tutors, the ancient historian Isobel Henderson and the classicist Mildred Hartley, had very much the same outlook on the world as Dorothy, and the three of them came to form a powerful alliance within the College in favour of more progressive policies. Dorothy moved easily back into the rhythm of College life, with its teatime appointments and dinners in Hall.

Her appearance made a great impression on the students. Barbara Chapman, who as Barbara Craig later became Somerville's Principal, had just arrived to read classics. She remembers seeing Dorothy at High Table,

> young and beautiful, with fair hair that, when caught by the sun, stood around her head like the halo of a stained-glass window medieval saint. Her distinctive step was light and springing. She had an engaging trick of giving one a little smile and wink as to a fellow conspirator.[1]

Barbara was one of a group of classics students interested in archaeology that Dorothy used to invite to her rooms. 'It was disconcerting,' she recalls, 'to find out how much more she knew about classical antiquity than an exhibitioner and two scholars admitted to read classics.'

As for Dorothy's own students, there were very few at first: only one or two chemists in each year at Somerville, although she also taught chemists from other women's colleges, and chemistry to the medical students. She found that chemistry tutors in other colleges expected to teach 'the whole of chemistry' in the course of three years. The physical chemist Tommy Taylor, who had written to Bernal on Dorothy's behalf two years before, advised her how to plan her work. Taking a postcard from his pocket during a chance meeting in Broad Street, he drew a grid with nine spaces, like a noughts-and-crosses game, and filled in a plan for each of the nine terms. There being no set syllabus or overall teaching plan for the University, that was all the training Dorothy received. However, she characteristically went her own way. She never tried to teach the whole of chemistry; she stuck mostly to inorganic chemistry and sent her students elsewhere for the rest.

She cared deeply about her students' progress and well-being, but undergraduate teaching never really came naturally to her. In her later correspondence, giving tutorials is usually described somewhat dismissively as 'seeing girls'. She often confessed privately to being ill-prepared. One of her most unrewarding tasks was to teach elementary physics to first-year medical students whose education, like her own, had left them seriously behind in the subject. Inevitably some of them failed the examinations, and she felt their disappointment keenly. For their part, students on the receiving end of her tutorials have described themselves as being 'utterly lost' as she talked on, completely over their heads. Others mention long silences, which she did nothing to break. She suggested they read original papers that she herself had found interesting or inspiring, but it never occurred to her to prepare them for examinations by setting questions from previous years' papers, as happened in some other colleges.[2] She fitted the tutorials around her other commitments and those of her students, never wanting to be away from the lab for long. In retrospect she realized that it might have been more sensible to restrict all her teaching to one or two days, leaving the rest free for research, but somehow she never managed it.

She also had to set and mark entrance examination papers and select students at interview, a chore she found disheartening as so few could be accepted. But it was a task to which she gave her wholehearted attention: 'I fought for every girl I could get.'[3] Amongst the first batch she had to consider was a girl whose father was unemployed, and who would be able to take up a place only if she won a scholarship. Like Dorothy at the same age, she had done no Latin.

I recommended her for a scholarship . . . I swore she would get through Latin in the time (judging by myself) and she did (and liked it). We gave her the largest scholarship we

had, and she worked very well, and though she didn't get
a first she did work in biochemical research all her life.[4]

There was one great advantage to Dorothy in the somewhat peculiar teaching arrangements of the Oxford college system. As
'Moral Tutor', or Director of Studies, of all the Somerville science
students, she had to arrange teaching for medics, botanists, zool-
ogists and physicists as well as chemists. This meant developing
links with scientists in other departments and other colleges, who
would undertake to teach her 'girls' the appropriate parts of the
syllabus, while she did the same for them. As her career developed, these links were to prove invaluable as a way round the
rather rigid barriers between departments that were typical at
the time, and which could have been a serious impediment to her
own cross-disciplinary research.[5]

Apart from her teaching commitments, she devoted herself to
her laboratory. Under pressure from Robert Robinson and the
need to accommodate Dorothy and her new equipment,
Professor Bowman had expanded the amount of space in the
Museum for crystallography. The upstairs room where Dorothy
had done her Part II research was now given over to undergraduate teaching, and Polly Porter and R. C. Spiller worked nearby.
Powell had organized an office for himself at the back of the small
mineralogy lecture room. (Only he and the professor ever lectured here, and audiences were typically in single figures.) A new
X-ray laboratory had been set up in a semi-basement room in the
north-west corner of the Museum, for the use of both Powell and
Dorothy; her only office space consisted of a table in this room.

Powell himself had by this time performed a valuable service.
At that time hardly any of the science departments had an AC
electricity supply, and the Museum was no exception. Dorothy's
new equipment would need an AC supply if it was to be used to
full effect. Fortunately Powell knew the immensely powerful and
wealthy professor from the Physics Department, Frederick
Alexander Lindemann, who at his own expense had installed a
400-volt, three-phase AC cable into his own laboratory. Powell
asked him to let the crystallographers tap into his cable, which
passed nearby, for the new X-ray crystallography laboratory in
the Museum. Lindemann, who knew nothing of X-ray

crystallography, wondered aloud what on earth mineralogists could want with so much power – but he agreed. A hole was duly made in the wall of the Museum – over 2 metres thick at that point – and the AC supply provided.[6]

A small gallery ran along the X-ray lab against the high windows. Here Dorothy kept her microscopes, under which she examined the tiny crystals before sticking them with shellac to the end of a length of glass fibre, ready to be mounted in the goniometer and photographed. She then had to descend a precipitous ladder, holding the precarious assemblage, to the room below. A less suitable environment for the conduct of experimental research involving tiny, fragile crystals, X-rays and high voltages could scarcely be imagined – but in Oxford such a situation was far from unique. The future President of the Royal Society, Cyril Hinshelwood, conducted his Nobel-prizewinning work in the Balliol–Trinity chemistry laboratories – a converted student bath-house.

Now that she was her own boss, Dorothy decided to do what she was never able to do in Cambridge, and see some crystals through to a complete analysis of their structures. There was plenty of work still to do on the sterols, the subject of her as yet unfinished PhD thesis. The Weissenberg photographs of cholesteryl chloride, bromide and iodide she had taken in Cambridge were still waiting for measurements of the absolute intensities of the spots. These intensities were the raw data which she hoped would lead to the structure.

Bernal had discovered that as well as being a good laboratory worker, Dorothy wrote with a simplicity and clarity of expression that was ideally suited to introducing sceptical chemists to this new field. While still a research student she had joined him in preparing the sections on crystallography for annual reports on progress in chemistry published by the Chemical Society. This entailed reading and commenting on the sum total of published work in crystallography worldwide for the preceding year, a job that at the time was not as onerous as it sounds. Moreover, it had the advantage that she was always on top of the latest developments.

The most significant of these in the early 1930s was the application of a mathematical technique known as Fourier analysis to find the exact positions of atoms in crystals. The technique was developed in the nineteenth century by Jean Baptiste Joseph Fourier as a way of representing any physical event that repeats at regular intervals. For the mathematically-minded, it is not an intrinsically difficult process, but, as Horace Freeland Judson put it, 'The high palisade that modern education generally erects between the hard and the soft, between those who have a clear sense for mathematics and those who don't, runs on the wrong side of Fourier analysis.' Put as simply as possible, the analysis involved adding a series of numbers derived from the positions and intensities of the reflections on an X-ray film, together with some idea of their phases.

Just like waves in the sea, waves of radiation have peaks and troughs. When the waves are in phase, the peaks and troughs combine and the waves become higher and deeper. If they are 180 degrees out of phase, a peak combines with a trough, and they cancel each other out. The intensity of spots on an X-ray photograph tells you the amplitude of the waves of scattered radiation, but not their phases. Exactly the same intensity could be associated with a peak or a trough – positive or negative phase. But the Fourier analysis demands for each spot a term representing the phase. With very simple structures it is possible to make an intelligent guess at the positions of the atoms and assign phases to the reflections on this basis. But such an approach is impossible with unknown structures containing more than a dozen or so atoms. Finding a solution to 'the phase problem' was one of the driving forces of advances in crystallography throughout the middle years of the twentieth century.

If the phases are known (or guessed reasonably accurately), then the sum of the terms in a Fourier series gives the density of the electrons at one position in the unit cell. By plotting these densities like a contour map, joining up the regions of equal density, you revealed the positions of the atoms, at the centres of the high density regions. The calculation was not too demanding for molecules with small unit cells, few atoms and few reflections on the X-ray photograph; with larger molecules, the number of terms to be summed quickly grew unmanageable until the advent of modern computers. After her return to Oxford Dorothy tentatively began to attempt Fourier analyses of some of the sterol structures she had worked on in Cambridge, initially without much success.

But she had barely started on this problem when a new and tantalizing possibility presented itself. Robert Robinson, through whose advocacy Dorothy had obtained the funds she needed to equip her laboratory, saw that research in his own field of organic chemistry stood to benefit considerably from the work of crystallographers. When she returned to Oxford Dorothy found him and his colleagues practically waiting on her doorstep. She was only too willing to help the organic chemists out, using the experience to get her new equipment running smoothly. Throughout the 1930s a series of papers appeared on a variety of compounds in which crystallography had clarified uncertainties about the chemical formula or molecular weight.

Robinson was not just using Dorothy as some kind of technical service. When he saw an opportunity to return the favour, he took it at once. He had acquired some pure crystals of a protein made by F. L. Pyman at the Boots Pure Drug Company, and, knowing of her work on pepsin with Bernal, gave her a 10-milligram sample to photograph. The protein was insulin.

It was not much more than a decade since Fred Banting and Charles Best had isolated insulin, the hormone produced in the pancreas that controls the balance of sugar in the blood. Their first cures of diabetic patients had seemed nothing short of miraculous, as Dorothy had read in a book she chose from a catalogue as a school prize. The book was a rather dry series of lectures on biochemistry, published in 1926. It was, she remembered, 'very far above my head'; but it contained an introduction to the pancreas and insulin by the eminent physiologist Sir Henry Dale that could not but whet her appetite for scientific discovery:

> Knowledge of the internal secretion by which the pancreas controls carbohydrate metabolism has been the subject during recent years of a development so rapid and romantic and so fruitful in practical therapeutic results that it has struck the imagination of the public in all civilized countries, with a force probably without parallel in the history of physiological discovery.[7]

Now Dorothy had crystals of this wonderful substance in her hand. It had first been crystallized in 1926, but no one had yet succeeded in taking X-ray photographs of it. What Robinson had given her was not just the chance to find the structure of a protein, but to find out how this remarkable molecule did its work of keeping blood-sugar levels on an even keel. She knew it would not be easy; she never guessed it would take thirty-five years just to get the structure.

When Dorothy first put the crystals under a microscope on 25 October 1934, she could see that they were promising. They were 'beautiful shining colourless rhombohedra' – but they were far smaller than grains of salt, too small for X-ray photography. Over the next three months, Dorothy read everything she could about how to grow larger crystals, experimenting all the while. Not until early in 1935 did she hit on the right recipe, based on a method published by the Canadian chemist D. A. Scott a few months before. Following his procedure 'somewhat slavishly', she redissolved the crystals, adding a little zinc and carefully controlling the acidity. She warmed the solution in a beaker to 60 degrees, and left it to cool for three days in one of the old insulated tanks that Henry Miers had used for growing crystals. She then 'madly filtered [her] precipitate, washed it with methyl alcohol and dried it'.

It worked, but only just. The crystals were less than a quarter of a millimetre across, and shaped 'more like flowers than perfect crystals'; but they were bright and shiny and, unlike pepsin, did not collapse when exposed to the air. Sitting in her window, she mounted one of the crystals on a glass fibre under the microscope, then descended the ladder with her fragile cargo. She set it up in front of the X-ray tube and left it for a ten-hour exposure. The result was all that she could have hoped. 'The moment late that evening – about 10 p.m. – when I developed the photograph and saw the central pattern of minute reflections was probably the most exciting in my life.' She wandered the deserted streets of Oxford in her elation, only to be questioned by a suspicious policeman before turning back to Somerville. She woke the following morning with a terrible thought. What if the crystals were not insulin after all? Before breakfast she rushed back to the lab to check that the crystals really were made of protein – they were.

Bursting to tell someone the news, she was on the point of sending a telegram to Bernal when she heard from Nora Wooster that he was seriously ill with a fever. So she compromised by writing to Eileen Bernal, on 17 February, asking her to tell him the unit cell measurements.

> If he is well enough would you tell him I've grown large enough crystals of insulin and taken photographs of them dry, that they're rhombohedral apparently with **a** taken hexagonally about 42½ Å and **c** much shorter, possibly about 30.

Within a few days Bernal replied, in terms that seem highly cryptic to the uninitiated; almost certainly there was an intervening phone call.

> Dear Dorothy,
>
> | Zn | 0.52 wt. per cent. |
> |----|--------------------|
> | Cd | 0.77 wt. per cent. |
> | Co | 0.44 wt. per cent |
>
> This gives slightly less than 3 in all cases. Nothing is said about the method of drying but they are certainly called dry.
>   I will send you the cadmium stuff as soon as I get back to Cambridge, probably Monday.
> S^8

What this terse missive meant was that Bernal had looked up the literature on the crystallization of insulin, and found that Scott had also made crystals in which he added other metals, cadmium and cobalt, instead of zinc. Bernal's letter told Dorothy the percentage by weight of each of these metals in insulin crystals, and that there were probably three metal atoms in each molecule. The significance of this was that it offered a potential solution to the phase problem, at that time an apparently insurmountable obstacle to the solution of large molecules such as proteins.

One way to discover the phases is to compare photographs of two molecules, in one of which a single atom has been replaced by another that is heavier. If the molecules are essentially identical in all other respects, the way the changed atom affects the intensity of all the reflections gives a clue about whether the phases are positive or negative. This is known as the method of isomorphous replacement. By 1935 the general idea had been talked about for a few years among crystallographers, but the method had been used successfully only for inorganic compounds such as the alums, which have only a few atoms in each unit cell. In the note from his sickbed, Bernal was suggesting that Dorothy try comparing photographs of zinc, cadmium and cobalt insulin, and indeed offered to send her some cadmium insulin as soon as he got back to Cambridge.

He was as good as his word, but in the first instance he urged Dorothy to write up her success in photographing insulin and publish it at once. She had already measured the positions and relative intensities of the spots on the photograph. From this she could deduce that of seven fundamental crystal systems established during the nineteenth century on the grounds of symmetry, the insulin unit cell had the form known as rhombohedral. Its molecular weight was about 37,200 (very close to the figure obtained by the Swedish chemist Theodor Svedberg using the ultracentrifuge). The molecule itself was in the shape of an 'oblate spheroid' – a flattened sphere. She also had a clear idea of how the molecules packed together to form the crystal: a rather more condensed structure than that of pepsin, which perhaps accounted for its greater stability in the air. She hurriedly wrote a short article to *Nature* and sent it off.

Meanwhile she was having once again to think about her future. Her original Somerville Fellowship would end in September, but there was clearly a strong possibility of a longer-term post there, if she wanted it. Her next letter to Bernal, dated 7 March, shows her uncertainty on this issue, as well as her continued anxiety about her insulin results.

> I've been offered and have accepted appointment as tutor here for one year only [the academic year 1935–6]. That is all right, isn't it? It settles nothing absolutely – next year

they say in their letter they intend to offer a five-year appointment which of course can be taken or left then – always supposing it materializes.

I'm rather worried about the 'insulin' . . . I wish really I'd waited the *Nature* letter till the biological tests were made. It'll serve me absolutely right if the thing is all wrong.[9]

On her behalf, Bernal had sent her crystals to Henry Dale himself, to have them tested for biological activity. Her fears were once again unfounded – a couple of weeks later he confirmed that they were the real thing. He was sufficiently impressed with her efforts to offer more help: 'I will certainly ask Dr Scott whether he can supply a further sample of the cadmium Insulin, in the hope that it may enable you to carry a little further your already highly important results.'[10]

As soon as the *Nature* paper was in the post, Dorothy turned her attention to cadmium insulin, hoping to obtain another series of photographs for comparison. But she was unable to put Bernal's suggestion into practice. Mid-March found her close to defeat over the problem of growing suitable crystals, in what was clearly a bad week all round.

The cadmium insulin came out this morning but not as desired . . . under the microscope the 'crystals' were all flaky masses with no birefringence.

The proofs of the *Nature* letter came this morning. The reproductions of the photographs are awfully bad.

I've had a frightful week with scholarship papers but I'll know a lot at the end of what science is taught![11]

Even when Dorothy did obtain usable crystals of cadmium insulin, they gave results that were too similar to those for zinc insulin to give any useful information about the phases. There seemed no other course but to abandon isomorphous replacement for the time being. She was ahead of her time in even attempting it. Not for another twenty years did isomorphous replacement begin to make an impact on protein crystallography. Even then, the technique generated such vast amounts of data for analysis that the solution of protein structures by this method had to wait for the invention of high-speed computers.

When Dorothy's *Nature* article appeared on 13 April 1935,[12] it was the first to be published under her name alone. Its importance established her, just short of her twenty-fifth birthday, as an original scientist in her own right, and brought her to the notice of figures at the heart of the scientific establishment, such as the Braggs and Dale. It convinced Robinson, if he needed further convincing, that X-ray work was going to be an invaluable adjunct to organic chemistry. 'Dear Miss Crowfoot,' he wrote soon afterwards,

> I am afraid that I am putting myself in the unfortunate position of being suspected of praising the role of X-rays for ulterior motives, and I have to confess that the advertisement of the value of your methods has certain consequences which may or may not be agreeable. To put it quite plainly, not only ourselves but a great many other people would like to take advantage of your good nature. I have four culprits to present to you . . . It is becoming clear to me that we must duplicate the apparatus and use the method as a matter of routine, whilst you will naturally develop the special investigations which interest you most.[13]

Robinson never did 'duplicate the apparatus'; Dorothy's complaisant nature and capacity for hard work perhaps made it unnecessary. In later years she urged crystallographers who worked with her always to make a point, when visiting other institutions, of calling on the Chemistry Department – that was the way to discover new and interesting problems. Perhaps she was thinking of her own early experience of contacts with the work of Robinson's large and energetic group.

She still sought Bernal's advice and approval on major issues, and, by her own admission, went back to Cambridge 'rather often' in the first year or so after she left. But although still outwardly diffident, her trademark self-reliance was never far from the surface, and she did not need Bernal's help to widen her acquaintance in the crystallographic field.

She gave her first public talk at a colloquium at Bristol University in 1935, feeling herself 'almost overwhelmed' by the welcome she received at an academic reception in the evening.[14] In November the same year she went up to Manchester, where the younger Bragg was Physics Professor, for a conference. The sessions were on the Saturday afternoon, so she travelled overnight the day before and arrived in time to spend the morning visiting Bragg's lab. Bernal was not at the meeting, and she reported to him after her trip.

> I had a very good time . . . Bragg was very good and gave me Beevers to take me round who wasted his entire morning on me. Then after the afternoon meeting we had a good gathering over tea – Astbury, West, Sylvia Dickinson, and a man from America whose name was something like Veinkochin [Isidore Fankuchen, who soon afterwards became Bernal's assistant]. He and Astbury both agreed your photos [of pepsin] were vastly superior . . . Also I actually said something at the meeting . . .[15]

The names of Arnold Beevers and his colleague Henry Lipson are engraved on the minds of older crystallographers for their invention of Beevers–Lipson strips. These were long strips of cardboard marked with sequences of figures representing the terms that had to be entered in the calculations involved in deriving maps of the density of the electrons in the unit cell from the diffraction pattern – the Fourier series. These electron density maps, always supposing that you had assigned the phases correctly, indicated the positions of the atoms in the crystal.

The strips each contained a row of figures from a table, so that crystallographers could simply line them up one above the other and sum the figures downwards. It saved the time that would otherwise be spent looking up the right figure in the table and writing it down. Not long before Dorothy's visit Beevers and Lipson had persuaded Bragg that it would be worth investing in the duplication of these strips for sale to other crystallographers. As she noted in her autobiography, on that

visit to Manchester Dorothy became one of the first customers. 'I
was amazed to find [them] quite young – Lipson was younger
than myself . . . They offered me two boxes of strips at £5 each –
I bought them.'

She was so quick off the mark that production had barely
started when she put in her order. Beevers was not able to deliver
her set, with custom-made storage boxes, until July 1936.

> We are sending the Fourier strips today . . . and are very
> sorry to have been so long about it. It may be some
> consolation to you to know that your set is, however, the
> very first of its kind that we have produced! The
> mahogany boxes and aluminium partitions are quite
> splendid, and until we get others made we are quite loth to
> lose them! . . .
>
> We do hope that the strips will prove really useful . . .[16]

At about the same time, Dorothy was learning another new technique, gleaned from her reading for the *Reports on Progress in
Chemistry*. The most significant paper that came under her eye in
this period was a report by A. Lindo Patterson in *Zeitschrift für
Krystallographie* in early 1935: 'A direct method for the determination of the components of interatomic distances in crystals'.

Patterson was originally from New Zealand, went to school in
England and took his first degree at McGill University in Canada.
In 1934 he had discovered that it was possible to compute Fourier
series on crystallographic data without the need to know the
phases. The results could be plotted as contour maps in which the
peaks represented not the atoms themselves, but the vectors
between them. A Patterson map does not show where all the
atoms are, but it may reveal the positions of the heaviest atoms
(the vectors between them producing the strongest peaks), and
therefore provide information about phasing that can be used in
a conventional Fourier series. The Patterson function gradually
became one of Dorothy's favourite tools for the analysis of large
molecules, and she used it with consummate skill. She began at
once on her insulin data, at first laboriously carrying out the calculations by hand, later using her new Beevers–Lipson strips to
speed things up.

Dorothy's rapid integration into the small but high-powered world of chemical crystallography left her little time for other interests, but she did permit herself occasional diversions. On visits to London, Margery Fry introduced her to her circle of literary, artistic and social reformist friends, including Leonard and Virginia Woolf. Through her Cambridge contacts, she found herself giving lunch in Somerville to a group of abstract artists, in Oxford for an exhibition of their work: they included Henry Moore, Barbara Hepworth, Ben Nicholson and John Piper. More adventurously, she undertook a trip to northern Spain with her old Somerville friends, Betty Murray, Alice Burnet and Janet Macaulay, in the Easter vacation of 1936. Whether through naivety, recklessness or curiosity to see for themselves what was happening, they planned this trip just as civil war in Spain was becoming inevitable.

The country had experienced increasing political turbulence since the beginning of the decade, and a workers' uprising had been violently suppressed at the end of 1934. In reaction to the repressive regime of the right, the left-wing Popular Front had been narrowly returned to power in the elections of February 1936. Almost immediately Fascist elements began to conspire with the military to launch an armed rebellion. The approaching conflict provoked intense concern among members of the British Left, and Dorothy would have been well aware of the situation. The young women, however, had no thought of involving themselves in political matters: they were going to look at churches.

The only account of their progress among Dorothy's papers is a series of postcards she wrote to her mother, perhaps less reassuring for the almost complete absence of any mention of the political situation.

3 April 1936, Santander
We all got given bouquets of mint and verbena by the old verger – picked out of this cloister [depicted on the postcard]. The cathedral is mainly 13'–14' cent. but with very clumsy provincial carving.

[and in a PS] The municipal elections are off, and the British Consul here says everything will probably be quite safe.

11 April, Leon
We arrived late last night here. The journey from Oviedo
over the pass was wonderful – we got up to the snow line
at one place. On the way we spent five hours at Pola da
Lena to see Santa Cristina, another 9' century church, very
small, situated all alone on a small hill in the middle of a
mountain valley.

12 April [Easter Sunday], Leon
We're still in Leon having found too much to do to pass on
yesterday . . . We're going on to Burgos this afternoon and
spending most of this morning between the Cathedral
mass and a Romanesque church on the outskirts.

15 April, Burguete
You will be glad to know that – if it is fine – we propose
walking across the frontier to France tomorrow . . . We
ought to reach London about 6 a.m. on Saturday and I
shall take the earliest possible train to Geldeston. If all goes
well I shall not write again. Could you please lay in stock a
shampoo for me to use when I get back?![17]

The photographs in Dorothy's files confirm the serious scholarly
purpose of this trip. The architectural details of the churches visited are all recorded – but there are no pictures of the visitors
themselves, or indeed of any people at all. Yet perhaps the
absences in the postcards and photographs give a misleading
impression. Betty Murray recalled how Dorothy persuaded them
to ignore advice not to travel by the trains used by workers as they
were 'unsuitable for females', and delighted the local miners by
exchanging Communist gestures with them. 'With great difficulty
she was dissuaded from joining one of the left-wing election meetings advertised in every town and village. Her friends feared that
their minimal Spanish and money would fail to bail her out.'[18]

Betty herself rediscovered her old role in protecting Dorothy
from her own exertions. 'Dorothy as usual was very tired and had
a rucksack full of textbooks which she did not use. These we sur-
reptitiously transferred to our rucksacks, and they were not
missed.'[19]

A letter from Betty to Dorothy a few weeks after their return contains a typically detailed summary of the views of an authority on Spanish church architecture, but nothing about the political situation. Dorothy herself has left no record of the trip and what it meant to her, other than the postcards. She seems to have forgotten the holiday altogether when writing her autobiography. As she spoke no Spanish, she would have been able to gather no more than superficial impressions from her visit, and was further limited by having companions who were more interested in architecture than politics.

From 1935 onwards, most of her closest friends in Cambridge were directly and intensely concerned with organizations that were using the advent of the war in Spain to warn against the advance of Fascism elsewhere, and challenging government complacency over the need for civil defence. The Cambridge Scientists' Anti-War Group had started in 1932 at Bernal's instigation as a loose affiliation between Communists, pacifists and Labour Party supporters, with an equally unfocused political agenda. Until 1935 its most public act had been the letter it circulated protesting about the militarization of scientific research, which was published in the *Cambridge Review* in June 1934. Dorothy, still in Cambridge at the time, had naturally been one of the signatories. The Spanish Civil War united CSAWG's disparate membership around an anti-fascism that was no longer strictly pacifist. Bernal, Wooster, Pirie and others took up the issue of Civil Defence and, through a series of practical experiments in a King's Parade basement, demonstrated that Home Office advice on how to insulate a room in your house against the use of poison gases was wholly inadequate.[20]

Dorothy, as one of Bernal's closest confidantes, would have been well aware of what he was trying to do, and why. In November 1936 they went to the Netherlands together; Bernal was lecturing to the Dutch Biochemical Society on sterols, and visiting other labs nearby.

> He made a bargain with me that he would give all the
> lectures and that I should write up a lecture text, which
> should be published . . . I find myself remembering . . .
> how every morning in Holland we hurried down to

breakfast to get the first news on the radio, of whether
Madrid had fallen or not. All that time it held out.

Back in Oxford Dorothy was necessarily distanced from the activities of the Cambridge group, although she willingly joined in
when she made her frequent visits there. Poignantly she remembered finding the Crystallography Lab empty one day and being
told that everyone was

> away in an old house near the station helping to set up an
> anti-war exhibition. I went over and joined them and
> found myself working with Julian Bell for the afternoon,
> sticking photographs of bomb damage on posters.

Bell, the son of Vanessa Bell and beloved nephew of Virginia
Woolf, was killed driving an ambulance in Spain in July 1937.

In Oxford there were occasional demonstrations, but the scientific Left lacked the organization of its Cambridge counterpart.
At Bernal's instigation Dorothy became a founder member of the
Oxford branch of the Association of Scientific Workers, but she
did little other than help with the arrangements for visiting
speakers, and then only at Bernal's prompting. Her top priority
was always her research. She completed her thesis – a detailed
examination of the chemistry and crystallography of around fifty
sterol compounds – while still working on her insulin crystals
and doing odd jobs for Robinson, and was awarded her PhD in
the summer of 1936.

In the spring of 1937 Sir William Bragg, the grandfather of X-ray
crystallography, invited Dorothy to use the more powerful X-ray
tube at the Royal Institution in London, to try to obtain better
photographs from which to draw Patterson projections. In the
event, her acceptance of this invitation did not advance the science by very much – but it changed her life immeasurably in
other ways.

She arranged to spend a week in London staying with Margery
Fry while she worked at the Royal Institution. It was the Easter
vacation, and Margery had other guests. One was Pamela
Wrinch, the nine-year-old daughter of Dorothy Wrinch, whose

mother was away in Vienna at the start of her school holidays. The other was Thomas Lionel Hodgkin.

Thomas was a cousin of Margery Fry's, exactly the same age as Dorothy. They had been students at Oxford at the same time, although they had not met. He had been a scholar at Balliol, graduating with a first-class degree in 'Greats'. For him, Oxford was home. His grandfather, A. L. Smith, had been a legendary Master of Balliol. Smith had seven daughters: the third, Dorothy, married Robin Hodgkin, who had lodged with the family before going up to the University and was then a historian and Fellow of The Queen's College. The Hodgkin family, like the Frys, had belonged to the Society of Friends since the early days of Quakerism. Despite the exclusion of nonconformists from the ancient universities until the end of the nineteenth century, many members of the family achieved distinction in medicine, the law and scholarship. The doctor Thomas Hodgkin (1798–1866), who first described the form of cancer known as Hodgkin's disease, was Robin's great-uncle, and his father, another Thomas, was a distinguished historian and successful banker.

The Thomas Hodgkin Dorothy met was slim, with fair hair and blue-grey eyes, and an air of boyish vulnerability. He was an idealistic, romantic, passionate figure; he would never have conformed to the conventions of the Oxford academic community, familiar as they were to him. His early career showed some interesting parallels with that of John Crowfoot. Indeed, he had thought of trying to work with Crowfoot after graduation, as Dorothy communicated to her father in the summer of 1932.

> Nearly a fortnight ago a Mrs Hodgkin asked me out to tea . . . She wanted me to write to you about her son, who would like to go to Palestine with you next year to Samaria . . . Anyway if you are through Oxford this summer, they'd like to see you to talk it over.[21]

Instead, after winning a 'demyship' (a graduate scholarship) from Magdalen College that enabled him to go and work abroad for a year, Thomas attached himself to John Garstang, who was excavating the ancient city of Jericho. According to Dorothy 'he loved Palestine, but not Garstang nor archaeology'. During this period he met Dorothy's parents and her sister Joan, then excavating at another site. Not long after the year was up he obtained, through Colonial Office connections, a position in the Palestine Government, including a few months as personal secretary to the British High Commissioner in Palestine, Sir Arthur Wauchope. He became a well-known figure, famous for having ridden from Bethlehem to Sinai on horse- and camel-back one December, and for falling asleep at dinner parties. He was vehemently opposed to political Zionism, and to the violent suppression by the British Army of Arab revolt against greatly increased Jewish immigration. He spoke out in support of the Arab cause and resigned his job, whereupon he was deported to Lebanon. With the help of the British Consul in Beirut, a former pupil of his father's, he travelled in Lebanon and Syria before returning to England and the sheltering roof of Margery Fry.

At the time Dorothy met him he was in a state of abject misery, smoking and drinking too much and with no clear future direction. He had joined the Communist Party and was selling the *Daily Worker* on street corners, training as a schoolteacher (for which he had no aptitude) and, thanks to an Oxford friend, reviewing fiction for the *News Chronicle*. Margery was so worried about him she had made him visit a doctor and a psychiatrist. All this Dorothy learned that first evening, because Dorothy Wrinch was late arriving to pick up her daughter, and the two young people waited up for her. Apart from telling her his life story, Thomas spent the evening reading her extracts from the books he was supposed to be reviewing.

The rest of the week Dorothy was out all day taking her photographs, Thomas with his hated classes. Margery tried to cheer him up by buying them tickets to see *Swan Lake* together, but 'Thomas slept most of the time.'

Dorothy returned to Oxford and began to write up her first serious paper on insulin. It was for the *Proceedings of the Royal Society*, and would be communicated on her behalf by Sir Robert Robinson. It mattered enormously to her that it should be as good as she could make it, and her first encounter with Thomas seems not to have distracted her unduly. But her father, who was as concerned as Thomas about the treatment of the Arabs in Palestine, was keen to meet him again, and invited him to visit

Geldeston at the beginning of August. Dorothy meanwhile had made plans to go to Yugoslavia for a holiday with Mildred Hartley, the Classics Fellow at Somerville. On 13 July she wrote from Geldeston to Thomas (who was in Oxford) to point out, with an unconcern that might or might not have been genuine, that they might miss each other.

> Dear Thomas
> Since my father wrote to you my plans for going to Yugo Slavia have got changed again and I'm supposed to be leaving England July 28th. My father thought I should warn you and suggest you would rather come some other time before then, say July 26th on. But it doesn't matter as all the others will be here August 1st – unless for other reasons you'd like to change. And don't bother to write except to alter plans. I'm coming to Oxford myself for a week on Thursday. The rest will be glad to see you whenever you come.
> Yours Dorothy Crowfoot

It is difficult to discern the degree of Dorothy's attachment to Thomas at this stage. He had certainly made an impression; but he was not, after all, the first in the field. On the same day she wrote another letter, rather incoherent but clearly proposing a withdrawal from a physical relationship, to Bernal.

> Sage dear
> Times for my coming to Cambridge seem very restricted – only about Friday July 23rd, possibly also Thursday 22nd. I've decided to go to Oxford next Thursday for a week.
> I'm feeling better, writing this in the garden and I expect anyway it was mostly sick inside. But I was so very very glad and happy yesterday – for myself – I should so like to keep that time alone. Do you think it would be very stupid to stay with you only for walking and talking?
> Love Dorothy[22]

Was the timing of this letter related to her new attraction to Thomas? Or was it simply part of her continuing effort to contain her feelings for Bernal in a framework she found more acceptable? She duly arrived in Oxford on 23 July for a week, so she thought, of work on her paper. Going from Somerville to the Museum one evening (according to her own account) she bumped into Thomas in the street, on his way to visit his grandmother in the Banbury Road. He was looking much better. He was lecturing at a summer school for the Workers' Educational Association at Balliol and had a job to look forward to, lecturing on history for the Friends Voluntary Service for Unemployed Miners in the West Cumberland Distressed Area. Adult education proved to suit him very well. Dorothy accompanied him to his grandmother's house, where the matriarchal Mrs A. L. Smith met them at the door 'with a bowl of porridge in her hands'.

The chance meeting changed everything. Over the next few days Thomas turned all his charm and passion on Dorothy, which took her by surprise and shook her so much she could not keep her usually disciplined mind on her Patterson maps. A scrawled, undated note reveals her confusion.

> I'll come with you tonight and stay with you tonight but I won't promise anything more because I feel all perplexed myself and a little troubled by your urgency – but not fully knowing you or understanding it's too difficult to be sure.
>
> I had to write this to put myself to rest for the day. I'm not nearly so unmoved by these things as I might seem and it is not possible to finish this paper under so great stress.
>
> Dear Thomas, don't mind too much and have a little patience.
>
> Dorothy

But Thomas's impulsiveness carried the day; almost at once it was agreed between them that they would marry. Another note from Dorothy reveals the sudden transformation of her feelings.

> I'm feeling still very exalted though also really incredulous. And I know there are so many more things you should know about me before you could have me. And perhaps you'll change your mind for any or all sorts of reasons. But

I think whatever happens this will be one of the happiest
days of my life.

Have you noticed how much more you can make the
beginning and end of a letter mean if you really mean it?
so that it becomes almost impossible to write
yours Dorothy

With the lack of consideration typical of new lovers, Dorothy
postponed her travel plans to spend us much time as she could
with Thomas before he went North to his job in Cumberland.
Mildred had to set off for Yugoslavia without her. When
Thomas came to Geldeston to visit the Crowfoots, Dorothy was
at his side, and her parents were the first to hear their news.
Dorothy's sisters recall that privately the family saw Thomas as
a slightly risky proposition, however likeable. But Dorothy's
happiness was undeniable, and that was what mattered to her
mother.

It was lovely to see how happy you were, and Thomas too.
May you continue to give each other happiness. It is a right
relation, to find rest in each other, as well as new vigour . . .
Now be very careful on this trip, [to Yugoslavia]
precious one – and come back only slightly sunburnt. Very
much love, yr loving Mummy[23]

Dorothy's father discreetly arranged a marriage settlement that
would help their long-term financial security, and offered
Dorothy £100 a year in the meantime. She declined for the time
being, asking only that she might reconsider if she found herself
unable to work as a result of having a child. Thomas's mother in
turn, although she had not yet met Dorothy, gave their union her
blessing.

At first (that is once I got Tommy's letter this morning) it
seemed impossible to write to you – not knowing you. But
now that the evening has brought some peace and quiet
for thinking it seems impossible not to write – to say how
we bless you for bringing him this happiness. It is what we
have longed for for him – and his letter to me shows that

this *is* what we've longed for – the best thing that life can give him.[24]

Dorothy spent the last day before her belated departure for Yugoslavia in London with Margery Fry, whom she immediately took into her confidence. Margery was devoted to both Thomas and Dorothy – and technically made the match between them – but according to Thomas's brother Edward she too had some reservations about their marriage. Thomas's health and prospects were both rather uncertain, while Dorothy was clearly on the threshold of a brilliant career. But Dorothy's first letter after their engagement gives no hint that Fry might have voiced these concerns.

> Dearest Thomas
> I've just been lying in the sun talking about you to
> Margery and finding it quite impossible to feel you were
> already hundreds of miles away and soon would be
> thousands. You're still so much about me I find all my
> private thinking turned into conversations to you.
>   Anyway I'm deplorably lazy about starting out – but all
> is set for tomorrow at 10.30 a.m. which means arriving at
> Bohinj early Sunday morning . . . I'm wishing all happiness
> into you and trying to think how soon it will be that we
> shall see each other again. It has been very lovely. Bless
> you and thank you.
>   With all love, Dorothy

Not liking to leave loose ends, she plucked up the courage while at Fry's house to break the news to Bernal, in a letter in which her concern for his feelings is almost eclipsed by her own bliss and contentment. For once, she addressed him by his Christian name.

> Desmond my dear,
> I've been wanting to tell you a little of all that has been
> happening to me this last ten days, because as you know
> you've meant more to me than anyone for so long – and I
> still find it a little difficult to measure differences. It's hard

writing these things though. But it has all had a sudden dreamlike quality that you more than most people would understand, two nights together in strange country places and days wandering through woods and then meeting all Thomas's friends – and I knew they all knew what had happened though no one said a word – but I just felt perfectly happy and oddly virtuous.

It's a queer thing for I can't begin to be perplexed or troubled. I shall not look for letters from Thomas four times a day now that he has gone, as I used to look for them from you. Nor shall I come thousands of miles to see his face as once I came for you. It doesn't seem to be the same sort of being in love, you know. But I'm extraordinarily happy and feeling blessed and peaceful. I expect I shall marry Thomas and if I do I can't believe I shall regret it, and if I don't I can't believe I shall regret this time.

It's queer, how the only thing that bothers me at all is that I didn't make you happier when I had the chance. I still can't bear to think of you miserable and want to keep you somehow deeply in my life.

Much love to you, Dorothy

Thomas is Margery's cousin, Thomas Hodgkin. Like him a little if you can for my sake – though I think you might for his own.[25]

Dorothy finally reached Bohinj and met up with Mildred Hartley on 8 August, two weeks after the date on which they had originally planned to leave together. The lakeside town, surrounded by mountains, is in modern-day Slovenia near the border with Austria. There they stayed in the Hotel Sveti Duh, with a cosmopolitain collection of other tourists presided over by a hospitable Herr Patron. They spent most of their time going for long walks together, during which Hartley chatted about the lives of her friends, few of whom Dorothy knew. The weather was variable and they both got soaked on one occasion but 'Mildred insisted on large draughts of cognac and no ill effects have followed.' In between these excursions Dorothy continued to work on her Royal Society paper.

She wrote long, chatty letters to Thomas almost every day. She missed him and longed to see him again, but still took careful note of her surroundings and reported anything she thought might interest him. She was also, with his encouragement, giving some thought to preparing for married life.

11 August
I'd love to have anything you could send – specially your *Labour Monthly* article . . . A section of the Yugo Slav army just walked past the window – almost shuffled, poor things, looking very hot and overburdened and generally war weary. I doubt that I'll have much chance of acquiring more useful information about sex till I come home. I read the whole of Marie Stopes when I was about 15 but was rather bored really and remembered nothing accurately enough. But it'll be easy to learn now.

17 August
I like this funny democratic international society. Yesterday it poured all day and in the evening everybody, maids and guests, crowded into the only available room . . .
    And why the nations of Europe ever have wars! All these people seem to have at least six possible nationalities . . . One reason I like going about with Mildred is that she has something of one of your qualities – though perhaps in you it is still more marked – a general friendliness to everyone she meets. It makes the world seem a much nicer place than probably it really is.

The plan was to stay for one week in Bohinj before moving on to Zagreb and then down to the Croatian coast to visit Split and Dubrovnik. But the hotel manager arranged to take them on an overnight trip into the mountains, which they felt they could not refuse, even though it meant staying longer. Interesting as it was, the trip was not an unmitigated success.

20 August
We had an awful argument with the Herr Patron . . .
Mildred started it by saying how frightful it was to think of

those completely isolated people being drawn into a war.
And he straightaway produced all the ancient arguments –
biological necessity of war, need for colonies and what not.
I got very involved trying to produce all the latest trends of
population figures, reproduction rates and what not but
both my German and his English broke down and we all
made ourselves rather angry and had to stop.

It was therefore with some relief that they finally left Bohinj for
the second stage of their holiday. Dorothy found the Venetian
architecture of the coastal towns very lovely, and only wished
Thomas could share her enjoyment. She was less impressed with
the standards in the Hotel Salome.

24 August
I had a quite ridiculous first night in Split. The hotel was
practically full and I got a room in an annexe which turned
out to be swarming with bugs. I'd never seen any before
and only realized gradually from their behaviour and
pictures I'd seen what the creatures were. I isolated one
and put it in a little bottle of spirit for identification by
Mildred in the morning to her great amusement (the spirit
bottle was provided by Sv. Duh's Herr Patron to house
another creature he thought I out [sic] to be interested in as
a scientist). I meant to go to sleep along with the bugs
because I thought it silly to mind them so much, but by
midnight I simply could bear them no longer so I dressed
rapidly and ran down and asked the night porter if I might
sleep on the sofa in the hall. He was very sympathetic and
let me . . . [she woke to find herself surrounded by water as
the rain had leaked through the hall roof] I've got a very
nice room now for my sins. But my face is a sight from
bites!

At last, on 29 August, they left Dubrovnik for the three-day train
journey back to England.
    Dorothy's return was timed to get her to Nottingham for the
annual meeting of the British Association for the Advancement of
Science, where Bernal and all her Cambridge friends, and others

from further afield, had gathered for a special session on the structure of proteins on 3 September. A delightful photo taken at the time by Gordon Cox, then at Birmingham University, shows Dorothy sitting on a wall with Bernal as he shows the distinguished American chemist Irving Langmuir 'reversed spirals in tobacco mosaic virus solution'. Dorothy's calm pose at Bernal's side reveals nothing of her heightened emotional state. Her friends were more observant than the camera, however. At the time only Bernal knew of her engagement. But when a month later she told the news to 'Fan' Fankuchen, he replied, 'I told Dina [his wife] after I'd seen you at the BA that there was something quite different about you – a sort of glittering in your eye.'

Normally she might have spent several days at the week-long conference, which annually drew all the top scientists in the country to talk about their latest work. This time she left immediately after the protein session and went North to be reunited with Thomas. Together they continued up to Northumberland, where Thomas's parents were on holiday at the family home in Bamborough, so that Dorothy could meet them for the first time. Parental approval for the marriage, already given in principle, was wholeheartedly confirmed, as Dorothy Foster Hodgkin wrote to Dorothy Crowfoot the next day.

> My dear Dorothy
> Today is sunny and gentle, the kind of day that I longed
> for you to have so that when you thought of Bamborough
> and Northumberland you should picture it like this. But
> there will be other times and I think we didn't feel the lack
> of sunshine.
>   It was a wonderful time – for T's parents full of
> thanksgiving. To see the change in him was so blessed –
> like watching sun and wind drive away clouds. He has so
> needed someone to be loved by – but could never have
> been content except with the best. Even in so short a time
> we could see how beautifully right this is for him. What a
> lovely thing he has found.[26]

In addition to Thomas and his younger brother Edward there had been a sister, Betty, who had died at the age of twelve.

Thomas's mother's joy at acquiring a daughter-in-law, Dorothy confided to her mother, might have been magnified by the fact that she had lost a daughter. 'It's partly as a result I think she is prepared to be almost frighteningly fond of me. But nobody has suggested I should give up my present work, which is rather understanding of them.'[27]

There was never any expectation in Dorothy's mind that marriage would stop her working, a position in which she had her own mother's full support (Molly even wrote to Thomas to reinforce the point). She had written to Helen Darbishire from Yugoslavia about the engagement, making it clear that she meant to continue if possible.

> I am finding it a little difficult to begin this letter but I would so very much like you to know. Just before I came here I got to know Thomas Hodgkin and we both rather suddenly decided we should like to marry one another . . . I've been very happy and very excited about this for the last three weeks – even if I feel sometimes a little appalled as to how I can fit in all the rest of my life. I should like to try to, though. It is still rather soon to be quite sure of ourselves, but I should like to come and talk to you when I get back.[28]

She confirmed this when, at the beginning of the next term, she wrote formally to offer to resign her Fellowship, which had been made permanent only the year before. All Fellows were still required to resign on marriage, although by this time those who wished to be were almost always automatically reinstated; Dorothy was of course no exception: 'I should be very sorry if it should mean the immediate end of my present connection with the College. I should much like to be able to continue, for a time at least, some of my work in Oxford.'[29]

As the news of her engagement reached wider and wider circles, the majority view seemed to be that it would be absurd for Dorothy to give up her work. Aside from the skill and dedication she brought to it and the satisfaction it gave her, it was more secure and better paid than Thomas's current employment. There are some hints that Thomas himself may have been uncertain at first. Years later Katy Antonius, wife of the Palestine scholar George Antonius, who was a great friend of Thomas's, wrote to Dorothy her recollection of a meeting between the four of them at about this time.

> Thomas stayed and talked with George and Katy went for a walk in the grounds of the place – and listened to the shy angel whose name was Dorothy – saying 'Thomas wants me to give up my work . . . when we marry' and stupid Katy said 'What is it?' and D. said 'I'm working with crystals and it means very much to me' and foolish K who hadn't the least idea what crystals meant . . . but who saw how much it meant to angel D . . . said 'My dear – never give up the work you're interested in for a man and marriage – Thomas must accept you and not stop your work – *please* don't give in – it would be most foolish of you if you care so much about your work of crystals' . . . and later cheeky K told Thomas 'I've told that lovely fiancée of yours that she must *not* give up her work – and you must arrange your life accordingly.' K loved Thomas from Jerusalem days – she'd not met Dorothy till that day . . . but she was completely struck by her frail beauty and her great wish to continue her work.[30]

One reason Dorothy was especially reluctant to let her marriage interrupt her research was that her career had just reached a significant milestone. She had acquired her first research student. Dennis Riley was a Part II chemistry undergraduate from Christ Church who came to work with Dorothy by his own choice. He was only a few years younger than she, and at least a head taller. A photo of the two of them together presents him as an almost avuncular figure in a double-breasted suit beside a diminutive and ethereal creature in a flower-print frock; the antithesis of the student–supervisor stereotype.[31] They had previously met through the efforts of Riley to help Dorothy breach that bastion of male exclusivity, the Alembic Club.

The Alembic Club operated on various levels. Its senior members were research students and members of the chemistry subfaculty, while the undergraduates had a junior version with its own committee. Both junior and senior branches held occasional open meetings with invited outside speakers. These were widely advertised, and non-members of either sex could attend, as Dorothy frequently did. No woman had ever been invited to speak, however.

In addition there were members-only meetings each week, held in students' or Fellows' college rooms, to discuss recent work on topics of general interest. These smaller meetings took the form of informal seminars and were 'a great part of the life of the chemistry school'. But it was only in her fourth year as an undergraduate that Dorothy discovered their existence, and that as a woman she was excluded from them. The bitterest moment came when she heard that Tiny Powell was to talk at one of these meetings on Dorothy's work on the thallium dialkyl halides. Understandably wishing to be present while her own work was discussed, she approached the President, the organic chemist Wilson Baker, whom she regarded as 'a good friend'. He put out some feelers, and came back with the message that it 'wouldn't be a good idea' for her to attend. That she 'really minded about'.[32]

Four years later, when Dorothy was established as a Fellow and Tutor in Chemistry and had a solid research record behind her, the Senior Alembic Club continued to ignore her existence. Dennis Riley, who was on the committee of the Junior Alembic, saw an opportunity to redress this. He and his colleagues invited her to speak to them and their fellow-members about her work on the sterols. She readily agreed, and Riley half-expected some sort of showdown with the seniors over his action. But the meeting was an 'unprecedented success'. Not only was there a good crowd of undergraduates, but 'a sizeable contingent of our seniors, who listened to Dorothy's talk with close attention and evident respect'. Almost immediately Dorothy was invited by the senior members to address them a few weeks later. It was a significant victory, but not the end of the war. In the mid-1940s one of Dorothy's Somerville students, Nesta Dean (née Jones) remembers that Dorothy once arrived for an open Alembic meeting to find a group of her students being kept waiting outside in the corridor until the closed part of the meeting had finished. She opened the door and barged in, whereupon her old tutor Freddy Brewer picked her up bodily and carried her out again. 'There was no bitterness, it was all very good-humoured,' says Dean. The Alembic Club did not vote to admit women as members until 1950.

After his success with her Alembic talk, Riley felt bold enough to approach Dorothy about doing his Part II with her. She was delighted – an extra pair of hands to deal with the steady flow of crystals into her laboratory was just what she needed. Riley remembered that his college, Christ Church, was less taken with the idea.

> This was . . . quite revolutionary and several eyebrows
> were lifted. Here was I, a member of a prestigious college,
> choosing to do my fourth year's research in a new
> borderline subject with a young female who held no
> University appointment but only a Fellowship in a
> women's college . . . [M]y tutor, Dr A. A. Russell, was . . .
> somewhat less than enchanted with the idea but did see
> Dorothy and discuss it with her. Having done so, he
> indicated to me the college's acceptance of the proposal.[33]

Dorothy had a quick meeting with Riley to talk about his work at the beginning of September, between arriving back from Yugoslavia and setting off for Nottingham. It left him in no doubt as to the style his new supervisor would adopt.

> Dorothy's conception of acquainting a raw research
> student with the complexities of the subject was to lead
> him to the deep end and invite him to dive in, without
> thinking of asking whether he could swim. Thus, she lent
> me a book on the polarizing microscope and a reprint of
> Bernal's 1926 paper on the interpretation of rotation
> photographs. She also gave me a tube containing crystals
> of dkp [diketopiperazine, originally to be the subject of
> Riley's research] and left me to it.[34]

She later showed him how to set up a crystal in the goniometer, by which time he had spent enough time reading up the subject in the library to know roughly what it was he was supposed to be doing. Fortunately Riley turned out to be able, amiable and hard-working, and the partnership was a success.

Not long after Riley arrived in the lab, their work took a new direction. Towards the end of September Dorothy fulfilled a promise made at the BA by going up to London to visit Sir Charles 'Bobby' Harington, her distant cousin, at University College. Harington had published a paper showing that insulin would react with iodine, leaving a few iodine atoms in the insulin molecule. Dorothy was hopeful that, because iodine atoms were relatively heavy, this derivative would help her interpret her insulin maps. But in the event the visit was more significant for introducing her to another protein altogether.

Harington had just two days before got out the first crystalline derivative of insulin and was very excited over it. So was I. He is going to send some to Oxford for when I get back. We worked out a grand programme – combined crystallographic and chemical – for a further attack involving a lot of new protein crystals. In the middle he realized one was being studied in the Lister Institute and we rang them up. Dr Keckwick there replied that they had already grown quite large crystals and would certainly give them me if I'd come and get them. So I went down to the Lister in the afternoon and brought back the bottle in my pocket.[35]

The crystals in the bottle were of lactoglobulin, a protein found in milk and isolated for the first time only three years before. By this time Dorothy had realized that she had made a big mistake in preparing her first insulin crystals. By letting them dry, she had allowed them to become slightly disordered. If she had photographed them wet, as Bernal did with pepsin, she would have had more reflections on her photographs and therefore more data for her analysis. The new lactoglobulin crystals were in two forms, both beautifully shaped, and she had no intention of making the same mistake again. She told Riley to put aside his diketopiperazine for the moment (a relatively simple molecule he had some chance of solving completely in the seven months available) and start work photographing the lactoglobulin crystals in their mother liquor.

They subsequently discovered that you could still get good pictures from crystals that were partially dried, as long as you dried them slowly. Riley soon produced the first series of photographs to show the same protein in both wet and dry forms – not a bad achievement for an undergraduate project. He and Dorothy saw that the protein molecule remained essentially unchanged as it dried, apart from shrinking along its long axis. Meanwhile they heard that diketopiperazine had been solved by Robert Corey in Linus Pauling's lab at Cal Tech, so there did not seem much point in going back to it. Riley continued to work on lactoglobulin for the next four years.

Dorothy had precious little opportunity to get to know her future husband, except through frequent letters and the occasional weekend visit. In late September, for example, they took a break together in Kent, staying overnight in a small bed-and-breakfast in Downe, the village where Charles Darwin lived for forty years. In October she joined him in Cambridge, where he was giving a lecture. Once or twice she went up to Cumberland, on one occasion returning infested with lice, much to her horror. Between these meetings Thomas wrote to suggest suitable reading to prepare her for their life together. With her trained scientist's mind, she was able to retain a degree of scepticism about the advice such books contained.

> I've finished your marriage book. Actually I find myself
> very much needing to control my authorities. The subject
> is horrible empirical. There's obviously a lot that could
> only be found out by proper experiments on intelligent
> individuals. If I weren't going to marry you I might
> seriously consider it . . .

She was scarcely more serious about his suggestion that they might converse on political theory during the honeymoon.

> I don't feel that I'd be very much good at sustaining a
> discussion with you on Marxism and literature – too likely
> to take your point of view which doesn't help
> conversation. And if we are to talk about Marxism I'd need

to take a few 'basic' books with me in order to be sure of what I was talking about! None of the Communists I know seem properly rigid. Dennis Riley has just expressed almost approval of my getting married in Church.

The marriage plans developed. Dorothy found herself caught between the high-minded principles she and Thomas had agreed would govern the occasion, and an onslaught of family pressure to do the thing according to all the prevailing middle-class conventions.

My dear, I don't think that it's our parents that will disagree over this wedding! It's a problem of where we come in . . . Your mother was a bit horrified when I said your idea was a small wedding with only about 15 relatives each – so much so I begin to think you must have said 50. However I gave in on that and said I didn't mind how many came. Do you? Really? The point I have much stronger feelings about is announcing the engagement in *The Times* (against of course). They offered to pay the cash required if only we'd do it!

The two sets of parents met for the first time on 3 October at Crab Mill, the old yellow Cotswold stone house in the village of Ilmington in Warwickshire that Thomas's parents had bought for their retirement. Robin had unexpectedly been asked to stay on as Provost of his college, Queen's, following the sudden death of the previous incumbent, so the house had become a weekend retreat. As Dorothy had predicted, the Hodgkin and Crowfoot parents presented a united front against all Thomas and Dorothy's ideas for a low-key event. Thomas's father had five brothers and sisters, his mother had eight; there were thirty-six first cousins altogether. Dorothy's mother insisted on inviting the whole of the village of Geldeston, where the marriage was to take place. At least the date was settled easily: 16 December, the first available weekend after the scholarship exams. Dorothy, however, had to dissuade her future father-in-law from securing the services of all the Queen's chemists to mark her papers for her, so that she should not be exhausted. Meanwhile Molly Crowfoot persuaded them

that the South of France would be preferable to the West of
Ireland for a December honeymoon.

Without Thomas beside her to stiffen her resolve, Dorothy
caved in on all the essential points, apparently without too much
regret.

> My mother, removed from everyone else's pernicious
> influence, agreed very well with us about our wedding
> arrangements. Perhaps that's not true – really I agree with
> her when she says she thinks it all quite unimportant and
> it's only you and me really whatever else is happening all
> round. One makes too many moral issues for oneself, don't
> you think?

As for a home, the couple decided to do without one at first, and
to continue to see each other only for weekends and holidays
after they were married. There were precedents for such an
arrangement among some of Dorothy's closest friends; Bill and
Tony Pirie, for example, had lived in London and Cambridge
respectively when they first married. Tony, now a young mother,
also had a Cambridge Research Fellowship and had just been
elected a city councillor. But Dorothy confessed privately to
Bernal that she had some anxieties about the arrangement.

> It's lovely for me of course because you know I don't really
> need someone desperately all the time; but it is delightful
> to have Thomas to turn to, to know that I shall see him in a
> week's time and there will be time for us to be together
> and talk and know one another. It's not all quite clear.
> Some things bother me. I think Thomas probably misses
> me more when I'm away than I do him – and would rather
> I were going to live with him more. While I have got so
> used to long absences what I have is luxury. So I think
> there may be a lot of practical difficulties.[36]

It took some effort on Dorothy's part to reconcile Bernal to the
idea of her marrying Thomas, and that this would necessarily
mean a change in their relationship. She made several efforts to
arrange a meeting – not only to talk to him about Thomas, but

because she was desperate for his advice about the new lactoglobulin work, and her progress on insulin.

> I do care immensely what happens to you. And I can't bear
> you minding my marrying. Sage dear, and a year ago I felt
> so hurt when you said why ever didn't I marry Wad, or
> why didn't I marry someone else.
>   All the same, while I'd dearly love to see you if you've
> time to spare I know you have got a great deal to do. So I
> won't try to attach too great importance to our meeting
> before Thomas speaks in Cambridge on 31st [October],
> knowing that something of you and me will last whatever
> happens.
>   Dorothy
>   But if there is a chance of seeing you I'll bring the
> lactoglobulin photographs![37]

Soon afterwards she wrote again, anxious that Bernal might not even make the Cambridge meeting.

> Dearest Sage
> Do if you can be in Cambridge next weekend. I've got that
> lactoglobulin set – the photographs are more beautiful
> than you can believe – really tetragonal – the sort of things
> that make me sick with pleasure and astounded that I ever
> thought of giving up crystallography.
>   . . . It would be nicest of all of course if you would come
> back on Sat night after the ASW [Association of Scientific
> Workers] dinner.
>   Dorothy[38]

To her disappointment Bernal could not or would not see Dorothy after the dinner in London which they both attended. But she finally managed to talk to him over lunch the next day, both about work and the future. This straightened things out between them to such an extent that Bernal not only undertook to be in Cambridge for Thomas's talk, but suggested the two of them might like to stay overnight with him and Eileen.

How Dorothy felt when she finally introduced the two men to

one another can only be imagined. But Thomas made a great impression on Bernal, who saw immediately that the younger man's idealism matched his own. Dorothy reported back on his verdict.

> I had a very pleasant walk down to the lab with Sage,
> talking about you and our future. He thought what you
> were doing was one of the best possible things and
> wondered if you'd be able to lead it on to a study of
> conditions in the distressed areas and radical proposals for
> their liquidation. We discussed what I should do if you
> wanted to stay in Cumberland and thought Newcastle the
> best hope – there is a job of the kind wanted going at
> Edinburgh now but that's not near enough you to make
> the change worth while! Sage developed a grand day
> dream of a floating college of protein structure – all of us
> that used to be in Cambridge now working apart but
> meeting in our new home once or twice a year.

Dorothy was forcibly confronted with other examples of the complexities of marriage and relationships as she delicately negotiated her own. Her sister Joan, who had experienced a long and somewhat fraught engagement, finally fixed the day for early October. There was trepidation among both families about her marriage to Denis Payne, who worked in a Cambridge bookseller's and had first met the three eldest Crowfoot girls when they shared a flat together. Dorothy herself, who almost invariably tried to see the best in everyone, confessed to Thomas that Joan and her fiancé never seemed to be 'wholly happy about each other or even with each other'. The marriage went ahead. Thomas did not attend, and Dorothy had to stay outside during the reception because Dennis Riley had gone down with scarlet fever, and she feared she might be infectious.

Almost immediately afterwards the quiet calm of Somerville was rocked by the case of a student who had been caught in the rooms of a Rhodes Scholar from The Queen's College. The Principal immediately told her that she would be 'sent down' – expelled from the college. The boy in the case was merely 'rusticated' – temporarily excluded – for one term. Dorothy was incensed. Quiet as she was, she was absolutely fearless in defending a cause she believed in, even when hopelessly outnumbered. She stormed in to see Helen Darbishire.

> She was very nice – she is – but it was simply hopeless and I felt sick and rotten . . . One gets up against a sort of machine and I can't bear being part of it. It's all wretched. Yesterday I felt too bad to write . . . I'm better now really having been strongly supported by Dilly . . . It's not that I think [the couple] a very meritorious case – I don't – but they're not bad.

She took her protest to the next Fellows' meeting and was also the sole dissenting voice in Council, the body that governed Somerville's affairs and included a number of outside members in addition to the Fellows.[39] A two-thirds majority of the students voted to oppose the expulsion. But Dorothy received very little support from the other Fellows and was unable to reverse the decision. Unfortunately the combative and unorthodox Fellow in French, Enid Starkie, who had been appointed at about the same time as Dorothy and was tutor to the girl in question, was away in Italy on sabbatical and heard about the controversy too late to add her voice to Dorothy's. She wrote to thank Dorothy for her efforts – taking the opportunity to urge her not to stop working after marriage.

Dorothy had taken similar action in a previous, less well-publicized case shortly after her return to Somerville in 1934. On that occasion she had threatened to resign her Fellowship if the girl was not pardoned – and more or less forced the Senior Scholar, Barbara Chapman, to put her own hard-won scholarship on the line. The miscreant was excluded for one term only.[40]

One further alarm intervened before the wedding. Dorothy had long enjoyed midnight cups of tea with a group of young émigré physicists in the Clarendon Laboratory, who like her tended to keep unsocial hours over their experiments. When they heard the news of her engagement, a delegation led by Nicholas Kurti hurried over. Did she realize, they said, that sitting around X-ray tubes all day could cause her children to be deformed, or leave her childless? She was momentarily 'rather shocked'. But after a detailed medical examination her London doctor gave her a clean bill of health and said there was no reason why she shouldn't marry. She wrote to reassure Thomas.

> I've thought later that X-rays and sterility was a scare I needn't have let you in for. For Kathleen Lonsdale has had several children and she has had a much longer X-ray life than I have under worse experimental conditions. I was a lot relieved myself when I remembered that.

Dorothy was never superstitious, but she did perform her own little ritual a few days before the wedding. Alexander Todd, one of Robinson's protégés, had sent her crystals of a substance related to Vitamin E, asking her to determine its molecular weight. It was a relatively unimportant task that could have waited until after the honeymoon. But remembering a medical students' song about Vitamin E, advising you to 'blast the hopes of Marie Stopes by taking it in your tea', Dorothy carried out the job just before she left for Geldeston 'in the hope of a happy future'.

A huge and 'very mixed' party gathered in the village church at Geldeston to see Dorothy married. She wore a medieval-style brocade dress of blue and green flowers interwoven with gold (chosen by Thomas after she had rejected his first choice of scarlet velvet[41]), and a light veil over her blonde hair. Betty Murray, who had made the long journey with Alice Burnet, remembered the guests nudging each other and whispering, 'Do look – you'll never see another so beautiful a bride.'[42] The wedding began at 3.30 p.m., as darkness began to fall outside. They sang 'Brightest and best', 'In the bleak midwinter' and 'Jerusalem'. Thomas had found a Communist vicar to conduct the service, who quoted Marx over the couple on the altar steps. Bernal did not come, but sent an affectionate letter. Afterwards an even larger crowd celebrated in the village hall, many of them gate-crashers. Dorothy's father later told her that she should take this as a compliment.

The newly-weds saw most of their guests on to the train at the end of the afternoon, staying for supper with Dorothy's parents before leaving themselves for London. The next day they set off by train for the Villa St Michel at La Croix, near St Tropez. For the next ten days they walked and talked together among the pine trees by the sea. It would be many months before they could enjoy so much of each other's company again.

5

'Nobody could be indifferent to the search for the truth about proteins'

Proteins and pregnancy, 1938–1939

By the beginning of 1938, proteins had emerged as the main focus of the work in Dorothy's laboratory. In addition to insulin and lactoglobulin, she began to take some photographs of the digestive enzyme lysozyme, although without much hope of success. And she was working with Fankuchen of Bernal's lab on the molecular weight of a plant protein, tobacco seed globulin. Of the seven proteins of which single crystal X-ray photographs had been attempted at that time, four had been investigated in Dorothy's laboratory and she had been closely involved with a fifth, pepsin. Since the heady moment when she had seen the first reflections from an insulin crystal, she had believed she stood a chance of being among the first to solve the structure of a protein – and perhaps the structure of all proteins.

It is difficult, from the perspective of the late twentieth century, to appreciate the challenge represented by protein structure at that time. Work on proteins has been eclipsed in the public imagination by the discovery of the structure of DNA by Francis Crick and James Watson in 1953, and the subsequent cracking of the genetic code. But in 1938 no one knew that genes were made of DNA, far less that a simple coded sequence of the four-letter DNA alphabet was all it took to manufacture the thousands of proteins at work in the living world. Proteins, on the other hand, were the key components of the living, working body. They not only provided its structure, but, in the form of enzymes, were key participants in the thousands upon thousands of reactions that kept it alive.

Their components, the twenty or so amino acids, were known to be common to all proteins. In each the components were mixed in different proportions, threaded into chains like necklaces of different-coloured beads. But how did these chains fold up into the three-dimensional molecules that both Svedberg's ultracentrifuge experiments and the early X-ray photographs suggested? Was there a common model, or were they all different? Until even one structure was solved, there were no answers to these questions. But to solve a protein structure by X-ray crystallography was a massive task. There were thousands of reflections in a good photograph, hundreds or thousands of atoms in each molecule, and the calculations involved in trying to deduce one from the other would take literally years with the methods then available. Such calculations could not even be attempted without a reliable way of assigning phases to the reflections.

Making some sort of sense of the bewildering variety of proteins became the goal of a small but highly select band of researchers. Protein structure was their Mount Everest, and crystallography was the means by which they would scale that peak. They knew it would take a long time, but not how long; the real Everest would be conquered before any of them reached their own summit.

From her first success with insulin, possibly even from the earlier work with pepsin, Dorothy dedicated her life to the ascent. Although circumstances forced her to make occasional detours from this hard route – detours leading to triumphs which in the eyes of the world only added to her distinction – her heart was always set on reaching the goal of a protein structure.

Others were setting out on the same journey. Bernal himself now spent little time on laboratory work, but he remained a leader in discussions about the implications of the results produced by Dorothy and others. In 1936 a young Austrian, Max Perutz, had joined his Cambridge laboratory to learn crystallography in the hope of applying it to biological questions. A year later he had his own protein to work on: haemoglobin, the protein that carries oxygen in red blood cells and releases it into the tissues. It made beautiful red crystals, and he soon had a series of X-ray photographs – but at a molecular weight of 64,500 it was several times larger than insulin, with thousands of atoms in each molecule. Perutz remained in Cambridge after Bernal left, and dedicated the next two decades of his life to solving the haemoglobin structure.

Bill Astbury in Leeds was one of the pioneers of protein X-ray crystallography, having been working for years on protein fibres such as the keratin that makes up hair and wool. Fibres have sufficient internal organization to diffract X-rays, but they produce streaks and smears on the film rather than the sharp spots given by single crystals. Fibre pictures could not lead to the positions of individual atoms, but they could suggest something about the overall shape of the molecule which could help in model-building. Astbury put forward the idea that proteins included chains of amino acids wound into a corkscrew twist or helix, and he interpreted his keratin photographs as suggesting that the height of each turn should be 5.1 Ångstrom units (one Å is one ten millionth of a millimetre). For many years this observation provided the main constraint on all discussions about possible structures for proteins.

All the protein structure work in the UK was in the hands of this close-knit group, whose academic ancestry led straight back to the elder Bragg's lab at the Royal Institution. Lawrence Bragg, his son, succeeded Rutherford as Cavendish Professor in Cambridge in 1939 and also became deeply involved in the protein structure work of Perutz and his colleagues. The members corresponded freely and frequently, and met at conferences and each other's labs. Then, in 1937, another major player came on the scene, in the formidable person of Linus Pauling of the California Institute of Technology. No one knew more than Pauling about the bonds that held atoms together in molecules. He had stolen a march on the Braggs in 1929 by publishing a set of tables that quickly became known as 'Pauling's Rules', specifying the relative arrangement of positively and negatively charged atoms in minerals, which helped to narrow down the possible options in a trial structure.[1] He looked at Astbury's papers and began to think about helical structures with a 5.1 Å spacing, but didn't immediately come up with a solution. Instead, he and his assistant Robert

Corey began a crystallographic study of the structures of the individual amino acids, hoping that understanding the component parts of the protein would shed some light on the solution of the whole. It was Corey who solved the structure of diketopiperazine, a small molecule made up of two amino acids, and the problem Dorothy had originally set for Dennis Riley.

For all these researchers experimental evidence was slow in coming, but there was a great deal of speculation and discussion about what protein structures might be. A prominent figure in these discussions was Dorothy Wrinch, the mathematics tutor Dorothy Crowfoot had met as an undergraduate at Somerville. This clever, passionate, bold and combative woman presents a fascinating contrast to her younger namesake, with whom she pursued a one-sided and uneasy scientific association for decades. Dorothy Crowfoot in turn was helpless to prevent the tutor she had once admired from squandering her gifts in pursuit of a vain idea. Recent studies, particularly in the United States, have attempted to rehabilitate Wrinch as a forgotten heroine of protein structure, suppressed by the male establishment.[2] But Dorothy herself never accepted this view, and looking at the different ways in which the two Dorothies worked, it is hard to see how she could have.

Wrinch had begun her academic career at Cambridge, where she graduated at the top of her year in mathematics, and published a stream of well-received papers in classical mathematics. Also interested in philosophy, at Cambridge she had moved in the same circles as Ludwig Wittgenstein and Bertrand Russell. She obtained DSc degrees from both London and Oxford, in the latter case the first woman to have been so honoured. She was, when Dorothy first knew her, 'gay, enthusiastic and adventurous, courageous in the face of misfortune, and very kind'.[3]

That the promise of her early distinction faded she owed to a combination of personal misfortune and errors of judgement on her own part. Principal among these was her determination to make her mark on the field of protein structure. It was this determination, combined with a lack of any real understanding of chemistry or biology, that ultimately proved her undoing and put a considerable strain on her friendship with the younger Dorothy.

By the late 1930s Dorothy Crowfoot knew Dorothy Wrinch well, and liked her. Through Margery Fry she had learned something of Wrinch's troubled personal life: her marriage to the Oxford physicist John Nicholson, his alcoholism and their divorce, leaving her with a daughter, Pamela, to bring up on her own. Through Bernal she knew Wrinch as an innovative thinker, keen to apply her mathematical and logical skills to biological problems. Wrinch had been one of the founders of the loose group known as the 'Biotheoretical Gathering' that met once or twice a year between 1932 and 1937 to try to develop a physico-chemical basis for understanding biological systems.[4] The other founder members were Bernal, the London-based philosopher of science J. H. Woodger, Conrad Waddington and Joseph Needham. Dorothy Crowfoot herself attended a meeting in 1935, at which she also met the philosopher of science Karl Popper.[5] One of its plans had been for an interdisciplinary research institute, in which Dorothy was to have been offered the post of *chef de travaux* in a department of 'Crystal physics of substances of biochemical importance' headed by Bernal. But their attempts to raise a very substantial grant for the project fell on stony ground.

Wrinch had no formal training in biology or chemistry, but she obtained a series of Fellowships and grants that enabled her to take time off from her teaching responsibilities in Oxford and visit labs in continental Europe to learn of the latest advances. In 1935 she received the accolade of a research grant from the Rockefeller Foundation, £500 a year for five years. Warren Weaver, head of the Foundation's natural sciences division, was making it his business to support research into the mathematical, physical and chemical basis of biology.[6] Some work Wrinch had done on mathematical aspects of the contraction of chromosomes had convinced him that she was worth supporting. Almost at once she embarked on a new project: to develop a coherent theoretical framework for studies of protein structure.

At first her ideas were taken as seriously as any others. With so little evidence to go on, Bernal, Dorothy and their friends all speculated freely about how peptide chains might arrange themselves into three-dimensional protein molecules, trying out different possibilities with ball-and-spoke models. It was from Bernal that Wrinch picked up the possibility of the 'cyclol link' – a form of bond between atoms in the peptide chain that would bend it round into a hexagon, then link the hexagons into sheets that Wrinch called 'protein fabrics'. She presented her ideas for the first time in a paper in *Nature* in March 1936, stating as a premise that 'there is general uniformity among proteins of widely different chemical constitution which suggests a simple general plan in the arrangement of the amino acid residues characteristic of proteins in general'.[7]

A year later she went on to describe how her two-dimensional cyclol fabrics could be curved round into three-dimensional 'cages', and the cage structure was what she proposed for the globular protein molecules. The ideas looked good on paper – perhaps too good – and the first few proteins to be studied appeared to have exactly the right molecular weights to supply the number of residues her patterns demanded. In addition, the work on pepsin and insulin seemed to suggest that protein molecules were highly symmetrical, as her theory required.

At first everyone was pleased to see such an elegant piece of work. Bernal wrote a friendly letter to Wrinch having seen a draft of her first paper for *Nature*, judging it to be 'quite excellent and even somewhat cautious in tone'.[8] But whereas in the worlds of mathematics or philosophy an elegant theory might survive on its own merits, in the world of physical science it had to stand the harsh test of what worked in real systems. Within a year or two, new evidence began to undermine what support there was for the cyclol theory. Lactoglobulin, haemoglobin and chymotrypsin (another protein studied by Max Perutz in Cambridge) did not have the high degree of symmetry shown by the earlier proteins. Molecular weights no longer suggested the exact number of amino acid residues needed for the protein fabrics. Proteins, indeed, were turning out to be so diverse that it seemed increasingly unlikely that a single structural theory could account for them all. There were also doubts, on purely chemical grounds, that the links required by the cyclol theory were robust enough to hold the molecules in stable configurations.

But Dorothy Wrinch didn't – apparently couldn't – give up. Her faith in the ultimate triumph of mathematics was absolute, and she continued to publish paper after paper. She chose insulin – Dorothy Crowfoot's insulin – as the molecule on which her theory would stand or fall. Beginning in June 1937, Wrinch began to publish her own ideas about the insulin structure, demonstrating, as she thought, that the idea of cyclol cages was perfectly compatible with Dorothy's findings. This put Dorothy in a difficult position; she never accepted the cyclol theory, but somehow she had to reconcile her loyalty to a friend with her integrity as a scientist. It was a conflict that disturbed her habitual tranquillity, as she reported to Thomas. Writing in 1938 about a seminar on proteins Wrinch had organized she commented, 'I was very annoyed and stupid and behaved very badly.'

Dorothy's problem was not that she was particularly wedded to any alternative theory, such as Bernal's idea that protein chains folded themselves into parallel layers in the globular molecules. Still less was she interested in developing a theory of her own. As a committed experimentalist, she believed any speculation about structure was quite unimportant compared with the need to collect more observations. She was quietly confident that, given time and a great deal of hard work, the correct solution would eventually drop out.

Wrinch, on the other hand, had no laboratory and never undertook practical experimental work. But even she recognized that in order to test her theory she had to have access to experimental data. She began by attempting to acquire a tame experimenter of her own by poaching Dennis Riley – an attempt made, as he recalled, 'over tea and sherry (the traditional Oxford formula)'.

> She had become aware of my existence as a budding
> researcher and, in effect, suggested that I desert one
> Dorothy for the other, offering to get me a research grant to
> work with, or rather for, her. When I declined, she asked to
> have access to all my experimental data on protein crystals
> anyway, in advance of my own attempts to interpret them.
> Using some diplomacy, I managed to prevaricate . . .
> Dorothy Crowfoot . . . was highly amused by all this but,
> as usual, left me quite free to make my own decisions.[9]

Having failed to recruit Riley, Wrinch began to put pressure on Dorothy herself. Wrinch's papers on insulin were based only on Dorothy's published analysis of her results. To go further, she decided she needed Dorothy's data, the original observations that were the basis for her substantial paper that had just appeared in the *Proceedings of the Royal Society*. These raw data, consisting of tables of numbers representing the intensities of the reflections in the X-ray photographs, were not usually published. But asked point-blank for them, Dorothy felt unable to refuse, although she procrastinated as long as possible.

> Dear Dot* (she wrote in October 1938)
> I'm sorry to have been so long but I really have had no spare time at all for ages . . . I never can feel it terribly important as the original X-ray intensities are arbitrary values and only the relative intensities of the Patterson peaks . . . have any meaning . . . I've given them to you however as on my sheets which I found when I was clearing out just before the BA [British Association for the Advancement of Science] meeting.[10]

Wrinch seems to have been unaware that it was insensitive of her to ask for someone else's hard-won data in this way. On the contrary, from then on she seemed to regard Dorothy as a collaborator, requesting each new set of data to be delivered as it appeared. For her part, Dorothy had long since ceased to see the cyclol model as having any usefulness, and began to say so in public. In her Royal Society paper Dorothy wrote of her Patterson maps:

> The patterns calculated do not appear to have any direct relation either to the cyclol or the various chain structures put forward for the globular proteins. From the cyclol structure one would expect many more peaks in the Patterson synthesis than do actually occur.[11]

She added that although the cyclol theory could account for the

---

*Dorothy Wrinch always signed herself Dorothy or with the Greek letter delta, but all the British crystallographers referred to her by the diminutive Dot. Although Dorothy Crowfoot herself did not like to have her own name shortened in this way, it never occurred to her that Dorothy Wrinch minded. Wrinch let it pass until 1946, when in a postscript she asked crisply, 'Could we drop the Dot?'

surprising three-fold symmetry of the molecule, it was 'doubtful whether the facts justify pushing this argument further'. By this time Wrinch should have realized that it was time to drop cyclols, or at least to put them on the back burner until more evidence emerged. At the beginning of 1938 she had fulfilled a cherished wish to present her ideas in person to Linus Pauling in the United States. He had demolished them point by point, exposing both the logical and scientific flaws in her arguments. He was also irritated by the amount of publicity she was attracting; one American paper called her 'the woman Einstein'. He reported his conclusions in highly unfavourable terms to the Rockefeller Foundation, thereby ending any possibility that her grant would be renewed.[12]

Wrinch reacted badly to criticism; not having a good enough grasp of chemistry to refute the counter-arguments convincingly, she fell back on the position that proteins must be an exception to the rules that generally prevailed in organic chemistry. She pressed on. Seizing on Dorothy's Patterson maps, she calculated the pattern that might be produced if the insulin molecules were indeed cages. She had an important ally in the respected American physical chemist Irving Langmuir, who took her ideas seriously. Together they published papers in several journals in which they conjured from a comparison of the cyclol maps with Dorothy's data a confirmation of the cage structure of the insulin molecule. 'Extraordinary to relate the miracle that has happened,' she wrote in triumph to the Rockefeller Foundation.

The crystallographic community was not convinced. At the end of 1938, British and European protein scientists met for a conference at the Royal Society organized by Sir William Bragg to discuss the latest advances. Wrinch had a place on the programme, but her hold on membership of this group was becoming increasingly tenuous. In the days running up to the meeting Bernal was in regular contact with Dorothy, marshalling evidence for an alternative theory, as she reported to Thomas.

Sage rang up – full of his latest theories on proteins and wanting more data and calculations from me. His ideas really sound rather good and make me feel as though something really was likely to come out and clear the air

by the time of this meeting. At the moment I feel capable of
tackling anything . . .

. . . I was so excited by the protein conversation I slept very
badly on Friday night and woke up a complete wreck on
Saturday morning quite unfit for carrying through any of
the suggested calculations. After various feeble attempts to
do something I went out and bought 1 nail brush, 1 tube of
calcium gluconate and a 1/6d detective story . . .

Sage turned up . . . we spent the whole morning on his
theories. They *are* nice and I think worth putting forward
but they're not by any means complete and there are a lot
of very sticky points . . . I'm a bit worried about the protein
meeting actually. According to Dennis who saw her on
Monday Dot is very much on the warpath and I don't feel
at all like a free fight at present! And . . . meanwhile we
think of more and more things that want doing and I begin
to doubt whether I can really cope with all of them.[13]

In fact things turned out all right on the day. Dorothy reported to
Thomas that despite being extremely one-sided, 'Dot's paper . . .
wasn't as bad as it might have been', and in their own presentations neither she nor Bernal made outright attacks on the cyclol
theory. Wrinch was invited to join a large and good-natured lunch
party that also included Dorothy and Bernal and friends such as
Astbury and Fankuchen. But the Royal Society meeting was
almost the last time that Wrinch was given the chance to present
her ideas in person among her former friends and colleagues.
The following month Langmuir defended the cyclol theory at a
meeting of the Physical Society in London. Dorothy was expecting her first child imminently and had gone home to Geldeston
by this time, but she kept in touch with Bernal by letter.

Dennis Riley wrote me a long account of the protein
meeting – it does puzzle me, this situation, how Langmuir,
Dot and Neville [a mathematician and lifelong friend of
Wrinch] can be so deluded. I'm glad you're writing to
Nature – and Bragg also.[14]

Indeed the letters pages of *Nature* fairly crackled with hostility to Wrinch's cyclol theory in the early days of 1939. Bernal, characteristically, led the way.

> Substantially this method is not new . . . what is new, however, is the use of certain additional assumptions and their application to cases where they are of extremely doubtful validity . . . Vector maps of Dr Wrinch's hypothetical cyclol structure bear no resemblance to those which have been derived by Miss Crowfoot from her observations . . . It can fairly be claimed that the scattering centre model derived from the cyclol hypothesis fails completely to account for the X-ray evidence for insulin . . . The discussion to which this attempt has given rise will not be wasted if it focuses attention on the need for an active collaboration by physicists and chemists in a concentrated attack on the structure of the protein molecule.[15]

The august figure of Lawrence Bragg, who clearly felt Wrinch's exploits in the field he created might give it a bad name, added his own voice to the argument in the same issue.

> The molecule of a protein such as insulin, for which Crowfoot gives Patterson diagrams, is . . . far beyond anything as yet analysed by X-rays. Experience with the difficulty of interpreting the Patterson of simple molecules warns us to be extremely cautious in basing conclusions upon the diagram of insulin . . . Exaggerated claims as to the . . . certainty with which a proposed detailed model is confirmed are only too likely, at this stage, to bring discredit upon the patient work which has placed the analysis of simpler structures upon a sure foundation.[16]

Fankuchen and Riley and several others weighed in against Wrinch and cyclols. She fought back every time, arguing that because Dorothy's data were so incomplete, it was not possible to say whether or not the cyclol model was incompatible with them. Dorothy herself had not put her name to any of the attacks. Direct confrontation was not her style – and probably more to the point, she was preoccupied with her new baby just as matters were coming to a head. But as the row dragged on for months, she suggested to Thomas that she might try more subtle methods.

> Dot Wrinch has written another rude letter to *Nature* about all of us and Sage has sent in a short reply trying to close down the controversy. I wonder a bit whether it would do any good if I wrote to her myself – a really sweet letter, you know, beginning 'My dear Dot' and so on.

She did write, and although the letter itself has not survived, Wrinch's reply has. She had by that time left her comparatively secure and familiar base in Oxford to move to the United States, believing that it was too dangerous to stay in Britain any longer with her young daughter now that war with Germany seemed inevitable. Isolated and vulnerable, she reveals in her letter the extent to which she had come to regard the objections of crystallographers to her ideas as personal attacks.

> Dearest Dorothy
> So pleased to get your letters . . .
>   As to the controversy and polemics . . . I my dear have not polemicized. I am out only for the truth about protein structure. Accordingly I attempted to interpret your data. Misstatements concerning this and my other works have to be corrected. Desmond etc were of course not the only attackers, since as I expect you have pointed out to me organic chemists and others of course hold fast to traditional ideas, even in the face of plain statements and deductions by physicists, X-ray crystallographers and mathematicians. Our chromosome count of course does not tend to weaken the desire to others to attack us, though Pauling (see forthcoming exhibition in *JACS*) judging from the disparaging remarks he made about Desmond when I was with him at Ithaca last spring, is naturally given to polemic and fails to see what a waste of time it is for him to leave his own field and repeat objections to my ideas, already answered, esp when nothing satisfactory has been

proposed to supplant them . . . I am of course delighted to
collaborate with you and will be most interested and
pleased to get your results on wet insulin . . .

And in a PS she added: 'What conflict therefore is there? I don't
see it.'[17]

Pauling's 'exhibition' was a paper jointly written with the
chemist Carl Niemann that came out in the *Journal of the American
Chemical Society* a month later. Pauling was characteristically
forthright, echoing the concerns of others about the X-ray evidence, but also arguing from his superior knowledge of bond
lengths, interatomic distances and the energy required to hold a
molecule together.

We . . . have reached the conclusions that there exists no
evidence whatever in support of this hypothesis and that
instead strong evidence can be advanced in support of the
contention that bonds of the cyclol type do not occur at all,
in any protein.[18]

He went out of his way to avoid implicating Dorothy Crowfoot in
his diatribe, describing her attempt to produce Patterson diagrams of insulin as 'interesting' and noting pointedly: 'Crowfoot
discussed these diagrams in a sensible way and pointed out
that . . . the X-ray data . . . do not permit the determination of the
position of individual atoms.'

Pauling's attack hit Wrinch at a particularly vulnerable time.
She had in fact more or less thrown in the towel by then, admitting to the Rockefeller Foundation that her conclusions on insulin
were premature, and telling Warren Weaver that she would give
up work on proteins. She was in a strange place, and needed a job
and research funds.

But characteristically she could not take his dismissal of her
cherished theory lying down. She insisted on a right of reply,
badgering the editor of the *JACS* until he gave her space. But her
rebuttal amounted to little more than saying she didn't agree
with Pauling's analysis. She had nothing new to say, yet still
clung on to a belief now shown to have no substance in reality.
Although she successfully obtained academic posts, first at Johns

Hopkins University in Maryland and later at Amherst, Smith and Mount Holyoake Colleges in Massachusetts, she retained a wistful desire to be included among the British protein chemists. That summer Dorothy Hodgkin had begun a new series of observations on insulin, this time keeping the crystals wet. The photographs were a great improvement, with many more reflections, extending out to positions that indicated spacings small enough to be between atoms within individual molecules. As soon as Wrinch heard about the work, she began to bombard Dorothy with requests for her data.

Dorothy made a point of keeping in touch, and wrote regularly with news of her progress. But she resisted the demands for her data, finding excuses not to send them. For example, in April 1940 she wrote:

> My present lot of photographs are most beautiful . . . I'm working them up in a rather careful way so that I observe most reflections twice, but there are hundreds of reflections (2 or 3,000 at least) and sometimes I gasp at the thought of what my series will be like . . . It would be silly to send you the list of intensities I used last summer – the present ones would be so much more reliable. But I don't calculate to be through with collecting them till the end of the summer.[19]

After more than a year during which Wrinch badgered her for numbers at every possible opportunity, in August 1941 she became even more blunt in her refusal. The same letter began by apologizing for having misrepresented some detail of Wrinch's ideas in a review paper, but her contrition was limited.

> I'm extremely sorry to have misread you but to be fair, I don't regard your criticisms of Desmond's theory as important in any way . . . None of this bothers me much at the moment or feels to me worth arguing about. I'm just rather cheerful from a mixture of motives – Russia coming into the war, and I'm going to have another baby and I finished two days ago some of my first calculations on my new wet insulin data and found a 5Å peak.
>
> I have every hope now that we are going to get

something out of the wet insulin data that will bring us information much nearer to atomic dimensions. But I'm afraid I'm not going to part with my intensity data to anyone yet . . . I'm doing preliminary calculations as we go along – but I don't want to let anything out till I'm reasonably certain of it.[20]

Reluctantly she did eventually send some data, but by that time the cyclol theory was dead in the water in the mind of everyone except Dorothy Wrinch. She continued doggedly along the same lines until well into the 1950s, asking Dorothy constantly not only to send her own data but to try to get her those of other workers such as Max Perutz, who was inching closer to a solution of the haemoglobin structure. This Dorothy clearly could not do. Her letters became less frequent, and when she was reunited with Wrinch on her first visit to the United States in 1947, she avoided the subject of proteins.

In 1950 Wrinch's much-loved second husband, the Botany Professor at Amherst Otto Glaser, died after a long illness. Dorothy's note of condolence was the catalyst for a renewed exchange of letters. Wrinch began by repeating a rumour she had heard that Dorothy thought she had 'stolen' her unpublished data. Dorothy tried once and for all to explain to Wrinch why she had been less than forthcoming in the past.

I am so very sorry you should have been unhappy about my attitude over insulin. I do assure you that I am not in the least distrustfull [sic], nor do I regard the data as having been given to you otherwise than entirely by my own free will.

It is true that at first I did not give them very willingly. I regard this as an imperfection in my character, but one which is perhaps understandable. It was in the middle of the war, I was working on penicillin and had deliberately put insulin aside as a subject that I ought to defer. Yet I was fond of the stuff and wanted some day to have the pleasure of working on it again . . .

The thing that inhibited my talking to you much about insulin and which has probably led to this feeling of suspicion, is quite different, and perhaps it would be best if I said what it was. I was only worried for your sake since it seemed to me that you cared a great deal that the cyclol idea should be right and that it would make you most unhappy if it should be proved wrong . . .

I may, of course, be quite wrong about cyclols and proteins but I just felt our attitudes to the problem were so different that we should probably only hurt one another by discussing it – and that therefore, perhaps it was best not to.[21]

This tactful letter restored the friendship, and evoked a partial admission from Wrinch that her constant demands on experimental workers may have been at the very least insensitive.

I am not fixated on the little cyclols: I am fixated on the protein: and I can distinguish between the two. I did I must admit long very greatly indeed for data which would make it possible to see if they were roughly correct or even on the right lines and I see now rather more clearly what a big sacrifice it was for you to let me see the intensities when the war made it impossible to spend time on them yourself. Again my deepest thanks for this: I appreciate now fully what it meant . . . I do realize that no one has any right to expect that data which have taken years to assemble should be made available to a theoretical worker . . .[22]

Unfortunately she then spoiled the effect by launching into a rambling complaint about Perutz's failure to give her his findings on haemoglobin, and pleading with Dorothy to get her sight of the intensities obtained by another worker, Barbara Low at Harvard, on a variant of the insulin molecule.

Dorothy Wrinch lived out the rest of her career comfortably enough, teaching at Amherst and Smith, and at the Marine Biological Laboratory at Woods Hole on Long Island in the summers. She was by no means excluded from the world of protein chemistry in the United States, being regularly asked to speak at conferences. But none of the research she did advanced understanding of protein structure any further. She died in 1976 at the age of eighty-two, a few weeks after her beloved daughter Pamela had been killed in a house fire at Woods Hole.

Dorothy Hodgkin wrote a sensitive and generous obituary in *Nature*, pointing out that 'many of [her] geometrical instincts and deductions were, in general terms, correct'.[23] But she vehemently rejected the view that grew up among some of Wrinch's colleagues at Smith College, that she had been badly treated because she was a woman. Writing to Marjorie Seneschal, who was organizing a conference at Smith in Wrinch's memory, Dorothy expressed regret that she had not turned her considerable talents to the real mathematical problems of crystallographic analysis that desperately needed attention from the start.

> We should probably have managed to convince Dorothy Wrinch (since we were her friends) to try herself to take the chemical evidence more seriously and help us to search for the real structure of proteins, had it not been for the war . . . Certainly we regarded her as one of the crystallographic community . . . Probably some of the intensity of feeling in the case of Dorothy Wrinch was due to the major importance of the scientific problem itself, the structure of proteins – nobody could be indifferent to the search for the truth about proteins.[24]

Marriage at first made little difference to Dorothy's daily routine. She continued to live in her room in Somerville, to teach her students, and to work on her insulin maps. A daily letter, often written late at night when she could hardly keep her eyes open, was almost her sole conjugal duty. Thomas was also an excellent correspondent. His weekend visits were treats to which she looked forward, but his commitments meant that he could not make the journey every week. So began a pattern of frequent correspondence, but little personal contact, which was to persist until the end of the Second World War. In many ways it was a lifestyle that suited them both, although it did not always mean that Dorothy could give her work her undivided attention.

> I'm rather shocked with myself over this term – I'm not conscious that I teach the girls very badly but I notice that I'm

not at all properly concerned about them – always thinking of last weekend or next weekend or the weekend after!

She was in excellent spirits. Her sister Diana, 'Dilly', whose company she always enjoyed, had come up to Somerville in October 1937. Partly due to Dorothy's persuasion, Dilly had allowed herself to be a guinea pig on a new combined science first-year course that had just been introduced. This meant that, as Somerville's only Science Fellow, Dorothy was Dilly's Moral Tutor. The warmth of their relationship, despite the eight-year age difference, was marked by the number of notes to 'Darling Dilly', unsealed and unfolded, that appeared in the 'C' pigeon-hole in the College lodge.

Bernal Sage made several visits, and apparently accepted the new basis for his relationship with Dorothy. Each time he came she found herself invited to the evening parties given in his honour, usually by his friend the South African zoologist Solly Zuckermann. As well as Oxford's top scientists, such as the German refugee physicist Franz Simon, these parties included such leading thinkers as Sir Bertrand Russell ('and his latest Lady Russell'), A. J. Ayer and Isaiah Berlin, and Labour Party activists including Frank and Elisabeth Pakenham (later Lord and Lady Longford).

Most of the discussion was of the world situation: the Japanese had invaded China the year before, the Italians had taken Abyssinia, the war in Spain was deadlocked and a wider war in Europe seemed inevitable. On the home front the political situation was volatile, with public opinion, especially among intellectuals, increasingly dissatisfied with Neville Chamberlain's policy of appeasement towards Germany. Dorothy attended lively Labour Club meetings, and went to hear the Labour leader, Clement Attlee, speak at the Town Hall.

There was a sort of mob excitement in the air. The crowd sang the Red Flag and the International and then surged into the street to be met by a mob of those who couldn't get in shouting 'We want Attlee.' Two lads raised the poor little man on their shoulders and then started carrying him up the High. Everyone followed shouting 'Down with

Halifax' . . . It wasn't an orderly procession – it occupied the whole street and went up the Corn, down the Turl and finally into Radcliffe Square where Attlee's car was waiting. Somebody in Exeter tipped a bucket of water onto the crowd as it passed along the Turl – not out of malice I think, but because the opportunity was too good to be lost.

She went to hear Margery Fry speak on the topic 'What we can do for China' and put her name down to work on a campaign to promote a boycott of Japanese goods. This entailed knocking on doors and asking people to sign a petition – an activity she found disheartening as so few agreed to sign. In practice most of the route she was allocated was taken care of by Betty Murray and Joan Blomfield (later Turville-Petre, who taught English at Somerville), as she found it so hard to tear herself away from her scientific work. Activism, however worthy the cause, was clearly alien to her retiring nature at this time in her life.

Betty and I, fired by the Attlee demonstration, went down with Helen [Megaw] and Janet [Macaulay]to see the China procession on Saturday afternoon and we walked in it part of the way and I hated it and wished all the time I wasn't there, in spite of the moral support of old [E. R.] Hughes [the Professor of Chinese] in a car plastered with posters at the head of it . . .

Murray remembered that Dorothy had made her walk on the outside to screen her from view.

Towards the end of the year Oxford became the focus of national attention as a by-election for the Oxford City seat opened up a crack in the mould of the three-party system. It was just after Chamberlain's Munich Agreement with Hitler, and A. D. Lindsay, the Master of Balliol, stood as an anti-appeasement candidate. The official Labour and Liberal candidates stood down in his favour, and he represented all shades of liberal and left-of-centre opinion in a single 'Progressive Front', in opposition to the Conservatives. His cause was fairly hopeless (if it had not been he probably would not have put himself forward), but it attracted an enthusiastic following among many of the younger

members of the University. Dorothy's regular attendance at the
Labour Club and a Thursday lunch club that was even further to
the left had earned her a place on the committee of the Oxford
University Labour Party along with leading left-wing thinkers
such as G. D. H. Cole and Christopher Hill. The OULP wholeheartedly supported Lindsay's candidature (despite opposition
from Labour headquarters in London which was deeply suspicious of the alliance of middle-class intellectuals and Communists
that it saw behind it). And Dorothy was caught up in the excitement that swept through left-leaning Somerville in the early
weeks of October.

> This election seems to be greatly stirring the SCR [Senior
> Common Room]. Isabel, the Lorry [Miss Lorimer], May,
> Mildred and I were all talking about it at lunch – the
> opening meeting is tonight – and someone started a
> suggestion we should take Eleanor Rathbone [one of the
> first women Members of Parliament] and Margery [Fry]
> down to the Town Hall after dinner as distinguished
> guests to Lindsay's first meeting. Afterwards the matter
> was broached in the common room and almost everyone
> wanted to come . . . We haven't of course found out if our
> distinguished guests want to be employed in this way!

> The plot of taking Margery and Eleanor Rathbone and
> Mildred Pope to Lindsay's meeting worked admirably –
> they and the Darb sat on the platform and all of the rest of
> the SCR went too except the unfortunate Lucy
> [Sutherland] who was left to look after the one remaining
> guest . . . The Town Hall was practically full – but rather a
> large proportion of university I'm afraid . . . I thought
> Lindsay was good . . . quite surprisingly good when it
> came to questions afterwards.
>   We are deeply disgusted by the press campaign suggesting
> a serious split in the socialist ranks. It's such an uneven
> split as far as Oxford Labour is concerned it doesn't count.

> . . . I decided to devote yesterday from lunch time on to the
> Election – not very usefully, I'm afraid – just got employed

making red and yellow rosettes . . . I said I'd organize a
sewing party in Somerville after hall – Mildred [Hartley]
and Joan Blom came and most of what I think are probably
the present JCR members of the CP . . . Mildred was
suffering rather badly from intellectual revolt at the state of
the election organization, the sort of people in it and the
kind of things to be done. I begin to feel all that much less
myself, I believe . . . And it's odd because I doubt whether
I've really progressed much in conviction since three or
four years ago when I used to lie awake at night
wondering whether to join the CP or not, a decision that
finally got shelved.

By this time Dorothy was in an advanced state of pregnancy, and
reasoning that this probably excused her from active canvassing,
she compromised by offering the services of her car with Dennis
Riley as driver to take people to the polling station on the day.
After that, as she put it to Thomas, there was 'nothing more a
woman in my condition can do except vote'. In the event Lindsay
was not elected, but his supporters took some satisfaction from
the fact that he had halved the majority of the sitting
Conservative MP, Quintin Hogg.

Infrequent as Thomas's visits were, Dorothy conceived within
three months of their marriage. 'The inevitable had happened,'
she later wrote; but to a modern working woman it seems surprising that she, of all people, should have rushed headlong into
starting a family. She was just beginning to establish a reputation
as one of the leaders of her scientific field; she was married to a
man who worked at the other end of the country, and with whom
she had never lived for more than a few days at a time; she had
no home; there was a war coming. She was not ignorant of birth
control methods, having read Marie Stopes and heard her lecture.
Before the wedding she had written to Thomas to report on a
medical examination she had just undergone.

[The doctor] said he usually advised not having children in
the first year of marriage for psychological reasons and
told me of a birth control method which seemed much

simpler and less likely to be harmful than any I'd read about. I wasn't sure we would want it but thought knowledge was always useful.

Later letters make it clear that a child was a dearly cherished wish. In February 1938, she wrote to Thomas: 'If I come and live with you like a cabbage I think then we should be much more likely to grow a child between us – & nice too, to have you there.' It seems unlikely, though, that she was seriously thinking of giving up her work – cabbagehood would have been too great a price to pay for the pleasure of living with Thomas.

She told him of her likely condition when she went with him to a residential summer school during the Easter vacation. The baby would be due at the end of December, almost exactly a year after their marriage. On her return, she set about dealing with this new situation by consulting the midwife at the local hospital.

Thomas darling, Mrs Radford says there isn't much reasonable doubt that I've conceived . . . If she's sure then I'll tell Helen Darbishire and we'll think what to do next . . . She seemed quite accustomed to steering academic women through childbirth – at least it didn't take her by surprise. She said coaching was a harmless occupation that could probably be continued within a month either side of the birth. But demonstrating or lecturing (which I don't do) should be avoided . . .

I told Dilly last night in order to have some right-minded person about me who knew. Dilly was deplorably practical. She led off 'Now do you want the child more or Somerville more?' I indicated that I didn't care two hoots for Somerville, and only regretted that I shouldn't be able to have such a nice summer with Thomas as if I could climb mountains. I was relieved to find that Dilly's obviously wide knowledge of methods of preventing yourself having children was not gathered from depraved Somerville but from her short stay in the theatre with Liz's company last summer. It is obviously very important to have such information if you're on the stage.

Two months into her pregnancy, and encouraged by the practicality and good sense of her midwife, Dorothy plucked up the courage to speak to the Principal of Somerville. No Fellow of Somerville – or indeed of any of the other women's colleges – had ever previously given birth while in post. For women Fellows to marry at all was still highly unusual.

> I was a bit taken aback – when I said that I thought I was
> going to have a child she said yes, she'd thought that too –
> from the way I'd looked for the last week or two.
> Depressing that it should be so obvious I wasn't feeling
> well . . . Helen Darbishire was very sweet and reasonable.
> She said that she would be very glad if I would come back
> for any part of next year that could fairly easily be managed –
> say the beginning of next term to see the first year settled
> in, and the Trinity term and perhaps part of the Hilary
> Term. But that if my doctors and relations and you thought
> I'd better resign, well the situation could be faced.

Somerville's support gave Dorothy the encouragement she needed to dispel any family doubts about her continuing to work. She did not resign; as her pregnancy progressed beyond some early sickness, her work barely missed a beat. Indeed, Dorothy was so preoccupied with writing papers, collecting data and teaching that she herself gave little thought to preparing for motherhood, but others did it for her. To begin with, Somerville was determined that she should suffer no financial disadvantage, although Dorothy herself found the idea of getting paid for doing nothing (the concept of statutory maternity pay was still some decades away) difficult to accept.

> I gather I've been give permission to stay away next term
> and probably a lot of sick pay as well which slightly shocks
> me – I said to the Darb I saw no reason why I shouldn't
> stay in the room and tell them about my baby myself but
> she kept me out on the ground that they had to discuss the
> financial situation. I tried beforehand to get Lucy
> [Sutherland] and Ann [Evans] to take the sensible line that
> the £100 I should have had for next term would just be

used by the college to pay for my pupils etc. But they said it would be a bad precedent and might mean that future married fellows would consider they couldn't have children and they didn't approve of interfering with the course of nature. Anyway it looks as if we should be quite well off out of it!

Thanks to Somerville's enlightened attitude, Dorothy became the first woman at Oxford to receive paid maternity leave. In 1944, when her third pregnancy coincided with Joan Turville-Petre's first, Somerville decided that in future all tutorial and administrative staff should be allowed three months' paid leave for the birth of children.[25] The University itself had no policy on maternity leave for women in academic posts until 1971, when, while noting that the number of cases had been small to date, it settled on a maximum of eighteen weeks on full pay. Statutory maternity provision was not enshrined in British law until 1975.

Meanwhile at the end of April Thomas returned to Oxford to do some job-hunting. The two of them set up home together for the first time in a house they rented for six months called Elder Stubbs on Shotover Hill, an area of parkland which overlooks Oxford to the east. The house had formerly been occupied by Kenneth Clark, later Lord Clark, who was Keeper of the Ashmolean Museum until 1934, before moving to the National Gallery in London.

It had a garden with a lawn and fruit trees and vegetables, and we paid for a gardener as rent for the house. We bought inexpensively the necessities of furniture – two beds, a number of desk chairs, a table, a supply of cutlery, kitchen utensils, a frying pan and two saucepans from Woolworths – with the help of Somerville friends.

Inevitably these friends included Betty Murray. She and Rosalind Beech-Thomas shared the house next door to Elder Stubbs, Ridings End. After Thomas and Dorothy had borrowed their house for a few days before their furniture arrived, Betty was under no illusions about their competence in household matters, and she decided to take charge.

We all went to D.'s house, unpacked china and things from Woolworths, and washed shelves for them to go on. On Tuesday morning I went with D. to shop. She had no list in her head or on paper. We wandered vaguely round the Co-op and I suggested things she might need. After that experience Rosalind and I spent the evening drawing up lists of possible needs.

. . . On Friday Alice [Burnet] and I were again at Shotover. The beds came but the bedrooms completely bare except for beds. No curtains anywhere and only a few mats. D. has carried off most of the rugs and chairs from her college rooms.

. . . I do wish T. were a little more capable of taking care of her and himself! She simply has no energy and is tired all the time. I think if she saw anyone who could take over her job she would thankfully give it up.[26]

Betty Murray was probably wrong in thinking Dorothy wanted to give up her work, but she was not mistaken about Dorothy's state of health. She was physically below par for much of the year, with a persistent streptococcal infection. Then, for no apparent reason, one of her fingers swelled up. But her London doctor diagnosed a 'torn tendon', rather than arthritis or rheumatism, which put her mind at rest.

Thomas, who had still not settled on his long-term future, did not stay long at Elder Stubbs. He spent most of the rest of the year back in Cumberland, returning for a fortnight's summer school in July, and the usual weekends. Dorothy spent some of September with him in lodgings after she gave up Elder Stubbs, then moved back into her Somerville room. She declared herself happy to move from Oxford if he found a job somewhere where she could continue with crystallography. She was confident, with good reason, that her network of contacts would not let her down. Arnold Beevers, who had moved from Manchester to Edinburgh, heard a rumour from Thomas's aunt Mary Smith while at a Friends' meeting that Dorothy and Thomas were thinking of moving there. He wrote at once. 'I hope if you are considering this, and if you are interested in continuing X-ray work, you will remember that I am just setting up an X-ray lab and that I am sure that satisfactory arrangements could be made for you to work here.'[27]

Thomas had indeed applied for an extramural lectureship at Edinburgh and at several other places, but nothing had come up so far. The plan was that Dorothy would go home to Geldeston for the birth of her baby, and then move into lodgings with Thomas in Maryport, on the Cumberland coast, for at least the first few months. After that they thought they might move into Crab Mill while Thomas continued to look for work. It was not a hugely practical scheme. It would have been very difficult for Dorothy to return to her teaching and research in Oxford while living at Crab Mill, which is a good hour's drive from Oxford on today's roads. But with the confidence born of two secure and supportive family backgrounds, they continued to hope that something would turn up.

Once it seemed likely that the baby would be born within the orbit of the Old House at Geldeston, Dorothy's mother took full control.

> Joan and I got busy this afternoon and visited Miss Hamby and her very nice little nursing home, but it is so very little that she usually only takes one patient and she already has one booked for December . . . Then I saw Uncle Harry [Wood-Hill, the husband of John Crowfoot's cousin Amy] . . . he would prefer you to be with Miss Hamby, but didn't at all veto your staying at Geldeston if you couldn't be taken in by Miss Hamby. (NB if you *have* any strong views as to Home v. Nursing Home in Beccles *now* is the moment to express them. It is also the moment to express your views on your doctor.) I rather took it for granted that it would be McLaren . . . but I believe that [Harry would] like to be persuaded into doing it, his confinements now total 3000! – if you really preferred having him . . . Darling thing – so sorry to bother but everybody here thinks I ought to have fixed you up before now![28]

At the same time Joan, who was expecting her first baby in the New Year, persuaded Dorothy to turn her thoughts away from proteins for a moment and towards baby clothes and maternity dresses.

Dorothy enjoyed the fuss that was being made of her, and enjoyed the reactions of her colleagues once the news was out. One of the first people she told was Bernal.

> I am in a rather horrid state of being constantly sick . . .
> Thomas and I think it may be the beginning of a child.
> Thomas is in the seventh heaven and I might be if I didn't
> feel so beastly ill most of the time. And I find it rather
> complicating to my future anyway. Don't please tell
> anyone because it is still rather early to be quite sure.[29]

For the first few months only other close friends such as Betty Murray knew (Betty plied her with barley sugar to prevent the sickness, and 'it seemed to work'.) To others, for a while she found herself being uncharacteristically economical with the truth. 'I had lunch with Tommy Taylor. He said would I lecture next year. I was jolly unwilling and he said really I ought to be stopping being shy by now. So I said well, I might in the summer term – to put it off as long as possible. I felt very deceitful.'

Once the news was out she admitted to joining with Joan in 'bragging' about their babies at an afternoon tea party. Both agreed that if anything the approaching conflict heightened their new sense of confidence.

> Joan said one of her first reactions to the crisis was 'thank
> goodness I'm going to have a baby' – that must be a very
> fundamental emotion, I had it too. While men . . . just think
> what an awful bad time to be bringing children into the
> world.

It was this confidence that carried her through the Royal Society meeting on protein molecules in November. Although she had an invitation, she had thought it might be unwise to give a definite acceptance to an event only one month before her baby was due. So she had told Bill Astbury that she 'hoped to be there', and did not expect to be asked to speak. She wrote rather breathlessly to Thomas the following day to tell him how the meeting had gone.

When I got there in the morning I found that my name was down among the official speakers – which gave me feelings of mingled shock and satisfaction . . .

The rest of the day got worse and worse. I got more and more harassed, thinking I really must try to write out what I was going to say. So I kept on moving in and out of the afternoon session – in to hear the X-ray people, out to try to write. Astbury was very bad and very amusing . . . Sage said it ought to cheer me up as I couldn't possibly be worse than Astbury.

Anyway I felt simply awful all the time I was speaking, I couldn't find my way in my notes, lost my way in my sentences, forgot half of what I meant to say altogether and felt as if I was shouting fearfully. Fan's assurance afterwards that I looked beautiful and he fell in love with me all over again (sic) wasn't entirely calculated to cheer me up . . . For my sins I now shall have to write a summary of what I wish I'd said – what I did say is beyond me to remember.

'Fan' Fankuchen was not the only one to admire her that day. Max Perutz, who was to become one of Dorothy's closest friends, had gone to the symposium excited about hearing a talk by Professor Theodor Svedberg of Uppsala, who had invented the ultracentrifuge and used it to demonstrate that proteins formed discrete molecules.

To my disappointment the great man's lecture was excruciatingly boring, but after him an attractive young woman took the stage and talked enthusiastically about her first X-ray diffraction studies of crystalline insulin . . . Dorothy lectured in that state to the Royal Society as if it were the most natural thing in the world, without any pretence of trying to be unconventional, which it certainly was at the time.[30]

Perhaps even less conventionally, Dorothy still retained her maiden name and despite her doctorate, styled herself Miss. It is unlikely that she saw anything remotely eyebrow-raising about this until her friend Flora Philpot, married to John Philpot, and herself a biochemist, walked up to her at the lunch break – accompanied by the great Professor Svedberg – and said, 'What the President of the Royal Society thinks about your lecturing under the name of Miss Crowfoot in your present condition I can't imagine!'

A week later Dorothy went home to her parents at Geldeston. They had settled on her giving birth at The Old House, with a midwife and doctor in attendance and a monthly nurse to look after mother and baby afterwards. While she waited she got to work finishing the diagrams for a massive paper summarizing the work she had done with Bernal and Fankuchen since 1932 on the structures of around eighty sterol molecules. Her sense of it being a race against time was not lessened by her mother's habit of looking at her with a critical eye and saying, 'It won't be long now.'

Thomas joined Dorothy in mid-December and Luke Howard Hodgkin was born precisely on time on the 20th of the month, to the great joy of everyone – especially the doctor and Dorothy's father who were hoping to get away to a sherry party. He was named, at Margery Fry's suggestion, after Thomas's great-great-grandfather Luke Howard (1772–1864), a Fellow of the Royal Society who had named the clouds and been dubbed 'the father of British meteorology'. It was a long labour, as Dorothy wrote to tell Bernal who had phoned up to wish her well.

> Thomas gave me your messages in the morning. I didn't have a really bad time at all. It went on rather long – I didn't observe the pains till 4 a.m. on Monday and the baby wasn't born till 5 p.m. on Tuesday. But I suspect the pains weren't as bad as some and therefore took a longish time to act – anyway I cowardly like got myself completely doped for the last hour. It was lovely waking up and being shown the baby.
>
> I think the baby is rather a nice one. He cries a good deal at the moment which tears my heart and my nurse (who seems a very good one) says all babies cry and often more than that, and won't let me feed him before his proper time. But really things are going very well with me and I'm very contented.[31]

Dorothy's contentment was short-lived. Confident of her own judgement only in the areas where she had special knowledge, she meekly deferred to the expertise of others where she had none. As far as the baby was concerned, the nurse's word was law. Dorothy was expected to do nothing but lie in bed and feed Luke at the four-hourly intervals decreed to be appropriate, a regime that has long since been wholly discredited. Luke was an alert, responsive baby; he frequently woke before the appointed time, cried pitifully, and then was too tired and upset to feed properly. Consequently he was hungry and miserable a great deal of the time, and failed to gain weight. Thomas went back to Cumberland when Luke was ten days old, leaving Dorothy to the tender mercies of the nurse.

> Nurse came up with my meat to find me gently crying into the remains of my soup. She said 'You're not weeping are you? You really mustn't – it'll spoil the baby's milk.' So I mayn't even shed a tear for you. We weighed Luke this morning on the Nurse's home balance – 6lbs 12. He had a very weepy night though. I shall try definite overfeeding this week.

But Nurse wasn't having any of that.

> I got into awful trouble with Nurse because when he cried at 2 last night I called out that I was awake. Nurse got McLaren to back her about the iniquity of midnight feeds and squashed Mummy and me quite flat. And all their good work was quite undone by a letter from Margaret [Gardiner] directly after (answering mine to Sage about Luke) describing how, as she couldn't bear to hear Martin cry, they decided to feed him as far as possible when he wanted to be fed. They kept a chart of the times he chose and found that fairly soon he settled down himself to a four hourly period. So it's all nonsense about the necessity of forming good habits at the beginning.

Incredibly, Dorothy admitted dreading the time when Nurse would come to the end of her four weeks and leave her alone with her mother to care for Luke. She seemed quite unable to trust her own instincts as a mother – which were certainly present in abundance – without the reassurance of a professional adviser. For his part, little Luke gave no particular cause for concern, except that (not surprisingly) he was still gaining weight more slowly than the doctor would have liked.

The plan was that when Luke was about a month old, Thomas would come down and collect mother and baby and take them back to his lodgings in the north-west. But just as the nurse's departure gave Dorothy the opportunity to gain a little more confidence, a new blow fell. She developed a breast abscess, quite possibly as a result of the anxiety of both mother and baby surrounding his feeds. The abscess was lanced, but as the days went by Dr McLaren's confidence that it would clear up in no time faded. It gradually became clear that Dorothy could not possibly leave on a journey of almost 300 miles for a single room in a small mining town far from her family. To make matters worse, McLaren was still worried about Luke's failure to gain weight, and began to suggest she give up the struggle and put him on to cow's milk. This Dorothy resisted, seeing such a move as an admission of her failure as a mother.

If all this were not upsetting enough, Dorothy found time to worry about her work, or lack of it. She had recently received a new set of insulin crystals from the Dutch pharmaceutical company Organon, which she wanted to work on as soon as she got back to Oxford. But Bernal wanted them photographed sooner, so she had to send them off to him at Birkbeck, much to her jealousy and regret. And there was still work to do on the sterol paper. She had hoped to have a meeting with Bernal in London on her way up north, but, as she wrote to him, that was out of the question too.

> It's beastly, it's all off as far as I'm concerned next weekend. I've had a breast abscess. It was lanced and cleaned out on Monday but it is still jolly painful and has to be dressed and the doctor won't let me travel . . . The abscess is a fairly superficial one and still may not prevent my feeding the child. Anyway I'm having a shot at going on.

Heilbron has asked me to talk at a Chem Soc discussion on March 2nd – on determination of mol. wts. by the X-ray method. I've, somewhat hopefully, accepted.

Tell me sometime about insulin. There's still a chance that I might be in London Monday evening – we ought to deal with those sterols.

O dear me.

Dorothy[32]

January wore on, and brought floods to Geldeston. Molly divided her time between caring for her daughter and grandson and organizing the distribution of free coal to the poorer villagers to help them dry out their cottages. The Hodgkin parents were putting Dorothy under pressure to go and live with them in Oxford, 'surrounded by doctors and nurses', rather than risk the wild north lands, a plan the Crowfoots enthusiastically supported. Dorothy confessed to Thomas, 'I'm rather worried and don't know what to think.'

At the end of January Thomas fell asleep while driving home and crashed into a brick wall. The accident put him in hospital with head injuries. That decided Dorothy: whatever her own condition, she must go straight to Cumberland to join him. The Hodgkin family saved the day. Thomas's brother Edward, then working on the *Manchester Guardian*, transferred him from the depressing district hospital in Whitehaven to a comfortable nursing home near Carlisle, while his mother collected Dorothy and Luke and took them to join him there. Dorothy's joy at seeing Thomas again soon turned to further anguish, as she recalled in her autobiography.

At the nursing home, where they had Thomas comfortably settled and safely bandaged up, they looked at me and decided I must stop nursing Luke, he must be otherwise fed, and my breast bandaged up and poulticed. For a time it was horrible: Thomas seriously wounded in one room, Luke weeping in another and myself in a third.

But Thomas recovered, Luke took to his bottle and soon they were well enough to move out of the nursing home to convalesce.

They were taken in by Sir James and Lady Moreton, the parents of one of Robin Hodgkin's students at Queen's, who lived in 'an enormous and very grand castle', Dalston Hall, nearby.

Eventually they were all sufficiently recovered for Dorothy and Luke to return to Oxford with her mother-in-law, and Thomas to his lectures in Cumberland. But Dorothy's breast was still infected, and when told she would have to have an operation she 'felt too ill to resist'. Luke was left in the care of his grand-mother at Queen's, and Dorothy went into the Acland Hospital for a fortnight. The hospital stay coincided with the Chemical Society meeting at which she had hoped to speak, so she quickly wrote out her talk and gave it to Dennis Riley to deliver on her behalf, 'which must have been rather overpowering for him'. After the operation she picked up another infection and ran a very high temperature for a while; but once that was past, she seemed at last to be on the way to recovery.

When she began to get up and about again, convalescing at Crab Mill for the Easter holidays, she found she was in pain all over and could hardly dress herself or turn on taps. At only twenty-eight years of age, she had suffered an attack of acute rheumatoid arthritis. Despite continuing pain, she returned to Oxford to make a second attempt at establishing a home for her family. She took over the few months' remaining lease on 315 Woodstock Road from Freddy Brewer, her former tutor, and set about engaging servants. She felt that her minimum needs, if she were to go back to work, were for a nursery nurse who would live in and take charge of Luke, a part-time cook to make lunch and dinner, and a cleaner for an hour or so a day. Even on her modest salary, an establishment on such a scale was just within her means. Whether she had been planning to work or not, it would have been almost unheard of for a young married woman of her social class to do without domestic help; both she and Thomas had grown up in households where there had always been at least two servants. The ready availability and low cost of this kind of help meant that even at a time when it was unusual for young mothers to carry on working, it was not difficult to do so. Had she been at the same stage in her career thirty years later, things might have been very different.

Almost at once she acquired Renée, the daughter of Thomas's

landlady in Maryport, who moved in very successfully as a nurse for Luke. The cook she engaged at first was more of a problem, daily conveying the impression that conditions at 315 Woodstock Road were not those that were met with 'in the best of households'; fortunately she found an excuse to leave and her replacement was a great improvement (until she left to have a baby). With domestic back-up in place, Dorothy returned to her teaching. As well as tutoring the Somerville 'girls', she now had to fulfil her promise to Tommy Taylor to give a course of lectures for the Chemistry Faculty. It began inauspiciously, as she told Thomas. 'First the lecture – well my audience was still there in spite of pouring rain, but I'm afraid they won't be next week – I felt myself definitely poor.'

Those who still remember Dorothy's undergraduate lectures describe them as always being sparsely attended, mainly by her own students from Somerville. When talking about her own special interests, she could sparkle; but she found it difficult to inject life into the drier fare of student courses, and took it for granted that people would be interested rather than trying to excite their interest. Powell had the same reputation as a lecturer. However, they both had the same problem: unless you are fired, as they were, with a desire to understand molecular structure, then the techniques of the crystallographer can seem complex, tedious and far removed from the concerns of everyday life.

Somehow she got through the term, still very stiff from the arthritis. To cheer her up, Thomas took her to Paris for a little early-summer holiday. She later remembered the agony of walking up the staircase of the little hotel he had found. Stopping in London on the way back, she went to see the Harley Street doctor who had treated her since childhood. He immediately referred her to Dr Charles Buckley, who ran a specialist clinic for arthritis and rheumatism sufferers in the spa town of Buxton in Derbyshire. Once again succumbing to the view of family and medical practitioners, she entered the clinic for treatment and spent most of the month of July there. The treatment, as she told Thomas, she found 'quite interesting'.

Mud packs on my hands are more primitive and I should guess much less effective than paraffin wax baths. One lies

with them on for 20 minutes. Then the bath in the Roman
style, a tank with steps down into it, but oneself all alone at
[illegible] degrees with douches at 105 degrees for the
hands. One feels very hot after it and has to cool down
wrapped round in towels to room temperature. The
patients are nicely friendly and mostly very north country.

Buckley also gave her a course of gold injections, impressed upon
her the importance of rest, and lent her the textbook on arthritis
he had written.[33] She found to her surprise that she was 'a typical
case: a young woman, under some stress, with an infection and a
history of rheumatism'. He was reassuring about her prospects
for recovery, but warned her that there might be recurrences in
the future. In both predictions he proved to be correct. For the rest
of Dorothy's life, and increasingly in her later years, her unique
capacity to focus also had to include overcoming physical pain
and disability.

Within a week in the clinic the pain had receded, but as a scientist, Dorothy was properly sceptical about the reasons for the
improvement. 'You'd be surprised if you saw me walking about
now – I'm so much better. I can't attribute it to the baths or cure
but just to having done so little, not only these last few days but
the week before.' Dorothy had been given a room to herself in the
clinic, with a table at which she could continue writing papers.
She was too far from Oxford to be troubled by many visitors or
demands for decisions. But she was not alone: her mother came
with her and stayed in a small hotel nearby, and not long afterwards Thomas's parents brought Luke and Renée to join her
there. Towards the end of her stay she was able to go out with
them and look at Poole's Cavern and other sights in the
picturesque Peak District. Whatever else she was getting from
her stay in the clinic, it was the first real chance she had had since
Luke's birth and difficult early days to recharge her physical and
emotional batteries.

When she returned to Oxford at the beginning of August to
start work photographing her new wet insulin crystals, she found
that her hands were so deformed that she could no longer operate the main switch on the X-ray equipment. Not to be deterred,
she got the laboratory technician, Frank Welch, to make a long

lever for the master switch. Thomas was home, back to his summer school lecturing at Balliol. And at last the prospect of a permanent home was in sight. Robin Hodgkin owned a large Victorian house in Bradmore Road, a quiet side street near the University Parks and extremely convenient for the Museum, which he had converted into flats. The top one would fall vacant in September, and he offered it to Dorothy and Thomas at very advantageous rates. They were delighted to accept.

At the end of August they went to Edinburgh together, Dorothy to read a paper on tobacco mosaic virus on behalf of Bernal at an international conference on genetics, Thomas to teach at another summer school. All was now well in the Hodgkin household, but not with the world. The conference seemed to be falling apart. The Russian contingent had pulled out only a few days before. Then the Germans did not arrive. The French received call-up papers.

> It was difficult to take scientific meetings seriously. We had already evacuated our boy to his grandmother in the country, but Thomas and I thought we had better go home. We stopped at Stoke on the way with some friends and heard Chamberlain's ultimatum to Germany. By the time we reached Ilmington the following day, we were at war.

6

'All this penicillin racket you know . . .'

War and penicillin,
1939–1945

To begin with, the war made rather little difference to Dorothy. Because of his precarious state of health (he suffered from narcolepsy, a tendency to fall asleep suddenly and unpredictably), Thomas was not called up for active service. He had obtained a new job, as a lecturer with the Workers' Educational Association in Stoke-on-Trent. In the heart of the region of Staffordshire known as the Potteries, Stoke was less than half the distance from Oxford of his previous post, but still more than two hours by car. Again he was living in lodgings during the week, but at least on their weekend visits Dorothy and Thomas could spend less time travelling and more in each other's company.

After an early air-raid alarm, which turned out to have been triggered by an Allied plane, Oxford saw no sign of enemy action. At the end of September Dorothy supervised the move from 315 Woodstock Road to 20c Bradmore Road single-handed. She soon felt sufficiently confident that the city would not be a target for bombers to bring Luke back from Crab Mill and settle him in their new home. From then on she tried to establish a routine that would allow Luke a little of her time every day – what textbooks for working couples now call 'quality time' – while a nursemaid looked after him during working hours and a cook took care of the meals. The idea was that Dorothy would get Luke up and dress him in the morning, come home for an hour at lunchtime and again for tea in the afternoon, after which he would go to bed and she would spend the evening working at home, back in the lab, or in college. This worked fairly well; the only problem was hiring a nursemaid to replace Renée, who decided on the outbreak of war that she must go home to her mother in Maryport, much to Dorothy's anguish. Over the next year or so her letters to Thomas feature regular domestic crises of this nature. Finding replacements was an unwelcome chore, but with Oxford full of European refugees desperate for work, not a difficult one. Thomas's mother was only too ready to look after Luke on the nursemaid's day off, or to step in in emergencies.

The austerity of wartime living was of little consequence to Dorothy, who was by nature frugal to the point of asceticism. She sold Maggie, her ancient car, for scrap, and turned her hand to making clothes for Luke, writing in triumph to Thomas that she had succeeded in cutting out two shirts from a single yard of fabric. She planted vegetables in the garden, and made jam (an activity nationally regarded as essential to the British war effort) with fruit from the garden at Crab Mill. During the Blitz in September 1940 thousands of evacuees from the East End of London were moved to Oxford and accommodated temporarily on the floor of the Majestic Cinema. Dorothy was at Crab Mill with Luke for the vacation, so was able to put up an evacuee family in her flat for a few days. A month later, although she was living there again herself, she volunteered to take in another. Her charitable zeal did not go down too well with Olga, the fastidious Viennese who at that time was caring for Luke and running the household.

> She nearly broke down at tea when a letter came . . . to say
> that Mrs Whitelock and babies would come to me
> tomorrow . . . She clearly thinks they're awful people. So
> worrying because if you think people awful they almost
> always become so . . . Poor Olga – she's torn between her
> nature and upbringing which require a perfectly tidy and
> ordered existence and her social conscience acquired
> through refugee experience which makes her know that it
> is really a good thing to take in the homeless etc. But she
> invents the most appalling reasons for not wanting them
> e.g. that they might have venereal disease.

Mrs Whitelock and her two children, a two-year-old girl and a baby boy, moved in at the end of October and stayed until January. She turned out to be 'a little dear', who eventually mollifted Olga by helping out around the house and cooking meals. Luke also learned to cope with the novel experience of having another child in the house.

> Luke and [Mary] are just of a size and get on very well. She
> has a sweet temper. When Luke hit her for reasons
> unknown to me all she said was 'Go away.' Olga scolded
> Luke who burst into tears and ran to me. But it all ended
> happily with Mary giving Luke a large kiss.

Nevertheless, Dorothy had to admit that she was relieved when Mrs Whitelock decided to move on to Wolverhampton, where most of her other former neighbours had gone, and they finally had the flat to themselves again. She had other evacuees to keep an eye on: her Aunt Dolly and maternal grandmother had moved from London into the ground-floor flat, which had just become vacant. Grace Hood was very elderly and quite infirm by this time, and most of her conversation was about religious matters – an obsession that could have surprising consequences.

> I had a nice talk with my granny in the garden. Do you
> know she is quite taken with the idea of our making
> friends with Russia – on the rather curious grounds that
> Stalin's mother intended him for the church. Still it's nice
> to find some point of politics on which we can agree.

There were evacuees in the lab as well, but they were an unexpected bonus, in the form of trained researchers from Bernal's lab. Research scientists were not expected to join up, but to stay at their present posts unless directed elsewhere by the Ministry of Labour. For much of the previous decade Bernal had been developing his thinking on the uses of science in peace and war; the result was published in 1939 as *The Social Function of Science*,[1] his most influential book. (Many of his ideas about government support for science, and the way it should be organized, are now common practice.) Already well known in defence circles for his experimental work with the Cambridge Scientists' Anti-War Group, he was given the post of scientific adviser to the Research and Experimental Department of the Ministry of Home Security, based in Princes Risborough. Senior civil servants anxiously queried the appointment on the grounds of his politics. The Minister, Sir John Anderson, overruled them exclaiming, 'I don't care if he's as red as the flames of hell!'[2]

Bernal threw himself into the task of evaluating the effects of aerial bombardment, first in field trials, later on the increasingly devastated streets of London. As the war progressed his influence increased; he was seconded first to Bomber Command, then to Combined Operations, where he gave personal briefings to the Chief, Lord Mountbatten. Mountbatten's main task was to plan what later became known as the D-Day landings along the Normandy coast. Bernal played a central role in carrying out studies of such factors as the beach gradients and methods of suppressing waves. On one occasion Mountbatten invited him to demonstrate the effectiveness of an inflated barrier to Winston Churchill in a bathroom on board the *Queen Mary*, using paper ships in the bath.

Research in Bernal's department at Birkbeck ceased, partly due to his absence but more pressingly because of the danger of bomb damage in central London; the Physics Department was indeed bombed in one of the early raids. His research team had to split up. Fankuchen and his wife decided to return to the United States, but Bernal arranged for the other members of the group, first Harry Carlisle and later Käthe Schiff, to come and join Dorothy's laboratory in Oxford. The extra hands were welcome, but what was even more so was the brand-new set of crystallographic equipment they brought with them. Harry Carlisle arrived at the end of October, followed shortly by a new transformer set, two new X-ray tubes and more goniometers.

Carlisle arrived with a great deal of junk from Birkbeck . . .
We just hope to get this lot cleared away before the main
lot arrives on Thursday. He seems nice and is evidently a
hard worker. So I have every hope that we may get
something done.

The new equipment was a godsend. Tiny Powell also had research students, and there had been tension between him and Dorothy over access to the X-ray equipment. Less than a year before, for example, she had written to Thomas:

> Dennis and I after being extremely annoyed with Tiny Powell for the last ten days for blocking an experiment of ours now just decided it was silly being enemies and we'd best be friends. So we made some quite decent efforts and now I feel really rather badly about my past view of the poor little man . . .

The arrival of a second transformer set and more tubes and cameras restored Dorothy to her previous independence. All the equipment had only recently been delivered to Birkbeck on the strength of a grant for which Bernal had applied to the Rockefeller Foundation in December 1938. This application had been dropped by the Trustees on the outbreak of war, and the equipment was still unpaid for.

Having solved the problem of keeping his equipment safe, Bernal then set about finding the means to pay for it and making sure that research would continue. He wrote to the Rockefeller Foundation on 16 January 1940 to suggest that it make a grant to Dorothy.

> The position of X-ray research on proteins and viruses in this country is at present in a promising but critical state . . . If this work can be maintained there now seems a direct way to attack the fundamental problem of protein structure . . . The position, however, is precarious. All research work which has no immediate bearing on the present military struggle is being carried on somewhat on sufferance, and funds for its continuation may be stopped at any moment. Even now it is difficult to find money to pay for apparatus and supplies already in use, and unless some support can come from outside the whole work on this side of the water may come to an end in a few months' time . . . I would like, therefore, to put the following suggestions through you to the Foundation.

Dorothy was born in Cairo in 1910; her mother Molly Crowfoot was one of the most important influences in her life. (Courtesy of Elisabeth Crowfoot)

'Pandora's Box', one of the plays performed by the Geldeston children under Molly Crowfoot's direction. Dorothy (aged about 11, centre) holds the hand of her sister Diana; Joan is right of Dorothy, and Elisabeth seated far left. (Courtesy of Elisabeth Crowfoot)

John Winter Crowfoot rented the Old House at Geldeston for the family in 1920; a magnificent cedar grew in the garden.

(Courtesy of the Hodgkin family)

Chemistry at the Sir John Leman School: Dorothy and her friend Norah can just be seen in the back row.

(Courtesy of Elisabeth Crowfoot)

Somerville College, the class of 1928: Dorothy, fifth from the right in the second-to-back row, seems to have something else on her mind. (Courtesy of Somerville College)

British Association Meeting, Nottingham, 1937: Dorothy looks on as Bernal demonstrates 'reversed spirals in tobacco mosaic virus solution' to Irving Langmuir.

(Photograph by Gordon Cox, courtesy of Judith Howard)

*Luke Howard Hodgkin was born in December 1938; a
month later, Thomas was injured in a road accident.*

Bernal, Isidore Fankuchen (left) and his wife Dina visited Dorothy in Oxford in September 1939. The Fankuchens returned to the US soon afterwards.

(Courtesy of the Bodleian Library, Oxford, Ms.Eng.c.5715, Folder J.7)

Dennis Riley, Dorothy's first research student, in the garden at 20 Bradmore Road with Luke and Dorothy.

(Courtesy of Judith Howard)

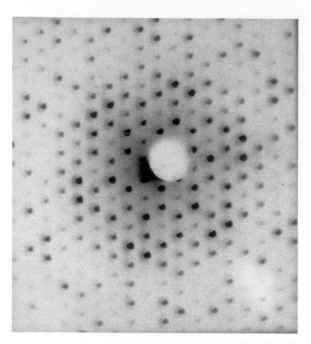

One of Dorothy's early insulin diffraction patterns. She first photographed insulin in 1935; the structure was solved in 1969.
(Courtesy of Guy Dodson)

FRS and mother of three: Dorothy with Toby, Liz and Luke on her election to the Royal Society in 1947.
(© Oxford and County Newspapers)

After being refused a visa in 1953, Dorothy had to fight to be allowed to return to the United States to visit friends such as Linus Pauling. (Courtesy of the Hodgkin family)

At the time of the Nobel prize announcement, Dorothy was in Ghana with Thomas.
(Courtesy of the Hodgkin family)

*In unaccustomed finery,
Dorothy and Thomas danced
at the Nobel ball.*
(Courtesy of the Hodgkin family)

*In 1970 Dorothy was
appointed Chancellor of the
University of Bristol; the
gown had been made for one
of her predecessors, Sir
Winston Churchill.*
(With permission from the University
of Bristol Arts Photographic Unit)

North Vietnam, September 1971: Dorothy was impressed by the self-reliance of the girls who defended the villages.
(Courtesy of the Hodgkin family)

Kyoto, 1972: Dorothy took office as President of the International Union of Crystallography.
(Courtesy of the Hodgkin family)

Bangalore, 1970s: Vijayan and Kalyani are to the right of Dorothy; Siv Ramaseshan stands behind his wife Kausalya.

(Courtesy of the Hodgkin family)

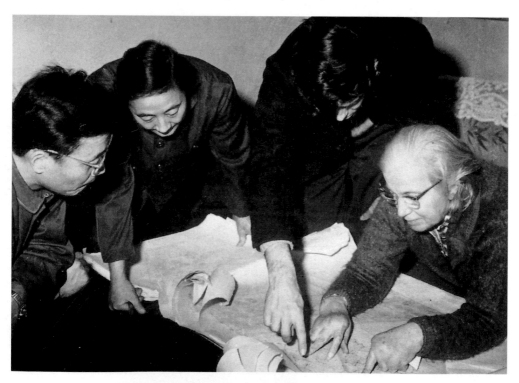

Beijing, 1977: Dorothy took Guy Dodson to compare insulin maps with the Chinese crystallographers.

(Courtesy of Liang Dongcai)

*Beijing, 1980: Dorothy accompanied Liang Dongcai
(behind Dorothy) on a visit to the Great Wall.*
(Courtesy of Liang Dongcai)

*Dorothy, President of Pugwash since 1975, arrives for a
peace conference with Joseph Rotblat (behind Dorothy).*
(Courtesy of the Hodgkin family)

In the kitchen at Crab Mill with Elizabeth: in the years after Thomas died Dorothy took comfort from the company of her children.

(Courtesy of the Hodgkin family)

With Guy Dodson at York, Dorothy continued to work on the insulin structure until the late 1980s.

(© John Olive, with permission from Chemistry Photographics, University of York)

Visits from great-grandchildren – here Dorothy holds the first born, Sam – were a particular delight.
(Courtesy of the Hodgkin family)

Dorothy was among an illustrious group awarded honorary degrees by Oxford University at the inauguration of Lord Jenkins of Hillhead as Chancellor in October 1987. Others pictured are Isaiah Berlin, Arthur Schlesinger and Iris Murdoch. (© Billett Potter)

Dorothy was one of the first to congratulate Louise Johnson (right) on her election as David Phillips Professor of Molecular Biophysics at Oxford in 1990.

(Photograph © Norman McBeath)

Tutor and student: Dorothy and her former student Margaret Thatcher attended the opening of the Dorothy Hodgkin Quadrangle and Margaret Thatcher Conference Centre at Somerville College in 1991.

(© Oxford and County Newspapers)

Despite her frailty, Dorothy insisted on travelling to the International Congress of Crystallography in Beijing in 1993. Eleanor Dodson (left) and Elizabeth Hodgkin (centre) accompanied her.

(© Deborah Elliott)

> That a sum of £1000 should be granted to Dr Crowfoot . . .
> for researches on proteins and viruses, with the object of
> carrying out more general and fundamental investigations
> than that which I proposed in my original application of 12
> December 1938 . . . A grant of this size would enable the
> work to be carried on in a satisfactory way for another year
> or two. There is little serious risk of destruction by war as
> Oxford is not considered to be a military target.[3]

The officers of the Rockefeller Foundation did not immediately
agree. A meeting between Wilbur Tisdale and Warren Weaver in
February concluded that

> it is not outside the question to help Bernal or Crowfoot at
> the proper time, but . . . that we could afford to consider
> the advisability of a further development at Cambridge
> after the war than to think of this uncertain proposal at the
> present moment.[4]

At the end of the year Dorothy sent them an account of the work
she had done on wet insulin crystals, using the new equipment.
It was taken for her by the evolutionary biologist Julian Huxley,
who (no doubt at Bernal's instigation), put in a word on her
behalf. In January she heard that her application for £1000 had
been approved. The grant provided Dorothy with enough funds
to pay for the Birkbeck equipment, to relieve her of teaching for a
term, and to pay for two research assistants. It was the beginning
of an association that lasted into the 1960s, one of the longest
periods for which the Foundation had supported any single scientist continuously. It also included Dorothy in a highly select
league of British scientists viewed by the Rockefeller as important
to its new strategy of applying the techniques of physical science
to biology. The Rockefeller officers, particularly Gerard Pomerat
who visited Dorothy regularly after the war was over, would
remind her regularly to let them know of her needs, and were not
in the least concerned when the demands of the war forced her to
switch the focus of her research away from proteins. It is difficult
to overestimate the importance of this friendly and consistent
support in establishing her research on a sure footing.

With her little group now grown to four – Dennis Riley was still in Oxford, though trying to find work more related to the war effort – Dorothy had to find them all projects to work on. Riley was completing his DPhil research on lactoglobulin, and had also participated in the work on insulin and helped Perutz with haemoglobin. She herself wanted to continue with insulin. Previously she had always measured the intensities of the reflections by eye, comparing the spots on the photographs with a reference set of spots obtained by exposing a piece of film to the same beam for different amounts of time. But although this method could be surprisingly accurate, she was not satisfied. To obtain more objective readings, she wanted to make use of a photometer, a device that would measure how much light was blocked by each of the spots on an X-ray photograph.

To set up the device and carry out the measurements she now had the assistance of Käthe Schiff. Schiff was Austrian by birth, a cousin of the philosopher Karl Popper; she had been doing a PhD with V. M. Goldschmidt in Göttingen when Hitler came to power. When Goldschmidt fled to Oslo Schiff, who was also Jewish, returned to her native Vienna and completed her thesis there. In 1937 she had to flee again, this time to England, and as a competent crystallographer she very quickly found herself added to Bernal's team at Birkbeck. She came to Oxford with a grant from ICI for one year, but once the Rockefeller money came through Dorothy had enough to keep her on as her research assistant.

That left Harry Carlisle. Originally from Burma, he had come to Britain on a scholarship to do a PhD, and had begun work with Bernal on the synthetic sex hormone stilboestrol and some of its derivatives. Dorothy still maintained her interest in the sterols, the subject of her PhD thesis and the soon-to-be published magnum opus with Bernal and Fankuchen for the *Transactions of the Royal Society*.[5] She and Carlisle published a short paper together on the research he had begun at Birkbeck. However, she saw his arrival as an opportunity to push things further. Because of her more recent commitment to proteins, she still had not completed the analysis of a single sterol structure. She suggested to Carlisle that he should take this on, and he agreed.

Of the dozens she had examined, one in particular seemed a promising candidate: cholesteryl iodide. The atom of iodine in each molecule was much heavier than the twenty-seven atoms of carbon that made up the bulk of the molecule, and therefore estimating the phases of the reflections on the basis of the iodine atom alone gave a good approximation to the true phases. She already knew from her preliminary studies that the unit cell of the crystal structure contained just two molecules, related in a way that would not cause undue problems in interpreting the maps. The chemistry of the sterols was by this time fairly well understood. With a little help from crystallographers such as Bernal, organic chemists had already worked out the basic sterol formula – the proportions of the atomic ingredients that go to make up the molecule – and knew how the atoms were linked into chains and rings. What remained to be determined was exactly how these chains and rings were arranged in three dimensions – a job for which X-ray crystallography was the only tool.

Dorothy was determined, though, that Carlisle should not rely on the chemical information in his analysis. She realized that it ought to be possible to find the structure of a largely unknown molecule purely by crystallographic means, and decided, as an exercise, that he should treat cholesteryl iodide in this way. The fact that its chemistry was in fact known simply provided her with a means of comparing her results with the work of the organic chemists.

The first problem, that of finding suitable crystals, was quickly solved. Carlisle brought with him 'a sufficiency' of crystals of cholesteryl iodide, the remains of a batch that had been given to Fankuchen a few years before by the organic chemist Ian Heilbron of Imperial College, London. Finding that they were looking a bit past their best, she dissolved the material and recrystallized it, producing two slightly different forms of crystal, both usable for X-ray analysis.

Carlisle 'started the work in early 1941 and completed the collection of the X-ray data in about three months'.[6] This included the laborious task of estimating the intensities of all the reflections, for which Carlisle used the traditional method of comparing them by eye with a standard set of spots. The next stage was to find the positions of the iodine atoms by calculating Patterson projections. The vectors between one iodine atom and another in the crystal stood out as densely contoured peaks. With the positions of the iodine atoms fixed, Carlisle could move on to calculate a projection of the electron density throughout the whole molecule, based on the phases contributed by the iodine atoms alone. From these, as Dorothy noted, it was 'relatively easy to pick out the outlines of the sterol ring system and the side chain attached to it oriented as expected within the crystal'.

What was 'relatively easy' for Dorothy was far from straight-forward even to Carlisle, who had carried out all the hard graft of collecting and analysing the data.

> I had calculated the electron-density map . . . of the B form where the two molecules in projection are reasonably well separated except for a slight overlap. At the time I could not make head or tail of it. After all, I had only used some sixty reflections for this projection and consequently the map was of poor resolution. Dorothy saw it and without difficulty sketched in one molecule; except for minor corrections of the atomic positions, her selection of the . . . coordinates was remarkably close to the correct positions when the work was completed.[7]

This was not the end of the job. A projection is a picture of what the molecule would look like if it was squashed flat; and Dorothy knew that cholesterol iodide was not flat. Two-dimensional projections were easier to calculate, but left you with the problem that atoms could be masked by others that overlapped. Only a three-dimensional analysis could give you an accurate picture of the lengths and angles of all the bonds that held the atoms together in the molecule. Carlisle next set about calculating the electron density along a series of lines perpendicular to the points on one projection that seemed most likely to indicate the positions of atoms, gradually building up a three-dimensional picture. He did this once using phase angles derived from the iodine contributions, and then, once he had a more accurate idea of the approximate positions of the carbon atoms, repeated the calculations taking their contributions to the phases into account as well.

He had barely started on the calculations when Bernal summoned him to work at Princes Risborough on defence research. But Carlisle was not to be put off his stride.

It was on the journeys to and from Oxford, in cold and ill-lit carriages, that I carried out the one-and-only set of three-dimensional calculations to obtain the whole set of bond lengths and bond angles using a slide rule and logarithmic tables . . . Not only that, but if I got tired of calculating – the train was often delayed because it was a single-track line – I would start drafting out parts of my thesis, for what was normally a half-hour journey in daylight could be anything from three to four hours in the blackout.[8]

It was a 'heroic operation' in Dorothy's eyes. By the end of 1942 they were able to make a model out of wires and corks that showed the positions of every principal atom – although as Dorothy later noted, it was actually a mirror image of the true structure. A method that would allow her to distinguish between the two was not developed for another ten years.

Carlisle went off on his own to present their results in a lecture that he gave at Cambridge in January 1943, before the great and the good of British crystallography. The response was all that Dorothy could have wished, and more, as she told Thomas.

I'm in a state of bliss at the moment, Harry having just rung up to say we've won a resounding victory! His lecture seems to have been an enormous success – he went on for an hour and a half – Bragg and Lipson repeatedly asking questions where they didn't understand! and Bragg at the end said he'd written in a recent review . . . that the younger generation of crystallographers hadn't the initiative to tackle really difficult problems and now he would have to write and withdraw it all!

Carlisle was awarded a DPhil for his work on the project in 1943, but it did not reach a wider public until the end of the war, when Dorothy wrote it up and Bernal arranged for it to be published in the *Transactions of the Royal Society*.[9] The solution of cholesteryl iodide was a significant milestone, both for Dorothy and for crystallography. Not only was it her first complete crystallographic analysis, it was the first biochemically significant molecule for which a detailed three-dimensional structure had been published. 'The crucial thing,' says Max Perutz, 'was that when she solved the structure it was the most complex organic structure yet determined.'[10] It showed that even for molecules of this type, the heavy atom method could provide enough information about phases to produce an interpretable map. Until then the conventional approach was still trial-and-error, based on assigning phases according to a guess about what the molecule ought to look like.

Others in the field were equally impressed. Jack Dunitz was then a young doctoral student in Glasgow, working with the highly respected crystallographer J. Monteath Robertson who had trained with W. H. Bragg at the Royal Institution.

> For our trial-and-error methods we needed a well-defined molecular model. Although Robertson himself had shown the power of isomorphous replacement in crystal structure analysis, 'heavy atom' methods were not current among his students. We had heard of the Patterson function, but the only applications we knew were for very simple structures . . . We were conditioned to think in terms of two-dimensional projections rather than in terms of the three-dimensional structure itself. I read some of Dorothy's published papers, especially the one (with Harry Carlisle) on the structure analysis of cholesteryl iodide, involving the use of three-dimensional diffraction data. I saw that three-dimensional methods were essential for the solution of complex organic structures . . .[11]

The success of the work on cholesteryl iodide suggested that similar methods could be used to find the structure of a molecule for which the formula was not known. Dorothy was therefore the obvious choice when the need arose for a crystallographer to examine a newly isolated compound of enormous clinical significance: penicillin.

In 1939 Howard Florey, Oxford's new Professor of Pathology, had begun to work with the biochemist Ernst Chain on naturally occurring compounds that had antibacterial effects. The most promising was penicillin, discovered a decade before by Alexander Fleming at St Mary's Hospital in London. Fleming reported that the penicillium mould produced a substance that killed bacteria, but pronounced the substance too unstable to be isolated and used as a drug. Florey and Chain, with their colleague Norman Heatley, were more persistent. Heatley developed an ingenious range of techniques for growing the mould in fermentation flasks, extracting the active agent from the broth, and testing its activity. In May 1940 Florey carried out a historic experiment. He injected eight mice with lethal doses of streptococcus, treating four of them with some of the first penicillin extracts. The untreated mice all died within twenty-four hours. The other four survived for days to weeks. The normally taciturn Florey said, 'It looks like a miracle.' The work, which Chain and Florey were at pains to emphasize they had begun out of scientific curiosity rather than any supposed benefit to mankind, now looked like leading to one of the most important advances in twentieth-century medicine.[12]

In Oxford every scientist walks along South Parks Road, the main thoroughfare through the Science Area, at least once a day. Dorothy was walking along South Parks Road the morning after this momentous experiment, where she met Ernst Chain 'in a very excited state'. He told her about their results, and added, 'Some day we will have crystals for you.' For the next year the pathologists continued their experiments, confirming penicillin's astonishing effects on laboratory animals, and moving on in February 1941 to treating the first human patients. At this stage they were still working with very impure samples of penicillin, but so potent was it that some of their early patients were literally brought back from the brink of death.

The authorities soon recognized the enormous benefits such a powerful drug could bring, especially in wartime. Soldiers wounded in the battlefield were more at risk from bacterial infections than from death in the line of fire. The recently introduced sulphonamide drugs were better than nothing, but could not deal with the range of bacteria penicillin appeared able to combat. There were still a great many problems to be solved, however. Heatley's methods of production, even working round the clock, produced barely enough penicillin for the experimental programme in Oxford. Large-scale production meant developing a reliable industrial process. One way to do this would be simply to scale up the fermentation process. Another approach would be to develop a method of synthesizing penicillin. That would be impossible, however, without knowing the chemical formula for the penicillin molecule.

The study of penicillin quickly became an international enterprise. To his disappointment, Florey had been unable to get any British chemical company to take on the task of developing the production of the drug at a time when they were fully stretched with other wartime requirements. So in the summer of 1941, taking Heatley with him, he set sail for the United States. They visited a number of firms, as well as the government research laboratories at Peioria in Illinois. Soon afterwards, the United States entered the war; within a few months, several American firms were working on large-scale penicillin production and a system was in place for providing the drug, through the US Office of Scientific Research and Development (OSRD), to people suffering from life-threatening infections.

In Britain the government belatedly woke up to the significance of what was going on in Oxford. Florey was put into uniform and sent to North Africa to supervise the testing of penicillin in the front line, and British companies began to enter the field of penicillin research. A Penicillin Chemists' Committee (PEN), consisting of both university and industrial chemists, met regularly and produced research papers which were circulated among members. In 1944 a second group, the Committee on Penicillin Synthesis (CPS) was set up under the direction of the Medical Research Council (MRC), largely incorporating PEN. Both PEN and the CPS communicated with their American counterparts, but only under strictly controlled conditions; from 1944 all communication was supposed to be channelled through the MRC and OSRD.

The Dyson Perrins Laboratory at Oxford was one of the principal centres for research into penicillin. The professor, Robert Robinson, was directly involved in attempting to discover its formula, together with his colleague Wilson Baker, and Ernst Chain and Edward Abraham from the Dunn School of Pathology. Dorothy did not immediately become involved, having other

things on her mind: early in 1941 she found that she was pregnant with her second child. Prudence Elizabeth,* otherwise
known as Lizzie Pru, was born on 23 September in the Radcliffe
Infirmary, Oxford's public hospital. Thomas was sent for by
telegram but did not quite make it in time and heard the news by
telephone from Banbury Station. The birth and its aftermath were
much less traumatic than Luke's, while Elizabeth proved at first
a placid and easily contented baby. Dorothy returned to research
and teaching as soon as term began in mid-October. Her letters in
the weeks after Thomas returned north are full of her feelings for
her children and their futures.

I've got Prudence Elisabeth on my knee getting up her
wind . . . it's 3 p.m. and I'm due at College at 3.30 . . .
    A nice scene greeted me this morning when I came out
from my 9 o'clock girl to my daughter's bath. There were
Mima [Robin Hodgkin], Mima Granny and Luke and Olga
all assisting to get her undressed. Your father said 'How
nice it is to think that in the year 2000 she may be watching
her granddaughter bathed.' I hope she will. Though it's
funny to think of this little thing ever being nearly 60 years
old.

I had a really triumphal entry to College yesterday. First
Auntie took me by car – I chatted to Ethel at the Lodge – she
very pleased as she always wished Luke had been a girl.
Then . . . found all the Fellows finishing their tea. I naturally
bragged about my daughter for the next ten minutes after
which we reluctantly began the meeting. The Bursar took
me home in her car in return for a view of the Baby.

I was thinking to myself when I was reading your letters in
bed this morning. Some sorts of happiness are perfectly
good in themselves and one feels about them one doesn't
mind what happens afterwards since such a time once
was. But children aren't like that. They belong to the future

---

*Elizabeth Hodgkin always uses this spelling. Dorothy tended to spell the name
Elisabeth, as her sister was named.

and one does desperately want them to have a good
future. And so I more than ever wish for some action that
might preserve us all.

But by the end of November the laboratory was exerting its pull
once more, and the children were having to share her attention
with that other new arrival, penicillin. Dorothy knew very well
that X-ray work on crystals of the substance would be enormously important, and she was determined to be part of it.

> I've just come back from visiting Chain and now it's 10.30
> p.m. I'm feeling disgustingly cheerful too as a result of my
> visit. The main purpose of Chain I may say is that he
> works on penicillin – you may remember the stuff Hugo
> [Cairns, Thomas's uncle and Nuffield Professor of Surgery]
> was talking about in the summer that is so active
> antistreptocci and staphylococci that it almost brings
> people back from the dead. Apparently it hasn't yet been
> crystallized after all – both Chain and Powell thought
> they'd got crystals of it about the time we went on holiday
> but both were mistaken and so far all attempts have failed.
> I found myself irresistibly drawn to follow Hugo's advice
> and 'inject myself into the situation'. Chain seemed quite
> keen to let me have some stuff to try to crystallize and I'd
> simply love to try. Though when I shall have the time
> goodness knows – perhaps after term? And of course
> Chain may draw back when it comes to the point. Or the
> other gang – Baker, Powell, may have got on further than
> Chain thinks.
>
>   Lisbeth in my arms. She weighed 9lbs 4 oz this morning
> and has gained an average of 7½ oz per week in the first 8
> weeks of her life.

From this point on, the chemists involved Dorothy in their
researches whenever anything emerged that might provide her
with suitable material for X-ray analysis. Her proximity was for-
tuitous; it was her proven expertise that led them to include her
in this momentous project.

With a whole new branch of research opening up in her lab, as much teaching as ever, and two young children at home, Dorothy needed another pair of hands. For the first time she turned to one of her own Somerville students to help her out with her research. Barbara Low finished Part I of her chemistry degree in the summer of 1942, and Dorothy had encouraged her to think about doing Part II with her. She was a determined young woman and an ardent pacifist; Dorothy also found her a fast learner and an extremely competent practical scientist. Under wartime conditions applications to do research had to be approved by the Ministry of Labour – and the Ministry turned Barbara down.

Although Barbara had not done as well as expected in her exams, Dorothy had seen enough of her work in the laboratory to know that she was the right person for the job. She immediately put her networking skills into operation. One of Low's external examiners, the inorganic chemist William Wardlaw, was now, by coincidence, working for the Ministry of Labour. Dorothy wrote to tell him that Low had worked with her during the summer vacation (paid for by Rockefeller money), and that she was convinced of her worth; she concluded that 'It is difficult to think of anything much more useful Miss Low could do next year than this research if it proves at all successful.' Wardlaw wrote back immediately in reply:

If Miss Low will send the completed card to me personally I will deal with the matter myself and secure her services for you. The research she will be associated with is, in my view, most timely and important and I agree she could not be better employed . . .[13]

Dorothy was jubilant, as she wrote to Thomas:

I'm in a state of great happiness . . . All this penicillin racket you know – but even if it's a bit of a racket, it's also really serious too . . . And we've got lovely photographs of this first mould stuff – claviformin or whatever they call it . . .

She quickly became caught up in the excitement of the new research.

I can't seem to take this term seriously at all. I seem to be
spending all my mornings and quite a lot of the rest of the
day in the lab. – though I have not yet induced penicillin to
crystallize, bad luck. We now, however, have three other
substances on hand – claviformin, terreic acid and 'mould
318'. The last is the most hopeful medically – but not so
good as penicillin.

Dorothy and Barbara Low worked first on the variety of other
mould products isolated by Chain, all of which turned out to be
too toxic to be useful. Penicillin was another matter; but penicillin proved to be surprisingly difficult to deal with. It took the
chemists until the middle of 1943 to be sure of the compound's
chemical composition. But its formula – the diagram that would
show how the atoms were connected together in the molecule,
an essential prerequisite for any attempt at synthesis – still
eluded them. And Dorothy was frustrated because neither they
nor she had managed to grow crystals of penicillin for her to
photograph.

There was some progress, however. The chemists succeeded in
breaking penicillin down into a variety of smaller compounds:
penicillamine, penillic acid and so on. These did make crystals of
sorts, and it was these that provided most of the work for
Dorothy and Barbara Low during that first year. It was a far from
easy introduction to the subject.

[Dorothy] really believed in throwing people in the deep
end. She expected you to work with crystals that you could
only just see under the highest power of the microscope,
and she expected you to manipulate them and mount
them. There were all sorts of gadgets in the lab, Bernal
gadgets and Fankuchen gadgets, and if you were expected
to do something you did it, there were no alternatives . . .
Sometimes I remember being told to mount on a little piece
of glass fibre a sort of nasty resinous mess with a little
crystal in the middle. I don't know who said if you can see
it as a birefringent speck it's a crystal and you can
photograph it, but certainly that was what I was taught
and one never thought anything else.[14]

The urgency of the work called for the highest expectations, but Dorothy certainly expected no more of Barbara than she expected of herself. Those beastly crystals of penicillamine, a fraction of the size of a grain of salt and 'embedded in a viscous glue-like matrix' caused her just as much trouble as they did Barbara, as she relayed to Thomas in a series of bulletins.

> The penicillin amino acid has turned up again – quite decent crystals to look at but simply awful to handle 1) they are immersed in a gummy fluid 2) they are extremely hygroscopic so that they are practically impossible to leave out in the air for more than a few minutes or so. I've spent most of the day – with intervals for teaching and family – trying to get them into little tubes to be photographed and have not yet succeeded to my liking.

> I'm feeling a bit fed up at the moment – fed up but not defeated, my very carefully and difficultly mounted crystal having decomposed during its exposure to X rays – a shame when we were so excited to see if there were any effects.

> One word of love – but it's Thursday and even worse than usual as a new compound of penicillin itself – sodium salt of dihydropenicillin turned up – horrible to handle as usual – I've spent my whole day on it looking down a microscope teasing things with a pin.

The main value of the work Dorothy and Barbara Low did during this year was to provide the chemists with independent checks on the molecular weights of the substances they were isolating, and a method of confirming their identity. It was partly due to their measurements that the chemists realized that there was something missing from their analysis. Wilson Baker carried out a further investigation on the penicillin degradation products. In July 1943 Dorothy was back in the clinic at Buxton having another course of treatment for her arthritis when Barbara Low wrote in great excitement.

> Red hot news! Penicillin and all its degradation products

contain sulphur. This is very hush-hush . . . The sulphur obviously explains the enormous oxygen content of penicillaminic acid. They are sending in a report about it today.

About penicillin and rheumatoid arthritis. Dr Abraham talked to Dr Gardner about it. He, Dr Gardner, says no work has been done on rheumatoid arthritis and he himself is not very hopeful. Penicillin does appear very specific in its properties and has a limited range of applicability.

But he does say that if you feel you would like to try it he is sure Mrs Florey would be very glad for you to. [Howard Florey's wife Ethel managed the penicillin treatment programme at the Radcliffe Infirmary.] He suggests that you get into touch with her. He said quite definitely that there is the penicillin there.[15]

One of the interesting features of this letter is that it reveals the extent to which penicillin was regarded as a wonder drug; it also reveals that Dorothy herself at this stage had rather little understanding of how penicillin worked, or of the nature of arthritis.

With the discovery of the sulphur atom, the chemists had at last completed their analysis of penicillin. In total there were 27 atoms in each molecule: 1 of sulphur, 2 of nitrogen, 4 of oxygen, 9 of carbon and 11 of hydrogen. But there was still room for doubt about the way the atoms linked together – the formula. Edward Abraham was one of those hard at work on this problem, and he recalled that there were differences of opinion.

[Robert] Robinson immediately suggested what became known as the thiazolidine-oxazolone structure which I didn't like, but he was quite sure about it. I didn't like it because . . . its stability was rather greater than one would have expected with this sort of structure. I proposed to Chain that the structure must be the beta lactam structure and Chain immediately accepted this . . . Robinson had already drafted a report with the oxazolone structure but we added to it the beta lactam structure. When he came back we had a meeting and to my dismay, he was furious about this structure. He said 'I know what it is. You think I'm getting old, that I'm getting past it.' . . . He had this characteristic of finding it very difficult to accept anything which didn't immediately agree with what he thought.[16]

Both structures consisted of two linked rings. In the thiazolidine–oxazolone structure there were two five-membered rings of atoms connected by a single bond; in the beta lactam structure one five-membered ring was fused to an adjacent four-membered ring. Most of the Oxford penicillin team took sides on the issue. Chain and Abraham continued to favour the beta lactam. John Cornforth, a younger colleague of Robinson's, is reputed to have announced that if the beta lactam structure was correct he would give up chemistry and grow mushrooms instead. (He does not deny the gist of the story, but thinks he said 'take up croquet' rather than 'grow mushrooms'.) Dorothy knew of both proposed structures, but had no strong feelings on the matter herself. 'We were all very gay. It seemed likely that one of the chemists would synthesize both proposed structures and easily decide which was correct. The true course of events proved otherwise.'[17]

Almost immediately afterwards news arrived by telegram from the United States. Chemists at the company E. R. Squibb had succeeded in crystallizing penicillin itself, as a sodium salt. As soon as she heard this, Dorothy rang Edward Abraham to ask if he could make some sodium penicillin. He replied that he had plenty already, but that it had to be kept in a desiccator (a container from which all moisture could be removed) because it took up water so readily from the air. He brought a tube over from the Dunn School to show her. She got to work straight away.

I put out a little on a slide for examination, and while we were talking together it picked up water from the atmosphere and set in a mass of crystals. I put one on the X-ray tube and took a couple of X-ray diffractions.[18]

Dorothy hoped that the sodium in the crystals would provide the heavy atom she needed to solve the structure, just as she had done with cholesteryl iodide. But the results were disappointing. The crystals were 'small and fragile and difficult to handle . . . it was also clear that the crystal structure of the sodium salt was of a complex type which it would prove extremely difficult to interpret in detail'. Abraham tried to make salts with other alkali metals, rubidium and caesium, but they were even worse.

In October 1943 Dorothy received a letter inviting her to attend the next meeting of the penicillin chemists' committee later that month, enclosing copies of all their past reports. (She was horrified to discover herself quoted in some of these reports on the basis of some 'very casual' letters she had written to the authors.) Not only did this raise her profile both nationally and internationally; it extended the range of her contacts among chemists in industry that was to prove invaluable in her future research. It also gave her her first glimpse of the political complexity surrounding the international effort to understand penicillin.

> I had quite a good time myself showing off photographs
> and models etc at the end. But an awful lot of the meeting
> was spent in semipolitical discussion of the construction of
> a new penicillin committee to deal with synthesis. I gather
> there's been a good deal of difficulty over interchange of
> information – especially with Americans – the Oxford
> group strongly feeling that they'd given more than they'd
> got.

But the Oxford group soon had reason to be grateful to the Americans. That autumn Robert Robinson visited the Squibb laboratories and brought back some of their sodium penicillin. It was a revelation. Comparing it with the sodium penicillin prepared in Oxford, the chemists found that British and American penicillin were two different compounds. They had the same basic structural features, but different side-chains. In scientific terms, the American form was benzylpenicillin, later known as penicillin II or penicillin G, and the British was 2-pentenyl penicillin, penicillin I or penicillin F. The important thing from Dorothy's point of view was that the American crystals turned out to have a structure that was simpler to interpret. She decided that the best hope for completing an X-ray analysis of penicillin lay in working with different salts of benzylpenicillin. Each contained twenty-four principal atoms, not counting the hydrogens which could be placed by following the rules of physical chemistry once the others were correctly located. To solve the structure of a molecule this large, without knowing the formula in advance, would break new ground.

The first problem was to obtain enough material. Penicillin G was originally isolated from a mould growing on a cantaloupe melon near the government research laboratories at Peioria, Illinois. All American penicillin production was now based on this strain of mould. Dorothy had to get her hands on some more American penicillin, so she went to the top. She wrote to Sir Henry Dale, Director of the Royal Institution since the death of Sir William Bragg in 1942, who had contacts with the American company Merck. In February 1944 a tube containing 10 milligrams arrived in London aboard a military aircraft. Dale entrusted it to his colleague Kathleen Lonsdale, who personally brought it to Dorothy in Oxford.

Kathleen Lonsdale had been a protégée of the elder Bragg's, and remained the senior research worker at the RI under Dale. The youngest of ten children of an Irish postman, her background could not have been more different from Dorothy's. As Kathleen Yardley, she had first caught Bragg's attention when in 1923 she obtained the highest mark for ten years in the physics final examination at London University. He promptly obtained a government research grant and took her into his laboratory, where she joined Astbury, Bernal and others who were laying the foundations of X-ray crystallography with their own hands. She soon married a fellow researcher, Thomas Lonsdale, and subsequently gave birth to three children. But although she followed her husband's career moves from London to Leeds and back again, he insisted that he had not married her to get a free housekeeper, and shared domestic tasks so that she could keep up her crystallographic calculations. When they returned to London, Bragg personally secured the funds for her to pay for extra help at home and welcomed her back into the RI.

At the time Dorothy came to know her well, Kathleen Lonsdale had made a number of distinguished contributions on a range of topics, although she did not normally work on the large biological molecules that were Dorothy's main interest. A Quaker and conscientious objector, she had won admiration in many quarters for choosing to pay a £2 fine for not registering a month in Holloway prison in February 1943 rather than register for war work or civil defence duties. At about the time she came to Oxford with a tube of sodium benzylpenicillin in her hand, Dale had just set in motion the delicate political manoeuvring that would conclude a year later with her election as one of the first two female Fellows of the Royal Society, of which Dale was President.

It would be easy to assume that the presence of another successful woman in the field helped to inspire Dorothy in her own achievements. In fact, there is no evidence that Lonsdale was a direct influence. Although Dorothy knew of her work (and had been reassured on her marriage by the older crystallographer's successful child-bearing), she was already well established in her own right before they developed much personal contact. Nevertheless, Dorothy certainly admired Lonsdale and valued her involvement in the penicillin enterprise.

> The new American penicillin was not in a state fit to work with when it came but we followed instructions and recrystallized about ⅓ of it and by lunchtime had crystals larger than any we had ever had before! So now we're trying to go one better with the remainder and grow them overnight.
>
> Kathleen Lonsdale did not stay with us most of the day – she had some books to read in the Bodleian so left her stuff with us to work on. Indeed she very nicely seems to regard her role as mainly to secure new supplies for us. I do hope it comes out well.

The crystal proved all that was desired, producing a complete set of reflections. The next stage was to get comparable crystals of other salts, and once again Kathleen Lonsdale acted as mediator, persuading Henry Dale to exercise his influence. By this time, because of the new arrangements for trans-Atlantic cooperation, Dale had to go through Sir Edward Mellanby at the Medical Research Council. In mid-March, Mellanby wrote to Dorothy, making clear the restrictions under which she must now work:

At Sir Henry Dale's request I sent a cable to the Committee on Medical Research in America for a supply of the potassium and rubidium salts of penicillin 2[benzylpenicillin], and I have just heard from Dr Richards that he will try to get this made and sent to England, but hopes that any information that you obtain as the result of your X-ray analysis of these two salts will be made available to the Americans.

In addition to this I want to tell you

1. That all information on the chemistry and production of penicillin is now on the secret list and may not be transmitted to anybody either in this country or abroad;

2. that for the time being no information of any kind on these matters is being sent to America, and this will hold until agreement has been reached between the Medical Research Council and the Office of Scientific Research and Development in Washington, which will allow of complete and free transmission of all information on these matters. It is hoped that this agreement will be completed in the course of the next week or two;

3. when this agreement has been made, no information can be transmitted on the chemistry and production of penicillin between Great Britain and the USA except through [MRC and OSRD], and on their part, the Council will be guided on what information is to be transmitted by Sir Robert Robinson, who is Chairman of the Penicillin Synthesis Committee of the Medical Research Council, and his colleagues.[19]

In the event the rubidium penicillin came from ICI in Northwich, Cheshire, and the potassium penicillin from Squibb in the United States. Over a period of three months, Dorothy and Barbara Low photographed all three. There was an immediate setback. Although potassium and rubidium penicillin had the same crystal structure, differing only in the weight of the heavy atom, sodium penicillin crystals were of a different form. This would make direct comparison impossible. Dorothy decided to undertake two parallel studies. For sodium penicillin she would proceed by the time-honoured method of finding a trial structure and refining it until she achieved a good match with the observed reflections. For the potassium and rubidium salts she hoped to be able to proceed directly from Patterson maps to electron density as she and Carlisle had with cholesteryl iodide.

In April 1944 the annual X-Ray Analysis Group conference had been held in Oxford – finding accommodation for the participants was another chore for Dorothy, although she managed to delegate much of the organization to Dennis Riley and Tiny Powell's student Freddy Wells. At the meeting she renewed an earlier acquaintance with Charles Bunn of ICI's Dyestuffs Division in Northwich. Bunn had been developing a new way of testing trial structures, originally suggested by Lawrence Bragg. It was called the 'fly's eye' method, and involved making an optical version of the X-ray diffraction pattern expected from a particular structure. The structure was punched as a pattern of holes in a metal mask, duplicated many times, which could then be projected on to a flat surface by passing a strong beam of light through it. The diffraction pattern produced could then be compared with the actual diffraction pattern obtained from the crystal. Conventional trial-and-error methods involved lengthy calculations to compare the actual and model diffraction patterns; the fly's eye greatly speeded up this process.

In the spring of 1944 Dorothy went to Northwich to see Bunn and try out some trial structures for sodium benzylpenicillin. On the basis of some of her early studies of the probable shape of the molecule, they tried out models that were 'curled up'. But because the most emphatic voice in Oxford was insisting on the thiazolidine-oxazolone structure, their models also included two five-membered rings, plus the six-membered benzene ring of sodium benzylpenicillin. None of the models was very satisfactory; no atom or group of atoms seemed to be in the right place.

Looking again at the intensities of the reflections, Dorothy decided that perhaps she had been wrong to curl the structure round. The chemists, too, did not like the relationship between the two five-membered rings in the curled configuration, because it brought some of the atoms too close together. So she decided to change to trial structures that had a stretched-out configuration. Such structures seemed to fit both the sodium penicillin unit cell and that of rubidium and potassium penicillin. She also decided to split the research effort into two, partly because she was 'afraid of failing to solve the structures through having too many other things to do'. So she handed over all the data on sodium penicillin to Bunn and his colleague Anne Turner-Jones to continue analysing with the fly's eye method, and left Barbara Low with the task of sorting out potassium and rubidium penicillin.

These crystals were not proving as hopeful as first thought. Although it was easy to spot the heavy atoms on the Patterson projections, they were in a special position in the molecule, right at one face of the unit cell. This meant that the positions of all the carbon atoms could not be revealed by assigning phases according to the heavy atom contributions to the reflections. So Barbara Low also had to fall back on trial structures, of the traditional wire model variety. The word from Cheshire was that the work on the sodium salt was going well – Bunn had found a model that seemed to match at least some of the data. In August 1944 he wrote:

> I really think there is a chance of solving this structure (approximately at any rate) by trial . . . I have done several more trials on the sodium salt, using fly's eye patterns and the Bragg and Lipson charts in conjunction . . . the fact that it is possible to get the intensities of the first few 001 and neighbouring reflections correct suggests that perhaps the present formula is something like the truth along the length of the molecule, although the sides may be more doubtful.[20]

Because of this apparent correspondence, Low too was told to stick to elongated models. It was a frustrating time for her.

> I was trying to find an elongated form of the molecule which could be oriented such that it gave large calculated values for strong observed reflections, and small calculated values for very weak reflections. I was getting stymied. I have notebooks with models after models and they weren't really getting anywhere . . . there were four reflections that I couldn't do any thing with, I couldn't move the model in any way to make them fit . . .[21]

Low felt keenly the burden of responsibility for taking the work forward. Dorothy had many other calls on her time, and was often away from the lab. For each model she tested, Low had to calculate Fourier series to evaluate its resemblance to the true structure. This was the most tedious part of the operation.

> All we had to do Fouriers were Beevers-Lipson strips and an electric calculator that literally went ker-plunk, and so it took a long time. And the way you used the strips, if you wanted to put in something different you really had to go back to square one, you couldn't put it in in any intelligent kind of way. So there must be dozens of Fouriers with different models at the time an effort was being make to fit the stretched-out model to the existing Fourier.[22]

Luckily there were others in the lab by then who Low helped out with a couple of the Fouriers: Gerhard Schmidt who had arrived in 1943 to work with Dorothy on a small, protein-like antibiotic called gramicidin S, and Flying Officer Humphrey Watts, a Canadian bomber pilot who spent his leaves working with Tiny Powell. (He was killed in action on one of the last sorties of the war.) But still they were getting nowhere. Low feared that Dorothy thought she was being insufficiently imaginative in her approach to the problem, especially when she went north to visit Bunn and see what he was doing.

> I remember when she went to see Bunn, she didn't say this, but it was perfectly obvious to me that she thought that I was doing something wrong, and that if she went it would all be cleared up.[23]

The autumn of 1944 was a bleak time all round. During the year Dorothy had unexpectedly become pregnant again. But whereas her previous pregnancies had made her bloom with good health, this time she found herself ailing. During August at Geldeston she had a couple of episodes of bleeding, and returning to work in September made things worse.

> I'm not feeling so well today – I've been sick a lot this

morning so I'm thinking of giving up work and going to Crab. At present it seems I'm just a burden on Barbara who spends time she might be spending on useful work looking after me . . . I think I'll just have to go and do more resting for three or four days . . . Awfully slack it seems.

While she was at Crab in mid-September she lost the baby. 'It was a sad episode', she noted in her autobiography, surely an under-statement of her feelings at the time. Thomas came down to spend a couple of days with her while she was in hospital, and she wrote a letter afterwards that one could read as deliberately calculated to reassure him about her state of mind.

I had a nice talk to McMullins [the Ilmington doctor] – asked him various questions – he said wait for 3 or 4 months before trying to have another baby. Also whether he had views on why it had all happened – he hadn't – said most mothers of large families had one or two misses.

Anyhow I feel lots better now and it was lovely having so much of you – otherwise I might have got low and miserable. You have been so good.

Now I've just got up and dressed and packed. I haven't found it a bit difficult though I do still feel a little wobbly. It certainly will be lovely to see the children again.

While Dorothy was staying with Thomas for a few days to recu-perate, she heard from Barbara of another disaster. Gerhard Schmidt had been working on some extremely delicate crystals of tobacco necrosis virus, grown by Bill Pirie at the Rothamsted Experimental Station. Like protein crystals, they needed to be photographed in their mother liquor, in a fine glass capillary tube. Such was the delicacy of the crystals that Dorothy (whose dex-terity in dealing with such tiny objects would have been extraordinary even without the deformation caused by her arthritis) had succeeded in transferring only one of them to its tube, ready to be photographed. Schmidt's first photograph was extremely promising, indicating that the size of the repeating unit in the crystal was very large indeed, but also that the arrange-ment of atoms within these particles was quite specific.

At Sir Henry Dale's invitation, Schmidt took the precious crystal to the Royal Institution to take further photographs with the more powerful X-ray tube in the Davy Faraday Laboratory. There to assist him was the elderly technician known as 'Smithy' who had overseen the efforts of Bernal, Lonsdale, Astbury and their fellows twenty years before. But Smithy's eyesight was beginning to fail; in passing he knocked the tiny capillary from its mount, and it shattered on the ground. Barbara told Dorothy the sorry story.

> Kathleen Lonsdale, who heard the shriek, rushed in and found the crystal on a fragment of glass and put it into another capillary . . . She feels rather anxious about trying to remount it herself. I suggested that perhaps Gerhard might bring it back as it is for you to remount . . . I feel so sad about it, everything was going so nicely, and it seemed such a glorious chance to do something with such crystals.[24]

Dorothy was still in no position to help. The crystal was lost for good when, on the advice of someone from Rothamsted, Lonsdale tried to rescue the crystal by adding extra liquid: it simply dissolved away. (Not until the 1970s did a group of Swedish chemists succeed in growing similar crystals for study.) With the penicillin work also apparently at an impasse, it seemed a cruel blow.[25]

The following year began on a much more optimistic note. For one thing, it was clear that the war was nearing its end. Then Bunn decided he had got far enough with the fly's eye method to produce an electron density projection of sodium benzylpenicillin using phases derived from his best model. When Dorothy saw it she was 'immediately very worried'. The benzene ring seemed approximately right, but even at first sight, the rest of the molecule looked so different from what she knew of the rubidium results that one or other of them must be wrong. Dorothy solved the conflict in a characteristically simple manner. She drew projections of the sodium and rubidium structures to the same scale, placed them one on top of the other, and rotated them until she found a position in which many of the peaks coincided. These, she concluded, must represent the molecule. The molecule they suggested was, as she had originally thought, semicircular or 'curled up' rather than elongated.

She was so thrilled she grabbed the first person who happened to be passing, Harry Carlisle.

> Dorothy asked me to pick out the molecule from the two maps – which I couldn't – and then, with almost childish pleasure, she showed me that both maps presented almost the same view of the projected molecule.[26]

Dorothy herself described the impact of this revelation in her own account of the penicillin work, published four years later.

> When this form had been established in the actual projections, the relation of the electron density peaks to a number of the atoms known by chemical methods to be present became obvious and, in turn, the relation of these atoms to the crystal structure became clear and very beautifully convincing.[27]

After that things moved very fast. Barbara was given permission to try curled-up models, while Dorothy suggested to Bunn that he try the same thing. Bunn had to accept that while his electron density projection was more or less right, his interpretation of it, based on the model he began with, was wrong. Both teams now had enough information about the positions of atoms to run Fourier series that would allow the rest of the atoms to emerge. Until the beginning of February 1945, they still assumed that what would emerge would be the thiazolidine–oxazolone structure. On 1 February Dorothy presented her results to a meeting of the Penicillin Committee, explaining that they were close to a solution. She tentatively suggested that although their models had been based on the oxazolone structure, the beta lactam configuration was turning out to be a possible alternative. The day after, Bunn wrote to tell her of his progress.

> We have been following up possibilities based on the curled molecular configuration, and have now found a set

of atomic coordinates which give better intensities than
any we have had previously . . . This is in agreement with
the conclusions in your last letter, and I am very interested
to hear that this sort of configuration seems to fit the other
projections for the rubidium salt . . .

The structure which has given such promising
intensities looks more like the beta lactam formula than
any other; and packing and coordination look very
reasonable . . .

As I said in my last letter, we were not entirely
convinced of the curled configuration by your argument
based on the electron density contours; but owing to these
recent developments in our study of the details of the
sodium salt structure, together with the consideration of
the packing of molecules and metal atoms, we are quite
converted and are now as strongly in favour of the curled
configuration as you are.[28]

Within a day or two, Dorothy produced electron density maps in
which the atoms in the central part of the molecule had shifted
much closer to the beta lactam structure. The excitement of nearing the goal emerges clearly from the letters from Bunn that
arrived two or three times a week.

6 February
It is remarkable that the two investigations are at a very
similar stage, and it is significant that present indications
are in the same direction; your letter tells practically the
same story as mine . . .

I am interested to see that the indications of your latest
electron density map are in favour of the beta lactam
formula – in agreement with ours on the sodium salt . . .
Things are at an exciting stage. There seems little doubt
that the precise chemical structure of penicillin will be
settled by the X-ray work, and that at a not very distant
date.

12 February
I am sending you a tracing of our latest electron density

map. More of the atoms are showing up individually, and although the details of the centre part of the molecule are still doubtful, I think it will not be long before we can be confident of all the atomic positions . . .

A postscript – It is almost uncanny that we write letters practically simultaneously, giving the same suggestion! This is about the third time it has happened . . . Your latest atomic positions show exactly the same modification as ours . . .

I thoroughly agree that the final report on the structure of penicillin should be a joint affair. The work has been a very close cooperation, and is a most striking example of the value of working on two different salts. I should like to say how much I appreciate the way in which you have kept us fully informed of developments – and indeed, we are very gratified to have had the opportunity of taking part in this important work, which now seems certain to reach a successful conclusion.[29]

To confirm the result, Dorothy decided it would be a good idea to calculate the electron density in three dimensions, rather than the two-dimensional projections they had produced so far. This would be a monumental computing job to do by hand, but she already knew that there was another option – an early type of computer, known as a Hollerith punched card machine. She had first heard of these machines, and their possible use in X-ray crystallography, from J. M. Robertson in 1937

By the way, there have recently been some discussions between Dr Comrie, who does computational work for the Nautical Almanac, and Messrs Beevers, Lipson, and Wooster, and myself. Dr Comrie is very anxious to try to do Fourier synthesis on the Hollerith calculating machine and establish some kind of service for research workers. The idea is to have a lot of punched cards corresponding to B and L's strips, and the machine sorts them out and does the adding. But the idea is in a preliminary stage.[30]

Dorothy met Leslie Comrie, who had by that time set up his

Scientific Computing Service in London, at the X-Ray Analysis Group meeting in Oxford in 1944. He mentioned that using Hollerith machines, it would be possible to carry out three-dimensional Fourier syntheses. By the end of the year she was negotiating with the Ministry of Supply and the Medical Research Council for permission (and funding) to use the service. With Dale's help both were granted. The following year, Barbara Low went to work with the Scientific Computing Service's George Hey on writing the first program. The programs consisted of sets of cards, punched by the women assistants at Comrie's London bureau, each of which represented one Beevers–Lipson strip. Low and Hey checked them, and took them to Cirencester where there was an American Hollerith machine used principally for tracking ships' cargoes. The penicillin program was run at night, when the machine would otherwise have been idle.

> The first night [the machine operators] ran it Hey had scribbled on top of the pack 'Fourier series of penicillin' or something like that – and what came out was absolute garbage. So we looked at this garbage and said 'Ah, the title's upset them.' We then invented a ship and did something so that they could treat this Fourier as though it were a ship's cargo. We gave it a new title, and it went through perfectly.[31]

Once the three-dimensional Fourier was calculated, Low designed a new type of display model. She had left Oxford for a Fellowship at Cal Tech before this could be made, so Dorothy enlisted the help of her sister to draw contours of electron density on a series of perspex sheets that could be stacked one above the other to show the full structure. No other form of model so successfully showed how variations in electron density could be interpreted as real atoms, large and small. She used it at the first opportunity she had to present the penicillin work in public, the meeting of the X-Ray Analysis Group in London in April 1947.

The experience of working with the Scientific Computing Service had two consequences for Dorothy. First, it showed her how dramatically machine computation could speed up crystallographic calculations, opening the possibility of solving larger structures. Second, it sowed in her mind the idea that she needed access to computing technology and expertise on the spot. Hey and Comrie, and their assistant Elizabeth Gittus, were highly competent. But there was a muddle about payment for time on the Cirencester computer – Dorothy had assumed it would be essentially free, and with the irrepressible Hey's assistance managed to run up a bill of more than twice her £1000 MRC grant. When, in January 1947, Oxford University circulated a tentative questionnaire about the need for a University computing laboratory, Dorothy's was the most enthusiastic (and informed) reply. As a result, later that year she was asked to chair a committee to investigate the possibility further.[32]

Although in the short term only the members of the CPS officially knew about the penicillin structure, the news quickly began to leak out. One of the first to congratulate Dorothy was Bill Astbury, whose daughter Maureen was studying chemistry at Somerville and keeping him informed of the mood in Dorothy's lab. He had also done some work on penicillin as a consultant to ICI.

> I've no definite evidence that you have got the thing out completely, but I feel you must have, and I want to be one of the first to congratulate you and to say how terribly bucked I am that you have pulled it off. It's simply great, and not a little of my pleasure is that you have kept it in the Old Country! To quote another letter of Maureen's, it is a triumph for (a) crystallography, (b) women, (c) Oxford and (d) Somerville – I don't know if that was her actual order, but anyway those were the headings.[33]

Ever cautious, it was not until May 1945 that Dorothy decided she could state definitely that they had found the structure, and that it was the beta lactam after all. She made a little model of wires and corks, and on VE day, as celebrating crowds spilled into the streets, she took it over to show Chain and Abraham. They, of course, were delighted. When she mentioned that she would have to break it to Robinson, Chain said, 'You'd better take a gun with you.' Robinson, true to form, refused to believe he was wrong. He seized on the possibility that the X-rays might have altered the structure of the molecule. Dorothy duly took a packet of strongly irradiated penicillin crystals to Norman Heatley and asked him to check their activity against bacteria. They were as active as ever. Later, when the biochemistry of penicillin began to be examined, it emerged that the beta lactam ring was crucial to the way it worked, in disrupting the integrity of bacterial cell walls.

Years later Dorothy recorded a conversation with Robinson, only a few months before his death. She found that he still clung to the possibility that at least during the synthesis of penicillin by the mould there was some sort of change from one structure to the other.[34] She compared his reluctance to give up a cherished idea with the case of Dorothy Wrinch and cyclols; the difference was that Robinson achieved so much in other areas that he was forgiven this one mistaken obsession.[35]

John Cornforth did not grow mushrooms, or take up croquet. He later won a Nobel prize, became Director of Research for Shell UK, and was knighted.

Bernal, despite his wartime responsibilities as a scientific adviser, nevertheless followed progress in Dorothy's lab closely. Barbara Low looked forward to his visits, because even at intervals of several months he would always remember exactly what point she had reached the previous time he called. Dorothy told the sociologist Hilary Rose an anecdote about his reaction to her solution of the penicillin structure.

> I remember sitting on the steps of the Royal Society . . . talking to Bernal and I was telling him that we had solved the structure of penicillin. He said 'you will get the Nobel prize for this'. I said 'I would far rather be elected a Fellow of the Royal Society,' and he said 'that's more difficult', which just shows how they were viewing elections at that moment.[36]

Outside the closed community of the PEN and CPS scientists, news of Dorothy's achievement at first spread by word of mouth only. Publication during the war had been restricted, ostensibly on grounds of national security. But after the war it became apparent that industrial secrecy was a prime consideration, particularly on the American side. In the autumn of 1945 the Royal Society held an exhibition to celebrate the fiftieth anniversary of Röntgen's discovery of X-rays. X-ray crystallography on proteins and other large molecules was to be an important part of the exhibition, and Dorothy was looking forward to presenting her work on penicillin. But she had to obtain permission from the CPS – and they said no. Kathleen Lonsdale wrote to Bernal to tell him the whole story.

> The Penicillin Committee has decided that only work carried out prior to July 1944 is to be released, and Dorothy has therefore been refused permission to speak about penicillin at the Röntgen celebration. She is as angry as her gentle nature will allow her to be.
>
> She believes, I think rightly, that further secrecy can only hinder progress and is intended to do so, in commercial interests. She has asked me to speak to Sir Henry [Dale] about it, and I will, but I thought you should also know, not only because it affects our programme, but also because it is a particularly vicious example of the kind of thing we were deploring . . . There can be *no* good reason for secrecy about penicillin now; don't you agree?
>
> PS Sir Henry is very angry about this and will speak to Sir Edward Mellanby, but the trouble really seems to originate from the USA side of the committee.[37]

Dorothy was even more upset when in December 1945 a brief summary of wartime work on penicillin by Sir Robert Robinson appeared in *Nature*.[38] Again, it claimed only to cover work up till July 1944, but in fact mentioned more recent results, without admitting the crystallographers had confirmed the beta lactam structure. Charles Bunn was equally angry.

> I was, like you, somewhat disturbed about the way in which the X-ray work on penicillin was referred to in *Nature*. The statement was inaccurate and misleading in more than one respect. So I am glad you have taken the matter up with Sir Robert Robinson . . . It is somewhat

unfortunate for us that the work has been secret so long. If publication had occurred freely, Robinson would have committed himself to the oxazolone formula, and our part in overturning that formula and establishing the beta lactam would have been clear in print for everybody to see.

We must not of course claim too much, for the work has after all been mostly chemistry – the greater part of the chemical formula was settled in the ordinary way, and we only came in at the end to settle the linkings of the last few atoms. All the same, the problem of those last few links did baffle the chemists; the deadlock caused by the ambiguity of the chemical evidence from different breakdown reactions was as complete as it could be; and our part in settling the matter ought to be made clear. Moreover, the fact that this is the first occasion on which X-ray methods have led to the revision of ideas on the details of a complex formula ought to be brought out . . . I think it is true to say that the complexity of the problem solved exceeds that of any organic structure solved previously . . .

Robinson is still very touchy about the beta lactam formula – so much so that it often leads him to make remarks which actually emphasize the part played by the X-ray work. So among people concerned with penicillin research, the X-ray contribution is fully recognized. It may be that the same factors will operate in publications intended for a wider public – I don't know. But the *Nature* article is not a good start.[39]

Dorothy's own account of the penicillin research was not published until 1949, when a massive tome called *The Chemistry of Penicillin* finally appeared. Edited by Hans Clarke at the College of Physicians and Surgeons in New York and published by Princeton University Press, it took years to assemble. Dorothy's chapter, co-authored by Barbara Low, Charles Bunn and Anne Turner-Jones, departs from the usual style of scientific writing in adopting a more narrative approach. Dorothy documents the failures as well as the successes of their enterprise in language that is limpid and for the most part readable even to the uninitiated. She concludes, in characteristically modest style:

Throughout the whole of the X-ray crystallographic investigation of penicillin we have been working in a state of much greater ignorance of the chemical nature of the compounds we have had to study than is common in X-ray analysis. We have, at all stages of our examination, tried to make any deduction we could of chemical interest, and we have seen some of these confirmed and others not. For the future application of X-ray measurements in this type of problem our errors as well as our successes have some importance . . .

The accuracy achieved in the present analyses is, in fact, much better than could have been anticipated at the beginning of the investigation; and it seems quite likely that in the future, under improved experimental conditions, a higher degree of precision might be reached.[40]

In the short term, Dorothy's work did not contribute to the mass production of penicillin that made it possible to treat Allied soldiers with the drug during the D-day landings. The beta lactam ring is difficult to synthesize, and only in the past few years have scientists begun to understand how the penicillium mould does it. Large-scale production is still a matter of growing the mould in huge fermentation tanks and extracting the penicillin from the broth. But in the post-war years Dorothy's work enabled pharmaceutical companies to develop a huge range of semi-synthetic versions of penicillin, which made it possible to tailor the drug for particular purposes, and gave us the arsenal of antibiotics that we have today. It was also a notable scientific success, because as in the case of cholesteryl iodide, it was the most complex molecule ever to have been analysed using the methods of X-ray crystallography.

Dorothy's status in international crystallography was assured by the success of her work on penicillin. Her status in Oxford was another matter. It was one thing to enjoy the respect of colleagues in chemistry and other departments. It was quite another to be recognized by the Byzantine system of boards and committees that controlled appointments to University posts. Although she had given lectures for the subfaculty of chemistry since 1939, she held no University appointment in either chemistry or mineralogy and therefore could not officially participate in decisions about the future of crystallography at Oxford.

This was a serious issue throughout most of the war years. In November 1938 H. L. Bowman, the Waynflete Professor of Mineralogy and Crystallography, had announced that he wished to retire the following summer. The kindly, violin-playing specialist in crystal optics had unwittingly presided over a major shift in the emphasis of the research in his laboratory. Classical mineralogy was in decline, while the X-ray work of Dorothy and Powell was closer to chemistry than to geology. Asked by the University's Council if there were any 'special considerations' to take into account before filling Bowman's chair, the Board of the Faculty of Physical Sciences recommended abolishing it. In its place, it suggested creating a Readership in Chemical Crystallography which would be attached to the Inorganic and Physical Chemistry Laboratory (under Cyril Hinshelwood); the Department of Geology could take over the teaching of mineralogy.[41]

With the addition of a further Readership in Mineralogy to look after the mineralogical specimens in the Museum, this plan was more or less adopted by the University, despite the protests of the outgoing Professor and his predecessor, Sir Henry Miers, about the dismemberment of their department. But putting it into action was delayed by the war. Bowman was persuaded to hang on for another two years while Hebdomadal Council, the University's governing body, took some more outside advice. Among those who were asked to advise were Lawrence Bragg and J. D. Bernal. In the spring of 1940 Dorothy wrote to Bernal to tell him how she saw the situation.

I'm glad you're on this committee to discuss the future of crystallography in Oxford. I wish I knew more about it but I only get told things by the way.

I believe the starting point was a committee that met to consider Bowman's resignation last year. McCallum [the Fellow in Physics at New College] was on it and he very nicely came with Dennis to talk to me when I was in the Acland. They recommended that the chair of crystallography should be dropped and two readerships substituted, mineralogy to belong to the department of Geology and crystallography the dept of Physical Chemistry. By one section J. M. Robertson was suggested as Reader in Crystallography. Two snags arose – one from the old mineralogy in crystallography side represented by Miers who was strongly opposed to the abolition of the professorship. The other, though it is quite unofficial (through Tommy Taylor to me) was from Robertson who apparently was approached, I gather unofficially, and was not keen to come for a readership alone.

You know my concern is largely to get better working conditions all together. I was very much taken with the idea of Robertson coming – I still think this would be best. But I don't know whether there's any chance of it even if the chair were preserved. Apart from that, I think the idea of splitting the department is quite a good one and I expect it's rather hard on Powell that there are all these plans to get another Reader when he might naturally drop into the job.

Only I wish that if the Physical Chemists take us on they would do so properly and consider whether we might not be housed more adequately elsewhere – it would surely be an advantage to have us in the new physical chemistry building for example (or perhaps add a wing!)

I find it dashed difficult being so much out of all these discussions – my own fault. I suspect. One should lead a more friendly sort of life and get to know people better. But I just don't know what I'm going to do myself anyhow, and that's the truth.[42]

Robertson chose neither to accept the Readership nor to push for an improved offer, leaving the field open once more. Bernal failed to turn up at the meeting of the Advisory Committee, and made no official recommendation. W. L. Bragg had flu, but sent a letter.

A strong research department . . . can play a very valuable part in the research of other scientific departments. You have a striking example of this at Oxford in the important work on proteins, and on complex organic substances.[43]

The only people working on such substances at Oxford were Dorothy and her students. Although she seems to have assumed Powell was the obvious choice for the Readership, there is little doubt that her own name was beginning to be mentioned in that connection.

Things moved on slowly. The University decided to suspend both new Readerships temporarily because of the war, and put R. C. Spiller, as the senior of the two Demonstrators, in charge in the meantime. Dorothy found this a great improvement over Bowman, as she told Thomas gleefully.

> There's a general atmosphere of making hay while the sun shines on Spiller's part – since whatever happens he isn't likely much longer to be acting head of the whole department. He's prepared to buy almost anything we ask him for! So we just go on asking!

It was not until early in 1944 that the University decided to act. At the end of February the electors to the Readership in Chemical Crystallography, who included Lawrence Bragg, Hinshelwood and the Biochemistry Professor Rudolph Peters, as well as the Vice-Chancellor, met and decided not to advertise the post. The following day, Bragg appeared unexpectedly in Dorothy's lab to see her – she had been at home unwell. Apparently she did not connect his visit with the Readership at Oxford, but with the possibility that he might ask her to join his department in Cambridge.

> It was very exciting Bragg turning up this morning. Apparently the VC rang up your mother to find out how I could be got on to and she said I was in bed but she was sure I'd want to see Bragg if possible. I . . . wonder as usual if I said, or did, the right things. We talked actually almost entirely about the penicillin research – me showing photographs and so on. But he did ask a few leading questions about the department here, staff etc, and said 'you're going to have a new laboratory, aren't you?' . . . It didn't sound to me though, honestly, as if he were thinking of me for Cambridge. Still I was flattered at his wanting to come.

A week later the Electoral Board met again and approved a short-list of people they proposed to ask to put themselves forward for consideration. A sheet of paper survives in the University's files, containing two handwritten lists of names, one long, one short. The name at the head of both lists is that of Mrs Hodgkin. The other names on the short list are Powell, W. H. Taylor (a physicist from Manchester University), Beevers, Bunn and Cox (Gordon Cox of Birmingham University). The selection procedure seems to have been perfunctory. Each candidate on the shortlist was asked to attend a ten-minute interview (neatly filling the hours between 6 and 7 p.m.) on 31 March, when they might all be expected to be in Oxford for the annual conference of the X-Ray Analysis Group. No one was asked to write an application or provide references.

Dorothy was genuinely surprised to find herself included in this list. She was pleased, but also unsure about the commitment. With the war turning in favour of the Allies, she and Thomas had begun to discuss their future options once again.

> I meant to have more time with you yesterday for seriously talking over plans – but somehow there wasn't much time, or perhaps also I thought us both rather tired.
>
> What I feel just now is that as things have happened I should go ahead as a candidate for the Readership. But I shall not be very disappointed or anything if I don't get it . . . And if I didn't get Oxford I would seriously consider doing what we've thought of all along – moving the family to where you are and coming to you for long weekends.
>
> And I think it would be nice if you went into politics and Parliament and so on – only I don't know that Oxford is a very suitable seat . . . Any way I'm not thinking this Readership is a *very* serious proposition.

Whatever she felt about the Readership, Dorothy was far from passive on the subject of Oxford crystallography. While in 1940 she had felt out of things, by 1944 her prominence in the penicillin field had put her in a position to campaign actively. She was one of the authors of a memorandum urging the University to provide new laboratory space for research in the subject, to coincide with its new management.

I'm feeling rather cheerful tonight. It's chiefly over the Crystallography 'new' department memorandum – I forget if I told you. It got left out of the White Paper for the University by whose agency we don't know so we've decided a new one must be drawn up. The (my) idea is to send one jointly from Spiller, Powell and me. I decided to go and chat to Robinson about it – rather against everyone else's opinion and had a lovely time. First he entirely held my view of where the new crystallography lab should be – i.e. built as an extension of his own new lab, facing the new PCL [Physical Chemistry Laboratory] in the centre of everything. He also said (with what truth I don't know) he had booked the site for us! He also said he hoped they'd appoint the obvious person as Reader by which I gathered – rather slowly and surprisedly – he meant me. I took it more as a compliment than seriously and suggested alternatives. Anyway I felt very cheered.

Robinson was not the only one who saw the post as appropriate for Dorothy. Because she never complained about her situation, even some of her closest colleagues in other universities did not know about her lowly status within Oxford. Arnold Beevers wrote in genuine puzzlement, when he received his invitation to apply for the Readership, 'Is it *your* post which you are relinquishing, or would it be a parallel post?'[44]

No records were kept of the deliberations of the Electoral Board, and none of Dorothy's correspondence reveals how her interview went. After meeting the five candidates (Taylor had declined the invitation, on the grounds that they really wanted a chemist, and that he was earning more than they were offering already), they decided to appoint Powell to the £750-a-year post. Why? It is easiest to see the decision as Oxford favouring its own over outside candidates, and not liking to appoint a more junior researcher over her superior. It is easy to assume that sexism came into play – perhaps too easy, given that the same year Ida Mann was elected to the Professorship of Ophthalmology. Powell certainly had a respectable research record, but most crystallographers today would argue that Dorothy's was at least as impressive, breaking new ground in the analysis of complex molecules. Yet her assessment of her own chances was probably realistic, not simply because of her sex, but because of her lack of administrative experience. This handicap did not apply, however, in the case of either Cox or Beevers, who were already running their own laboratories at respected universities. Soon afterwards Beevers was promoted to a professorship at Edinburgh, and Cox moved from Birmingham to a professorship at Leeds.

Dorothy received a brief note informing her of the electors' decision two days later. Beevers wrote to commiserate, but added, 'I feel quite relieved not to have been appointed myself as I am very well dealt with up here [at Edinburgh].'

Dorothy was not 'well dealt with' at Oxford. Aside from the privations of her dungeon-like laboratory, she was personally 'deeply in the red' by the end of the war, having failed to make ends meet on her meagre Fellowship. Most of Thomas's similarly modest salary went on his own living expenses. Matters had been made worse by Somerville's decision, as a wartime measure, that all fees for outside teaching should go into College funds, rather than to the tutors themselves. It slowly dawned on Dorothy that while she was attempting to survive – and support a family – on a College Fellowship alone, many of her male colleagues had parallel University appointments that effectively doubled their salaries. (Again it is important not to leap to hasty conclusions about discrimination based on gender. In the previous decade, William Hume-Rothery had laid much of the groundwork for the modern science of metallurgy in Oxford while surviving on outside grants and the goodwill of various professors who provided laboratory space. He did not receive a College Fellowship or a University post until after his election to the Royal Society in 1937.[45] A common factor that unites him with Dorothy was that both worked in new research areas that had no established place in the University structure.)

Having failed to get the Readership, Dorothy decided to ask Hinshelwood, her Head of Department under the reorganization, for help in obtaining a more junior University post. He acted at once, authorizing Powell to approach the Board of the Faculty of Physical Sciences to ask if Dorothy could be appointed University Demonstrator 'to assist in the work of the laboratory of Chemical Crystallography'. Powell accordingly sent a memo on 9 June 1944, pointing out that in peacetime 'heavier demands than those before the war will be made for practical courses and lectures'; that as Reader his administrative responsibilities would leave him less time for teaching; and finally, that Mrs Hodgkin had already been giving lectures and supervising advanced students for some time.[46]

The Secretary of Faculties, the senior University administrator in charge of academic matters, replied to Hinshelwood that it was 'apparently not an urgent matter' and that it 'ought to wait until Hilary Term [the following spring] when University demonstrators are normally considered'. He then asked for a statement of Mrs Hodgkin's qualifications, and whether she was to work full-time. There is no indication in this correspondence that he had any idea how close Mrs Hodgkin had come to the Readership. She was duly proposed again by Hinshelwood at the proper time, and in May 1945, almost a year after he had first suggested it, she was officially appointed University Demonstrator in Chemical Crystallography. Having kept Oxford University at the forefront of research in the structure of organic molecules for ten years, she became a University employee for the first time. She wrote to Thomas in excitement. 'I've got that University Demonstratorship – it appears to mean £350 extra a year! Seems rather wicked now, but you'll be able to get a nice new car, and we'll get some things for the house.'

Meanwhile Dorothy's hopes that Chemical Crystallography's lot would be improved by being taken into Hinshelwood's empire turned out to be unfounded. There was to be no place for her work in his gleaming new Physical Chemistry Laboratory. As early as April 1940 Douglas Veale, the Registrar, wrote to reassure Hinshelwood that 'it has always been envisaged that crystallography would stay in its present quarters'.[47] Robinson's vague promise to Dorothy that he had 'booked' a space next to the Dyson Perrins laboratory for a new lab also came to nothing. Dorothy, Powell and their colleagues were not to move out of their cramped and unsuitable quarters in the Museum for another twelve years.

Dorothy had another reason to celebrate the arrival of peace. Thomas had successfully applied for the post of Secretary to the Delegacy for Extramural Studies at Oxford – effectively, the directorship of Oxford's pioneering adult education centre. Since the beginning of the century the Delegacy for Extramural Studies had been running evening classes and summer schools for working people not only in Oxford but in other parts of the country. The Workers' Educational Association, for which Thomas had been working throughout most of the war, also owed its origins to enlightened Oxford thinkers such as his grandfather A. L. Smith, A. D. Lindsay and R. H. Tawney. At last, thought Dorothy, the family was to be united. The only cloud was that Bernal was once again talking about setting up a research institute – but having finally got Thomas to Oxford, even that would not tempt Dorothy to leave.

> Sage rang up last night with more news about his research institute. He said [Sir Henry] Tizard had just told him it could be financed by Nuffield (secret secret). I warned him about your job and that I might not be in on it full time. After he rang off I walked round feeling very jealous of the idea of this kind of research group going and me not altogether there. Then had the brainy idea that if you did get this job I'd intrigue with the Nuffield trustees – i.e. JV [Janet Vaughan, just elected Principal of Somerville] – to have the whole thing moved to Oxford! however we must see what happens. Because Sage is likely to be coming and going all over the place anyway.

The institute, like its predecessors, never materialized; Bernal remained in his Birkbeck department until his retirement. Thomas moved back to Oxford in the summer of 1945. During the war Dorothy's grandmother had died, so that her own family had been able to move down to the larger ground-floor flat at 20 Bradmore Road. Dorothy immediately went to see her friend Flora Philpot, the biochemist who had worked on some of Chain's moulds, and who was struggling with an over-large house full of evacuees. Like Thomas, Flora's husband John was home only at weekends.

> [Dorothy] was extremely kind to me. I was in hospital after my second child was born, and she came along and said

'would you like to move into the top flat?' This was in
1943, and we didn't know what was going to happen
next . . . I was only too delighted to move into a central
heated flat with a big garden and other children.[48]

Flora's children Jane and Andrew were a little younger than Luke
and Liz, but they managed to pair up somehow.

Luke was the sort of child who taught himself algebra one
day and astronomy the next, and wasn't really a good
companion for my daughter who was horsey. But they did
find ways of combining. And Liz was a nice ordinary child
who played with dolls. Andrew was a very mild little boy
who played with animals, and they got on, playing in a
wigwam in the garden . . . My dealings with the Hodgkin
family were mainly at the child level, encouraging the
bicycle club, going round the garden putting toys away –
the Hodgkin household wasn't very good at putting things
away. Or going round to the Hodgkin house and retrieving
navy blue raincoats that had got left there and not been
noticed – I noticed they had gone, but they didn't notice
that there were extra ones . . . Everything was so gentle
there. Luke I found crying in the garden because my
daughter Jane had rigged up a little high jump and she
could jump higher than he could. So I told him that his
mother could do all sorts of things that I couldn't do, and
people were like that.[49]

Dorothy's own domestic establishment now consisted of Joyce,
who had replaced Olga as the children's nurse, and Edith, a
middle-aged evacuee from London who had taken on the cooking and housekeeping. Thomas's parents were still very much
part of the local support network, and having the Philpots as
neighbours also helped.

Nice episode yesterday. It was rather cold and I at college
when Luke was due to be picked up off the bus at 4.15 so
Joyce took Liz upstairs to the Philpots. When Joyce came
back she was already having tea – so stayed there,

perfectly happily, apparently, till about 5.30. Not like Luke ever that I can remember.

Luke had started school in 1942, going on the bus every day with his nurse, and later with other children, to a nursery school in the north of the city that served the Cutteslowe council estate. The area has achieved a certain notoriety in Oxford's history, because in 1934 residents in a private development adjacent to the estate constructed a wall more than 2 metres high to divide them from the council tenants, closing streets in the process. An attempt by students and left-wingers to demolish it led to a confrontation with the police. Oxford City Council finally had the Cutteslowe Wall taken down in 1959. Dorothy and Thomas began with the intention that Luke should be educated with the children of working people. But although Luke remembers being happy there (despite being nicknamed 'Luke Poshkin'), the school had little to offer him academically. He had read fluently from the age of about three years old, he was fascinated by numbers, and he had an unquenchable thirst for facts. Visitors, even the most academically distinguished, were constantly astonished at his precocity.

> Lunch with Sage was fun – Luke putting in intelligent remarks at intervals which interested Sage a lot . . . Sage suddenly said, 'My God, he's looking things up in the index' half laughing. Luke being rather mopy almost started to cry but I smoothed it over and explained Luke had been looking things up in indexes for months, if not years. But it makes me feel how bad it is we haven't kept accurate records of these remarkable occurrences.

The faint disapproval of some of her North Oxford friends and relations, together with her own observations, caused Dorothy to have misgivings about her choice of school. When the time came for Luke to move on at seven, she and Thomas decided that he would be better off at the kind of school more usually favoured by academic families. They abandoned their socialist principles and sent him to the Dragon School, a private school very near their home that prepared boys (and a few of their sisters) for entry to the more prestigious public schools. Thomas had gone there himself. After that the Cutteslowe experiment was not repeated. Liz started at a small private nursery school that opened near their home just as she reached the right age.

In May 1946 Dorothy gave birth to her third child, Toby, a sweet-natured soul with white-blond hair. Liz had constantly badgered her mother to have another baby, but perhaps Dorothy just wanted to make up for the one she had lost, and to celebrate peace and a united family. It was a happy time all round. A year later Dorothy was elected a Fellow of the Royal Society. The first two women, Kathleen Lonsdale and the Cambridge biochemist Marjorie Stephenson, had been admitted as Fellows in 1945, although the eligibility of women for membership had been legally established since 1922. Dorothy's research successes and the rising importance of the field of crystallography ensured that she would quickly follow them, even at the relatively early age of thirty-six. Even so, her certificate as a candidate for election, recently released from the usual fifty-year embargo, shows that she had to wait a year.

The certificate was read to the Society on 13 December 1945. Dorothy was proposed by Bernal, and seconded by the chemist Ian Heilbron. The other signatories were Bill Astbury, J. M. Robertson, Howard Florey, Franz Simon (the Oxford low-temperature physicist), Lawrence Bragg, William Hume-Rothery, and Kathleen Lonsdale. The citation, betraying the hand of Bernal, focused on her work on sterols, proteins and viruses. Its reference to penicillin, still unpublished and officially secret, is more oblique:

> During the war she has shown that it is possible to derive the complete structure of organic substances of unknown chemical composition by X-ray methods alone. Her contributions to this field has [sic] placed her in the forefront of X-ray crystal analysts.[50]

But the Royal Society's Council chose not to nominate her (the prelude to almost automatic election by the Fellows) for the election of 1946. That year the botanist Agnes Arber of Cambridge was elected the third woman Fellow, and the Oxford penicillin chemist Wilson Baker was also honoured.

Once a certificate has been properly drawn up and registered, it remains 'suspended', in the Society's term, in subsequent years. Dorothy's name came up again in 1947, and this time she was nominated and duly elected, together with the mathematician Mary Cartwright. Privately to Thomas, she admitted she was basking in the attention.

I've had a jolly nice week owing to the mechanics of this election. Council first nominates, that's last Thursday, then sends the proposed list round to all Fellows and they have to approve the nomination on March 20th. Result is, first one gets told by one's friends on Council – i.e. last Monday, then all through the week and particularly yesterday and today all one's Oxford friends who are Fellows ring up and congratulate. Simon was sweet – he was the first, rushed round about 9.30 on Thursday morning and was quite disappointed that owing to Astbury's letter I knew already. Then Henry rang up, and Le Gros Clark and Bowen and Hinsh have written and HR [Hume-Rothery] came round – it's been fine. I've been feeling kind of dotty all the time.

Immediately afterwards letters of congratulation began to flow in from further afield, emphasizing the significance of her achievement.

It is an honour very well deserved; and to our X-ray fraternity in particular it will give the greatest pleasure to see one of its brightest stars join Mrs Lonsdale in making history as the first women fellows. (*Sir Lawrence Bragg*)

May I add an expression of my personal pleasure in your election. It was a landmark in our history because your predecessors were somewhat more senior – we made up some lost opportunities. I am equally proud as an Oxford chemist. (*Sir Robert Robinson*)

I had always heard that once the barriers were down you would be one of the first in – and now you are. I am glad. (*Jacquetta Hawkes, archaeologist*)

I think it is magnificent that you manage to combine looking after a family with research, not to mention University teaching. I complain when I have to wash the dishes of an evening. (*Alan Hodgkin, Thomas's cousin, later a Nobel prizewinner for physiology*)

I hope your knees will not knock together as much as mine did. (*Kathleen Lonsdale*)

If a woman FRS can have three children, anyone might do anything. (*Justin Waddington*)

7

'The molecule that appears is very beautifully composed'

America, Russia and Vitamin B$_{12}$, 1946–1960

With the ending of the war came opportunities for Dorothy to travel further abroad and meet other scientists working in the same field. In August 1945 she wrote to the Rockefeller Foundation, which had paid for her equipment and research assistants throughout the war.

> I should greatly welcome an opportunity myself to visit America for a short time, if this could be arranged, to discuss more fully our present researches and further plans with you and others. We have had a most interesting, not to say exciting year, of which we should like to give you details.[1]

She received encouraging noises, but did not immediately pursue them when she realized that she was pregnant again. In July 1946 Gerard Pomerat, the Assistant Director of the Natural Sciences Division at Rockefeller, on his first visit to British laboratories since the end of the war, noted in his diary that the Miss Crowfoot whose research had so impressed the Foundation all these years had an alter ego.

> Called on Dorothy Crowfoot at the Museum . . . C. is Mrs

Hodgkin and admits that she has been married 8 years and
has 3 children, one of them quite recent. All this to show
that if the research urge is there it will go on even in
women . . . She looks astonishingly like Jeanette
MacDonald![2]

In February 1947 Dorothy wrote once again to say that a trip later
that year was on the cards. She was originally thinking in terms of
a month or so, but Rockefeller's travelling fellowships assumed a
visit of at least three months. Pomerat assured her that she would
find this the minimum necessary.

If your experiences are to resemble those of Miss [Honor]
Fell of the Strangeways Laboratories, you would find that
a visit of one month is almost more tantalizing than it is
productive. Miss Fell tells us that she has found Americans
very sympathetic to British women scientists and that she
will have great difficulty in compressing within the
confines of her four month visit here the many stimulating
invitations she has received from important research
centres.[3]

Thomas accepted that the family would survive without Dorothy.
Joyce had left in 1945, but they still had Edith to help with cooking and cleaning, and they took on another nurse to help with the
children. The University gave her leave of absence for
Michaelmas Term, during which she would hold a Rockefeller
travelling fellowship. On Pomerat's advice – 'you should try if
possible to get something on one of your nice big British ships' –
she booked a passage on the *Queen Elizabeth*, to sail for New York
on 26 September, returning in time for Christmas.

Dorothy has left a very full account of her trip.[4] She landed in
New York on 3 October, only to find that her 'usual economical
practice' of travelling third class meant that she would be last off
the boat, keeping her hosts waiting on the quayside. The slight,
ethereal figure who came down the gangplank (at 5 feet 5 inches
tall, she weighed only 7½ stone[5]) presented an unusual problem
to US Customs. Typically of Dorothy, she had packed only one
suitcase for a three-month stay – and it contained, along with her

modest wardrobe, her Perspex electron density model of penicillin.

> As the model occupied about half the space I thought I had best mention it. [The customs officer] was very interested and asked me to explain it. Then he said 'It may not seem right to you, but I think it would save a lot of trouble to us if I just recorded it as "one scientific model worth less than one dollar". Then you may take it in.' I thankfully agreed.

Dorothy's first hosts were Hans Clarke and his wife, who lived in a beautiful house on the Hudson River outside New York. Clarke was the editor of the still-unpublished volume on wartime penicillin research. In his office at Columbia University Dorothy was shocked to find the manuscript of her chapter for the book still unopened – especially as she had paid out of her own pocket to send it airmail. She also found his colleagues in the Biochemistry Department sceptical about her structure, and was 'appalled' to realize that she still had work to do to persuade them that it was correct.

'Fan' Fankuchen, who knew everyone through the crystallography summer schools he ran at Brooklyn Polytechnic, had worked out an itinerary for Dorothy that involved 'visiting almost every important crystallographer in America'. As well as visiting laboratories, she wanted to meet up with friends and former colleagues who had settled in the United States. One of the first to receive a visit was Dorothy Wrinch; Dorothy spent a weekend with her and her husband Otto Glaser at Amherst in Massachusetts on her way to Harvard and MIT. The visit seems to have passed amicably, and Dorothy wrote warmly to thank them.

> I shall remember for a long time the marvellous colour of the woods, and the lake. It is very good too to have the insulin Patterson complete and not still to be wondering whether it would be worth while having or not. [Wrinch had arranged to have a three-dimensional Patterson calculated on IBM's computers from Dorothy's data.][6]

In the course of five weeks on the East Coast, Dorothy visited twelve cities and even more institutions, and took part in a meeting of the American Society for X-Ray and Electron Diffraction. She was most in demand to talk about penicillin, but her own priority was to look at X-ray crystallographic work on proteins, and to compare the equipment and organization of American labs with her own. In the course of these visits she met every X-ray crystallographer and protein chemist who had contributed anything significant to the subject, as well as a number of other leading scientists in related areas. She received valuable advice about equipment from Martin Buerger at MIT, and talked about computing to von Neumann at Princeton. She spent a happy afternoon with Lindo Patterson at Bryn Mawr, amazed to discover that the inventor of her favourite tool had 'not very much apparatus in a rather small laboratory and as far as I could see, one research assistant'. She was fascinated by photographs of virus crystals taken with the electron microscope by Ralph Wyckoff in Bethesda, the first that she had seen.

On 9 November Dorothy left the East for California, to spend a month with Linus Pauling and his colleagues at the California Institute of Technology in Pasadena. It was the first time she had been able to discuss her work in detail with Pauling, although they had corresponded and had met briefly in Oxford when he and his wife visited England earlier in the year. Dorothy had a very high regard for Pauling, chiefly based on his work on the chemical bond and his theoretical contributions to structure analysis. She had already arranged for Barbara Low to go to Cal Tech for a year; Low had arrived the previous November, funded by the Rose Sidgwick Memorial Fellowship of the American Association of University Women. But first Dorothy, with Pauling's help, had to negotiate an unexpected hurdle.

Linus answered 'Yes, delighted' as expected, but the American Women replied that although they would certainly give her an award Pasadena did not accept women students . . . It was the first time I had come across the difficulty of women doing research in the USA. Luckily, although I hadn't known this, Linus was a strong supporter of women in science . . . So Barbara and I had our way, and began a long relationship with Cal Tech.

Having always thought of Pauling as a theoretician, she was surprised to discover that so much practical protein structure analysis was going on under his direction. Unlike the British protein researchers, he was trying to break down the problem by working on individual amino acids rather than tackling whole proteins. Dorothy soon found kindred spirits among the workers in his lab. Chief among these was Eddie Hughes, whose office she shared while she stayed at Cal Tech.

Before she left, Hughes drove her from Pasadena to Berkeley and Oakland to visit laboratories. At the North West Regional Research Laboratory in Oakland she particularly wanted to see Dr Palmer, who had first prepared crystals of lactoglobulin like those she had studied with Dennis Riley. Low had told her he now had beautiful X-ray photographs of the enzyme lysozyme. But when they arrived they found the laboratory was shut. Nothing daunted, Hughes burgled Palmer's lab and found the photographs while Dorothy lurked in a hotel nearby. As a result she was fairly confident that in the course of her trip she had seen 'all the X-ray single crystal photographs which have been taken of any protein crystals in the States'.[7] They returned along the Pacific Coast Highway so that Dorothy could see the beauties of Big Sur.

The friendships Dorothy made at Cal Tech were genuine and lasting, especially with Pauling himself and his wife Ava Helen. Happily the farewells when she left were no more than au revoirs. In 1946 crystallographers from all over the world had met in London to set up the International Union of Crystallography, the latest in a growing number of subject-based international scientific unions. In 1948 its first International Congress was to be held at Harvard. Dorothy was to be an official delegate, and of course all her new acquaintances would be there. Even better, Pauling and his family would be living in Oxford from January to June 1948; he had been appointed George Eastman Visiting Professor at Balliol.

Before returning to New York to catch the boat home, Dorothy had originally intended to do a bit of sight-seeing, including a visit to the Grand Canyon. But last-minute invitations to speak in Iowa, Illinois and Michigan changed her plans. The timetable depended on an absolutely reliable transport system. But she found herself held up for a day, travelling by train from Albuquerque to Kansas City as winter storms began to play havoc with the flight schedules. This trip proved to be one of many in which Dorothy showed herself to be an adventurous and enthusiastic traveller, completely unconcerned by departures from her planned itinerary.

> I woke up next morning in a different world, white and snow-covered, but fine . . . I took a taxi to the airport to find if planes were flying. There was one in about half an hour to Peioria [in Illinois, site of the US government research laboratory, where much of the early work on penicillin production had been carried out], where I had a date for lunch; I quickly booked a ticket and rang them up with my time of arrival, so the chemists of Peioria were at the airport to meet me . . . Before we left the airport I noticed advertisements announcing that one could book a plane which would take one 200 miles for fifty dollars, to any destination. It was clear that if I did this I could get to Ames [Iowa] for my lecture. So I booked a plane for about 3.30, rang up Ames to say I could come, and then went back to a good lunch talking over penicillin . . . Then I went quickly to the airport and found my little plane. The pilot was anxious to go, saying we must reach Ames by sunset, as it had no equipment for landing by night. It was the most wonderful flight I've ever done. I sat beside the pilot on the front seat . . . He put a map on his knee on which he drew a line between Peioria and Ames. We were near enough to the ground to watch the map and see that we took the right way . . . The sun was sinking and the western sky red around it as we landed at the little airport at Ames where [Bob] Rundle was on the tarmac, waving us in.

In December the *Mauretania* docked at Liverpool, bringing Dorothy back to her family in time for Christmas. She wasn't sure that nineteen-month-old Toby recognized her, but if not, she wrote to a colleague, he seemed to take to her again very quickly. Thomas and the children announced that in her absence they had

had chocolate semolina for pudding every day – 'and as for the bills we didn't pay any, they are all ready for you'.

Travelling parents was something the Hodgkin children just had to get used to, as Dorothy and her sisters had before them. In 1948 it was Thomas's turn: he was invited to visit the Gold Coast (later Ghana), Nigeria and the Sudan to lecture and advise on setting up adult education systems in African countries as they worked towards independence from British rule. He also met many of the leading figures in the independence movements, including the charismatic Kwame Nkrumah of the Gold Coast. The experience had a profound effect on him; on his return he was 'totally unset-tled' according to Dorothy. No longer satisfied with a quiet life in Oxford, he began to write about African history and devote him-self to the cause of African nationalism. Within a few years disputes with Oxford University over his tendency to fill all tuto-rial appointments with members of the Communist Party led to a parting of the ways, and Africa absorbed his full attention. A charismatic speaker and fluent writer, he quickly established an international reputation and a vast acquaintance among those working for the establishment of post-colonial governments. Knowing little about Dorothy's scientific achievements, her chil-dren and their friends saw Thomas as 'the towering figure with everyone revolving around' – not until she won the Nobel prize in 1964 did they realize that she was just as distinguished as he.

Thomas's lack of secure employment left Dorothy once again in the position of principal, if not sole, breadwinner for her family, with only her College Fellowship and her modest demonstra-tor's salary to call on. Her daughter Elizabeth recalls that compared with those of her schoolfriends, her family never seemed to have enough money; it was a matter of 'lurching from one financial crisis to the next'. (A former research assistant remembers that while attending a conference in Canada Dorothy camped in her sister Diana's garden to save on hotel bills, despite having a heavy cold.) To make things worse, Thomas decided that they must move from the small but convenient flat in Bradmore Road to a house on Boar's Hill, a wooded retreat about 5 miles from the centre of Oxford colonized by wealthier dons around the turn of the century. Powder Hill, as the large brick house was called, had several bedrooms and a garden 'full of broom and tree lupins'. Its owner had died and left it to All Souls College. His will specified that if none of the Fellows wanted to live there they should let it to Thomas Hodgkin, who had once expressed a desire for it. The family all went up to have a look, a day Elizabeth Hodgkin, then ten years old, still remembers. 'It was a snowy day, I remember being absolutely in love with it and hoping we would come to live there. I dropped a coin in the snow as a charm to make them go there.'

Dorothy was not so sure. At Bradmore Road she could walk to and from the lab in less than twenty minutes; Powder Hill was almost a mile from the nearest bus stop, followed by a two-stage ride into town. There were no shops nearby. The big house would be a lot for Edith and her friend Alice, who had joined the household, to manage, although there was a little cottage attached where they could live. Toby could go to the village school, but Liz, once she passed the 11-plus examination, would need to travel in to Oxford High School every day. By this time Luke was away at boarding school. He had won the top scholarship to Eton; it was not the kind of education his parents favoured, but who would turn down a top scholarship? Thomas himself planned to spend extended periods in Africa. Dorothy, whose physical vigour and mobility were increasingly compromised by her arthritis, could not see how it would work. 'I said "We can go and live as you want in Powder Hill or you can go to West Africa, but how can you do both?" But Thomas, of course, in his generosity of spirit, decided to do both.'

They moved to Powder Hill in 1951. The children led very active lives, allowed to run free in the woods around the house. There was no television, so in the evenings, encouraged particularly by their paternal grandmother, they enjoyed playing cards, pencil and paper games and jigsaw puzzles. Charades was a popular favourite; when on holiday at Geldeston, more elaborate plays were produced, usually written by Luke. If he was at home, Thomas would always take the lead in these activities, organizing riotous games of 'Crusaders and Saracens' for birthday parties. Any visitors, whether African politicians or timid students from Somerville who thought they were just coming for tea with their tutor, were compelled to join in, their own coats and scarves commandeered as costumes.[8] At tea-time the children would make toast round the fire, and in the evenings someone, Thomas if he was there but Dorothy too, would read aloud. Kipling's *Puck of Pook's Hill* and *Rewards and Fairies* were favourites of hers; she knew most of the poems by heart.

Discipline, Elizabeth recalls, was maintained with a light touch.

> Dorothy never used a bad word to you – I remember very vividly when I was about ten she called me a donkey, and I went away and burst into tears because that was the harshest thing she ever said to me in her life. My father was tougher, although not by some standards. I remember Thomas saying that if he punished Luke he was immediately tremendously upset and repentant, if he punished me I was oppositional and rebellious, and if he punished Toby he would just laugh.[9]

But if the children were indulged, they also had to learn to be independent, and to accept the absence of one or both parents for long periods. For Elizabeth, it was not always easy.

> When Dorothy went for ten days to the Soviet Union, I remember one moment of being very upset, and cycling round the lawn waving a pair of scissors that then dropped down and cut my head. And I remember once when she was going away and there was an epidemic of German measles at the school, and I said 'Well, if I got German measles you wouldn't go, would you mum?' And she said, 'Well yes, I think I would.'[10]

A year after they moved into Powder Hill, Thomas set off for a six-month tour of West Africa. Before he left, Dorothy put an advertisement in the local paper offering free accommodation to anyone who would help with driving and child care. The ad caught the eye of Don and Maureen Mackay, an Australian couple who were living nearby but finding it hard to make ends meet on Don's scholarship; he was doing a DPhil in history at Balliol. They came for a visit, liked the friendly, easy-going household and moved in almost at once. Both could drive, so they did most of the journeys up and down to town, taking Dorothy and Elizabeth and doing all the shopping. Maureen also took Toby to and from school. In the evenings Don read aloud to six-year-old Toby from Thor Heyerdal's *Voyage of the Kon-Tiki*, which he loved. It worked out well enough, though occasionally the strains of living in such close proximity began to tell; Elizabeth remembers a row with 'Mack' over her bursting into the Mackays' room without knocking.

The arrival of the Mackays had an unexpected advantage for Dorothy: it turned out that Maureen had a degree in chemistry. 'As soon as she realized that I had a science degree,' recalls Mackay, 'she was interested in getting me involved in her research.'[11] Although when she had followed her husband to Oxford Maureen had had little thought of pursuing a career in science, she enthusiastically took up the offer of part-time work. When Thomas returned from Africa and the Mackays moved out of Powder Hill, Dorothy made Maureen a full-time research assistant. She helped with the work on Vitamin B_{12} that was the main preoccupation of the lab at the time, but also had her own project, the structure of morphine. The paper she published with Dorothy in 1955 on this structure was her first; soon after her return to Australia in 1956, having separated from her husband, she embarked on a PhD in crystallography and ended up as Reader at La Trobe University in Melbourne, with her own lab. 'If it hadn't been for Dorothy I would never have gone into crystallography,' she says now.

The presence of Don and Maureen also made it possible for Dorothy to consider joining Thomas in Africa for a while before he returned home. As he had been extremely ill during his travels, she was anxious to see him again. But making the decision to travel was not easy, as she explained in a letter to him. 'Here I can't really get serious advice – the usual sides having formed – your mother and the children . . . wanting me to stay, my mother, Janet [Vaughan], Tony [Pirie] etc wanting me to go. The Macks are neutral but prepared for any event.' She did go, and spent two weeks in March 1953 travelling through villages in Northern Nigeria with Thomas and a friend who was showing a 'March of Time' newsreel film reporting the death of Gandhi.

I'll never forget showing this film in one Northern

Nigerian village with the whole population out in the open watching it, and how a great groan went up from the whole audience as the shots rang out. It wasn't, perhaps, the most obvious film to show to a country just hoping for independence itself, but may have been useful as a warning of the troubles which could overtake you.

The trip convinced Dorothy that Thomas was 'effectively settled in his mind in Africa', and that she would have to find a way of facing further absences while she pressed on with her research.

In the post-war years a steady stream of new research workers passed through Dorothy's lab, although the total number never grew very large. Riley, Carlisle, Schiff and Low had all moved on; after Cal Tech, Low went to Harvard and then Columbia, never returning to Oxford as Dorothy had once hoped she would. Somerville continued to yield the occasional Part II student. In 1947 these included Margaret Roberts, who worked for a year with Gerhard Schmidt on the antibiotic gramicidin S. From the perspective of the laboratory, Roberts was not one of Dorothy's success stories; she obtained a second-class degree and eventually gave up chemistry for law. Years later, as Margaret Thatcher, she became leader of the Conservative Party and Prime Minister of Britain. Her time in Dorothy's lab coincided with a period of heightened political awareness – the Conservatives had been heavily defeated by Labour in the 1945 election – and although Baroness Thatcher recalls that she and Dorothy never discussed politics when she was a student, she has no doubt that each was aware of the other's views. Despite their differences, they always remained on good terms; at the time, Dorothy's main disappointment was that Roberts was clearly not going to make a crystallographer.

As well as home-grown talent, young crystallographers from around the world were wanting to come and experience her approach for themselves. She welcomed all-comers, especially if they brought their own funds; if not, she usually found ways of funding them. In 1946 Jack Dunitz asked if he could come from Edinburgh to work with her, curious to learn more about three-dimensional Fouriers and heavy atom methods. He first came to talk to her in the Museum one day in June.

I was directed to her room, just across from the collection
of life-size skeletons of prehistoric animals . . . When I
knocked on the door, punctually, at the agreed hour of the
afternoon, Dorothy greeted me with her serene, pre-
Raphaelite smile and explained that she was just
concluding a tutorial. As the two Somerville students were
preparing to leave, one of them enquired politely, 'And
when should we come back for our next tutorial, Dr
Hodgkin?' Dorothy seemed to consider the question with
great concentration before replying, 'Tuesdayish'. 'And at
what time should we come?' 'Threeish.'

Dorothy arranged that he should come to work in the laboratory
in October that year, and asked what he would like to work on.
He replied that he had doubts about a statement she and Bernal
had made in their big paper on the sterols, to the effect that calciferol, or Vitamin D, had the same basic shape as cholesterol.
Despite the apparent challenge to her judgement, she agreed that
calciferol would be a good problem to work on.

When Dunitz arrived, he needed to find a calciferol derivative
with a heavy atom, in order to solve the phase problem. The first
to make such a compound was Rita Cornforth, a gifted practical
chemist who worked with Robinson in the Dyson Perrins
Laboratory. She had come to Oxford on an 1851 scholarship* from
Australia in 1939 to undertake graduate study in Robinson's lab,
and had married John Cornforth (another 1851 scholar who had
come over on the same boat) two years later. Rita Cornforth made
a calciferol derivative that contained iodine and formed deep
yellow crystals. (Years later when her husband, a future Nobel
laureate, tried to make more of this compound he could not get it
to crystallize. In desperation he added to his solution the scrap-
ings from her original tube – and it set in a mass of crystals.[13])
Once he had the crystal, Dunitz was soon able to solve the structure, presenting it in triumph to Dorothy on her return from the

*1851 science scholarships were established by the Royal Commission that
managed the profits of the 1851 Great Exhibition, to bring students from the
Empire – later the Commonwealth – to undertake graduate degrees in British
universities. Eleven former scholarship holders have won Nobel prizes.

United States in December 1947. It showed that although Dorothy had correctly calculated the unit cell dimensions, she had misread the way the molecule sat in the unit cell.

> She said then since I had done this when she was away, I should publish it myself. But I said, 'Not at all, it's in your lab – if you hadn't done the earlier work I should never have dreamt of choosing this structure.'[14]

Others came from further afield. David Sayre was a young American crystallographer who had become fascinated by the mathematical aspects of solving crystal structures. Having worked with him on radar at MIT during the war, he had joined Ray Pepinsky at the Alabama Polytechnic Institute in Auburn to work on the design and construction of the first-ever dedicated crystallographic computer. This was a machine called X-RAC – the X-Ray Automatic Computer – a remarkable analog device covered in dials and switches that computed Fourier series by generating sine waves and adding them up. Dorothy had seen a demonstration of X-RAC in 1948, when she was in the US for the first International Congress of Crystallography at Harvard. Sayre had been present, and had also heard her speak on calciferol at the Congress.

In 1948 Sayre became involved in a row over the fact that his wife Anne, an ardent Socialist, was teaching at the all-black Tuskegee Institute. The upshot was that he lost his job. Thinking it would be advisable to leave the United States for a while, he thought of Dorothy.

> I wrote a letter to the Director of Admissions at Oxford University and said that I'd like to come there as a graduate student. and at the same time I wrote a letter to Dorothy saying the same thing. A few days later I got back a puzzled letter from somebody at the University saying there isn't any such thing as a director of admissions, and I got a letter from Dorothy saying come ahead, it's all set.[15]

Disregarding a reference she received from Pepinsky that stressed Sayre's youth, immaturity and tendency to tackle problems too big for him, Dorothy went to some effort to secure him a place in the University as a DPhil student, and an attachment to Balliol College. He had been depending on receiving a Fulbright scholarship to fund his stay in Oxford, but there was a further setback – none were being offered for study in Britain that year.

> So David trudged off to see Dorothy [recalls Anne Sayre] to say 'well it was nice but goodbye', and I'll never forget her reply because it was so Dorothy. She said 'I hope you won't mind, but I feared this might happen . . . so when in New York I took the liberty of obtaining for you a Rockefeller grant.'[16]

The Sayres stayed in Oxford for two and a half years, and remain eternally grateful to Dorothy for helping them so effectively when they most needed help. David worked for his DPhil on another sterol structure, lumisterol, but spent much more of his time working on mathematical ways of solving the phase problem. Sayre's ideas prefigured what have come to be known as direct methods, which are used routinely in modern crystallography. But Dorothy was surprisingly indifferent to his efforts.

> [In] a lot of other crystallographic labs – for example Bragg's lab at Cambridge – the phase problem was regarded as really a problem of great importance and great interest. Anybody who had such an idea in Bragg's lab would have had Bragg beaming, picking up the idea, carrying it further . . . Dorothy – it didn't strike her that way, I can't say any more than that. She was perfectly supportive and happy . . . But no structure was solved at Oxford using direct methods. Dorothy was the queen of the Patterson function, that was her tool and she was unbelievable at it. She did not have a symbolic, mathematical mind, she had a much more concrete mind. She thought in terms of maps . . . Direct methods didn't really start to be used in crystallography for a number of years.[17]

Today Sayre's work is recognized as ground-breaking, although ahead of its time as far as protein crystals were concerned. In the early 1950s two other Americans, Herbert Hauptmann and Jerome Karle, independently developed a similar approach, which eventually won them the Nobel prize. Sayre confessed to Dorothy at the time of their discovery that 'the spice had gone' from crystallography as far as he was concerned.[18] In 1954 he went to work for IBM, working at first on crystallographic computation, later joining the team that developed the programming language FORTRAN. Not until much later, when fast, powerful computers became available, did direct methods begin to make a real impact.

The Rockefeller Foundation's continued support enabled Dorothy to buy new equipment to replace Bernal's, which had gone back to Birkbeck, and to employ a series of research assistants. The post-war period was a golden time for science: the contribution of scientists to the Allied victory prompted a new focus on science as a major contributor to progress in peacetime. Suddenly there was much more money available, and it seemed that Dorothy had only to ask. Kathleen Lonsdale wrote in 1946:

> How are you off these days for money for apparatus? I was talking the other day to Sir Henry [Dale] and he said that if you needed any, he would see that you got it. He has never said that to me![19]

Dorothy obtained her first government grant from the Department of Scientific and Industrial Research in 1948, and soon afterwards a much larger grant from the Nuffield Foundation, mainly to help pay for computation. This put her among the highest earners of outside grant income in the University, something which today would be celebrated, but at the time was seen by the University bureacracy as potentially worrying. Papers in the files of the University for 1949 referring to Dorothy's grants reflect this anxiety.

> Council has to look rather carefully when a Department suddenly begins to attract large grants from outside

sources . . . it was certain that this work did not involve
any concealed commitments . . . Plaskett is looking into
this and will be prepared . . . to reassure Council that this
laboratory is not getting unduly inflated.[20]

By this time Dorothy had expectations that she would soon have a
new laboratory in the new Physical Chemistry Building. She told
Pomerat, when he visited Oxford in 1948, that she hoped the
University would fund at least one new permanent post when the
lab was ready, and in the meantime did not plan to ask Rockefeller
for further funds, 'to force the hand of the University'. But there
was no move to Physical Chemistry; now Dorothy was promised
space in the planned extension to Inorganic Chemistry, as yet
unbuilt. Dorothy had to make do with moving from her ground-
floor office up to the larger room in the Museum where she had
originally worked with Powell – and there was no funding for an
extra post.

Despite the conditions – on one visit to her room Warren
Weaver noted that 'like most British labs, it looks like the corner
of a dusty old barn' – Dorothy's lab was a friendly place.
Everyone was on first-name terms. This solved the awkward
problem that while male scientists at that time usually called
even their best friends by surname alone, women conventionally
were addressed as Miss or Mrs. It is touching, reading Dorothy's
correspondence, to see how during the 1940s she and her male
colleagues gradually make the transition to first names. Henry
Lipson's first venture is typical.

Dear Dorothy
Mrs Lonsdale recently said to me that she found the
American practice of using Christian names more refreshing
than our usual English custom, so I am taking her advice
and trying it out on you. I hope you don't mind.[21]

It was 1948 – he had known Dorothy for thirteen years. While on
the subject of names, Dorothy continued to publish under the
name Crowfoot until the late 1940s. As she explained much later
to a historian of science, John Sheehan, she had never intended to
change her name on marriage at all.

But Robert Robinson told the University authorities to change my name in faculty lists while we were on our honeymoon. I hadn't the heart to change it back on University lists, Thomas' family being well known in Oxford. But I published as Crowfoot. As years went on it got a bit awkward, explaining the difference. Hans Clarke's secretary at Columbia worked at the proofs [of the penicillin chapter] disapprovingly and said, 'After all, you and I are never going to change our names again.' I agreed with her, but somehow couldn't bring myself to change it then and there. I changed it on the next proof I had, the first B$_{12}$ note in Lester Smith's paper. He was very cross. He said 'Everyone knows Crowfoot on X-ray analysis, no one knows Hodgkin.' After that, I put them both in.[22]

If Dorothy's lab was 'a haven of gender equality',[23] things remained less equal in the world outside. Dorothy, who never considered her gender a disadvantage in her chosen career, was genuinely astonished to discover that female graduate students who were married were expected to live on a lower level of DSIR grant than their student husbands. With indignation, in 1955 she took up the cause of her student Jennifer Kamper, who had just seen her grant cut from £325 to £245 per year on her marriage to a fellow student.

I am writing to ask, as a matter of public policy, that the decision to reduce maintenance grants to women on marriage be reconsidered.

It is a commonplace that large numbers of trained scientists are now needed and that women as well as men must be employed if these numbers are to be found. At the same time both men and women now are marrying young, often within a year of taking their first degrees at University. It is therefore essential . . . that these young married women should be positively encouraged to continue scientific work. In my own experience they are usually anxious to do this . . .

If a young married woman is to carry out serious scientific work she must live the same kind of life that her

husband, engaged in the same kind of occupation, expects
to live. She must not be overburdened with household
duties and cares. She cannot contribute to easing the
family expenses by cooking and housework . . . To speak
more personally, I could never have carried out the
amount of scientific research I have achieved if I had not,
at the time of my marriage, been earning a sufficient salary
to permit me to pay for help in our home.[24]

The first response from the DSIR indicated that they could not see
why a women living with her husband needed any more money
than one living with her parents. But Dorothy persisted, and
eventually Kamper's grant was raised for her second year. A personal note from the Secretary of the DSIR, who claimed to have
'some sympathy' with Dorothy's point of view, nevertheless
implied that she had won a battle but not the war. He undertook
to 'see that justice was done' in future cases, but declined to make
the change in policy official.

Much of the buzz in the laboratory was generated by work on a
new problem Dorothy had taken up in 1948. Vitamin B_{12} is essential for a variety of physiological functions. It prevents pernicious
anaemia, in which red blood cells are abnormal, leading to a variety of neurological problems such as numbness and difficulty in
walking. It was discovered by the American clinical scientist
George Minot in 1926, when he observed that patients suffering
from pernicious anaemia recovered when fed with liver. Research
chemists at Merck in the United States managed to isolate and
crystallize the active agent in liver, initially known as pernicious
anaemia factor, in 1948. Lester Smith of Glaxo achieved the same
result later that year. Smith, who had been a member of the
Penicillin Committee and so knew of Dorothy's work, immediately told her of his success.

I have recently isolated from liver as red needle crystals the
factor that is specific for the treatment of pernicious
anaemia, and we are anxious to obtain as much
information as possible on its crystallographic structure.
The factor has a molecular weight of about 3000 . . . We

wondered whether you would be sufficiently interested to undertake some X-ray measurements on the crystals . . .[25]

Dorothy never could resist a well-formed crystal. Smith brought his specimens with him when he came up to Oxford for a Biochemical Society meeting, and she had a couple of photographs to show him before he went home again the next day. She took further pictures in the weeks that followed, although at first she does not seem to have thought of taking it on to a full structural analysis.

> All the measurements recorded were made on 3 of the very nice, but still very small, crystals on the microscope slide which were sent last. I was surprised at the excellent X-ray photographs the crystals gave . . . Certainly your crystals are remarkably interesting, and I am very happy indeed to have had the opportunity of working on them.[26]

The formula of the factor was unknown, and its chemical composition still under investigation. But almost immediately the Glaxo chemists made a discovery that changed Dorothy's attitude completely. Smith's colleague Dr Macrae rang up to tell her that a molecule of the pernicious anaemia factor contained a cobalt atom. Cobalt would be heavy enough to show up on a Patterson map, the starting point for Dorothy's preferred method of approaching a structural analysis.

> I thought it was very marvellous to find a natural product with cobalt inside it, but cobalt was of a rather light weight to solve a totally unknown molecular structure . . . But I began, of course, to think about it from that day.[27]

At once she urged Smith to send her more, and bigger, crystals as soon as he could. He was of course delighted, but thought he should let her know that others were also taking an interest in the factor.

> We are . . . very glad that the presence of cobalt in the molecule encourages you to proceed further with the X-ray

work . . . I think you will be interested to learn that we
have agreed to provide Professor Todd with relatively
large amounts of the crystals for chemical work. He has
promised to put some of his best people on the job and
expresses confidence that we might even now get ahead of
the Americans in establishing the structure and possibly
devising a synthesis. I mention this because I am sure he
will be more than grateful for any assistance the X-ray
method can provide.[28]

Alexander Todd, soon to be knighted, was an organic chemist
who had done his DPhil with Robinson at Oxford in the 1930s,
then worked in Manchester before moving to Cambridge to take
up the chair in organic chemistry in 1944. As in the case of penicillin, it would help Dorothy if the chemical analysis could give
some clues to the composition of the B_{12} molecule, so having
Todd's team on the case was a distinct advantage.

B_{12} was interesting for a number of reasons. It had a clear clinical value, and there would be enormous interest among chemists
and biochemists in knowing how it worked. In size it was intermediate between penicillin and the proteins, with something over
100 atoms excluding hydrogen – certainly a serious challenge,
but with Dorothy's experience, not an impossible one. It had the
all-important heavy atom. The difficulty would be the increased
amount of computing involved. To carry such large calculations
out by hand would be a frustratingly slow process. Punched-
card machines could speed things up considerably, but Dorothy
would have to pay to have such work done elsewhere – there
were no such machines in Oxford. She talked over the problem
with Janet Vaughan, who had been elected Principal of
Somerville in 1944.

Vaughan was a pathologist, the first scientist to be elected head
not only of a women's college, but of any Oxford college. She herself had studied the effectiveness of treating pernicious anaemia
with liver extract before the Second World War, and had then
gone on to play a key role in the establishment of the London
blood transfusion service. After coming to Oxford she set up a
unit carrying out research into the pathology of bone, and the
effects of radiation.[29] Dorothy had lobbied hard behind the scenes

for her election to the Principalship (the other main candidate was Lucy Sutherland, herself a Fellow of Somerville), and the two had become friends and allies. Under Vaughan's Principalship, the number of young women opting to study science at Somerville was steadily increasing.

Janet Vaughan was an influential figure, both within and beyond Oxford. Significantly, she had just become one of the Trustees of the Nuffield Foundation. Set up by Lord Nuffield, who had made a fortune through his Oxford-based Morris Motors, this fund was a major supporter of biomedical research. Vaughan encouraged Dorothy to put in an application – which she did, for £3000 per year for five years for computing and research assistance. It was granted almost immediately. Dorothy hired new assistants to work on the B$_{12}$ project. First came June Broomhead (later Lindsey), who had just obtained a PhD from Cambridge, to collect data on the air-dried crystals sent from Glaxo. These crystals tended to degenerate over time, so a year later, in 1950, Dorothy welcomed Clara Brink (later Shoemaker), a student of her old friend Caroline MacGillavry in the Netherlands, and asked her to collect a new set of data on wet crystals as she herself had done for insulin.

There was rivalry between Merck and Glaxo over which would be the first to crack the B$_{12}$ formula, hence Todd's desire to 'get ahead of the Americans'. Merck also had contacts with a crystallographer – John White, a British scientist working at Princeton. White was collaborating with Karl Folkers at Merck in the same informal way Dorothy was with Smith at Glaxo: Folkers had given him crystals of B$_{12}$, which he had begun to photograph, in air-dried form, in the autumn of 1949. One crucial difference was that the Merck chemists were so anxious to protect their proprietary rights on work done in their laboratories that White was denied access to confidential information on the results of their research in organic chemistry. He, on the other hand, had to agree to 'keep Merck informed of the progress of [his] investigation' in exchange for the crystals.[30]

He had just begun his work when he received a visit from Cecily Darwin (later Littleton), a vivacious Somerville student (and descendant of Charles Darwin) who had completed a Part II research project with Dorothy. She was now spending time in the

United States, working with Lindo Patterson, who had moved to the Fox Chase Cancer Centre in Philadelphia. Hearing that White was working on B_{12}, she told him that Dorothy's lab was working on the same problem. There was, and still is, an informal code of honour among crystallographers that different groups would not work in competition with one another on the same molecule. In January 1950 White wrote to Dorothy expressing surprise that she was attempting an analysis of B_{12}, having been under the impression that she was doing only preliminary studies. Dorothy was certainly not to be deterred from her new project, but neither did she wish to cause bad feeling. She suggested diplomatically that the problem was big enough for two groups, and that they might keep in touch on progress. June Broomhead visited White in the summer of 1950. He was planning to spend some time working on the X-RAC with Pepinsky, now at Pennsylvania State College, and it was suggested that June might usefully do the same.

White began work on the X-RAC in September, aiming to calculate a three-dimensional Patterson map. But almost at once he heard from Dorothy that she already had one. Benefiting from the experience with penicillin, she had sent the first set of B_{12} data to Elizabeth Gittus at Comrie's Scientific Computing Service, to do the computation on a Hollerith machine. The map looked much more encouraging than she had dared to hope, and she wrote to White with a proposition.

> I think you cannot help but get out the structure and neither can we. There will be a great deal of work on the way, but nothing like as much as at one time imagined. I would be very glad, if you liked the idea, to decide to compare all our conclusions and to arrange for some form of either joint or simultaneous publication . . . If you decide you'd rather go ahead on your own we'll quite understand.[31]

White agreed at once, and urged that June should come over with all the Oxford results as soon as possible. The two of them used an average of the two sets of data to produce an electron density map of the dry form of the B_{12} structure. Dorothy later commented that the two commercial companies must have regarded White and herself as 'wholly unreliable' for colluding in this way.[32]

Pepinsky's computer lab, where White and Broomhead produced their map, was full of British workers in 1951. Bill Cochran, a senior physical chemist from Cambridge, was paying a visit, and his advice was very valuable. There was also a former student of Arnold Beevers at Edinburgh, John Robertson. Robertson and his wife Inge were increasingly unhappy at Pennsylvania State College with Pepinsky. They wanted to come back to England, so Robertson wrote in some desperation to Dorothy to ask if he might work with her.

> Looking back it seems amazing that she wrote back and said yes. She took on a lot of different people from all over the world. Where she got the money from I don't know. So that's how I went, essentially as a refugee.[33]

In fact Robertson neatly filled a gap left by June Broomhead, who soon afterwards married, moved to Canada and gave up crystallography – a great loss, in Dorothy's view. His arrival coincided with the appearance of a new crystal, a derivative that contained selenium as well as cobalt; that became his project.

The drill was the same with all three types of crystal (dry, wet and selenium derivative): take photographs, index and measure the intensities of the reflections, calculate a Patterson map to find the heavy atoms. In each case the cobalt-cobalt vectors stood out clearly as peaks, so that even a novice crystallographer could fix the position of the cobalt atom in the molecule. What excited Dorothy more, though, was that surrounding the cobalt peak she could see a less well-defined ring of other features, close enough to represent atoms that were connected to the cobalt. 'Through the confused pattern and overlapping produced by the Patterson function we traced peaks that could belong to four five-membered rings as in a porphyrin.'

The way the red crystals absorbed light suggested that the molecule might contain a porphyrin-like structure, a flat ring made up of four smaller rings called pyrroles (although data from spectroscopical analysis showed that the ring system could not be

a true porphyrin). Porphyrins exist in a number of other biological molecules, notably haemoglobin. So Dorothy's hunch, as
was usually the case, was backed up by sound chemical evidence. But hardly anyone else shared her conviction that the
vague blobs on the map meant anything significant. Serenely
confident, Dorothy moved directly to the next stage: calculating
electron density maps using phases derived from the heavy
atoms alone. She, White and Broomhead had reached this point
with the air-dried crystal when the second International
Congress of Crystallography took place in Stockholm, in the
summer of 1951. This was a much bigger affair than the inaugural meeting three years earlier. Naturally, Dorothy took the
opportunity to present some of her preliminary work on B_{12}. In
the audience was David Phillips, then a young PhD student at
Cardiff.

> I remember her in this seemingly diffident manner
> showing slides of electron density maps . . . This map had
> a nice big mountain in the middle which was clearly
> cobalt, surrounded by vague contours that no one else
> thought anything. But Dorothy said in her prescient way
> 'It looks a little bit like a collection of pyrrole rings,' and
> everyone looked at her blankly because they couldn't see
> anything at all. That was really my first introduction to
> Dorothy and her imaginative, inspirational way of going
> about the subject – her dependence on the interpretation of
> electron density maps backed up by chemical
> understanding that was very rarely brought into the
> foreground.[34]

For those who worked with her, such prescience could be infuri-
ating. John Robertson has written about this in some detail.

> When shown an oscillation photograph, still wet, of some
> brand new crystal, she was capable, after an apparently
> casual glance, of gaily pronouncing what the space group
> must be, to the consternation (even humiliation) of the
> young man who had just developed the picture; yet, two
> or three days later, after the appropriate zero and first layer

Weissenberg photographs had been made, dried, indexed and analysed, Dorothy's remark would turn out to have been correct . . .'Women's intuition', it was often said; but really, it was the product of her phenomenal knowledge of relevant chemistry and physics, her long experience, her marvellous memory for detail and her tirelessly active mind.[35]

By the autumn of 1953 progress had slowed. With the help of the Cambridge chemists who could give them some idea of what to look out for, Dorothy and her colleagues had with some confidence fitted atoms into the outlying parts of the molecule. But the porphyrin-like nucleus was causing more trouble. John White persisted for a while with assuming a conventional porphyrin structure, but the further he proceeded, the worse his maps looked. On the basis of the first electron density map derived from John Robertson's selenium derivative of B$_{12}$, the Oxford team began, 'with great hesitation', to think about a modified porphyrin structure in which two of the rings were directly joined, rather than having an atom in between. Such a structure had never been described before.

At just this point another new crystal appeared. John Cannon, an Australian researcher working with Todd, was trying to make a B$_{12}$ derivative that contained only the central nucleus. He was having little success, and out of sheer frustration he threw every solvent he could think of into the mixture and left it while he went on holiday. When he returned a rock-like clump of red crystals had formed in the bottom of the flask. His colleague Alan Johnson sent them to Dorothy as a matter of course, with little hope that they would be useful. Carefully she cut from the mass of crystals one that could be photographed. It turned out to be the best yet, giving a mass of reflections. The molecule was indeed a fragment of B$_{12}$, its hexacarboxylic acid, containing the cobalt and surrounding group of flat rings, without the outlying parts of the molecule. Better still, the fragment molecule sat in the unit cell in a much more useful position, making angles with all three of the axes; in B$_{12}$ itself the central group was close to and almost parallel with one of the unit-cell edges, giving a confused and overlapping picture.

Dorothy decided to make solving the structure of the new crystal a priority, ignoring a belated message from Cambridge that the chemists thought the lump of crystals was insufficiently pure. She had a new assistant to work on the project: Jenny Pickworth (now Professor Jenny Glusker of the Fox Chase Cancer Institute in Philadelphia), one of her Somerville students who had done a Part II in infrared spectroscopy, but now wanted to learn crystallography for her DPhil. John Robertson was also working on the new project, but Dorothy told him not to tell Pickworth anything about the tentative conclusions they had reached so far, to 'see what she came up with'. Pickworth threw herself into the task.

> It started out by my doing a Patterson map to find where the cobalt was. I thought it would be complicated to do it in three dimensions so I did it in two dimensions, and everyone said that's ridiculous but in fact it worked . . . I did that myself by hand, that was not too hard. And then we had to do a three-dimensional Fourier, electron density map, and that took about six weeks with a Hollerith calculator, punched cards everywhere, it was really hard work.[36]

Thanks to the Nuffield grant, Dorothy had been able to hire an early type of Hollerith machine from British Tabulating Machines, which was kept in the basement of the Mathematical Institute nearby. It could only add, not subtract, so that cards had to be turned upside down to deal with negative values. But the result showed unequivocally that the vitamin contained a ring system unlike any that had been seen before (it was later given the name 'corrin').

> Our realization, from a study of the peaks around the cobalt atom in a map of the hexacarboxylic acid phased on the cobalt atom alone, that the two five-membered rings were directly joined, was a memorable event for me, John Robertson and Dorothy . . . This time there was no question about the location of atoms, no possibility of error.[37]

At about this time Gerard Pomerat paid one of his annual visits, and while Dorothy was off attending to some domestic matter he spent the afternoon with the rest of the group. The comments he recorded in his diary reveal how different Dorothy's lab seemed from others that he visited.

> All of them took turns in describing the highlights of their research and a nicer, friendlier lot GRP has yet to meet. Without Robertson it is possible that they would be too young a group by usual RF project standards, but they are a knowledgeable lot and there is no question but what they are kept under good strong scientific discipline by their gentle lady director who can outthink and outguess them on any score. A lovely small show reflecting the quality of its director.[38]

It was a characteristic of Dorothy's that she would not even consider publication until she was certain of a result, whatever the danger of being overtaken by another group. Until this point the only paper on B$_{12}$ she had published was a very preliminary classical, optical and X-ray description of the crystals, co-authored by Mary Porter and R. C. Spiller. Lester Smith, ever fearful that Merck might get in first, had been dropping hints since 1950 that she ought to publish as she went along.

> I am lost in admiration for the elegance of your technique! So far as I recall the structure you deduce for the 'kernel' of this B$_{12}$ fragment is identical with a diagram you showed me earlier derived from the analysis of B$_{12}$ itself.
>   Scientifically speaking, this work certainly ought to be published and my colleagues and I see no reason for advising any delay.[39]

Dorothy did send off a quick note to *Nature*, although it went somewhat against the grain, as she admitted in the introduction, to 'present evidence of part only of a crystal structure'.[40] But it was still only the beginning. Jenny Pickworth's map contained, in addition to the peaks that represented real atoms, a large number of spurious peaks. To refine the map until all its contours homed in on all the real atoms and nothing but the real atoms would take several more rounds of calculation. The idea of spending all that time over the already antiquated punched-card machine was daunting to say the least. But by one of those extraordinary strokes of fortune with which Dorothy seems to have been blessed, a new alternative presented itself just at the critical moment.

The previous summer a genial young American crystallographer, Ken Trueblood, had dropped in at the lab while on a sight-seeing tour of Britain with his parents. Trueblood had got to know Jack Dunitz when the two of them had coincided in Linus Pauling's lab at Pasadena a year or so before. Now he was working at the University of California at Los Angeles. UCLA was home to one of the most powerful computers in the world, the National Bureau of Standards Western Automatic Computer, known as SWAC. Trueblood and his graduate students Bob Sparks and Dick Prosen were developing programs for SWAC that could do crystallographic calculations on timescales that seemed nothing short of miraculous – hours rather than weeks. They had never tested them on a really large molecule. Meeting Dorothy on 8 July 1953, it occurred to Trueblood that this might just be the opportunity he needed. That evening he noted on a sheet of writing paper with the letterhead of the Royal Hotel, Ashby de la Zouch: 'Talked with Dorothy Hodgkin, John Robertson and Jack Dunitz. Offered help on 3-dim Fourier and SF [structure factor] calcs for calciferol (40 atoms, 2500 refl) and Vit B_{12} (112 atoms?) if SWAC seemed feasible.'[41]

In November he wrote to confirm the offer, pointing out that he was able to use SWAC free of charge. Dorothy was 'very doubtful about allowing our various unknown but hopeful-looking crystals to be worked on by somebody whose work we didn't know'.[42] She first sent him parameters for calciferol – 3000 reflections and thirty-seven atomic positions out of forty-one – for which she already knew the structure. It took him a while to get down to the job, but in May 1954 he wrote to report that all thirty-seven atoms had come out in the right place, and the four missing ones had also turned up in plausible positions. Dorothy was ecstatic.

It is a great achievement on your part to get this
through . . . One of the things that I like most is that, of the
last four atoms which appeared, one is not in the expected
place (or at least not where Jack and I expected it). It is in a
perfectly reasonable place . . . Can you face more
calculations? We have an awful lot of possibilities for
you . . .[43]

It was at about this point that Jenny Pickworth's first electron
density map gave them the confidence that they knew the positions of twenty-six out of the seventy-three atoms in the 'red
fragment' of B$_{12}$. Completely convinced of Trueblood's and
SWAC's reliability, she sent him the coordinates for these atoms
and the data on all the reflections on 16 July 1954. From then on,
barring occasional breakdowns of the computer, the analysis proceeded more or less like clockwork, thanks largely to the
dedication of Trueblood and Prosen. They worked at night, when
there was less demand for access to the computer, and because
Trueblood had teaching responsibilities during the day.

What it involved was sitting at a card punch typewriter
with a stack of IBM cards in a machine, and you hope
you get all the numbers in the right places. And first you
type up the intensity data, 3000 pieces of data each with
a triple of indices, so you type 7 4 10 and then 193, and
then 7 4 11 and 20, and then 7 4 12 37 and so on. And
then you print them out and proof read them and correct
your errors. Then you take another set of punched cards
and you put in the positions of each of the atoms that
they've so far identified. . . . Dick Prosen and I worked 12
hours at a stretch, all night. It increased the speed at
which you could do this by a factor of maybe 100, so we
could do in one night what would have taken three or
four months.[44]

The sense of anticipation as they approached the structure
emerges clearly from letters written between Trueblood and
Dorothy, and from Jenny Pickworth to her fiancé Don Glusker in
Pasadena. In September 1954 Jenny wrote:

We are very excited about the way this new Fourier
calculation from UCLA is turning out. All the atoms I
chose parameters for have come up beautifully in the right
positions and now I must look for a structure in the
remaining peaks.[45]

Less than two months later there was a setback. In calculating
the Fourier phased on positions for fifty-four of the seventy
atoms, Ken Trueblood made a mistake in one atomic position. He
wrote to Dorothy in despair.

Consequently all that labor was totally wasted . . .We'll
start over as soon as our morale recovers from this shock . . .
Please pardon my depression – the blow, coming on top of
only about 14 hours sleep in the last three nights, is just too
much. It is conceivable that we may try to get this done
much sooner than I indicated above – but don't count on
it – it depends on who else is working graveyard shifts,
what Dick's wife thinks about his never being home at
night, how tired we are tomorrow etc.[46]

Dorothy immediately cabled back 'CHEER UP SEND EVERY-
THING AIRMAIL'. She examined the map based on the series
with the mistake in it, and was encouraged to find that
although the rogue atom produced a spurious peak, a weaker
one still turned up in the right place. This gave her confidence
that other positions were correct, and not artifacts of the positions
chosen for the phasing. Almost as soon as Trueblood was ready
to make another attempt SWAC broke down, and was unusable
for more than two months. But by the spring of 1955 the structure of the fragment was more or less complete, and by
implication, the structure of the whole B_{12} molecule. It needed
only a few more rounds of calculation to leave the structure clear
for all to see.

By May 1955 Dorothy was sufficiently certain of the fragment structure to consider a more detailed article in *Nature*.
She wrote to John White, with whom she had been out of touch
during all the excitement about the fragment, to bring him up
to date.

Such a lot has been happening this year, I hardly know
where to begin.

First we think the fragment structure is almost
completely solved. It started coming out very rapidly from
the series we had calculated by Ken phased on 26 atoms.
We've had a few setbacks, particularly over the last four
atoms, but we're hoping that the Fourier series Ken is
calculating now, on 73 atoms, may be essentially the last.
We can write a formula for this fragment, which I enclose.
There are one or two questionable details, as you can see,
and at least one region in which it differs from B$_{12}$.

We have calculated two partly-phased series, one for
wet and one for dry B$_{12}$ . . . and have sorted out all of the
molecule as we think it is, from both of them . . .

I am inclined to think that we should publish a little
note on the fragment soon. I'll send you a draft to see
when I have one. Then we can follow up with B$_{12}$ itself in, I
hope, a few months from now.

Todd quite approves the formula. He says it can fit all
the known chemical facts.[47]

Alexander Todd was to publish a paper on the chemical evidence
alongside Dorothy's. John White immediately became concerned
that he would receive no credit for the work he had done on B$_{12}$
since 1949.

I have thought a good deal about the publication question
in general and it seems that there are two viewpoints. One
is that there are different crystal structures which shouldn't
be published till they are complete. But the chemists' is
that there is one B$_{12}$ molecule and your and Todd's notes
will be taken as the announcement of the structure of it.
After working on this molecule for six years I think I
should be able to say something about it myself . . . I don't
like to raise questions of this sort but I had to fairly soon or
never.[48]

Dorothy solved the problem to everyone's satisfaction by including White's name, along with those of Jenny Pickworth, John

Robertson, Ken Trueblood and Dick Prosen, as authors on the paper, and including a tentative structure of the whole B_{12} molecule partly based on White's results so far.[49]

Dorothy was always modest about her achievements, but she believed in giving credit where it was due. Even as she reassured White that his role would be recognized, she found herself having to defend the achievements of her own group. In early July, before the *Nature* papers had been published, a conference of the Chemical Society was held in Exeter, and Todd was billed to talk about 'some new nitrogen-containing compounds'. Only a day or two before, he had been in Oxford discussing the *Nature* publications with Dorothy, and had said nothing about the Exeter meeting. But somehow she got wind that he might be going to announce the B_{12} structure. She leapt straight on a train to be there, as Jenny Glusker remembers.

> She said 'I have to go down and hear that talk.' And indeed he was announcing the structure of Vitamin B_{12}. He was not expecting her, but she stood up at the end and said this was how it was done. And after that she insisted that whenever Todd was speaking we all had to go to his lectures and give a comment at the end.[50]

Todd then went to the International Congress of Pure and Applied Chemistry in Zurich at the end of July. As he was not allowed to give a formal presentation because of the short notice, he 'saw no point in trailing [Dorothy] over to Zurich'. He did, however, submit an abstract based on the two unpublished *Nature* papers, give an impromptu colloquium to a packed audience in the laboratory of the eminent chemist Leopold Ruzicka, and give an interview to a journalist from the *New York Times*. A full column appeared there on 26 July, headed 'Britons discover structure of B-12'. It began: 'The solution of one of nature's most formidable puzzles – the three-dimensional structure of Vitamin B-12 – has been achieved by a team of British chemists at Cambridge University', and went on: 'The team that won the race . . . was headed by Sir Alexander Todd of Cambridge University Chemical Laboratory . . .' Not until the seventeenth and eighteenth paragraphs respectively did the article acknowledge the 'assistance' of 'a team of X-ray crystalographers [sic] of the Department of Chemistry at Oxford', and of the UCLA computing team.

Todd blamed the bias of the article on incompetent journalism, himself sending Dorothy a copy of the *New York Times* cutting, which she had almost certainly seen already.

> I was extremely annoyed when I saw it for I had been at particular pains in Zurich to play down the chemical side and especially my own minor contribution to getting the answer . . . It is really hopeless trying to control newspapers and the only consolation is that they are ephemeral. I am however very angry about this particular article . . . [51]

He backed up his position by sending a letter to the editor of the *New York Times*, published a week or two after the original article, in which he gave full honours to the Oxford researchers.

> The main credit for the progress which has been made should be given to Dr Dorothy Hodgkin of Oxford and her colleagues Miss J. Pickworth and Mr J. H. Robertson . . . and to Drs K. N. Trueblood and R. T. Posen [sic] . . . I feel strongly that Dr Hodgkin's outstanding contribution to the structural elucidation of vitamin B$_{12}$ should be recognized . . .

Not strongly enough, it seems, to have let her give the first presentations on the subject herself. At the last minute she managed to get herself on to the programme of a conference in Brussels at the beginning of August, where for the first time she was able to describe the work herself. Dorothy hoped that time and the *Nature* publications would clear up any misconceptions, and did not make any direct protest to Todd. But she allowed something of her feelings to show in a letter to Ken Trueblood. 'I found it rather trying myself when I arrived in Brussels to have so many people asking me what I thought of 'Todd's' structure for B$_{12}$.'[52]

For her part, Jenny Pickworth was furious that Todd had, in her view, underplayed the achievement of the crystallographers. 'I think Todd really felt this was his work and the crystallographers were just the technicians, and so he wanted to be the first to report the structure.'[53] If this was the case, it must have been hard for Todd to accept that mere 'technicians' could by now run spectacular rings round traditional chemists when it came to solving unknown structures. He himself confessed to Dorothy that the chemists at the Zurich colloquium were 'divided between admiration for your work and an unconscious fear that you and your colleagues would one day put the organic chemist out of business!'[54] Among crystallographers, the success with Vitamin B_{12} was immediately recognized as setting a new standard: Sir Lawrence Bragg himself described it as 'breaking the sound barrier' and 'in a class of its own'.[55] Linus Pauling wrote with a gracious tribute.

> I am writing to congratulate you on the wonderful job you have done on Vitamin B_{12}. I find it hard to believe, although very satisfying, that the methods of X-ray crystallography can be used so effectively on such a complex molecule.[56]

The success with Vitamin B_{12} gave hope that even proteins, ten or a hundred times larger, might one day succumb to the power of the X-ray. Despite her diversion into other problems, Dorothy had never stopped thinking about proteins, especially insulin. Unlike some sceptical chemists, she never believed that protein structures were insoluble. And in the post-war years, some chinks of light were beginning to emerge. During his stay in Oxford in 1948, Linus Pauling had come up with the idea that proteins might include a common structure which he called the alpha helix, a winding of the amino acid chain through precisely defined turns that seemed to fit some of the available X-ray evidence. He hit on the model while in bed with flu, trying out different possibilities with scissors and paper. The breakthrough came when he realized that it was not necessary to have an exact number of amino acid residues in each turn of the helix. In 1951 he published the first papers on the discovery, which generated intense excitement. To draw together new theories and findings on protein structure, he organized an international conference at Pasadena to take place in October 1953.

Of course Dorothy was invited; it would have been her fourth trip across the Atlantic (she had been to conferences in 1948 and 1949) and a welcome chance to revisit the Paulings, Eddie Hughes and other friends in the Pasadena lab. But she had reckoned without the anti-Communist hysteria that was blighting the careers of thousands of Americans with left-wing connections. As long ago as 1948 Jean Wyart, who was to lead the French delegation to the International Congress of Crystallography at Harvard, had been refused permission to enter the country on suspicion of being a Communist. One year later it was the turn of Dick Synge, an organic chemist from the Rowett Research Institute in Aberdeen, who had acquired samples of gramicidin S from Moscow at the end of the war and given them to Dorothy for X-ray analysis. Another future Nobel prizewinner, he asked Dorothy to read his paper at the Cold Spring Harbor protein conference in 1949 because he could not get a visa. Pauling himself, who with his wife Ava Helen's encouragement had become involved in anti-nuclear campaigning, had been denied a passport to come to Britain for a protein conference at the Royal Society in 1952.[57]

Dorothy filled in her visa application in early 1953 with touchingly naïve thoroughness. She included every organization she had ever belonged to, from the Girl Guides to the Oxford University Archaeological Society and the Labour Party. Crucially, she included a number of organizations concerned with world peace and nuclear disarmament that had sprung up since the dropping of the atom bomb in 1945. These included the Atomic Scientists' Association, the Oxford Area Peace Association (of which she was briefly vice-president), Science for Peace and the National Peace Council. To her astonishment her visa was refused. So was Bernal's, but he had never made any secret of his Communist affiliations. Dorothy had never been a Party member, but one or two of the organizations she had listed were suspect in the eyes of the State Department. Science for Peace, for instance, was a British organization that flared up in 1952 from the embers of the old Cambridge Scientists' Anti-War Group, with committee members including the Piries and, inevitably, Bernal. It remained, in Gary Werskey's words, 'the principal platform for the old scientific Left' for the next five years.[58]

Dorothy's association with such organizations made her

'statutorily inadmissible' under the terms of the Immigration and Nationality Act. Both she and her friends in Pasadena found the situation unbelievable, and were sure they could expect help from the Scientific Attaché at the US Embassy in London, Ralph Wyckoff. Wyckoff was himself a crystallographer (and future President of the International Union of Crystallography) whom Dorothy had met on her 1947 visit, and had even helped to obtain crystals in the past. But his response contained no grounds for hope.

> I did not know before the receipt of your letter that your visa application had been turned down and I am certainly sorry about it.
>
> Under the old law there was a way in which special consideration could be requested in Washington . . . Such things, however, always take a long time and I don't think that there is any possibility such an appeal could be carried to a decision in time for Pauling's meeting.
>
> Not that it's of any help now but I would be very glad to discuss the matter further when we next meet.[59]

The conference took place without her and she was sorely missed, although Eddie Hughes compensated by showing home movies he had shot during her first visit to Pasadena in 1947.

Bernal, meanwhile, had been asked to join a delegation of scientists invited to visit the Soviet Union in mid-September the same year by the Soviet Academy of Sciences. This move towards cooperation was a new development – for example, although Russian crystallographers had been involved in setting up the International Union of Crystallography in 1946, worsening East–West relations had prevented them from attending the first two Congresses in 1948 and 1951. Bernal rang Dorothy and asked her to join the delegation. She would have preferred to go to the protein meeting, but as there was no chance of that, she took the opportunity. She had herself made tentative enquiries about a visit to Moscow the year before. Her days in Cambridge had taught her to think of Soviet Russia as an ideal society, a view reinforced by Thomas. In the week after Elizabeth's birth she had written to him about a book she had been reading on Soviet society.

Trouble about books about Russia, specially now, is that
they make me think of Soviet Britain and begin to cry. All
those descriptions of the children's schools and parks –
how lovely it would be to think of Luke and Elisabeth
going to grow up in such places and enjoy that sort of
atmosphere. But not much prospect of it. Perhaps they'll
make it possible for their children but we seem likely to
prove a washout.

The stories that emerged in the post-war years about Stalin's
murderous regime troubled her, but she interpreted them at first
as anti-Communist propaganda. Her comment to Thomas on the
death of Stalin early in 1953 strikes something of a chill from a
modern perspective: 'Stalin's death comes as a sad blow. Here
very mixed and conflicting accounts of his life appear in the
papers – as you would expect.'

Bernal himself wrote a fulsome tribute to Stalin in the *Modern
Quarterly*, a weighty intellectual journal controlled by the
Communist Party. The same year he was rewarded for his loyalty
to Soviet Russia by the award of the Stalin Peace Prize.[60]

Now Dorothy had a chance to see the Soviet Union for herself. She was not as impervious as she might have appeared to
the dark tales that were circulating, and the night before she
left her anxiety was increased. Another member of the delegation, the Oxford Mathematics Professor Henry Whitehead, met
her for dinner in London and disclosed that several members of
the family of his friend Kate Field, including her American
Quaker husband Hermann, had been arrested in the Eastern
Bloc. Nothing had been heard of them for three or four years.
Kate Field had asked Whitehead to try to find out what had
happened to them. This personal evidence that all was not
entirely well cast a cloud over Dorothy's departure, but it was
dispelled during a one-day stop in Prague. Seeing three Polish
scientists she knew waiting to meet their plane, she remembered, 'All my fears of going into this dangerous part of the
world disappeared, as it was obvious we should find friends
there.'[61] A day later, the evening of her arrival at the Metropol
Hotel in Moscow, she reported to Thomas that she was feeling
much more cheerful.

Here I am, really pretty drunk I am afraid after a fantastic welcoming dinner and an orgy of speeches (I made two, one in reply to the toast of the women of Britain, one to a speech of Sjrkin's about Robert Robinson and chemistry).

We were bowled over at Moscow by being met by about eight members of the Academy of Sciences, including Schubikow [sic – A. V. Shubnikov was the grand old man of Russian crystallography, having started work in the field in 1906; he came to London for the inaugural IUCr meeting in 1946] who greeted me like a long lost friend, and a girl with a bouquet of flowers for me and a welcoming speech . . .

Sage turned up about 6 p.m. having caught a later plane. Then about ten academicians turned up to have dinner with us, a marvellous incredible banquet, with speeches and toasts on and off all the way through, to the detriment of eating . . . We really are all terribly drunk now.

My rooms are like a princess's with marvellous lace counterpanes and fruit and drinks set ready for me on arrival.

A few days later she was ready to admit to some frustrations at the lack of choice the visitors were able to have in their programme.

We are having a rather fantastic time. Everything has been rather thoroughly arranged for us at a very high level – explanations of academicians about the whole organization of Soviet science interspersed with lengthy feasts. We ought to have been delighted, but time is short, and we all began to feel quite desperate about our chances of getting into Soviet labs. However that has happened in the last two days and we are now all feeling much better. (We were all in a bad way on Sat. night when we returned from a nice opera at 11 and Henry called for champagne to cheer us all up. We thought our nice little interpreters were so upset by our behaviour (general atmosphere of revolt and riot) we'd wrecked Anglo-Soviet relations for good).

But even apart from the labs – which were entirely

friendly and exciting – we've had marvellous times. The new university is magnificent – marvellously spacious and enormous and grand.

Then they were whisked off to Leningrad and shown round the Hermitage by one of the country's leading archaeologists, being given privileged glimpses of treasures not on public display: the gold of Scythia, rugs from Central Asia, and recent finds from the Caucasus. Dorothy was given 'a helmet to hold, and an axe'. It was all 'absolutely fantastic' to Dorothy, but time was slipping by and still no one had done anything about Hermann Field and his relatives. Henry Whitehead seemed to have forgotten about them.

> I remember well walking back beside the Neva, with Henry in a very drunken state. One of our party walking behind was clearly feeling that he was letting down the side, but he and our guide, Kiselov [the archaeologist], were arm-in-arm . . . with Henry singing occasionally. When we got back to the Asturias [Hotel], though, he suddenly became totally sober again and said: 'We ought to think about what we ought to do about the Fields.' And so we went and had a talk with Bernal in his room.[62]

Bernal made enquiries in Moscow and later in Warsaw, but apparently not with any immediate effect. Hermann Field was in fact alive; he was released in Poland a year or so later and reunited with his wife, and they moved to the United States. His brother Noel and sister-in-law were released in Hungary a little later. Their adopted daughter Erica languished in a labour camp for a few more years, apparently forgotten, before her own efforts led to her release.

Dorothy had no more success with some timid enquiries she made about the whereabouts of some Russian scientists.

> Kathleen Lonsdale had given me a long list of people, saying that it would be nice if I could find out where they were. I had this list with me, but somewhere during my first day or two in Moscow I lost this list, and I became

extremely worried about it; I thought, if it's found it will
do none of us any good, and particularly the people
concerned. And I was curiously quite frightened, and
everything suddenly seemed very suspicious all round – I
thought perhaps they had it already. Two days later I
found it inside the book I'd been reading, just used as a
bookmarker. Then my suspicions disappeared and I
thought, really, we make our own suspicions of the
Eastern world.

It is interesting to reflect that the reappearance of the list, rather
than of the people it named, was apparently enough to calm
Dorothy's fears. Since the late 1930s many scientists had been the
victims of Stalin's terror. In particular the state-ordered rejection
of the science of genetics in favour of a spurious notion pro-
pounded by T. D. Lysenko, that characteristics acquired by an
individual organism through environmental influences can be
passed on to its offspring, had seen large numbers of biologists
lose their jobs if not their lives. Lysenko's main opponent, the
leading geneticist N. I. Vavilov, had died of neglect in prison.
Many formerly left-leaning scientists in the West became disillu-
sioned with Soviet Communism at this development which,
combined with the greatly improved conditions for scientific
research in the West after the war, largely extinguished the socialist fervour that had sprung up among scientists in the 1930s.[63]

Bernal, however, did not immediately change his position. He
remained the leading apologist for Lysenkoism in Britain until
Lysenko himself fell from grace in the early 1950s. Simultaneously
he acknowledged that the 'facts' of Mendelian inheritance were
correct, and was absolutely delighted by Crick and Watson's discovery of the structure of DNA. Dorothy later explained his
apparent ability to accept two contradictory points of view by
saying that he 'held theories lightly'. She believed he thought of
the death of Vavilov and others as due to 'madness and war'
rather than to the system, or to the action of powerful individuals
such as Lysenko or Stalin.

It is difficult to tell how much Dorothy herself knew or
believed in 1953 of the terrors of Stalin's dictatorship, which left
millions of ordinary Russians dead or imprisoned in labour

camps. If she did know, she took her cue from Bernal in suppressing any criticism in the interests of promoting Anglo-Soviet scientific cooperation. She was enchanted by the optimism and fervour of some of the young people she met on that first visit, especially the students at the grand new university. For the first time, tentatively, she began to write and speak in support of the USSR, revealing her convictions beyond her immediate circle of acquaintances. Typically she avoided socialist sloganizing, couching her beliefs in highly personal terms.

After her return from this first visit she drafted a long and rather light-hearted article, intended for *The Times*, entitled 'Last Day in Moscow'. It was chatty and anecdotal: how she managed to cut the 'enormous 3.30 or 4 p.m. lunch' in order to have more time visiting labs; how her translator was ordered to return her at once on the grounds that 'We can't possibly send her home to her husband in her present condition. She's much too thin'; how the delegates were cajoled by their hosts into preparing a press statement that included the Soviet desire for world peace; how Henry Whitehead stole the show at the final press conference by describing how kind Muscovites had given him directions when he was walking the streets of the city alone. The piece concluded in a more serious vein.

> It would I think be impossible in a fortnight's casual visiting to track down deep seated evils in any country one visited. And so I cannot say whether or no many of the evils ascribed to the Soviet Union exist. And yet, and yet. I shall find it very difficult ever to believe that Soviet civilization which has grown the very many able, intelligent and amusing people I met, is wholly bad.[64]

The following year a Soviet delegation attended the International Congress of Crystallography in Paris; it was a source of great satisfaction to Dorothy to believe that she had had a hand in bringing about this rapprochement. It probably did her no good in relation to the US visa issue, however. Wyckoff, who attended the conference as a member of the US delegation, filed a despatch to the Department of State on his return headed 'Communist Participation in Union of Crystallography'. It reveals that far from being sympathetic to Dorothy's problems, he regarded her as a threat to US relations with the Soviet Union.

> Two of the five-membered voting British delegation were: Professor Kathleen Lonsdale of University College, a well-known Quaker pacifist of strong Russian sympathies, and Dr Dorothy Hodgkin of the University of Oxford, who was this winter a member of a party of British scientists that visited Russia under the patronage of Professor J. D. Bernal of Birkbeck College, whose Communist sympathies are well established . . . These persons vigorously urged the immediate entry of Russia into full membership of this Union . . . It is perhaps significant that the marked public cordiality shown by these British delegates throughout the conference was quietly received but not reciprocated by the Russians . . . The foregoing reaction of the Leftist British delegates was of course to be expected, but there was a somewhat surprising failure of the Conservative British representatives to give a more balanced position to the British delegation as a whole . . .
>
> It is this Attache's opinion that in our coming dealings with Communist scientists their lack of understanding of the real circumstances under which we work and live will be a serious obstacle . . . and it is as sources of mis-information about us that anti-American Left-wing Europeans are in a position to do us harm. It is important that they should not be allowed to manoeuvre into being intermediaries between us and Communist scientists.[65]

In subsequent years other members of the American crystallo-graphic community did their best to help Dorothy obtain permission from the Attorney General for single-entry visas to attend conferences. In 1957 she was to be in Montreal in July for the International Congress of Crystallography, and Bill Lipscomb, then at the University of Minnesota, invited her to give a talk immediately afterwards. She replied with some regret.

> I would love to come and visit you but do you really think I could? You see, I was formally judged inadmissible any

more to the USA . . . Thomas having been at one time a member of the Communist party, and my having various doubtful-in-the-light-of-this-fact associations . . . But even though times have changed now, I think it might be hard for me to get a visa with so much down in black and white against my name (all deplorably accurately remembered and recorded by myself), and Eddie [Hughes] thought I would need some very high up backing to the Secretary of State level. It's a great pity.[66]

Lipscomb immediately wrote to the Consul-General at the US Embassy in London protesting about her case.

Dr Hodgkin is considered to be the most able person in the world in her research field . . . it would seem to be a shame that a scientist of Mrs Hodgkin's calibre could not give a lecture in the United States because her husband had formerly been a member of the Communist party.[67]

Through Lipsomb's intervention, Dorothy was encouraged to re-apply. But the wheels of bureaucracy ground so slowly that the conference date came and went without any decision being reached. The State Department's excuse was that it had been unable to obtain various documents necessary to 'complete her file' before putting the case before the Attorney-General. By this time it was gradually dawning on the State Department that its policy was having a very negative effect on international percep-tions of the United States. Three years before, hard-line bureaucrats who wanted to refuse Pauling a passport to go to Stockholm to collect his Nobel Prize for Chemistry had been overruled for this reason.[68] In the autumn of 1957 Lipscomb again invited Dorothy, and she also had an invitation to give the keynote speech at a celebration of forty years of X-ray crystallog-raphy in America that Pauling was organizing in late December. She at last received a visa a few days before she was due to leave. Thomas was already in the United States, giving a series of lec-tures at Northwestern University, and he joined her in California. (It was a little ironic that he had had been granted a waiver despite admitting to former Party membership.) Amidst much joy at the return of the popular couple, the hospitable Eddie Hughes and his wife Ruth gave a champagne party to celebrate the Hodgkins' twentieth wedding anniversary.

The 1950s were a decade of astonishing achievement for scientists working on biological molecules. In 1953, James Watson and Francis Crick, working in Max Perutz's laboratory in Cambridge succeeded in discovering the structure of DNA. Their work was also based on X-ray crystallographic studies, carried out by Rosalind Franklin and Maurice Wilkins at King's College London.

Franklin's name has become one of the best-known of any woman scientist, largely on the grounds that she was a victim of scientific injustice, and she died young. She was an extremely able scientist; one of her Cambridge tutors had no hesitation in attributing to her the 'first-class mind' that is the ultimate Oxbridge accolade.[69] Before coming to King's she had spent a happy and fruitful few years working in Paris. But the contrast in her new job was a shock. First, she found that Wilkins thought she would work under his direction, when she expected to be working independently on DNA. Second, there was a mutual incomprehension that made it impossible to resolve their differences. Among French colleagues, Franklin's direct and combative personal style aroused no comment – vigorous and heated debate was a normal feature of scientific discourse, and no one took offence. At King's, only her assistant Raymond Gosling gave as good as he got, and they became friends; Wilkins responded to attack with immediate withdrawal. Their styles were so incompatible that they barely spoke in the two years she was there. Less important but still an irritation to Rosalind was the discovery that women were not permitted in the Senior Common Room, where staff met for lunch each day.[70]

Franklin, with Gosling to assist her, worked on alone. Her experiments brought her close to the solution of the DNA structure, but her approach was completely different from that of Watson and Crick. Like Dorothy, she was extremely cautious about accepting any theoretical model without the evidence to back it up. But unlike Dorothy, she rejected model-building as an approach to finding that evidence. She opted to find the solution the hard way, through calculating Patterson functions. She was still some way from succeeding when Wilkins, without her knowledge, showed Watson one of her X-ray photographs – a photograph that told the American immediately that a helical model would be correct. It took only a few more weeks before he and Crick built the model that represented the single most important discovery in modern biology.

Franklin meanwhile had decided to leave King's, and DNA, and move to the more congenial environment of Bernal's lab at Birkbeck. There she began a hugely fruitful collaboration with Aaron Klug on plant viruses, which lasted until her untimely death from cancer in 1958 at the age of thirty-seven. Because Nobel prizes are never awarded posthumously, she never shared the glory for the DNA discovery, despite the crucial role of her photograph; she was doubly disinherited by the caricatured image of the bespectacled bluestocking 'Rosy' (a nickname only ever used behind her back) presented by Watson in his book about the discovery.[71] In recent years the full complexity of the story and her role in it has emerged. It tells of an embattled and somewhat lonely figure, full of talent but, by a combination of her own stubbornness and the inability of others to accept her on her own terms, denied the opportunity to let it flower.

It is a story that contrasts vividly with Dorothy's, emphasizing the futility of drawing simplistic conclusions about the experience of women scientists. The two of them would undoubtedly have met many times; on Dorothy's frequent visits to Birkbeck, at meetings of the X-Ray Analysis Group and the International Union of Crystallography. Dorothy had a high regard for her technical competence; the photographs Franklin brought to Oxford to show Dorothy soon after her arrival at King's were the best she had ever seen. But Franklin lacked Dorothy's comprehensive grasp of the chemistry behind the structures that so fascinated her. Jack Dunitz remembers one exchange between the two of them, as they looked at the DNA photographs on the big tables of the museum laboratory. Dorothy remarked that the photographs were so good that it ought to be possible to derive from them the space group – the set of symmetry relations governing the way the molecules formed a repeating pattern. Franklin eagerly replied that she had already narrowed the possibilities down to three. 'But Rosalind!' exclaimed Dorothy, and immediately pointed out that two of these were impossible. Franklin could not see why, and so Dorothy asked Dunitz to explain. What Franklin had failed to take into account was that all the sugars in a molecule of DNA have the same 'handedness'. Two of the three space groups suggested by Franklin required both left- and right-handed forms. The episode is just one example of the insight Dorothy could bring to problems that she herself had never worked on directly.

Dorothy and Dunitz were among the first to go to Cambridge and see Watson and Crick's model, which they immediately realized must be right. Success with DNA was followed a few years later by success with proteins, and again the honours went to Cambridge. In 1955 the biochemist Fred Sanger published the sequence of amino acids that make up the small protein insulin. He found that each molecule consisted of two chains, A and B, connected to one another by bridges between sulphur atoms in the cysteine residues. Again, Dorothy followed his work closely. As early as February 1952 Sanger had sent her a brief letter including what he was 'fairly certain' was the sequence of the A chain of insulin. The B chain followed in due course. But knowing the insulin sequence was not enough to reveal its three-dimensional structure.

Dorothy began to turn her attention back to insulin as soon as she had completed the structure of Vitamin B_{12}. By this time not only was the insulin sequence known, but other proteins were close to a structural solution. Max Perutz had never been diverted from his devotion to solving the structure of haemoglobin. Yet for a long time the problem seemed impossible: the beautiful haemoglobin crystals gave thousands of reflections, but no means at all of estimating the phases. The conventional wisdom before 1951 was that heavy atom or isomorphous replacement methods, such as those Dorothy had used to solve cholesteryl iodide and penicillin, would be no use with proteins. The argument was that because there were so many light atoms in a protein, the contribution of one or two heavy atoms to the reflections would be swamped.

But in 1951 Perutz carried out an experiment showing that he and others had been completely mistaken in this view. Proteins were known to be 'weakly diffracting', requiring long exposures to produce photographs with a good number of measurable reflections. Perutz's experiment, which calculated the exact fraction of the incident beam of X-rays that produced each reflection, showed for the first time why this was so. The fractions – known as the absolute intensities, to distinguish them from the relative intensities usually used in crystallographic calculations – were much smaller than he expected, and he realized that the scattering contributions of most of the atoms in the crystal were simply cancelling each other out through interference. Just a few were in a position to reinforce each other and produce a reflection. If that were the case, then a heavy atom would indeed make a difference to the intensities, and could be used to find the phases.

Perutz and his colleagues crystallized haemoglobin with a mercury salt, and obtained crystals that had the same structure as haemoglobin, but for the addition of two molecules of mercury. They gave X-ray pictures with very similar diffraction patterns to the natural haemoglobin, but with some variation in the intensities – precisely what Perutz needed. He 'realized at that moment that now the protein problem was solved'. To his great satisfaction, he was able to report on this result at Pauling's protein meeting in Pasadena in September 1953.

> That was a marvellous meeting. I was very proud because my unit produced the best papers. I came with the heavy atom method showing that phase problems could be solved, and Watson and Crick came with DNA, and Hugh Huxley came with the sliding mechanism of muscular contraction.[72]

This elation was somewhat short-lived, because although the mercury derivative enabled Perutz to produce his first electron density map of haemoglobin, it was a two-dimensional projection of a very large unit cell, and could not be interpreted. It was Dorothy, whom Perutz had invited over to see his map, who suggested a way out of the problem: what he needed was a second heavy atom derivative, with the heavy atom in a different place in the molecule. Then he would be able to solve the structure in three dimensions. But in fact it was another three years before he succeeded in obtaining further derivatives. By that time, somewhat to his chagrin, his colleague John Kendrew had pipped him to the post. Kendrew, who came to work with Perutz in 1946, had chosen to solve myoglobin, a protein found in muscle that was related to haemoglobin but a quarter of the size. Using Perutz's methods, and with help from others in the group, he managed to make a number of heavy atom derivatives of sperm-whale myoglobin. By this time Cambridge had a digital computer, which Kendrew was able to use to calculate the electron densities. In March 1958 he published the structure in *Nature*, not yet refined sufficiently to show the exact positions of all the atoms, but nevertheless the first ever to show how protein chains contort themselves to produce a three-dimensional structure. It was not at all as anyone expected. 'The arrangement seems to be almost totally lacking in the kind of regularities which one instinctively anticipates, and it is more complicated than has been predicted by any theory of protein structure.'[73]

A year later Perutz solved the structure of the much larger haemoglobin molecule at about the same level of resolution – the completion of a task that had absorbed him for twenty-three years. Dorothy was one of the first to congratulate him, ringing up to say, 'I hear you have a fantastic model of haemoglobin. Can I come over and see it?' Her joy in her old friend's achievement was characteristic, but it concealed her own disappointment that she was not to be first in the field with proteins. This was not something she talked about openly, but an incident reported by David Sayre hints at the very real anguish she must have felt.

> For some reason she and I both had to go to Cambridge one day, and I drove her in our 1932 Austin 7. On the way back I said how much I admired the fact that instead of spending all her time on insulin, she went off to either side, doing cholesteryl iodide and penicillin – B_{12} hadn't happened yet – and each time she did this she moved the science another giant step towards the goal of a protein. And she almost bit my head off. She reminded me that back in 1939 Bernal had made that back-of-the-envelope calculation to the effect that a heavy atom ought to make enough difference to the diffraction pattern of a protein to enable phasing to take place, and with her voice trembling with emotion she told me how wrong I was. I think the

implication was that she was wrong to have done what she did. That's the only time I ever saw Dorothy betray violent emotion of a not entirely happy kind. I think she was hurt by the success that was apparently on its way for haemoglobin and myoglobin, and that she was going to come along later.[74]

If it were true that Dorothy regarded her own successes as second-best, then she was the only one who thought so. Recognition of her achievements continued to pour in. In 1955 Oxford University promoted her to Reader in X-Ray Crystallography. As well as providing a much-needed boost to her income, with a salary of £1650, the appointment limited her college teaching to six hours per week, leaving her more time for research. A few years later the Chemical Crystallography Laboratory, including both Dorothy's and Tiny Powell's groups, at last moved out of the Museum and into rooms on the ground floor of the Inorganic Chemistry Laboratory's new extension.

The following year the Royal Society awarded her its Royal Medal. She was the first woman to receive this honour, the highest in the Society's gift. The citation described her work on B$_{12}$ as 'the most beautiful and complex analysis which has yet been achieved in this field'. Both her parents were by this time increasingly infirm, and did not expect to be able to see her receive the medal, on 30 November 1956. But Dorothy arranged comfortable transport and accommodation so that at least her mother, who had first encouraged her, could be there. As Molly Crowfoot wrote later, it meant a great deal to both her parents.

It was marvellous to get to London and see you receive the medal, and thanks to you, was not nearly so tiring as I had expected. To be driven everywhere and taken care of made it so much easier.

Daddy was very pleased with me for going . . . he said he almost believed he could have done it himself – we both felt very happy when I got back.[75]

Working to the last, aided by her daughter Elizabeth, on Anglo-Saxon burial goods, on textiles from the caves where the Dead

Sea Scrolls were discovered, and on books on Middle Eastern handicrafts, Molly Crowfoot died a few months later, aged eighty. Her husband, whose heart was failing, survived her by little more than a year.

Around this time Dorothy and her immediate family underwent another domestic upheaval, but one which proved ideal all round. Dorothy's second sister Joan's fraught marriage had finally ended, a matter of some relief to the rest of the family. Only a few years before Molly Crowfoot had written to Dorothy in indignation that Joan had been forced to give up a good job in Cambridge when her husband came close to a nervous breakdown.

> Joan is put in the antique category of females who mustn't undertake such work, or be bound by its rules – who must put the whole of their life at the disposition of lover or husband. Well Joan being a modern can't live like that can she? The outlook is a bit gloomy I think.[76]

Joan was looking for work and somewhere to live cheaply with her five children. Dorothy, although she had come to love Powder Hill, found it difficult to manage the journeys in and out of town, especially when Thomas was away. The sisters decided to look for a house together in Oxford, and Dorothy bought the end of a lease on a large Victorian house in North Oxford at 94 Woodstock Road. (The idea of a joint household may have been prompted by Thomas, who had already suggested to his cousin Mary Jameson, herself a single mother of four, that she might think of moving in with Dorothy.[77]) The two families moved in in 1957, and Joan found work at the Ashmolean Museum, cataloguing its collection of ancient flint tools. Once more Dorothy could walk to the lab. The two eldest children were now at university – Luke went up to Balliol to read mathematics in October 1956 – but the other six had easy journeys to school.

Many friends and scientific colleagues have since written about visiting that household. Not only the eight children and their friends, but students and other visitors from abroad would often be staying, invited either by Dorothy or Thomas. There was a green baize board in the hall with crossed tapes, such as might be found in a boarding house, to take the day's letters for whoever might be in residence. It was a standing joke that when Thomas ran out of things to say to new acquaintances, he would invite them to dinner. When at home, he would cook enormous and delicious meals, and dominate the dinner-table conversation until he fell asleep in his chair. Dorothy, meanwhile, would sit quietly with a faraway look in her eyes, her mind on the latest structure problem. But the comfort of her guests was always her first concern.

> One thing one noticed was how Dorothy was able to combine making sure the flowers were put in somebody's room and that they had clean sheets, and caring a lot about that, and yet caring about her work at the same time.[78]

Edith, now quite elderly, and her friend Alice were still on hand to cook lunch and help around the house, but Joan oversaw much of the household management. Responsibilities were shared among everyone: Joan, Elizabeth and Toby, being first up in the mornings, would organize the breakfast between them. There was a strict rota for daily chores like washing up after meals. Elizabeth remembers very few disagreements.

> Dorothy was accustomed to come into the room where we were having breakfast and start combing my hair, and Joan objected and said it was messy. And I remember Dossie running out into the garden and weeping, and I ran out to comfort her and Joan did too – and she said, 'There aren't so many things I can do for her, so that I want to be able to do that.' I must have been sixteen or seventeen.

From their first arrival in Woodstock Road a regular visitor and friend of the family was Anna Davin, daughter of Dan Davin, the writer and Oxford University Press editor, and his wife Winnie. By then Luke's girlfriend, she joined the Hodgkins for a summer holiday in Austria in 1958. As she returned to school to prepare for the Oxford scholarship examinations, she discovered she was pregnant. She and Luke decided that they would marry as soon as possible, and that Anna, despite her brilliant school record, would give up plans for university entrance. At the time Thomas was on a three-month fellowship in Montreal, Canada, so Dorothy had to break the news by letter.

> They want to get married at Christmas. In the back of my
> mind I suppose I half expected it, and yet I feel so astray . . .
> Joan just said 'Oh the little dears, how very nice. Of course,
> they can live in the cottage. How lucky we didn't let it
> yet . . .' It seemed so nice and simple and ordinary.
>   In the middle of the night, lying awake, I suddenly
> thought – if I get the Nobel Prize in Chemistry next year
> the newspapers will headline it 'Grandmother Wins Nobel
> Prize' and burst into helpless giggles.

The development tested Dorothy's liberal principles to the limit. Her declared belief in free love would not let her condemn what had happened, especially as Anna had been more or less living under her roof; at the same time she could hardly be unmoved by the disappointment of Anna's parents at the blow to her educational prospects. Worst of all was the anguish of her own mother-in-law, who 'cried and cried', so much that Dorothy wished she had not told her. The marriage was quickly arranged, for the day Thomas returned from Canada, and the pregnancy kept as quiet as possible. Luke and Anna, and their baby Dominic when he arrived, took up residence in the cottage in the garden of Number 94.

The Hodgkin household was scarcely typical of the way academic families in Oxford ran their lives at the time. Visitors encountered a total disregard for convention that most regarded as a breath of fresh air, but which could sometimes be disconcerting: on one occasion Dorothy told Linus Pauling and other guests arriving for dinner that she was just off to meet Thomas from London airport, leaving them to help themselves from the cooker.[79] Elizabeth gradually became aware how her parents' broader outlook set them apart.

> I feel we weren't in the swim of Oxford society. I later
> heard people talk about Oxford society and we weren't
> part of it. We were part of an international crystallography
> society, and an international African society. But we were
> out of this kind of high, college, intellectual society, dinings

on high tables and the great Oxford families. We never had this kind of 'you have a dinner, and we'll have you back' sort of thing – hospitality is free, you never think you're going to be paid back in hospitality by others.[80]

If Dorothy was not part of Oxford 'society', she and her family were certainly part of the Oxford scene, and she felt disinclined to uproot them. But it seemed that she might have to if she wanted a more senior position. By 1960 she had been approached by a number of other universities to ask if she would consider accepting a professorship. She was seriously considering an offer from Leeds, which had a good track record in crystallography, when a new opportunity arose. Lord Wolfson gave a donation to the Royal Society to fund a professorship in any science, which would free the holder from teaching responsibilities and allow him or her to engage in research full-time. It would provide a salary of £3000, with a further £5000 annually for research assistants and other laboratory expenses, and could be held in any university. Dorothy's name immediately went to the top of the list. Early in May 1960 she heard the news from Kathleen Lonsdale, who by that time was Vice-President of the Royal Society.

All this is a preliminary to saying how *glad* I am that you were quite *unanimously* chosen as the first Wolfson professor if you wish to take it on . . . I think it is quite remarkable that the RS could be so remarkably sensible in such a united way![81]

When the offer finally came through, Thomas was in Ghana. Not wishing to accept without consulting him, Dorothy tried to get through to him on the telephone. It took a while to track him down, but Dorothy was paying to keep the line open until he could be found. When at last the conversation was concluded, the operator remarked: 'My word, what a fuss about a chair! Now that you are to have it I do hope you will find it comfortable.'[82]

Oxford University's reaction to Dorothy's appointment was surprisingly lukewarm. Although today there are a number of Royal Society Research Professors in the University – until recently there were five in Zoology alone – Dorothy was the first in Oxford, and only the second in the country. (The other was her cousin by marriage, Alan Hodgkin in Cambridge.) The files suggest that accommodating this illustrious figure was seen as a problem rather than a privilege, as in this letter from the Registrar to the Vice-Chairman of the General Board.

> What it would come to, I think, would be that Mrs
> Hodgkin . . . would be authorized to continue to use
> facilities in the Chemical Crystallography Laboratory . . .
> Clearly this is a new and confusing problem, which is not
> made any easier by the fact that the ICL is thought to be
> too small and that one of the proposals . . . is to extrude the
> Chemical Crystallographers elsewhere.[83]

The University's officers knew that Professor Patrick Blackett at Imperial College had offered Dorothy 7000 square feet in his brand-new Physics Building if she wanted to bring her chair to London. She had expressed a preference for staying in Oxford, but her loyalty gained her little advantage.

A few days later Hebdomadal Council, the University's executive body, debated the issue and concluded that 'no objection should be raised to an early announcement by the Royal Society'. The report of the meeting notes that the demand for computing generated by Dorothy's research had been a 'major factor' in the University's bid to the University Grants Committee for funds to purchase a successor to the Mercury computer installed two years before. (They might also have reflected on the central role she had played in establishing the Computing Laboratory in the first place.) However, the announcement was held up for another ten days while Cyril Hinshelwood, the Professor of Inorganic Chemistry, calmed Powell's anxieties about the possible growth of Dorothy's research group. He eventually reported that Powell and Dorothy had agreed to '"make do as they are" for the time being, subject to longer-range plans being made'. The decree accepting the award from the Royal Society that was eventually published explicitly stated that there was no obligation on the part of the Professor of Inorganic Chemistry to provide the Wolfson Professor with facilities.

The other issue that exercised the administrators was that of

Mrs Hodgkin's 'status'. Once she was off the University payroll, it was thought, she would lose all authority within the institution. A note to the Registrar reads as follows:

> She is . . . at the moment only a Reader working under the direction of the professor in charge of the ICL; after her resignation [from the Readership] she will have no formal status at all . . . But perhaps her personal status is such as to make formal provision in the decree unnecessary.[84]

She was eventually given the title of Professor, although what that meant in terms of her rights to space and facilities was left vague. The issue was more serious than it might appear. The General Board, while welcoming the Royal Society appointment and Dorothy's continued presence in Oxford, raised a doubt about whether she should henceforth have the right to free access to the University's computing service, which she was then using for around 1000 hours per year (at a notional cost of £40 per hour). It referred the matter to its Standing Committee on Finance for consideration. Almost two months later the Committee ruled in her favour, up to a limit of 1000 hours. Dorothy wrote to thank the Committee, adding, with characteristic understatement, 'I would really have felt very sad otherwise.'[85]

The Wolfson Professorship was in many respects the perfect appointment for Dorothy. It gave her a comfortable salary with no teaching or administrative responsibilities beyond running her own research group. It gave her a regular sum of money to use as she liked to employ research assistants, clerical and technical help. It gave her the freedom to spend more time with Thomas, wherever his various activities might take him. It made her independent of the normal machinery by which Oxford careers were advanced or stalled. This suited her temperament, disinclined to intrigue or empire-building, although it did have some disadvantages: she risked being left out of the loop when decisions were being made that might affect her. But if Oxford's administrators persisted in regarding her status as 'uncertain', elsewhere it was about to be confirmed with the highest of accolades.

8

'I seem to have spent much more of my life not solving structures than solving them'

The Nobel prize and insulin,
1960–1969

By the middle of the 1950s many of the greatest names in crystallography were prepared to state, both publicly and personally, that Dorothy was the supreme exponent of their art. Despite her legendarily modest demeanour, she was far from indifferent to such tributes, or to the honours and recognition that could be expected to follow. Her Fellowship of the Royal Society made her one of the scientific élite; the Royal Medal confirmed her high standing among her peers. Her solution of the structure of Vitamin B_{12} immediately put her in contention for the ultimate in recognition by the world scientific community, the Nobel prize. Her correspondence with family members shows that Dorothy more or less expected this as her due.

Although Alfred Nobel had originally envisaged that his prize would be awarded for work carried out in the previous year, in practice several years usually elapse between a discovery and its recognition. In 1956, the first year that the selection committee could possibly have noticed Dorothy's work on B_{12}, the prize for Chemistry went to her Head of Department at Oxford Cyril Hinshelwood and his Russian fellow chemist N. N. Semenov, for their work on chemical reactions. Dorothy wrote home about the excitement in the department, and her mother tellingly replied:

Darling
I was most interested in what you told me about the two
scientists who received the Nobel prize, and we all hope
that it will be your turn before long, it was wonderful to
get so near it. Even as far as the photograph![1]

The following year the prize again came very close to Dorothy,
but this time it was harder for her to share in the rejoicing. The
1957 Nobel Prize for Chemistry was awarded, unshared, to Sir
Alexander Todd, for his work on 'nucleotides and nucleotide
coenzymes'. Anyone who knew Dorothy well could guess what
her feelings might be. Ken Trueblood wrote from California:

I was pretty astonished and disappointed to hear Todd had
won the Nobel prize, but since the only citation I saw
mentioned his nucleic acid work (in other terms though) I
presume he didn't get it just for B_{12}. He has certainly done
lots of fine stuff over the years and I certainly know too
little of that work to be able to evaluate it. I just hope you
didn't win it for him. Anyway, there are lots more years,
and I'll not give up hope.[2]

It was only to members of her immediate family that Dorothy
confessed the depth of her disappointment. The award of the
prize had been a possibility that was talked about openly at
home. Elizabeth remembers how in the late 1950s the family
would congregate around the radio each year to hear the prizes
being announced. Thomas reported that eleven-year-old Toby's
reaction to his first plane flight, travelling with his father to
Toronto in September 1957, was that 'he'd like you to win the
Nobel prize, so that we could fly continually!' Thomas's mother,
Dorothy Foster Hodgkin, grasped something of the complexity of
Dorothy's feelings on Todd's triumph, so soon after the death of
her mother, and with her father ailing.

. . . I think I did guess that it was for your Father that you
felt the bitterest part of the disappointment about the NP. I
can understand that it must have been (must still be) a
steeper time even than last year – coming so very near to

you, to this Camb. man; and your Father alone, and
Thomas away from you.[3]

The following year Thomas was away in Canada again, this time
in Montreal. Once again, the prize announcements brought disappointment for Dorothy; once again, the prize for chemistry
came tantalizingly close. Fred Sanger won it for his work on protein sequences, particularly that of insulin. In the same year, 1958,
Boris Pasternak informed the Nobel committee with regret that
he could not accept the prize for literature because of what the
award would be taken to mean 'in the society in which he lived',
a circumstance that only added to the anti-Russian feeling in the
West that so distressed Dorothy. In a letter that was more than
usually revealing of feelings of which she felt a little ashamed, she
wrote to Thomas:

> . . . All these Nobel prize troubles. Lady Hayter . . . gave
> me the news about Boris Pasternak's refusal of the prize
> and was making v. anti Russian remarks which depressed
> me. I found myself wondering whether it would be any use
> writing a little personal letter to Ilya Ehrenberg to try to
> make peace. I might ask Sage when I see him tomorrow . . .
> And Janet was being very comforting over Fred Sanger.
> And I hadn't the heart to tell her that what partly perturbs
> me at present that it's just possible I'm still in the running –
> seeing they haven't done medicine yet. But I think of all
> the other medical triumphs than B_{12} – polio etc. And I
> think it's more likely they do one of the others this year . . .
> I meant not to care. Sanger is so very nice and good,
> absolutely worth a Nobel prize.

In the event the prize for medicine went to the American geneti-
cists George Beadle and Edward Tatum, for work done nearly
twenty years previously showing that genes work by making
enzymes.

Dorothy's hopes were not just wishful thinking. Although the
selection process is supposed to be a closely guarded secret,
inevitably there are leaks. Dorothy knew that Robert Robinson
had nominated her at least twice in the years following the B_{12}

solution; he had enlisted her help in gathering papers to support his nomination. According to Max Perutz she was once even rung up by journalists mistakenly telling her that she had won, perhaps in error for her cousin-by-marriage Alan Hodgkin (who won the prize for physiology in 1963). But as time went by, it began to look as though Dorothy's chance had come and gone.

In January 1960 Lawrence Bragg proposed her along with Perutz and Kendrew for the prize for physics, while suggesting Watson, Crick and Wilkins for chemistry.[4] Two years later his advocacy paid off – for most of his nominees. Watson, Crick and Wilkins won the 1962 prize for medicine, and Kendrew and Perutz won that for chemistry. The prizes were a triumphant vindication of the value of X-ray crystallography in biology – yet there was no place in the line-up for Dorothy.

Perutz himself was keenly conscious of this failure to recognize her. 'I felt embarrassed when I was awarded the Nobel prize before Dorothy, whose great discoveries had been made with such fantastic skill and chemical insight and had preceded my own.'[5] But now, wearing his new Nobel laurels, he was in a position to do something about it. The following summer at the 1963 International Congress of Crystallography in Rome he buttonholed Gunner Hägg, a Swedish crystallographer who was on the Nobel committee, and asked him about Dorothy. Hägg encouraged him to propose her, assuring him that the fact she had been proposed before was no obstacle. So Perutz set about acquiring the necessary support from other laureates. He began, reasonably enough, in Oxford. But although Robinson had actively lobbied for Dorothy in previous years, this time both he and Hinshelwood had already decided to support other candidates. Perutz turned to his own colleagues, Bragg and Kendrew, who were only too pleased to help. 'It was easy to make out a good case for her,' wrote Perutz; and the result was everything he could have wished. Dorothy was announced as the sole winner of the Nobel Prize for Chemistry on 29 October 1964.

The headlines were predictable. 'British woman wins Nobel prize – £18,750 award to mother of three', announced the *Daily Telegraph*. In a feature published later in the year, just after the award ceremony, the *Observer* reported that the 'affable-looking housewife' Mrs Hodgkin had won the prize 'for a thoroughly un-housewifely skill: the structures of crystals of great chemical interest'. (More endearing was the report in the local paper of her childhood home: 'Nobel prize for former Norfolk girl'.) These reports implied that for a woman to have done such a thing was completely exceptional (and therefore not something that other women might seek to emulate). They identified Dorothy first and foremost as a wife and mother, only grudgingly admitting that she was also a university professor and Fellow of the Royal Society. They were entirely at odds with Dorothy's own experience, in which she had never knowingly found her gender or marital status to be an obstacle to acceptance of her worth as a scientist. They serve as a salutary reminder of the prevailing attitudes in the world beyond the small scientific community in which she flourished, and perhaps go some way towards explaining why so few able women scientists of the same generation were able to achieve so much.

The manner in which Dorothy received the news of her prize was in many ways typical of the slightly chaotic Hodgkin lifestyle. The telegram from the Royal Swedish Academy of Sciences arrived at 94 Woodstock Road. But Dorothy was with Thomas in Ghana, where he had been appointed by President Kwame Nkrumah in 1961 as the first Director of the new Institute of African Studies at the University of Ghana. That telegram was followed by many others, offering congratulations. It was left to Dorothy's niece Jill to decide what to do with them. Ever conscious of the need to save money, she put them all in an envelope and sent them to Africa by sea mail. (They arrived about three months later.)

Meanwhile a couple of young reporters from the *Ghana Times* had been despatched to the University to get an interview. They found Thomas first at the Institute, who double-checked that it was not another false alarm, then took them to find Dorothy working quietly in the library of the Chemistry Department. And it was from them that she heard the news even though, as she wrote later, 'they didn't know what the Nobel prize was'. So the first to share in her celebrations were her African friends and colleagues, one of whom was hastily despatched from Legon to Accra to buy wine for the party. A few days later, at a function for the Ghana Academy of Sciences, Nkrumah himself announced that Dorothy had been elected a member of the Academy. 'I'm sure,' she later wrote, 'it was the first they'd heard of it.'[6]

Dorothy's one regret was that Bernal, her great inspiration, did not share the award. Whenever she talked about her achievements she always cited two critical moments in her career in which Bernal had played a key role. One was his success in photographing the first pepsin crystal in 1934, which suggested for the first time that one day it would be possible to solve the structure of proteins using X-ray crystallography; the other was the letter he sent a few months later (see page 111) implying that she could use isomorphous replacement to solve the phase problem in her analysis of insulin. But the terms of the Nobel committee are rather rigidly defined. Scientists are rewarded for discoveries, not for being inspirational. Bernal himself, who the previous year had suffered the first of many strokes that gradually incapacitated him, celebrated Dorothy's award with a laudatory article in the pages of *New Scientist*, in which, whether deliberately or absentmindedly, he somewhat exaggerated his supervision of her successes.

> Her early work was on the sterols, vitamins and antibiotics, largely carried out in my laboratory at Cambridge. She excelled both at extensive studies of a large number of related compounds and at detailed analysis of particular crystals. It was in this way she scored her first public triumph during the war by finding the structure of penicillin.[7]

Given Dorothy's own frequently declared debt to Bernal's support and inspiration throughout her career, she would doubtless forgive him for obscuring the fact that she spent only two years in his lab at Cambridge, and that penicillin was solved more than ten years after she moved back to Oxford. The article prompted Robert Robinson, who was himself inclined to claim Dorothy as his protégée, to hint at his own part in her elevation while acknowledging Bernal's important role.

> My dear Bernal
> I have read your article in 'New Scientist' on Dorothy

Hodgkin and, as one of her sponsors in connection with the award and also as a personal friend, I am extremely grateful to you for this generous estimate of your old pupil. I think it is generally known how much she owes to you.

Doubtless she should have been joined with the earlier recipients of awards in this field and I was terribly afraid that if she did not succeed this year it would be a question of missing the boat. However, everything has worked out well, especially the fact that she receives the full prize for the year.[8]

The Nobel ceremony on 10 December 1964 was a great family event. At the time of the announcement everyone was scattered – Thomas and Dorothy in Ghana, Luke, Anna and their three young children in Algeria where Luke was teaching at the University, Elizabeth teaching in a school in Zambia, while Toby was spending a pre-university year travelling in India. All except Luke and family made it to Stockholm, together with Dorothy's sisters Joan and Elisabeth, and several of Joan's children. Only Martin Luther King, who received the peace prize that year, had a larger entourage. Jean-Paul Sartre had refused the prize for literature, and a Swedish newspaper carried a photograph of him in a Paris café with the caption 'He was not there'. Below a neighbouring photograph of Thomas, resplendent in white tie and tails and fast asleep, the reporter added, 'And neither was he.'

In her Nobel lecture, Dorothy briefly outlined her introduction into the world of crystallography, then gave a lucid, if somewhat technical, account of the work on penicillin and Vitamin B_{12} for which the prize had been awarded. She spoke firmly and clearly, a surprise to Elizabeth because at home she spoke so softly. To her scientific colleagues it was nothing unusual; she had been speaking in public about her work for almost thirty years. But to the family it was a novel experience to see Dorothy in effect giving a performance – at home it was always Thomas who occupied centre stage.

She concluded her lecture with a brief reference to insulin, the structure of which still eluded her and which at that time occupied most of her attention. Her comment shows a humility in the face of science's mysteries that was entirely characteristic, even at the moment of her greatest triumph.

> I should not like to leave an impression that all structural problems can be settled by X-ray analysis or that all crystal structures are easy to solve. I seem to have spent much more of my life not solving structures than solving them.[9]

In addition to her formal lecture, Dorothy was chosen to address the Swedish students who greeted the prizewinners with songs following the banquet the day after the ceremony. She commented on the fact that she had been chosen for this role because being the only woman made her somehow exceptional.

> The situation in which I find myself will, I very much hope, not be so uncommon in the future that it will require any comment or special treatment – as more use is made of the many gifts which women share equally with men.[10]

More than thirty years later, this hope has still not been fulfilled.

The Nobel prize changed Dorothy's life. She soon realized that it gave her the capacity to exercise influence far beyond the world of science. The money was part of this. Apart from using some of it to bring members of her family to the ceremony in Stockholm, she made no extravagant personal use of the prize. Instead she put it in a deposit account, and over the years quietly made donations to causes that seemed worthwhile. These included support for overseas graduate students at Somerville and the newly established Linacre House (later College); funds to start a college nursery at Somerville; £1000 to the International Union of Crystallography to start a prize fund in honour of Paul Ewald, one of the founders of crystallography; another donation in memory of Isidore Fankuchen; and numerous small gifts to individuals in need.

But far more important was the national and international recognition accorded to her as a Nobel laureate, the first (and, at the time of writing, still the only) British woman scientist to be so honoured, and the fifth woman to receive the prize for science in six decades. The only other women to receive the prize for chemistry were Marie Curie in 1911 and her daughter Irène in 1935.

Honours beget further honours. Hardly had Dorothy finished answering the letters and telegrams of congratulation for her Nobel than, on her return from a trip abroad in March 1965, her sister Joan and niece Su met her at the airport with 'a very large, black-rimmed envelope from the Queen'. Dorothy immediately wrote to Thomas.

> I opened this in a blasé, casual way, expecting the DBE
> [Dame Commander of the Order of the British Empire],
> which I would refuse – but the letter offers me an OM,
> rather different really; I remember you once saying that the
> Order of Merit was the only decoration you would accept.
> Churchill's OM, I suppose, very queer.
>   The trouble is, I all the time doubt the judgement that
> places me in this class – better perhaps to have been like
> Sartre and not to have taken on this role – only, I also
> dislike the answer, no. My instinct is to say yes – but please
> send me a telegram if you feel strongly no.[11]

The OM – Order of Merit – is the highest honour any British citizen can receive, awarded for greatness in the arts, sciences, or public life, and is the personal gift of the Queen. There are only twenty-four members at any one time; new members fill dead men's shoes. The expression in this case is almost entirely apt: Dorothy was the first woman to be appointed since Florence Nightingale in 1907. Vacancies had just been created by the deaths of Sir Winston Churchill and the poet T. S. Eliot; their places were offered to Dorothy and the composer Benjamin Britten.

Of course Dorothy accepted the OM. Despite what she says in her letter to Thomas, it is difficult to believe that she would ever have done something as controversial – as frankly discourteous – as to refuse an honour of this nature. As it was, she induced a certain amount of agitation at the Palace by delaying her reply until she had heard back from Thomas. Given her declared dislike of the answer no, one wonders whether in fact, if it had been offered, she would really have refused a DBE. Both Kathleen

Lonsdale and Janet Vaughan were Dames – surely Dorothy would not have embarrassed her friends by rejecting an honour that they had been happy to accept? Certainly it irritated her when, as frequently happened, ignorant correspondents addressed her as Dame Dorothy; she had never liked titles, and it pleased her infinitely more to have the letters OM after her name than the word Dame before it. But to have refused would have been completely out of character. It was either a stroke of fortune, or an astute judgement on the part of someone at the Palace, that she was saved from having to make a decision that would force her to confront her own ambivalence on the subject. When the news became public, it was time for another celebration.

> The news of the OM actually broke as far as we were
> concerned at about 4.30 yesterday when newspaper chaps
> descended on the lab and the telephone started ringing etc . . .
> I collected everyone in the lab . . . and we had a very nice
> impromptu party for about an hour, drinking the
> Carlsberg beer [she had received a crate as a gift] in mugs
> and 2 beakers (luckily I'd never taken it home), talking
> about prizes and decorations and whether they should
> exist and listening happily to the telephone ringing from
> time to time in Tiny's room which we couldn't get into.

She had no problems in accepting the Freedom of Beccles, an honour that the little market town where she spent her school-days hastily invented for her. And she gradually accumulated a formidable list of honorary degrees and academy memberships from around the world. There were other, perhaps less desirable consequences, notably a vast amount of unsolicited mail. Before 1964 Dorothy had received an occasional invitation to appear on programmes such as *Woman's Hour*, or circular asking for her signature on a petition, but most of her postbag concerned scientific matters. A high proportion of the young admirers who wrote from all over the world beseeching her to find a place for them in her lab ended up as valued colleagues. But once she joined the ranks of the Nobelists, the floodgates opened. There are several files in her archive containing nothing but requests for autographs. An even larger number invite her to give prizes at school speech days, or lectures to women's groups, or to undertake other public speaking engagements. These are of course in addition to the invitations for her to give keynote addresses at scientific conferences, or to visit labs in every continent. She accepted the vast majority of these invitations, declining only when she genuinely had another engagement (often on the other side of the world).

It was a punishing schedule, but one which she adopted with surprising vigour. In her mid- to late fifties, Dorothy was no longer the frail, ethereal figure of a decade before. Her eyes still dazzled with their extraordinary brilliance, but in a face that had filled out and softened; the cloud of golden hair had now turned white and wispy, held in place with a tortoiseshell slide. In homespun tweeds, floral print frocks or wool cardigans, she had taken on a sturdy appearance, and the stamina to go with it. David Sayre, returning to England for a visit around this time, remembers that when they went up to London together for a Royal Society meeting she 'walked the legs off' him. An Oxford resident remembers seeing Dorothy parking her bicycle outside Somerville, hands red with cold, looking 'for all the world like a farmer's wife coming in to market'. One thing the Nobel prize certainly did not change was her complete lack of personal vanity. She liked to wear her best dresses on special occasions, but, remembers a colleague, 'She had the same best dresses for twenty years.'

Of necessity, Dorothy's increasingly frequent and prolonged absences meant that she had less time to devote to managing her laboratory in Oxford. Her office, with its huge table piled high with unopened mail, unfiled letters and even uncashed cheques gave the impression of administrative chaos: in fact in the eyes of Tom Blundell, who joined her as a post-doctoral researcher in 1967, she had 'perfected the art of never doing anything administrative'. Yet this impression is not quite fair, and the evidence of the enormous amount of administration she did undertake is there to be seen in her archive. During the 1950s she had little clerical help, and dealt personally with such matters as the extraordinary amount of red tape involved in importing a new type of camera from the United States. Once she became Wolfson Professor she had a secretary, and would begin the day by dictating replies to her correspondence, swiftly and economically; on any contentious issue these were usually models of tact and diplomacy. She was punctilious about making sure that her visiting overseas researchers had somewhere to live, and about providing references for students and colleagues when they moved on. But she had her priorities, and a fine sense of what could be put on one side. What she did not do was make any effort to integrate her laboratory more formally into the University's departmental structure.

Throughout the 1960s she was running a research group of between twelve and fifteen doctoral students, post-docs and senior research workers, plus clerical and technical staff, not one of whom was on the permanent University payroll. Her last Rockefeller grant ended in 1964. The Foundation had funded her research for more than twenty years – five was their usual limit. They stopped funding her only because once she had her Wolfson Chair she stopped asking. From 1960 her grant from the Royal Society paid her own salary and those of a couple of research assistants, technical and clerical staff, but did not cover equipment. She became increasingly dependent for other funds on the Science Research Council (a government funding body, which had taken over the functions of the Department of Scientific and Industrial Research).

Perhaps because her long and cordial relationship with the Rockefeller Foundation had given her such an easy start, she found it hard to understand why other funding bodies required more from her in the way of regular reports, consistency between what she said she wanted the money for and what she spent it on, and deadlines met for grant renewals. That the grants were paid at all owed more to her reputation than to any administrative skill on her part – indeed, some of her younger colleagues remember SRC officers tactfully prompting her to fill in applications, and even slipping them through after the critical meeting to consider applications had been held.

There were frequent muddles about which grant was supposed to pay for which assistants, and the occasional gentle rap on the knuckles from the Royal Society for overspending on her Wolfson account. Correspondence on these matters was an irritating distraction to Dorothy. But she was quick to take the SRC to task for decisions she saw as irrational, unfair or procrastinating. Delays in the payment of grants provoked uncharacteristically acerbic protests about the way her research was being held up. Another source of friction in the later 1960s was over the rate of pay for her most senior post-doctoral researcher, Guy Dodson, who for years was paid less than the going rate for someone of his age. But the anomaly dated from the time of his arrival in the lab, when Dorothy herself had accepted a lower rate because he was 'much younger and generally untried and the country seemed to be hard up'.

Another telling case was that of Tom Blundell. A few months after he joined Dorothy in 1967 he discovered he was the only person in the lab for whom no contributions were being paid into the national pension scheme for university workers. It appeared that Dorothy had failed to obtain a grant for his salary, and so was paying him with money intended for equipment. Diffidently, he tackled Dorothy on this point.

> She looked at me in absolute amazement and said 'Oh Tom, I never had any insurance at your age! You're young and healthy, I shouldn't worry.' And afterwards I discovered that if I had been identified with some sort of insurance it would have been evident that I wasn't a piece of equipment and my salary would not have been forthcoming.[12]

Dorothy was perfectly aware of her own shortcomings in this respect. Before her appointment to the Wolfson Chair, Oxford had briefly considered making her Head of the Department of Inorganic Chemistry. Giggling at the recollection, she later told her colleague Eleanor Dodson, 'I'm sure they realized that the whole thing would have fallen apart in about three weeks if I'd had any responsibility, so it can't have been a serious suggestion.' But she also thought, with some justification, that a tidy desk was irrelevant to good science. 'After all,' she would observe, 'Rutherford's desk was even worse!'

What Dorothy began to think she needed was a deputy, someone with sufficient seniority and scientific calibre to manage her motley crew of students, post-docs and overseas visitors in her many absences. She had long had her eye on David Phillips, who had impressed her as a post-doc when she met him in Canada in 1952. In 1956, through her recommendation, he had returned to Britain to work with Lawrence Bragg at the Royal Institution.

Kathleen Lonsdale had left the RI in 1946 for a Readership and soon afterwards a Chair at University College London, and research work of any kind in the Davy-Faraday Laboratory had been in decline since then. When Bragg took over as Director in 1954, he was keen to restore the lab to the glory days it had seen under his father. One of the first people he had approached, in May 1955, had been Dorothy herself.

> I may be making quite a wild proposal which you will turn down right away . . . If you liked to come and work in the Royal Institution, I believe I could provide you with a centre and facilities which would really give you full scope. This idea has floated through my mind many times in the past, but rather idly because I thought that your husband's work made living in Oxford essential for the Hodgkin family. But I understand he is now more independent of any special base.
>
> I cannot tell you how thrilled I should be if you were working here. We should have one of the very few great X-ray analysts in the world, and the fame it would bring the RI cannot be exaggerated. The attraction to you might be that I could support you with a first-rate workshop, any gear you want, and plenty of room for the young people who would want to work with you. I am sure we should have no difficulty in getting the necessary financial backing if you were here. You would be free of tiresome lecturing and tutoring . . .
>
> I think I am only brave enough to suggest you coming here because I have always felt so strongly that you ought to be given much more scope to get on with your research . . . I should like to tell you what has been happening here, hoping that perhaps you might feel inclined to play the role of leading lady in the new RI I am trying to build![13]

It sounded like an offer she couldn't refuse, and she certainly thought hard about it. Visiting Dorothy a week or two later, Gerard Pomerat of the Rockefeller Foundation recorded her thoughts in his diary.

> Had Bragg made her this offer a year ago she admits that she would have been sorely tempted. She is still giving the matter deep consideration but she is now almost certain that she will stay on here. She has her Readership at last; the family is settled well in a new house on the outskirts of Oxford; none of the children want to live in London; she will be getting nice new labs in a couple of years . . . What she doesn't say too sharply is that she has security here and knowing the husband GRP [the writer] is inclined to suspect that that was a fairly important point.[14]

Dorothy had made amends by recommending two names to Bragg: Jack Dunitz and David Phillips. Both had been working in North America at the time, and she had been keen to see them back in Britain. She had long hoped Dunitz would return to the fold, and had also recently failed in an attempt to lure Phillips to Oxford. He was interested in her invitation, he had told her, but not if it meant being employed as a research assistant on one or other of her grants.

> I am sure that the experience of working in your laboratory in any position would be most valuable but, as you expected, I would much prefer a position with more responsibility and closer ties with the University than the one you have to offer.[15]

Dunitz and Phillips had both gone to the RI. Soon afterwards Dunitz, again with Dorothy's recommendation to speed him on his way, went to the ETH in Zurich where he finally settled, developed a flourishing laboratory, and has remained ever since. Phillips had stayed with Bragg and established his own research group, working in collaboration with John Kendrew on myoglobin, and developing with Uli Arndt the first diffractometers, instruments which made it possible to collect more accurate data by measuring the intensity of reflected X-rays

directly. Dorothy had been an eager visitor to the lab, as excited
as anyone when the first myoglobin structure came out in 1958.

Soon after her appointment to the Wolfson Chair in 1960,
Dorothy renewed her efforts to get Phillips to move to Oxford.
After a visit to her lab in November 1961, he set down in writing
the kind of position he was seeking, were he to move from the RI.

> I would like best to supply or supplement the crystallography
> in a laboratory in which other techniques were also being
> used to study biological molecules and systems . . . I have
> been wondering how readily an expanding group working
> on biological molecules with . . . technical support can be
> accommodated in your present laboratory, and what
> individual responsibility I might have in it.
>
> Secondly I wonder what are the longer term prospects
> for a new laboratory.
>
> Thirdly I wonder what University and College positions
> might be open to me and what teaching might be
> involved.[16]

Dorothy was not immediately able to give him very satisfactory
answers to these questions. Meanwhile John Kendrew added to
Phillips's misgivings about Oxford's readiness to take him on,
and about Dorothy's expectations of his role in Oxford.

> I had a long talk with Dorothy . . . I had the impression that
> this project won't come to a head for quite a while . . . I saw
> Bragg subsequently . . . He mentioned that Dorothy was
> under pressure from her husband to spend 6 months a year
> in Africa; and added that *his* impression was that D. wanted
> you there to run her lab. while she was away! Dorothy
> didn't mention all this to me so I cannot comment . . .[17]

In the meantime Phillips had obtained crystals of another protein,
lysozyme, and had gained Bragg's blessing to go ahead and work
on a solution of its structure. By 1965 he had succeeded. Looking
back, he is frank about his reasons for not taking the new problem
to Dorothy's lab.

> I couldn't have taken it to Oxford to work on it there. If I

was joining Dorothy's group, I should have had to work on Dorothy's problems. And I suppose I may have felt too independent-minded to do that. She was single-mindedly dedicated to solving problems, she needed help, and she expected the same commitment and dedication from the people who came to work with her. At the end they were Dorothy's problems, and it was probably that that gave me pause.[18]

Dorothy did not give up. On her own she knew she could not provide the research environment that Phillips was seeking, one modelled on the newly established MRC Laboratory of Molecular Biology in Cambridge. This was a major initiative in a purpose-built laboratory next to Addenbrooke's Hospital, of which Max Perutz, whose work had been supported by the MRC since 1946, was the first director. There crystallographers worked alongside biochemists and molecular biologists in an integrated approach to understanding biologically important molecules that was to generate a string of Nobel prizes, the most recent in 1997. Oxford had nothing comparable. Dorothy's own group was based wholly on her own research interests, which were rather narrowly focused on the structures themselves. Its very existence was dependent on her presence – it had no formal status as part of the University's structure, squatting for historical reasons like a rather noisy cuckoo in the nest of Chemical Crystallography.

Having always obtained research support from outside sources, Dorothy had never engaged in the power play necessary to establish a permanent footing in the University. Getting anything changed in Oxford takes years of patient lobbying, as proposals wend their way slowly from one committee to another. It was not how Dorothy wanted to spend her time. As long as grants and hard-working assistants continued to flow – and they did – her 'lack of status' in Oxford terms did not bother her. Belatedly, she realized that if something was not done, crystallographic work on large molecules at Oxford would cease on her retirement, not much more than a decade away. Yet crystallography had a vital role to play in the new science of molecular biology that was poised for an explosive expansion.

Although she sat on no committees, Dorothy knew everyone

worth knowing. She enlisted the support first of the Professor of Biochemistry, Sir Hans Krebs, and then of the Professor of Zoology, John Pringle. Both realized that there was a strong case for building up a unit at Oxford with the cross-disciplinary skills necessary to renew the attack on biological systems at the molecular level. They were suitably impressed by David Phillips as a key figure to lead this development. There followed two years or more of hard bargaining. The outcome was that Phillips was offered a personal Chair in Molecular Biophysics at Oxford, a spacious new laboratory, and permanent jobs and College Fellowships for several members of his group from the RI, after Bragg's retirement in 1966.

Having set up all the initial contacts, Dorothy herself took no part in the detailed discussions. Much of the time she was in Africa, or travelling on other business. Lord Phillips (he was knighted in 1979 and raised to the peerage in 1994) recalls that her attitude to any difficulties was to say, 'Oh, why don't you just come, it'll be all right when you get here.' In contrast Krebs and Pringle, with the support of other powerful Oxford figures such as Howard Florey, backing from the MRC and some behind-the-scenes manoeuvring by Bragg, were able to wield sufficient influence to get everything Phillips wanted.

Not only did Dorothy not pull strings on Phillips's behalf, she almost forgot to pull them on her own. She may have started out thinking that Phillips would effectively be her deputy, but that was never his intention. In fact, he says, exactly how their two groups were to be related in Oxford was 'never explicitly discussed'. On at least two occasions hasty adjustments had to be made to the plans when the University authorities discovered that Dorothy had been making assumptions about the move's impact on her group without ever actually voicing them in the discussions. The long-term plan was for Phillips and his new Laboratory of Molecular Biophysics to be housed in the spacious Zoology/Psychology Building due to be completed in 1971. John Pringle, whose own interests in the biophysics of muscle fibres accounted for his enthusiasm for the new group, allocated a generous amount of space for the lab. Until it was ready, Phillips and his group were to move into vacant rooms in a building known as Old Physiology. While Phillips drew up detailed lists of the people, equipment and space he required, Dorothy casually let drop, less than a year before the move was due to take place, her own assumption that the two groups would work alongside one another.

At the end of January 1966 the University Registrar, Sir Folliott Sandford, confessed to Tiny Powell that 'discussions in the last few days about Dr Phillips and Professor Hodgkin have left me rather breathless'. On hearing of her wishes, Pringle left Sandford in no doubt that Dorothy did not form part of his plan to accommodate Molecular Biophysics in his new department.

I note with interest from your letter that Professor Hodgkin wishes to join up with Dr Phillips not only in October 1966 but also in the new building . . . I hope the Building and Development Committee appreciated that this would make it necessary for Professor Hodgkin to be allocated some additional space in the new laboratory; we could not find room for her group in the part at present being planned for Zoology and Molecular Biophysics.This means presumably she would have to occupy some of the space in the north west corner . . . [which] will not be built until Stage II . . .[19]

A series of hastily arranged compromises found Dorothy's group split between three different sites when Phillips arrived in October 1966. Since 1961 some of her X-ray equipment had been housed in a dingy basement lent to her by the Pharmacology Department. A couple of extra rooms in Old Physiology were cleared out for her insulin group, so that they could be near Phillips's team who also worked on large molecules. Meanwhile her own office and those of her group working on smaller molecules stayed behind in Chemical Crystallography with Tiny Powell. When the new Zoology/Psychology Building was ready, she was allocated space in the opposite half of the building from Phillips, which housed the Department of Experimental Psychology. She and her team eventually moved there in 1971, some months later than David Phillips's group.

Despite the fact that Dorothy made no systematic efforts to defend her interests or control events throughout this period (nor did the University authorities think to ask her what she would like to happen), everything worked out tolerably well on both sides. Phillips was not her deputy; he was free to run his own group independently as he wished. Yet she and her colleagues benefited from the fact that he had gained a strong University base for biological crystallography for the first time. Tom Blundell found that Phillips's presence made a big difference.

> He was the person that Dorothy always needed. He was a brilliant scientist, but also a fantastic organizer and I found him personally very helpful as well. David brought the infrastructure in his part of the laboratory that previously was lacking.[20]

The benefits were not all one way; for example, workers from Phillips's group would come to Eleanor Dodson in Dorothy's group for advice on computing problems. The two groups met daily over coffee, and engaged in friendly exchanges of ideas. But they remained separate entities, a point that Phillips has sometimes felt the need to stress.

> I sometimes say to people who think that I worked in Dorothy's lab that she worked in my lab, which is nearer the truth. At no point were we part of her team . . . I saw her as too powerful and influential a figure to collaborate with on equal terms.[21]

Phillips's judgement was almost certainly accurate. Since the solution of B_{12} there was only one mountain left to climb for Dorothy, and that was insulin. Insulin was unfinished business, the protein she had chosen for her own in 1934, and whose solution continued to elude her. She had a powerful sense of time running out: at that time she expected to retire in 1970, when she reached her sixtieth birthday. The need to care for Thomas in his increasingly precarious state of health, not to mention his mother who was in her eighties, and to meet all the obligations that came with her status as a Nobel laureate, meant that she herself could play only a small part in the laboratory work. She was anxious to keep up the momentum. Perutz, Kendrew and later Phillips had shown that protein structures could be solved. For insulin, it must only be a matter of time and effort.

But insulin was not an easy target. Although a much smaller molecule than haemoglobin, with a molecular weight of 6000 compared to 67,000, it presented peculiar difficulties. The most promising crystals were in the form known as rhombohedral, in the shape of flattened cubes. Sanger's work on the insulin sequence showed that the 'molecule' Dorothy described in her first paper in 1935 was actually six molecules: the unit cell of rhombohedral insulin contains three pairs of molecules around a central axis. This unit cell has three-fold symmetry, meaning that the contents of the cell can be rotated by 120 degrees to generate an identical structure. Most protein crystals have two-fold rotational symmetry. Where there is two-fold symmetry, the phases of a subset of the data can only take two possible values, differing by 180 degrees. There is therefore no need to give the phase angles exact values; they can simply be described as plus or minus. These special properties greatly simplify the effort to locate heavy atoms in the crystal, and to analyse their contribution to the reflections. But insulin offered no such short-cuts to a solution.

The first task, itself not an easy one, was to find good heavy atom derivatives. One of the first whom Dorothy enlisted to renew the attack on insulin was Marjorie Aitken (now Marjorie Harding, recently retired as lecturer at the University of Liverpool), who came to Somerville to study chemistry in 1953. Through her tutorials – again interspersed with those famous long silences – she caught Dorothy's enthusiasm for structure, and stayed with her for Part II. In 1957 Dorothy took her on as a DPhil student, although Harding recalls that it was a near thing.

> I can remember a crisis day in February when Dorothy suddenly started ringing up somebody in the administration and saying, 'What's the last day for DSIR grants to go in, because this one should have been in?' She realized the deadline had passed – I hadn't even realized the deadline was approaching.[22]

Fortunately all was well. Aitken began by joining in the work on gramicidin S, still unsolved and still under investigation in

Dorothy's lab. She worked alongside Beryl Rimmer (née Oughton), who had assisted Dorothy for almost ten years on a variety of problems. But after a few months Dorothy switched both of them to insulin. In 1956 a Danish chemist called Jorgen Schlichtkrull, who worked for the pharmaceutical company Novo Terapeutisk in Copenhagen, succeeded in producing very pure samples of pig insulin, which produced perfect rhombohedral crystals, eventually up to a millimetre in size. Schlichtkrull himself had a personal, bitter battle with diabetes: his own daughter was a brittle diabetic, suffering from a particularly dangerous form of the illness in which the sufferer's response to insulin is unpredictable. The aim of his work was to improve the quality of the insulin used for treating diabetics: the benefits to crystallographers were incidental. But Schlichtkrull appreciated the efforts Dorothy and her team were making and was generous with his crystals which, weight for weight, were worth more than gold.

He found that he could produce insulin with a minimum of either two or four zinc atoms per six-molecule unit. This discovery was hugely important to Dorothy. If there were only two zinc atoms in a unit cell with three-fold symmetry, they must themselves be positioned along the central three-fold axis; zinc anywhere else in the unit would have to come in multiples of three. Schlichtkrull gave her a small quantity of both forms in 1957, and from then on he supplied all the insulin she used in her quest for the structure. Marjorie Aitken had the job of growing crystals according to his recipes, then taking a complete set of X-ray photographs with the laboratory's new precession camera. This instrument, designed by Martin Buerger at MIT in the United States, took much of the slog out of indexing reflections by moving the camera so that the reflections appeared in a very simple lattice, rather than the distorted one generated by a Weissenberg camera.

Aitken's photographs provided the first new set of insulin data obtained in Dorothy's lab since she and Dennis Riley had worked on wet insulin crystals almost twenty years before. She also carried out some experiments to try to get heavy atoms into the crystals, soaking them in a variety of solutions, and succeeded in obtaining one or two derivatives that seemed quite promising. It was an optimistic time, as Harding remembers.

Insulin looked good in that it was a small molecule. The
other favourable thing was that Sanger had got the
sequence. There was a lot of work going on in Cambridge
with heavy atom derivatives of other proteins, so there
was plenty of precedent or encouragement to try to take
that forward, even though there was no obvious reason for
a beginner to see that she could get right through to the
end. I suppose I just didn't know how difficult it might
be.[23]

At first sight the new photographs looked very promising. In
particular they appeared to show slight differences in intensity
between symmetrically placed pairs of reflections, known as
anomalous scattering effects, that sometimes arise in molecules
with heavy atoms. A decade or so before the Dutch crystallographer, J. M. Bijvoet, had shown how these effects could be used to
fix the absolute configuration of atoms in a molecule. Previously,
as in the case of penicillin, it was not possible to distinguish
between one possible configuration and its mirror image. More
importantly, anomalous scattering also provided a way round
the ever-present phase problem. Dorothy had seen the technique
at work in a follow-up study on Vitamin B_{12} carried out by a
Dutch colleague, Aafje Vos. Because of insulin's symmetry problems, she realized that anomalous scattering could provide her
best hope of arriving at some trial phases to put into electron
density calculations.

But anomalous scattering was useful only if you also knew the
positions of the heavy atoms. Try as they might, Harding and
Dorothy could not interpret their Patterson maps to find these
positions. One of the problems that hindered Harding's progress
was that neither she nor Dorothy had fully understood the role of
salt, specifically the chloride ions, in forming the two types of
insulin crystal. If salt concentrations were too high, then the 4-
zinc form would be produced. This led to a lot of 'messing about',
as Harding puts it, as they tried to compare maps drawn from
2-zinc insulin data with those of heavy atom derivatives that,
unbeknownst to them, had switched to the 4-zinc form. But even
without these setbacks, hindsight seems to suggest that the technology simply had not developed far enough to make a solution

of insulin possible. 'What we really needed,' says Harding, 'was a much better derivative and much better data collection.'

Dorothy seemed unperturbed by her student's apparent lack of progress on her DPhil thesis.

> When I offered her chapters, she came back with helpful
> comments, but she never pushed me to get on with it . . .
> She would drift into the research rooms and say 'How are
> things?' and look round to see what people were doing,
> and from time to time take away pictures and have a think
> about them herself.[24]

So Harding, desperate for something concrete to put in her thesis, turned to a smaller molecule in which an organic compound combined with zinc, and had the satisfaction of producing a result at last. She also occupied herself learning to program the new Mercury computer that Oxford University finally acquired in 1959, a development in which Dorothy played a key role. Although Dorothy herself never, to anyone's knowledge, wrote a computer program in her life, she immediately understood how important computing would be to crystallographers. At every stage in the development of crystallographic computing, she had research assistants working alongside programmers and learning how to use the latest machines: Barbara Low with George Hey on penicillin; June Broomhead with Ray Pepinsky, and later Jenny Glusker with Ken Trueblood on Vitamin B_{12}.

In 1955 Dorothy welcomed John Rollett, who had developed a reputation as a computer whizz kid while working at Cal Tech as a post-doctoral researcher, into her group. He spent the first few years developing programs for crystallographic work to run on the DEUCE computer at the National Physical Laboratory, work which benefited the entire British crystallographic community. Durward Cruickshank, his lifelong friend and another computer pioneer who carried out analyses of wet B_{12} data for Dorothy on the Manchester computer, thinks his role has been underestimated.

> The programmes he produced were so good that many of
> the users in this country and abroad had no real idea of
> what John had done for them. A few users (including

Dorothy) certainly had that appreciation, but I do believe
that his name ought to have appeared as co-author on
many papers reporting crystal structure determinations.[25]

Rollett later moved to Oxford's new Computing Laboratory,
where he was instrumental in persuading crystallographers at
other institutions to standardize the way they prepared their
data for analysis, so that the same programs could be run on a
range of different computers. Dorothy played no direct role in
this, but by bringing Rollett back to Oxford she indirectly gave
impetus to his contributions. She was also an early source of
inspiration to Rollett: her lab at Oxford had been his first choice
for doctoral research back in 1949, but at that point she had no
openings and he went instead to her old friend Gordon Cox in
Leeds.

By the beginning of the 1960s the general availability of computers was making it possible to experiment with new ways of
looking at the data, as well as to cope with unwieldy amounts of
calculation. It was more or less essential that every crystallography lab included someone who was at home with computers.
After Rollett moved to the Computing Laboratory, Dorothy did
nothing about replacing him – he was, after all, only just down
the road, and Beryl Rimmer and Marjorie Harding had proved
adept at acquiring the new skill. When she did recruit a new
computer specialist, it was completely by accident. In 1961 a
young Australian, Eleanor Coller (now Eleanor Dodson), arrived
in Oxford with her husband, who had a post-doctoral position.
She wanted a job, any job; but with her arts degree in maths and
English, she was turned down as overqualified for the menial
jobs for which she applied. Hearing that Dorothy needed a new
technician, she went to see her and was given the job on the spot.

Dorothy was a very good draughtswoman, as was her
previous technician. I was supposed to take this girl's
place. After my first attempt Dorothy said 'Well, perhaps
you'd better do something else for us, dear.' The fact that
she appointed me was typical in a lot of ways of how other
parts of her life were run. I just walked off the street, there
had been no advertisement placed. I was the apple that

had just fallen off the tree, and it was simpler to take that apple than to try and climb the tree to get a better one.[26]

Dorothy soon discovered that even if Coller could not draw to save her life, she was a very able mathematician, and a more than competent programmer. Perhaps not even consciously, Dorothy's approach to running a laboratory was to let everyone develop his or her own strengths, and become the local 'expert' in a particular field. Coller became the computing expert. What she needed to know about crystallography, she learned from books.

> Although the mathematics was not difficult, it was complicated and messy and made more complicated by the restrictions on facilities that we had at the time. You had terribly limited [computer] memory in those days. There were 480 words on which you could do calculations, so you were taking the data, which for insulin even then was about 8000 observations, and you were moving them in and out of storage. And this is book-keeping, it's not technically interesting, and I'm sure Dorothy had no interest whatever in how I managed to shuffle the data in and out of the memory banks.[27]

But Eleanor Coller did not stop at book-keeping. She and Marjorie Harding became caught up in a new mathematical approach to insulin that originated in Cambridge. Perhaps because of its history of association with W. L. Bragg and its origins in a Physics Department, Perutz's lab at Cambridge tended to attract more of those who were interested in the theory of the subject than did Dorothy's at Oxford. But the close friendship between Dorothy and Perutz ensured that ideas were always freely exchanged. As the new decade opened two young Cambridge researchers, Michael Rossman and David Blow, were working on an idea that seemed particularly relevant to insulin, and Perutz suggested that they discuss it with the Oxford group. For Harding and especially for Coller, it was a welcome break from the drudgery of feeding the computer.

> We used to spend an enormous amount of time arguing.

We would go over and argue all day in their office. Michael once sent a postcard saying 'I think I've made an even number of mistakes today, so maybe this result is going to be correct.' Both Michael and I were equation people, we thought in equations.[28]

What Rossman and Blow had developed were mathematical methods of analysing the data from an X-ray photograph to show up relationships between closely similar sub-units in any crystal. Insulin was an ideal test case, with its six sub-units arranged in pairs around the three-fold axis. Rossman and Blow's methods, called rotation and translation functions, predicted that the members of each pair would be related to each other by an approximate two-fold axis, at right angles to the three-fold axis. David Blow, recently retired from Imperial College, London, still remembers how Dorothy reacted to the discovery.

Eleanor and Marjorie were extremely interested in this, and we all got together and thought a lot about it and worked some things out. We showed Dorothy the evidence we had for this two-fold axis, and what it meant was that the Patterson function would have certain features. Dorothy had of course the three-dimensional Patterson of insulin ready to hand, and we explained to her what we felt we had seen about this by calculation. And Dorothy turned through the pages of the Patterson and it was clear that what was happening was that she was bringing the whole three-dimensional form of the Patterson into her head. She turned through ten or twenty pages of these contour maps, and she said 'Yes, I can see it!'

That was the time when I directly saw one aspect of the amazing technical insight that she had. She was not a theoretician, but she understood theories when people explained them to her, and she had this wonderful three-dimensional mind and memory which could actually analyse what people said, and that was really impressive.[29]

Eleanor Coller was equally impressed, knowing as she did what those maps meant to Dorothy.

She had calculated these by hand when Luke was born,
she knew where every little ripple was, she was familiar
with the information content of her data. I think that's
something that's been lost with more automation and more
computing, that sort of intimate knowledge of what your
observations are telling you.[30]

The work done by Rossman, Blow, Harding and Coller has
become embedded in the methods used by crystallographers
right up to the present day. But it did not immediately lead to a
solution of the insulin structure. For Harding, the satisfaction of
working on these new methods was tinged with disappointment.
First, she was having to leave Oxford because her husband's job
was taking him to Edinburgh. She immediately obtained a job in
Arnold Beevers's department there, but computing facilities were
'primitive'. (Oddly enough Beevers, who with Henry Lipson had
developed the very first calculating aid for crystallographers,
'never really caught on to electronic computing', to use Harding's
words.) Second, she was leaving Oxford with very little published work to show for the years of thoughtful, creative and
technically accomplished research she had done there. She was
not the first to find Dorothy difficult to persuade that a paper that
did not contain a structure solution was worth publishing.

I tried to write up some of the rotation function stuff and
some of the early stuff, and I did get frustrated then – I
don't know whether Dorothy didn't want them written up,
I think she was just probably preoccupied with some other
problem – but whenever I went down with these papers I
got nowhere.[31]

Not until 1966 did Dorothy put her name to a couple of papers,
one covering the work Harding had done for her doctorate before
1960, and one on the two-fold axis. As far as the published record
is concerned, these two papers ended a long silence on insulin:
the previous paper was her note to *Nature* in 1939, co-authored by
Dennis Riley, in which she reported the first measurements on
wet insulin crystals.[32]

By the time these papers came out, the research had moved

into a new phase. Marjorie Harding's place in the laboratory had been taken by Guy Dodson, who had just completed a PhD in New Zealand.

> Towards the end of my thesis I came across the B_{12} papers which I read with astonishment. They're absolutely wonderful papers, clear, tremendously easy to follow, simple ideas, clearly written, with astonishing results . . . My supervisor eventually got fed up with me going on about it and saying, 'Why aren't we doing things like this?' and he said, 'If you think so much of the bloody woman why don't you write to her?' So I did. And the letter arrived the day Marjorie Harding said she was leaving.

Dodson became another apple that fell off the tree. He is not aware that Dorothy took up any references before accepting him into her laboratory, funded by the tail-end of her Rockefeller grant. However, she was the external examiner for his thesis. When he arrived in her office one cold, dark day in January 1962, there it was sitting on her desk. The sight amazed Dodson, but what amazed him more was how this legendary figure, whom he had revered from the other side of the world, seemed to disregard the difference between her status and his.

> She did two things: she stopped me calling her Professor Hodgkin and said, 'You must call me Dorothy – we in this laboratory follow the American custom of using first names.' Which I immediately found very easy to do. Then she took me round the lab 'to see what I wanted to work on'. I still don't understand why she did this; we had agreed that I wanted to work on insulin. She took me round all the labs to see what they were doing, when we got back to her room she said, 'What do you want to do?' And I said, 'I want to work on insulin,' and she said 'Fine.' If I'd said, 'B_{12}', she probably would have said, 'Fine.'[33]

Dodson brought some much-needed optimism into the insulin work, but as he himself admits, it was optimism based on ignorance of the difficulties. Marjorie Harding, as she worked out her last few months in the laboratory, let him know that she did not think the solution would ever come out. The methods existed, but with the equipment then available, the data were simply not good enough to see the tiny changes in intensity that would provide information about the phases of the reflections. Patterson map after Patterson map proved to be uninterpretable. At the time Dodson arrived the problem about the two different forms of insulin – 2-zinc and 4-zinc – had been sorted out, and the attack was starting again with just the 2-zinc form. But the problem Dodson faced of obtaining good heavy atom derivatives seemed worse than ever.

> The crystals were stinkers, they were complex crystals by any standards, and chemically they were very unreactive. In most other proteins there were ways of getting heavy atoms in, but not with insulin. Everything was soggy, nothing worked, or if it worked, it worked too well, so that instead of one site you'd have dozens. We spent years soaking it in all sorts of reagents and getting either no changes or huge changes, losing isomorphism, or the crystal would just crumple completely.[34]

Dodson, with Eleanor Coller and later Margaret Adams who came as a DPhil student having read chemistry at Somerville with Marjorie Harding as her tutor, struggled on for two years or more without getting anywhere at all. It was disheartening, and in almost any other laboratory it might have led the most competent researcher to give up the struggle. But somehow, says Dodson, Dorothy kept them going.

> The question was how long would we wait. And this is where Dorothy gets great marks, because she somehow generated enormous confidence that it was going to come out. Sure, it wasn't going to be next year or the year after, but it would come out. The whole way we looked at the structures and the maps, all of which were failures, was with the feeling that sooner or later things would come right – she was just unfailingly optimistic. That was of course typical of Max Perutz as well. He told me that Dorothy really encouraged him to keep going through

some very black moments. I don't know of anyone who encouraged Dorothy. She was disappointed, but she was never down. I think that was not unique to Dorothy, but it was so pervasive and undemonstrative, confidence and optimism was picked up by everyone.[35]

The other advantage was that for those who worked there, Dorothy's lab was such a congenial place to be. It was the 1960s, most of the group were very young, up to half were visitors from overseas, and all were prepared to venture strong opinions in debate on almost any topic. They formed close and lasting friendships: Guy Dodson and Eleanor Coller married in 1965. A casual visitor to the lab might gain the impression of a chaotic scene, papers piled everywhere, passionate arguments going on about something completely unrelated to research, on one occasion a baby (the Dodsons' first) suspended from a doorway in a baby bouncer. Teatime gatherings at the end of the corridor (at this point they were still in Chemical Crystallography) were an important part of the day, and if it was anyone's birthday he or she would bring in a cake to share. When she was there, Dorothy would drift vaguely through the chaos, with a quiet word here and there, humming old hymn tunes to herself. Margaret Adams remembers that, at a particularly bleak point in her research, she 'realized that what Dorothy was humming was "Through the night of doubt and sorrow" – and that was actually quite supportive!'[36]

Tom Blundell arrived in Chemical Crystallography in 1964 as one of Tiny Powell's Part II students. He had spent most of his undergraduate career as a political activist, conducting anti-racism campaigns and playing in jazz bands. But even he was unprepared for the informality of the Hodgkin laboratory.

The first thing you saw on entering the laboratory was Guy Dodson and a number of others playing cricket down the corridor [they used a rolled up electron density map as a bat and crumpled paper as a ball] . . . My main impression of the laboratory at that time was of total disorganization. The first thing I ended up doing, much to my surprise, was joining together with Ted Maslen who was a senior visitor from Australia and getting some seminars going where everybody gave a presentation. Nothing like that was in existence, there was no regular infrastructure or organization.[37]

Nominally in charge of this chaos was Tiny Powell, promoted to Professor of Crystallography in 1964 and still Head of Department. (Ironically Dorothy, whom he had beaten to the Readership back in 1944, had latterly sat on the committee that reviewed his appointment every seven years.) But he had long since given up trying to control what went on in Dorothy's group, and, as Guy Dodson gradually came to realize from incidents that occurred, the relationship between them remained as awkward as ever.

> He had to carry the can for some keys to the Museum being lost. And he asked Dorothy if she had the key and she couldn't find it. And a long time later she found this key, and she said to me, 'Let's go the short way, I've got a key.' And she was just unlocking the door and Tiny walked by and she said, 'God – I told him I'd lost this key and now look what he's seen.' And they didn't discuss it. There were lots of unspoken accusations between them, more on Tiny's side than Dorothy's. She was always apologizing to herself for making Tiny's life difficult, which she did . . . There was that pattern of Dorothy going entirely her own way, using her own judgement, and Tiny being dragged along like Pooh Bear, bump, bump, bump.[38]

In Tom Blundell's view, it wasn't so much that Powell had a bad relationship with Dorothy, it was that no relationship existed. Powell kept to his own daily rhythm, ignoring as best he could the mayhem that surrounded Dorothy. He would shut himself in his office all morning, appear in his lab for about half an hour and then go to lunch with his friends in the all-male back bar of the King's Arms. Of course, he and Dorothy were always civil to one another in public. But Keith Prout, who joined the Department as lecturer after Dorothy was appointed to the Wolfson Chair, once heard Powell describe Dorothy as 'the most bloody unbusinesslike woman I've ever had the misfortune to meet'. Dorothy, for her part, confessed to Guy Dodson that 'Tiny was a source of trial to her and she was an even bigger source of trial to him.' Yet despite their differences they had a genuine respect for each other's work. When Dorothy's Nobel award was announced, Powell rushed down the corridor in the laboratory opening all the doors and shouting, 'Dorothy's won the Nobel prize!' Even though she was not there, he organized a celebration in Chemical Crystallography so that they could all toast her success.

Within the laboratory, Dorothy's management style was unlike anything her colleagues had previously experienced. She never told anyone what to do, but would ask questions such as 'Don't you think it might be interesting to try such and such?', or 'Wouldn't it be nice if you could do so and so?' For some visiting researchers, it was several months before they realized that these hints were the nearest Dorothy would come to an order, and that they had better get on with following up the suggestion. When junior workers diffidently suggested their own ideas, she was never less than encouraging; if she wanted tactfully to steer them away from a dead end, she would say, 'I don't know, but I think you might find . . .' Often she would make a comment that showed she had been thinking all along about an idea someone had suggested long before, which at the time it seemed she had barely noticed. This apparently casual approach got results; most people who have been through Dorothy's lab claim to have worked harder and more effectively there than at any other time.

And although even the insulin researchers themselves may not have realized it in the exuberant days of the 1960s, they were making progress. The first step forward came when two visiting Swedish chemists from the Uppsala University, Bror Strandberg and B. Tilånder, told Dorothy of a discovery they had made. They had found that you could strip zinc out of crystals by soaking them in a substance called EDTA, and then replace it with other metals. Immediately Margaret Adams and Guy Dodson got to work to try this out on insulin. Crystals of 4-zinc insulin just fell apart; but a tiny fragment of a 2-zinc insulin crystal kept its structure even after the zinc had been removed.

The next step was to put in another metal. Adams and Dodson soaked the zinc-free crystals in solutions that contained lead, and did the same with cadmium. For the first time they had derivatives that looked really promising. 'We knew then that it was solved,' says Guy Dodson.

> We'd got the lead in, we had cadmium, we had the zinc-
> free series, so between those three series we ought to have
> been able to solve it. Nowadays it would have been a
> doddle. But the data weren't good enough because the
> equipment wasn't good enough, even though it was the
> best there was at the time. Out of that we got our first
> map – we saw a feature like a helix and where the
> histidines were. But the maps were messy, we couldn't go
> any further.[39]

It was not until Tom Blundell, who was a gifted organic chemist, began to experiment with uranyl derivatives that some of the problems were solved. The two uranyl derivatives helped to establish where the lead was in the zinc-free insulin – it did not simply replace the zinc – and now there was a series that really could provide the answer, if only the data were good enough. The machine they were using at the time to collect the data was a linear diffractometer, developed by David Phillips and Uli Arndt in the late 1950s. This device dispensed with photographic film and measured the intensity of the reflections directly, recording the results on to punched tape that could then be fed into a computer. It measured blocks of data automatically, but had to be adjusted manually to move from one block to another. During the 1960s Phillips and Arndt developed new diffractometers, which made all the adjustments automatically and fed the results directly into a computer. When properly adjusted, these instruments worked with an accuracy beyond anything Dorothy and her team had been able to achieve before.

In 1965 she approached the Science Research Council for the funds for an automatic diffractometer, which would cost about £50,000. She was told, rather curtly, that Tiny Powell had also applied for one, and that perhaps they might like to make a joint application. Whether or not she had known of Tiny's application – she may not have done, given the nature of their relationship – her reply showed her impatience with this parsimonious approach.

I should be very happy myself to share part of another
diffractometer if we could have one in the laboratory with
Dr Keith Prout, or with Professor Powell, but the fact is,
the department could very easily take up space on several
diffractometers.[40]

She decided to wait a year, because an even better model, called
the 'four-circle' diffractometer, was likely to be available then
from the manufacturers Hilger and Watt. She renewed her application in 1966, but it took more than a year, until September 1967,
before the SRC eventually indicated that they would give her the
funds to buy the new machine. It did not finally arrive in her
laboratory until early the following year.

The four-circle diffractometer arrived just as the work on
insulin was entering its final phase. By this time the insulin group
was settled alongside David Phillips's Laboratory of Molecular
Biophysics in its temporary home in Old Physiology. Tom
Blundell recalls that the atmosphere was just the same as it had
been in Chemical Crystallography.

I can remember David looking into our room which was
absolutely strewn with papers, with Guy and Eleanor and
myself usually in full, excited conversation about
something or the other, not always to do with
crystallography. And I could see on David's face the
thought that there was really very little chance that anyone
in this room would ever solve the insulin structure.[41]

Another visitor, Ted Baker from Auckland University in New
Zealand, was given the job of setting up the new diffractometer
when it arrived. He was soon joined by M. Vijayan, a post-
doctoral researcher from the Indian Institute of Science in
Bangalore. Vijayan was the latest in a line of Indian researchers
who had spent time in Dorothy's lab, all of whom had greatly
impressed her (see Chapter 9). He had another factor in his
favour: Dodson encouraged Dorothy to take him on because
his name meant 'Victory' in Sanskrit. Vijayan joined in the task
of collecting yet another set of data on five different heavy atom
derivatives, a total of 60,000 reflections. With the new machine,

they could collect data faster and more accurately than ever before. For once, says Guy Dodson, the end really seemed to be in sight.

> We worked extremely well as a team. We spent a year with Vijayan collecting the data, Tom doing the chemistry and soaking, me doing photographs, a bit of soaking and some data collection, Eleanor doing most of the computing and the refinement calculations. They were very happy days . . . Dorothy was a pretty invasive observer. She would come and look at the maps, and talk and encourage, and disappear. We had some very subtle Pattersons, we all worked like dogs on them. It was actually one of the more testing times, because these maps were affected by the extent of the data and the quality of the data, but they were all right, though we had all sorts of reasons to be worried about them. And sorting those Pattersons out, with Dorothy going through the arguments, it was bloody marvellous.[42]

And that was all it took: 'It was just a question of accuracy and precision,' says Dodson. Once more the team put into effect all they had learned about the combined effects of anomalous scattering and isomorphous heavy atom derivatives on variations in intensity, in the hope that the next electron density map would at last be interpretable.

Dorothy became increasingly convinced that they would have a result, or at least something interesting to say, by the time of the International Congress of Crystallography in August 1969. Not wanting to break up the team, she urged Vijayan to stay a year longer than he had originally intended. But there was a problem. Vijayan had promised another young crystallographer, Kalyani, that he would return to India and marry her. Not sure how to explain such a personal matter to Dorothy, he eventually consulted Guy, Eleanor and Tom, who had noticed that he was not his usual ebullient self. They immediately told him to tell Dorothy the whole story. Her instant response was to create a part-time job for Kalyani in the lab and set about finding her a Fellowship so that she could come to

England. To everyone's disappointment Kalyani failed to get one of the prestigious 1851 scholarships, for no other reason than that the Indian authorities did not submit their list until after the deadline. But Dorothy managed to make some other arrangement.

> Kalyani came about 10 July . . . Insulin was absolutely in top gear, so Dorothy said, 'You can get married over the weekend and come back to work on Monday'. Which we did. We were married on Saturday, 14 July, and the marriage was registered in St Giles. The next day we had a party – the summer that year was extraordinarily beautiful, and Dorothy, Guy and Eleanor and the rest of the group were just like a family to us. Then both of us were back in the lab, Kalyani started helping us by drawing some of the insulin maps.[43]

Kalyani soon joined the group working on smaller molecules, and solved the structure of another antibiotic, cephalo sporin, using direct methods. By the end of July there was a new electron density map of insulin. Although it was not as clear as some ('the penultimate map, I think', had been David Phillips's comment) it was possible to trace the insulin structure through it. When Dorothy came in one day and saw the map, drawn up on perspex sheets and stacked into three dimensions by Guy Dodson and Vijayan, she was in the seventh heaven.

> I used to say that the evening I developed the first X-ray photograph I took of insulin in 1935 was the most exciting moment of my life. But the Saturday afternoon in late July 1969, when we realized that the insulin electron density map was interpretable, runs that moment very close.[44]

At the centre of the map they could see the zinc atoms. But now, attached to the zinc, they could make out each of three amino acids, histidines, and stretching away from them more areas of density in the form of the alpha-helix described by Linus Pauling. With the electron density map on one hand, and Fred Sanger's amino acid sequence on the other, they could begin to build a plastic model of the insulin molecule, plugging the chains of amino acids together with steel wires to support them in three dimensions. In one extraordinary weekend, remembers Guy Dodson, the insulin structure was born.

> Dorothy, Vijayan and I just worked our way through it – it took us about two days. Dorothy worked so hard; her feet swelled so much she had to take her shoes off. She was in great pain, but every time we got another residue she would look at the map and say, 'The next one's a proline,' for example. Everything was working, we were just building up the sequence as we went.[45]

When the drive to finish something, to get it right, took hold of Dorothy, everyone and everything, in the words of Eleanor Dodson, 'became a bit shadowy'. Full of excitement, humming as she worked, she was entirely preoccupied by the insulin molecule. On this occasion her much-loved sister Diana, visiting from Canada, had to wait for two days before Dorothy spent any time with her. By then, the model was complete. Then it was time to share their excitement with others. Marjorie Harding was enormously touched to receive a call. Dorothy had taken her departure rather hard, and, as Harding put it, 'a curtain had come down' between them. But she found that all her early efforts, so demoralizing at the time, were not forgotten. When her husband picked up the phone, there was Dorothy, almost squeaking in her excitement, saying, 'Alan! Insulin is out!' Max Perutz received a call from Guy, inviting him to come over and celebrate. Pausing only to pin a handwritten notice on the board at the LMB – 'Late night news from Oxford – INSULIN IS SOLVED', he grabbed a magnum of champagne someone had given him belatedly to celebrate his Nobel prize and hurried over. 'But when we extracted the cork, all the CO_2 had evaporated and it tasted, as David Phillips remarked in his usual tactful way, just a little peculiar.[46]

The next step was to announce the result officially to the wider world, and for this the timing could not have been better. The Eighth International Congress of Crystallography was due to be held in August that year, at the State University of New York at

Stony Brook on Long Island. Dorothy, naturally, was planning to be there. Blundell was already in the US. He had been chosen to give a talk at the Congress some months earlier, when a preliminary map showed the overall shape and symmetry of the molecule. He had booked three weeks holiday in the US beforehand, and so missed the final days of the complete structure solution. But he was the first to give a preliminary talk on the structure, mainly concentrating on the earlier, low-resolution map, at a conference in Buffalo a week before the International Congress. Dorothy reached the United States in time for that, still effervescent with excitement as she wrote to Thomas.

> The most exciting thing was Guy's coming – I had just sent off a telegram to you and to him on Thursday morning, explained to other people about his not coming, taken my place in the front row for the opening ceremony – looked across the audience and there was Guy, sitting beside Siv [Ramaseshan], grinning – and I started laughing so much it quite disturbed the organization. Apparently after I'd rung him he began to hesitate and Eleanor said, 'Do go.' So he took the train to London, got a visa at the US Embassy in half an hour and caught a 6 p.m. plane, arriving here by 10.30 p.m. – our time! It's very nice having him here and I hope he now thinks it worthwhile . . .

It turned out that one of the plenary lectures to the International Congress, on the chemistry of moon rock recovered from one of the Apollo missions, had to be cancelled because the rock had not been subjected to the necessary biological safety precautions. The day before it was due to take place, Dorothy was offered the vacant slot, in a vast lecture hall seating 3000 people. She accepted – and then suggested to Blundell, the most junior member of the team, that he might like to give the lecture. It was a gesture of generosity, made partly to compensate Blundell for the fact that he had missed out on the euphoric excitement that accompanied the final days of the solution. And he accepted the challenge.

> I got all of the facilities of Stony Brook and Brookhaven

and made some large lantern slides and did some drawings and ended up with four different kinds of visual aid. Dorothy got up on the platform and said how she'd started working on [insulin] in the 1930s, and how none of those who had worked on the solution were born at the time she started. At that point she handed over to me and I was left with this huge audience. It was really quite a nice experience. I arranged all the slides across this huge white wall across the back of the auditorium. Dorothy always used to hum when she was happy. To my shame I can't remember what it was she was humming, but I wrote the music on one overlay. So I was able to show on one of these pictures the experimental data, on another the interpretation, and Dorothy played a major role in that, and on another the music she was humming. And almost the only thing she said to me after this lecture, which was quite an ordeal for somebody in his twenties with a huge audience and no preparation, was that she really didn't know she hummed that tune.[47]

After this *tour de force* it was Guy Dodson's turn; invited by John Kendrew, he travelled on almost immediately to the International Congress of Physics and Biophysics to present the same results. By this time *Nature* was practically begging for a paper for its centenary issue, only a few weeks away. Dorothy and Dodson quickly wrote up the work for publication; it came out in September.[48] (Unfortunately, as they realized too late, in their haste they had put one of the amino acids in the wrong place.) The list of authors included all the principal researchers who had worked on the project from Beryl Rimmer onwards, ten names altogether. The acknowledgements began with the sentence 'Our research on insulin has continued for so long that the line we draw between authors and those who contributed to our solution is necessarily arbitrary . . .' They went on to list another twenty-three people, beginning with Käthe Schiff who had worked on insulin in 1941–2. One of those thanked, Siv Ramaseshan, observed on seeing the paper that 'any one who has sneezed or coughed near the insulin programme has been given an authorship or profuse thanks'.[49]

It was typical of Dorothy to want to share the credit for the solution in this way. She wrote at length to Walter Sullivan of the *New York Times*, taking him to task for giving her all the glory in his report on the insulin discovery.

> I am nearly 60 and by now have had a great deal of fame; in recent years I have found it practically impossible to carry out most of the essential processes of crystal structure analysis, changed as they have been by many new inventions since I began . . . The crystal growing, and measurements on which the structure of insulin is based today were all made by members of my research group working with me in Oxford and particularly by the last four in, Guy and Eleanor Dodson, Tom Blundell and M. Vijayan . . . There are others still further back . . . The fact is this kind of work needs many kinds of talents; it takes a great deal of time, care and intelligence, and it is lucky there are so many able young people willing to spend years of their lives solving difficult and fascinating problems such as that of the structure of insulin.
>
> My part in the present insulin research has been largely one of discussion and of grant-raising for apparatus and to keep everyone going. Only for one glorious week, the last week of July, did I return to full-time research and help the others build the model . . .[50]

But in the shorthand of history, insulin will remain forever chalked up against Dorothy's name, and hers alone. There are plenty of other examples of leading scientists whose reputations are made by the efforts of their junior colleagues; work done 'in X's lab' almost inevitably becomes 'X's work', however much or little the great figure contributed. In the case of Dorothy and insulin, she certainly put in less time than many of the others in the years that led to the solution. But Guy Dodson, who has perhaps more right than anyone to claim a larger share of the limelight, is adamant that posterity is correct in crediting the insulin solution to Dorothy.

Her insight into protein structure, electron density and how these two aspects of crystallography came together were as good as anybody's. And she built that model with me – Dorothy, Vijayan and I built it together, and I wouldn't say her contribution was any less than mine for a moment.

If you say solving the structure is keeping the integrity of the effort going, then she solved the structure. I wasn't doing that, I wasn't raising the money. I think I was useful in keeping the experimental side up and running well, but that was just a job that I happened to be doing. And that's why I have no difficulty in saying she solved insulin. She set up the group – in a sense, we were the experiment.[51]

The structure reported in that first paper was based on data collected to a resolution of 2.8 Å, good enough to see the overall shape of the molecule, but not to define the atomic positions exactly. Triumph that it was, it opened a new chapter rather than ending the story. Now that the structure was understood, would it be possible to explain how insulin worked in the body? Three research groups, in China, Germany and the United States, had succeeded in synthesizing insulin in the mid-1960s. Could knowledge of the structure enable chemists to make even better insulins? Sanger and his colleagues had moved on from pig insulin to find the sequences of insulins from twenty or more other species. How did the small variations in sequence from one species to another affect the structure, and hence the activity? These questions fascinated Blundell, Guy Dodson and others who joined the group later. Dorothy herself was also keenly aware of their importance. But, recalls Tom Blundell, she was reticent about moving outside her own specialist area.

I think her view was that there were other people more expert than us who probably should be doing it – she saw herself as a chemist and a crystallographer, and thought that others would have the insights into biology.[52]

But the gulf between the crystallographers and the biologists was wider than she anticipated, as she discovered when she invited Sanger and the biochemist Philip Randle to come and see her model for the first time, and give her their thoughts on how it worked. After a brief silence, which Dorothy discouraged her own colleagues from breaking, Sanger said, 'Ah, I got the disulphides right.' As Blundell says, none of them had ever suspected for a moment that there could be any doubt about the three bonds between sulphur atoms Sanger had described in 1953.

> Dorothy looked slightly disappointed. She turned to Philip and said, 'What do you think?' After a bit he put his hand up – he had these huge hands – and pointed towards one of the residues. I thought he was going to say, 'Ah, this is the active site,' but actually he said, 'Is this a tyrosine?' He was still trying to work out what it all was.[53]

Blundell, Guy Dodson and an American visitor, Dan Mercola, put a great deal of time into thinking about the biological and chemical significance of the structure, and eventually wrote a substantial review paper for the journal *Advances in Protein Chemistry*, which came out in 1972.[54] Dorothy's name was on the paper, but she let Blundell and the others know that she was not happy about it.

> Dorothy was very unenthusiastic about our publishing it, because she thought we weren't the best to make these inferences. The arrangement was that Guy, Dan Mercola and I would write major sections and Dorothy would write the introduction. We produced all of our part, but Dorothy's introduction was very slow in appearing. She said we oughtn't to rush, there were lots of things to find out and probably we needed to discuss it with other people . . . John Edsall, the editor, started sending messages, and eventually Guy and I felt so embarrassed we didn't know what to do.[55]

The article was eventually sent off, with Dorothy's introduction but more or less without her blessing. She consoled herself with the thought that when the article came back from the editor they would have the opportunity to do some more work on it. But it was accepted as it was, and went on to become one of the most cited papers in the scientific literature.

Dorothy's reluctance to pronounce on biological matters had nothing to do with a disregard for the practical application of the knowledge she generated. She cared deeply about diabetes, often beginning lectures with a slide of a child first at death's door, then brought back to life through insulin treatment. She was delighted to hear of advances in treatment made possible through knowing the insulin structure. And she was thrilled to be asked to give the Banting Memorial Lecture to the American Diabetic Association in June 1972, celebrating the fifty years since Banting and Best's discovery.[56] She began with a few words about the chance reading of a scientific article that inspired Banting to attempt the isolation of insulin from the pancreas. Then she launched into an account of the structure determination that made few concessions to her audience of medical practitioners and endocrinologists. But her conclusion had a disarming humility.

> We have come a long way these last fifty years, but we still
> do not know how insulin really works, or how patients
> dying from diabetes can be restored to life . . . I fear I have
> taken everyone through many scientific facts that must
> seem very dry. They cannot be more dry than the sentences
> from Moses Barron's paper that stirred Banting into action.
> I should like to think that there may be something in the
> facts I describe to start another Banting on his way.

Dorothy's personal goal was different. By her standards, the 1969 electron density map and model were sloppy. She would not be happy until every atom was firmly in its place. Two more years of hard work brought a structure that was accurate to a resolution of 1.9Å, and still she was not satisfied.[57] By her retirement in 1977 the group had broken up: Tom Blundell went to Sussex University in 1974, Guy and Eleanor to the University of York in 1976, most of the rest of the overseas visitors went back to their home countries. But still she worked on. Her last paper on insulin came out in 1988 in the *Philosophical Transactions of the Royal Society*, when she was seventy-eight years old. It was an 87-page magnum opus, with ten co-authors, describing the structure of insulin at a resolution of 1.5 Å in the most exquisite detail, right down to the atoms in the water molecules that squeezed themselves into the spaces in the protein.[58] Once again, her principal lieutenant was Guy Dodson.

> We finished up with a structure for insulin in which we identified the position of every water molecule – there isn't a single atom that we haven't been able to describe in terms of its electron density. It's one of the most complete X-ray analyses of a molecule that's ever been done and ever will be done, because it took such a long time. Dorothy and I went to every water molecule, we interrogated it as a friend and said 'Who are you interacting with?' It took us four years, and halfway through we realized that something had gone seriously wrong. And so we had a serious and depressed conversation, and went right back to square one and started all over again. This was in '84, '85, '86, she was coming up here [to York] for two weeks at a time, she never wavered. I remember Eleanor was a bit shocked, and certain people in the lab thought we were mad. But she was determined to have a structure in which she knew the position of everything. She wanted a piece of work that was as complete and finished as B_{12} and penicillin had been.[59]

Dorothy's work on insulin is perhaps the best illustration of how she approached her science with the soul of an artist. However well her work was received, whatever its significance for the wider world of science and medicine, her personal satisfaction depended on nothing less than perfection.

9

'Born not for herself but for the world'

China, Africa, India, education and peace, 1959–1988

International peace and understanding had been a concern of Dorothy's since childhood, initially due to the influence of her mother. The loss of the four talented Hood uncles as a result of the First World War was a family tragedy in which they all shared. As an impressionable teenager Dorothy was greatly moved by the 1925 General Assembly of the League of Nations to which her mother took her. Molly also showed a complete lack of racial prejudice in the friendships she formed with women in Egypt, Sudan and Jerusalem, and Dorothy naturally emulated her mother in this respect.

Reaching adulthood during the 1930s under the influence of Bernal and her other Cambridge friends, she was exposed to the thinking of the Cambridge Scientists' Anti-War Group, and through personal contacts followed the progress of conflicts in Spain and China, and the rise of Fascism in Germany. Although in Oxford she was in little personal danger during the Second World War, the London bombing brought refugees of all sorts to her door, and close friends were suddenly victims of xenophobia or genocide. Max Perutz was interned as an alien and sent to a prison camp in Canada until the efforts of his colleagues secured his release. Gerhard Schmidt spent the first few years of the war similarly interned in Australia before returning to join Dorothy's lab in 1943. Then there was poor Frau Goldschmidt, who killed herself rather than be deported to the nameless horrors of Auschwitz–Birkenau.

After the war, and particularly the devastation of Hiroshima and Nagasaki, Dorothy willingly added her name to campaigns by scientists and others against the further development, testing and stock-piling of nuclear weapons. She was a member of Science for Peace and the Campaign for Nuclear Disarmament, a cause which her children took up with even greater enthusiasm. At 94 Woodstock Road in the early 1960s it was not unusual to find Dorothy entertaining visiting scientists to sherry in one room while Toby and his friends held Youth CND meetings next door. With Dorothy's blessing they joined the protest marches to the nuclear weapons research laboratories at Aldermaston, and Elizabeth, while a student at Cambridge, once managed to get herself arrested at a sit-in (a story Dorothy later related with some pride).

But it was not until comparatively late in her life, once her Nobel prize made her a public figure, that she began herself to campaign publicly. If Dorothy had an ideology, it was that international relations were best fostered by dialogue, preferably face to face and in private, between nationals of countries with different outlooks. It was a philosophy she personally put into practice with great enthusiasm: the total distance she travelled in her lifetime must surely be close to the record for a scientist. She also encouraged others by pulling strings to find grants for scientists from overseas to come and work with her. The sense of being part of a world community was one of the aspects of Dorothy's lab most valued by her younger colleagues.

Dorothy's personal political outlook was grounded in this internationalism. Her brand of socialism was similarly idealistic rather than ideological, driven by her concern for humanity and the betterment of standards of living. Although she never joined the Communist Party, she found much to admire in the socialist regimes of the USSR, China and North Vietnam. A vision of self-organizing communities of happy, hard-working people, living modestly but comfortably and benefiting from excellent schools, universities, parks and hospitals, seemed to her eyes to be becoming a joyful reality in the socialist countries she visited.

In letters to Thomas she expressed regret that Britain was not organized on similar lines. It is only in private, to Thomas, that Dorothy expresses such direct sentiments, and one always has to consider the possibility that she did it out of love for him rather than personal conviction. On the evidence of years of correspondence, it is apparent that Dorothy never took a contrary position to Thomas on a political issue (or, indeed, on almost any issue). Thomas was always far more likely to talk publicly about the need for socialist reconstruction and the evils of capitalism. The choice of the *Daily Worker* as the newspaper of the Hodgkin household must surely have been made by him.

Yet Dorothy did share Thomas's idealism. She was not blind to the tyranny of Communist regimes, but believed that the corruption of the Socialist ideal in one state or another did not mean that the ideal itself was unworkable. Like others of the Old Left, she defended what others perceived to be indefensible on the grounds that any state that was ostensibly working towards such an ideal should not be condemned for mistakes it made along the way. She persisted in hoping that things would improve in the future, and that her best chance of helping with the development of these countries was to remain on friendly terms.

There were no exceptions. Visiting Ceauşescu's Romania for a scientific conference in 1980, she met Elena Ceauşescu, who held the title of First Vice-Prime Minister and President of the National Council for Science and Technology of Romania, and found herself agreeing to contribute a signed preface to the English edition of Madame Ceauşescu's book on the chemistry of synthetic rubber. She was well aware that conditions for scientists were far from ideal, and that industrial pollution in Romania was raging unchecked, although she may genuinely have been ignorant of some of the more barbaric features of the Ceauşescu regime. After her return she regretted agreeing to sign the preface, but under pressure from the Romanians came up with a characteristic response. She put aside the sycophantic draft provided by Madame Ceauşescu's aides, and composed her own version. This provided her with an opportunity to make a plea on behalf of Romanian scientists, but it was so tactfully worded that it could not possibly cause offence.

> My interest in scientific progress in Romania is recent,
> grown out of a visit that my husband and I made three
> years ago . . . At the end of our stay I was able to meet Dr
> Elena Ceauşescu . . . and to have with her and her
> colleagues extremely interesting discussions on the
> scientific problems before Romania . . . There is no
> shortage of [problems] for all the young, very intelligent
> scientists growing up under her guidance, if all the needs
> of the people of Romania are to be met and the country
> preserved still as beautiful as we saw it.[1]

She would certainly have called herself a socialist, but her uniquely non-confrontational approach to human and international relations prevented her from wearing her socialism like a badge. In other respects too, she resisted labels. She campaigned against American intervention in Vietnam, and against nuclear weapons, but unlike Kathleen Lonsdale she would not have called herself a pacifist. She encouraged women to succeed as scientists, both by her example and by direct support to women colleagues, but gave short shrift to women writers who tried to adopt her as a feminist icon.

Perhaps because of this reluctance to identify herself too rigidly with any ideological perspective, her socialism and anti-militarism never prevented her from moving comfortably among the highest levels of the British and international scientific establishments. While Bernal had been voted off the Council of the British Association for the Advancement of Science in 1949 because of his pro-Soviet views, Dorothy was elected its President for the year 1977–8, to add to all the other scientific honours she had received by then. She accepted Foreign Membership of both the US National Academy of Sciences and the USSR Academy of Sciences; the latter awarded her its coveted Lomonosov Medal. She was a universally popular choice for the Presidency of the International Union of Crystallography from 1972 to 1975, and of the Pugwash Conferences on Science and World Affairs from 1975. Individual scientists from every corner of the globe declared their undying admiration and affection for her after benefiting from her unobtrusive generosity with her time and connections. Her efforts were fuelled by a hope, not always fulfilled, that as long as people could be brought face to face and talk through their differences, all problems could be solved.

There was no corner of the world to which Dorothy would not travel, and especially after her Nobel award she had every opportunity to do so. She visited laboratories all over the world, gave lectures and received further honours. A trip to Australia and New Zealand in 1967 was particularly poignant. She was reunited with her old nurse, Katie Collins, whose husband Jimmy had made contact after reading about her in the newspaper. In a gesture typical of Dorothy, she then paid for her sister Elisabeth, who had been more attached to Katie than any of them, to visit the following year. Once the difficulty with visas was more or less resolved, she travelled frequently to the United States and Canada. Russia and the other Eastern European countries were regular ports of call. But three other countries she came to know well perhaps deserve special mention: China, Ghana and India.

Through her encounters with China, during and after the period when it was closed to the rest of the world, she demonstrated her belief that science knows no national boundaries. She visited the country eight times in all, but received her first impression much earlier. A fellow student at Somerville was an earnest and idealistic young woman called Liao Hongying.[2] Hongying was the daughter of a Confucian scholar in the small town of Changting in the mountains of southern China. Her childhood was spent in rural isolation and material poverty, but with a high regard for learning; she studied the Chinese classics with her father and brother, and also learned something of the world beyond China's borders in mission schools. Fired with a sense of the injustice of traditional Chinese society, she became an ardent revolutionary while at secondary school in her early twenties. Friends in the mission system eventually arranged to send her to England for her own safety, where she spent three years improving her English and preparing for entrance to university.

Hongying joined the Quakers in 1929, and had heard of Margery Fry, one of the movement's most prominent members. She decided to try for Oxford, having been disgusted to discover that Cambridge did not award full degrees to women. With a great deal of hard work, she succeeded in being admitted to

Somerville in 1930 to read chemistry. Her one aim was to use her education to help the cause of socialist reconstruction in China, and she planned to specialize in agricultural science. But she found the teaching uninspiring and struggled to keep up. Dorothy, who was five years younger than Hongying but two years ahead in her studies, offered to help. During her last year at Oxford, while undertaking her Part II research, she found time to give Hongying extra coaching sessions in her rooms in Richmond Road. For her part, Hongying communicated to Dorothy her fervent desire to help in the transformation of her poor and backward country by means of socialist revolution. Dorothy was so inspired that she looked into the possibility, through Hongying's contacts with an Anglo-Chinese group in London, of going to work there after graduation.

Hongying returned to China in 1936, teaching at universities in Wuhan and Chengdu. In 1944 she married a British diplomat, Derek Bryan. The British authorities took the view that having a Chinese wife (especially one as anti-American as Hongying) would compromise his impartiality, and while on a visit to Britain in 1951 Bryan was told he would not be sent back to China. He resigned from the Foreign Service, and together he and Hongying threw their energies into the Britain–China Friendship Association. The BCFA membership consisted largely of British Communists keen to support China's position in the face of uncomprehending and largely hostile public opinion.

In 1959 the BCFA was asked by the Chinese chargé d'affaires in London to help select a British delegation to attend celebrations of the tenth anniversary of the revolution in China. The Chinese were anxious to have a delegation including distinguished academics who were also interested in China. The association was chaired by Joseph Needham, whom Dorothy had known as a biochemist at Cambridge, and who had since devoted his life to a study of the science and civilization of China. Its Arts and Sciences Committee included Bill Pirie, also an old Cambridge contact. Once the President of the Royal Society (Hinshelwood) had declined because of another engagement, Dorothy's name came to the top of the list of those who might represent British science. The rest of the delegation consisted of the author and critic Herbert Read and the agriculturalist Frank Harold Garner.

Hongying and her husband were to accompany the delegation as interpreters, returning for the first time since 1951.

The visit made a huge impression on Dorothy. As in the case of her trip to the USSR, she was briefed before leaving by Kathleen Lonsdale, who had herself visited the country four years before. Lonsdale gave her a list of the names of Chinese crystallographers whom she might try to contact.

> I am sure you will enjoy going to China and do, if you possibly can, go to see the crystallographers in Manchuria who are very keen and more isolated than those in Peking.
>
> Please give them my kind remembrances! And do ask them if there is any hope of their coming to Cambridge next year [for the 5th International Congress of Crystallography].[3]

Dorothy already had one or two connections of her own. Tang Youqi (now Professor of Biophysics at Beijing University) had met her at a seminar in Pasadena in 1947, where he was a young researcher in Pauling's laboratory. Amongst the crowd of Americans at the seminar they were the only foreigners, and Dorothy was the only woman, so he particularly noticed her. On his way back to China in 1951, encouraged by Eddie Hughes to meet some English crystallographers, Tang called on Dorothy in Oxford. He was impressed to discover that while fully occupied with her work on Vitamin B_{12}, she was still 'emotionally attached to insulin'. 'She was overwhelmed with excitement when she told me about Dr Sanger's work on the amino-acid sequence of insulin. She predicted that Sanger's work would eventually kindle renewed interest in research on insulin.[4]

In the late 1950s scientific research in China was virtually at a standstill. Before the establishment of the People's Republic of China in 1949 many talented Chinese had trained in Europe or the United States. Many stayed, but some, like Tang, returned to help build new scientific institutes in their own country. To begin with the Chinese government looked to the Soviet Union to provide technical help, training and equipment. Western visitors with strong Communist sympathies, such as Bernal and Kathleen Lonsdale, had also helped chemists and crystallographers to acquire some up-to-date equipment and access to the main scientific journals.

The Great Leap Forward, launched by Mao Zedong in December 1957, was an attempt to break away from dependence on Soviet ideas and to build a uniquely Chinese form of socialism. With its emphasis on collectivism and physical labour, it was a potential threat to scientific research in laboratories. But, says Tang, some science was allowed to continue.

> In 1958 the young students were asked what they wanted to do. They didn't know much, but they wanted to do something great, so they chose to synthesize insulin. In fact our government spent a lot of money on that. The solvent used in the insulin synthesis could fill a small swimming pool! The amino acids also cost a lot of money. In China we cannot go to the moon, but I think for a country of 800 million people to spend that much money was something of an experiment.[5]

The task of insulin synthesis, undertaken by teams of chemists in Beijing and Shanghai, had become possible since Fred Sanger had published the sequence of amino acids in the molecule. Dorothy first heard that this work was under way in China during her first visit, when she gave a lecture on the B_{12} structure in Beijing, for which Tang was her interpreter. She was enormously interested, and although on this first visit she did not visit the biochemistry laboratories in Shanghai where much of the work was taking place, she took careful note of the key contacts. Meanwhile students and researchers crowded round with questions after her lecture, delighting her with their enthusiasm. Insulin, recalled Tang later, was the means of establishing an 'intimate and lasting friendship' between Dorothy and Chinese crystallographers.

On this first visit science was only part of the programme. It began with the anniversary banquet, 1000 guests sitting down to dinner in the Great Hall of the People – Khruschev was there, and Ho Chi Minh, Zhou Enlai and Mao Zedong. Dorothy herself did not meet Mao, although as leader of the British delegation, Herbert Read did. It was, as Derek Bryan recalls,[6] a very tense time politically, the year before the Sino-Soviet split that was to send shockwaves through Communist organizations in Britain and elsewhere. Khruschev, who had been openly critical of the Great Leap Forward, was one of the national leaders who spoke during the banquet.

The British delegation was later taken on a tour of the country, privately noting the poor growth of the crops. The Great Leap Forward, which had amalgamated collective farms into larger communes, had failed to produce an efficient system of agricultural production, and this had been compounded by poor weather. The agriculturalist in the delegation made few allowances for the circumstances of China's recent history and criticized practices on the collective farms they visited. 'Hongying was very cross about his disapproval,' Dorothy remembered. But much later, when mortality figures for the next few years became available, it was apparent that his criticism was justified: millions had died of starvation.

They went on a 'rather stormy' boat trip down the Yangtse River, through the Three Gorges from Chungking to Wuhan. They visited communes and factories, travelled on the new railway, and were shown round universities. They were able to talk quite freely to those they met during their stay. But as the visit drew to an end, Dorothy realized that Hongying was troubled. She and her husband had been refused permission to stay on at the end of the visit and go to her home town of Changting, which was in Fujian, a part of China closed to foreigners because of its proximity to Taiwan. Bryan recalled that the senior cadre who had been assigned to look after the delegation was 'very bureaucratic and very rigid politically'. Hongying argued with him all day, sitting in a room in the little hotel in Beijing where they were staying. But he did not relent until Dorothy intervened on Hongying's behalf. Bryan does not know exactly how she did it, but she certainly went over the head of the obstructive cadre, and the result was that Hongying alone was allowed to visit her family.[7]

For Dorothy, meeting the Chinese scientists and hearing of their interest in insulin was the highlight of this extraordinary trip. There was little chance of following their progress – no Chinese was allowed to publish in Western journals at the time –

without going back to see for herself. Only a few years later she
found the opportunity she was looking for. In 1965 the British
Council invited her to spend two weeks lecturing in Japan as
part of a major exhibition on British culture it was staging in
Tokyo. It immediately struck Dorothy that she could make a
diversion to China on the way back, and with the help of the
Royal Society and the Chinese Academy of Sciences, she secured
the funding and the necessary invitation. The Japan part of the
trip was rather more formal than she would have liked, as she
hinted in a letter to the scientific counsellor at the British Embassy
in Tokyo before she set off.

> Your programme sounds pretty overwhelming but I expect
> one will survive. I suppose my real trouble is that I think it
> would be very useful for our own research here, if I had
> had just a bit more time to see Japanese scientific research.
> This seems to be completely left out of my programme.[8]

Apart from set-piece lectures in Tokyo and Kyoto, she was
required to attend various official receptions, the Scientific
Counsellor being careful to advise her to wear a hat at those when
royalty (Japanese or British) were present. More to her taste was
a day spent in the company of representatives of the Japanese
Association of Women Scientists visiting a traditional home. With
much laughter, they persuaded her to dress in a kimono and to
pose for photographs pretending to sleep Japanese-style on a
mattress on the floor. She wrote to Thomas that the beauty of a
Japanese garden she visited in Kyoto was worth coming for on its
own.

But she was keen to move on to China. She knew that as well
as the Chinese, a group in Pittsburgh under Panayotis
Katsoyannis and a group in Aachen under Helmut Zahn were
trying to synthesize insulin by making the A and B chains sep-
arately and then trying to put them together. There was a
conference on insulin synthesis coming up at Brookhaven in the
United States. The Chinese would almost certainly be absent –
at that time travel to overseas conferences was almost unheard
of for Chinese scientists – and Dorothy wanted to be able to
report on how far they had got. She found when she arrived in

Shanghai that Wang Yinglai and his colleagues had already successfully synthesized bovine insulin, but like the German and
American groups, had not yet succeeded in getting it to crystallize. She encouraged them to pursue this, impressing on them
the importance of completing an X-ray analysis in order to compare the structures of natural and synthetic insulin. Her own
work on insulin was at this stage looking quite hopeful,
although even she did not realize how much longer it was going
to take.

In the spring of 1966 the Chinese Academy of Sciences held a
conference at which the insulin researchers reported that they
had succeeded in crystallizing synthetic insulin. The Academy
decided to set up a team, involving groups from institutes in both
Beijing and Shanghai, dedicated to solving the structure. Tang
Youqi was asked to act as leader of the group of younger workers
who would undertake the research. Today he says it was not an
obligation he accepted very wholeheartedly, knowing that the
insulin structure was Dorothy's project.

> That was a decision made by the authorities, by the
> community. I wasn't extremely happy, but I couldn't
> refuse. In fact, because I was quite sure what kind of
> person Dorothy was, I knew I could very frankly explain
> to her. But as an individual I would not have done that,
> because I knew Dorothy was working on [insulin], and she
> was not an enemy. If she had been an enemy it would have
> been different, but she was our friend! Of course in China
> at that time no one would care if we heard someone in
> another country was starting the same work – there was no
> bond between us.[9]

The same year Dorothy attempted to get the Chinese insulin scientists invited to a Chemical Society conference to be held at
Exeter University. She overcame opposition from the British end
after offering to pay the travel costs of the Chinese scientists herself, only stipulating that it should be made to look as if the
Chemical Society was paying. The organizers accepted this compromise; but she was defeated by events in China. The Chinese
Academy of Sciences turned down the invitation.

Now, the great proletarian cultural revolution is being
carried on vigorously in our country and we should
accomplish our task with even better results while taking
an active part in this cultural revolution. Therefore, no
scientists concerned will be able to spare their time to go to
your country for the meetings.[10]

The Cultural Revolution brought chaos to China as Mao
Zedong, urged on by his wife Jiang Qing, incited the youth of
the country to reject their own cultural traditions and defy the
authority of their elders. Students and intellectuals were
ordered to undertake 're-education' through labouring as peasants in the countryside. In many areas social order broke down
completely, as rival groups of Red Guards battled for
supremacy and neighbours denounced one another. By the
time order was restored a million were dead, millions more
displaced or persecuted. It was a situation in which no scientific research could possibly be expected to continue – but, says
Gu Xiaocheng of the Institute of Biophysics in Beijing, who was
a member of the newly established insulin team, their research
was an exception.

All the universities were closed, and almost all the
scientific research came to a stop in 1966. That lasted for
quite a few years, but the reason [structural work on
insulin] was still going on, or restarted after a brief stop,
was because the government said that 'even during the
Cultural Revolution we want to have some basic research
going on to show that we put great emphasis on promoting
basic science'. At that time this one was almost the only
project that was really going on intensively. So our project
was unique and went on uninterrupted – in other
universities very little was achieved.[11]

The group began its work in earnest in early 1967. One who
joined it at this time was Liang Dongcai, now a Professor at the
Institute of Biophysics in Beijing, who had spent the previous
fourteen months in England on an exchange programme between
the Royal Society and the Chinese Academy of Sciences. He

worked first with Charles Bunn at the Royal Institution, then transferred to Dorothy and her insulin team in Oxford.

> Dorothy led me into protein crystallography, a very
> important step. I knew it would be very important for
> China. So I worked and studied very hard indeed. In
> Oxford Dorothy looked after me very well, and let me do
> all sorts of protein structure determination, crystal growth,
> and seeking heavy atom derivatives. It was important for
> me, the first step I took into molecular biology, not only
> protein crystallography. I had a good background in small
> molecule crystallography, but didn't have any background
> in molecular biology.[12]

Liang's stay in Oxford was cut short at the beginning of 1967 when he received a message from the Chinese Embassy telling him to return to China immediately. He joined a group of around thirty young scientists – at times the number reached as many as sixty – dedicated to solving the insulin structure. Conditions were very different from those in Oxford. The sheer number of people employed was designed to compensate for the lack of good equipment. They were divided into groups of five or six people, each group doing part of the job. One grew crystals, another collected data on a linear diffractometer, running it twenty-four hours a day. Gu Xiaocheng and the rest of her group sat together doing calculations ten hours a day on slide-rules. Another group traced out the maps.

After four years' work they solved the structure independently, two years later than Dorothy and her group in Oxford, but to a slightly higher resolution. Dorothy learned of this just after returning from a trip to Vietnam in 1971, and was 'pretty sick' that she hadn't stopped off in China on the way back. The next year the International Congress of Crystallography was to be held in Kyoto. Dorothy had just been nominated unanimously as President of the International Union of Crystallography for a three-year term, and would be formally elected during the Congress. Now adept at using all official travel to maximum advantage, Dorothy fitted in a trip to Beijing on the way out to Japan. She took with her her own insulin electron density maps, hoping to make a direct comparison with the Chinese structure.

The moment when the two maps were placed together, both having been drawn to the same scale, had both a practical and a symbolic significance. And the first reaction was 'acute concern' on both sides. The structures did not seem to be the same at all. But almost at once they realized that there was a simple explanation: the two teams had drawn their structures opposite ways up. When one was turned through 180 degrees the correspondence was very close, though not exact. And there were smiles all round. Dorothy was so excited that she immediately wrote a long letter to her colleagues back in the lab in Oxford.

> Their crystallization work is beautiful and should be imitated by us. They have grown crystals very large – 3–4 mm across . . . The main find in heavy atom derivatives was the whole series of alkyl mercury chlorides, which goodness knows we should have tried . . . They think and I agree that their zinc position is likely to be more accurate than ours.
>
> They are a marvellous group. Somewhere we must plan a meeting of all forces – when the final maps come through.

Dorothy flew at once to Kyoto and gave a full account of insulin research in China to the International Congress. Her words were published on the front page of the Congress newsletter, copies of which the Beijing scientists still treasure. Dorothy's promotion of their work brought enormous benefits to them, not only abroad but at home.

Once the Chinese insulin structure was published in 1971, the group had been disbanded. Liang went for 're-education' to his home province of Guangdong, in the south of China, and did not return to work in Beijing until 1978. (He was summoned briefly to meet Dorothy during her 1972 visit, but could not tell her at the time that he had stopped working on insulin.) Gu found herself on a farm, 'raising rice seedlings, chicks and ducks'. Their achievement seemed to mean nothing to their own government until Dorothy proclaimed to the world that the work was as good as could be found anywhere else. At the same time, her announcement in Kyoto brought requests from Japanese crystallographers to provide Japanese translations of their work, and soon afterwards letters arrived from others around the world saying that they would like to come and visit.

Three years after the Kyoto conference Dorothy published a short article in *Nature* headed 'Chinese work on insulin'. Here she summarized the latest work published in *Scientia Sinica* (at that time Chinese scientists could publish only in domestic journals, which were little noticed elsewhere) and brought it to the attention not only of crystallographers but of the whole Western scientific community. She was generous in her assessment.

> One might not wish, in all cases, to see complete
> duplication of the X-ray analysis of a protein molecule – so
> much work is involved. But there are great gains in the
> present case from having two views of the insulin crystal
> structure . . . The present Peking map at 1.8Å resolution is
> the most accurate map available of the insulin electron
> density defined by experimental, isomorphous phase
> angles – and may well remain so.[13]

She went on to say that her own efforts to refine the structure further involved some rather experimental computing procedures, and that the availability of the Chinese analysis would provide a very valuable comparison. She concluded, with some feeling: 'It will be splendid if we can some day soon all meet and talk over the very interesting observations that are accumulating, East and West, on the structure and function of insulin.'

Dorothy went to Beijing again in 1977, this time taking Guy Dodson with her, again comparing the improved maps from both groups. But China's long isolation, to which she had built one fragile bridge, was about to end. Dorothy had since the early 1960s been trying to encourage the Chinese to join the IUCr and come to its congresses, a move fully supported by the secretariat. But China was not prepared to join any organization that recognized the separate existence of Taiwan. Despite her excellent personal relations with the Chinese Academy of Sciences and with individual crystallographers, Dorothy was not able to alter this position during her presidency of the IUCr. But the fact that lines of communication were kept open throughout this difficult period meant that, after the fall of the Gang of Four, and the decision of the People's Congress of March 1978 that China should participate in the interchange of international science, Chinese crystallographers were rapidly able to meet their Western counterparts. A delegation led by Tang Youqi and including Gu Xiaocheng attended the 11th International Congress of Crystallography in Warsaw in 1978, and applied for membership of the Union. Dorothy explained the voting procedure to Tang, and assured him that she was certain China would be admitted. She was right, of course, as Gu remembers.

> We all saw that it was a unanimous vote. I think that without her introduction and her efforts it would not have happened. And at that conference we met people from all over the world, and they congratulated us, and a lot of people said you are long overdue, you should have been here, you have joined us many years ago. And we were surprised that so many people knew about the Chinese group. And almost all of them said, 'Well, we first got the news from Dorothy.' So that was the kind of impact, and her great contribution in introducing the Chinese crystallographers to the world.[14]

After the Congress Dorothy arranged for the delegation to come to England and visit labs around the country, as well as attending the Bath meeting of the British Association for the Advancement of Science – she was its President that year. And she happily entertained them all in her garden at Crab Mill. In the years since, most of the laboratories with which Dorothy had good connections – Oxford, Cambridge, Bristol, York, Durham – have set up regular exchanges with Chinese groups, and some very fruitful research partnerships have grown up as a result.

When she next visited Beijing in 1980, recalls Tom Blundell who accompanied her, 'the whole hierarchy of the Communist Party turned up at Friendship House to see Dorothy. *They* came to see *her*.' On the same trip Liang Dongcai discovered to his surprise that in four previous visits Dorothy had never visited the

Great Wall. Quoting the expression 'One is not a hero (*haohan*) if one has never been on the Great Wall', he arranged the trip. Dorothy, then aged seventy, made the strenuous climb with great enthusiasm, in a borrowed coat and fur hat against the cold wind – although her status as a hero in the eyes of Chinese crystallographers was never in doubt.

While China exerted a pull all of its own, Dorothy followed in Thomas's footsteps to Ghana. But Ghana still occupied a special place in her affections. Formerly the Gold Coast, it was the first British colony to pass peacefully to independence with a democratically elected black majority government, and it carried the hopes of anti-colonialists all over the world for a new dawn in African politics. Thomas was an ardent supporter of Ghana's bid for self-government, and of Kwame Nkrumah, from his first visit in the late 1940s. Soon after independence in 1957, he had been appointed one of the secretaries of a commission set up to advise on the development of higher education. One of the commission's recommendations was the establishment of an Institute of African Studies at the University of Ghana in Legon, just outside Accra. In 1961 Thomas was appointed its Director by Prime Minister Kwame Nkrumah, 'rather against his will,' wrote Dorothy, 'for he had urged [Nkrumah] to appoint an African head'.

This meant that Thomas would be in Legon effectively full-time. Beginning in 1962, Dorothy would spend periods of a month or more with him a couple of times each year, involving herself in the problems of a new university in a new country. To begin with they were full of optimism. Dorothy was with Thomas in November 1963 when the Institute was officially opened by Nkrumah. Dancers from the Institute's own troupe (the deputy director was a musicologist) performed at the ceremony, and the same week the girls in one of the halls of residence gave a ball that went on until three in the morning. What Dorothy described as 'nice and interesting characters' came from all over the world as Fellows of the Institute, and 'interesting dissidents from every nation' took jobs at the University. Conor Cruise O'Brien, the Irish diplomat and writer, had just been appointed Vice-Chancellor, and he and his wife Maire became friends of the Hodgkins.

Thomas . . . and other friends would often go round to the
Vice-Chancellor's lodgings and stay till the early hours of
the morning, playing Shakespeare or acting parts (a
favourite one would be Thomas as an American
millionaire trying to buy the University from Conor to
rebuild it in the grounds of his mansion in the States).[15]

During the day Dorothy would work quietly in the Chemistry
Department. The only crystallographic equipment it had was an
old X-ray tube, set up by a student of Tiny Powell's many years
before. This was the province of Adjei Bekoe, a crystallographer
who had previously worked in Nigeria, and his one PhD student
to whom Dorothy occasionally gave a helping hand. For herself,
a quiet spot in the library, pen and paper was all she needed to
write up work that had been carried out in Oxford for publication, or to check past results. She held a visiting professorship,
and did a little lecturing.

But all was not as well as it first appeared. The University had
been set up to match the highest standards of any university in
Britain. This meant that it could cater for very few Ghanaians at
a time when secondary education in the country was itself available only to a privileged few. Not only that, but under the
previous Cambridge-educated Principal a curriculum had been
developed that bore little relation to the needs of the country: it
offered courses in Latin and Greek, but none of the applied subjects that might assist with national development. At the same
time Nkrumah wanted to use the university to promote his own
idiosyncratic brand of socialism. A rift opened up between the
government and the University. O'Brien and his staff resisted
interference by the government on the grounds that it represented a threat to academic freedom. Meanwhile Nkrumah's
assumption of the Presidency and failure to maintain the democratic process that had brought him to power hardened opinion
against him among former sympathizers in the West.

In January 1964 Dorothy, then in Oxford, received word that
Thomas was seriously ill. She flew out at once, and found him in
hospital with dengue fever. He was beginning to mend, and she
persuaded the doctors to let him return to their house. But she
found the University campus in a ferment. Six academics had

been served with deportation orders. Wild rumours were circulating about Nkrumah's mental state following an assassination attempt a few weeks before. There were government-orchestrated demonstrations by local people against the privileges of the University community, with windows being broken and rooms wrecked.

There was a general feeling that if anyone could persuade Nkrumah to reverse the deportation orders, then it was Thomas and Dorothy. They did succeed in paying a visit to the President, who was not unfriendly, but argued that there was too much evidence against those accused to reverse the orders. One was charged with falsifying his academic record; two senior figures from the Law Department, both Americans, were suspected of having CIA connections.

> All the time we were talking, Thomas was breaking into most awful fits of coughing and being unable to speak. He was obviously not at all well and most probably should not have been out. Kwame was very much concerned about his situation, and said, 'When I get into this state my doctor always orders me large doses of Vitamin A.' . . . The same afternoon we were rung up in the middle of the afternoon from the Institute of African Studies to say that there was a large police car there with a message from Kwame. When it reached us, the driver handed over a large bottle of Vitamin A.[16]

The deportations went ahead. After a couple of weeks things calmed down, and Dorothy agreed to go with Ann Seidman, an economist and the wife of one of the deported lawyers, to try to persuade Nkrumah to let Ann's husband Bob return.

> We sat on either side of him on an oriental sofa at Christiansborg Castle, to which he'd retreated from his usual offices at Flagstaff House . . . At the end we had the feeling that he would surely arrange for her husband to come back; but he said, 'It is very difficult, but yes he should certainly come back, but I won't be able to act quickly.' Ann remembers him asking why she thought Bob

was deported, adding, 'It's as my old mother used to say:
If only you could take off the man's head and look inside,
you'd know what really went on.'[17]

Bob Seidman did indeed return to Ghana soon afterwards.
Despite these troubles, Thomas and Dorothy refused to be disil-
lusioned. The photographs printed in the *Observer* colour
supplement at the time of the Nobel prize ceremony, taken in the
autumn of 1964, show Dorothy and Thomas relaxed and happy
in their garden in Legon, Dorothy wearing a dress of printed
Ghanaian cotton. She later described these photographs as being
among her favourites. In 1965 she was awarded an honorary
degree by the University of Ghana, and was touched that the
citation began 'O Daughter of Africa!'

But like so many who had come from all over the world to support Ghana in its struggle to become a truly independent nation,
Thomas and Dorothy lost their second home in the military coup
of February 1966 that swept Nkrumah from power. Neither was
in Ghana at the time – fortunately, as Thomas was one of ten
Nkrumah appointees declared *persona non grata* by the new government. Returning to Oxford, he was given a Fellowship by
Balliol, and a lecturership in the Government of New States. Soon
afterwards, with all the children grown up and scattered, the
combined Payne–Hodgkin household was dissolved. Joan
bought a cottage just outside Oxford, while Thomas and Dorothy
moved into Crab Mill, the old house in the Warwickshire countryside bought by Thomas's parents thirty years before. They
kept a pied-à-terre in the Bradmore Road flat that had been their
first real home.

Dorothy's relationship with India was different yet again.
Politically it automatically gained her sympathy and goodwill as
a nation still adapting to independence from British colonial
authority. She had some personal connections too: Jawarhalal
Nehru's daughter Indira Gandhi had been a student at
Somerville when Dorothy was a young fellow, and she knew Sir
Sarvepalli Radhakrishnan, who became President of India, when
he was a professor at Oxford earlier in his life. She was aware
early in her career that the country had produced distinguished

work in X-ray physics; she was photographed in 1948 at the first International Congress of Crystallography at Harvard, viewing an exhibition with Bernal and the tall, turbanned figure of the Nobel prizewinner C. V. Raman, who had studied the scattering of X-rays in liquids. She was therefore extremely receptive to the idea that Indian scientists might come to her lab to learn her particular brand of crystallography as applied to biological molecules. The succession of able Indian scientists who passed through Oxford during the 1960s gave her a personal stake in the development of the subject in India itself, which she later followed up with a number of visits. For their part, Dorothy's Indian colleagues still write and speak of her as devotees might of their guru.

The key figure in Dorothy's relationship with India, although he was not the first to meet her, was Sivaraj Ramaseshan of the Indian Institute of Science in Bangalore. In the early 1950s he was given the task of building up an X-ray crystallography group in the Physics Department there, and in 1954 he left for the United States to spend a year working with Fankuchen at Brooklyn Poly. There he realized that the physics of X-ray diffraction was now substantially complete, and that the next wave of advances would come in the application of its techniques to chemistry and biology. Fankuchen encouraged him to develop these applications in India, and mentioned Dorothy's work as a particularly good example to follow.

Five or six years later Ramaseshan's younger colleague K. Venkatesan came to work with Dorothy at the suggestion of Jack Dunitz, who had examined his PhD thesis and arranged a Fellowship for him to come to Zurich. Dorothy had just got her hands on some new crystals, of a substance called cobyric acid that was isolated from sewage sludge. Cobyric acid was part of the Vitamin B_{12} family of molecules, with exactly the same corrin nucleus. The first photographs showed marked anomalous scattering effects, the variations in intensity within pairs of reflections that could provide clues to the phasing. Knowing that Venkatesan had worked on anomalous scattering for his PhD, she suggested he might try to solve the structure using only this method.

She said very mischievously, winking her eye, 'But it might

mean measuring thousands of reflections – one could
always solve the structure by traditional methods. But if
you want to use the Bijvoet effect, that's fine.'[18]

She then announced that she would call him Van, there being no
short form of his name, and that he must call her Dorothy as
everyone else did. When he recovered from his astonishment at
the informality of the lab – Guy Dodson pressed him into joining
in their games of cricket – Venkatesan set to work with a DPhil
student, David Dale, to measure the intensities of almost 2000
reflections. Their work produced phase angles that were so accurate that the first electron density map contained every principal
atom, and the final version even showed the hydrogen atoms as
clear peaks. For much of the time Dorothy was in Ghana, and
Venkatesan kept her informed of their progress by letter.

> When we finished she was all excited and happy. David
> and I had made a model, and as soon as she arrived she
> said, 'Van, could I have a look at your model?' What had
> taken us months she finished in about forty-five minutes,
> correcting a few things here and there. The whole structure
> was before her eyes. I was really amazed, it was a
> remarkable experience for me.
>   As soon as she had seen that everything was perfect, she
> immediately rushed to the insulin room. Marjorie and Guy
> were there, and she told them about the success of the
> anomalous dispersion for this molecule – it was the biggest
> molecule to have been solved by this method. Her thinking
> was immediately insulin. She wanted to inspire them to
> think about that next. She was always thinking of the
> application of new methods to higher and higher
> systems.[19]

Dorothy later made a point of describing this work in her Nobel
lecture, which the Indian crystallographers regarded as a great
tribute. After Venkatesan went back to India, the next to arrive
was Ramaseshan himself, or 'Siv', as he had been known since his
days with 'Fan' Fankuchen. Dorothy arranged for him to stand in
for her as the senior scientist in her laboratory, keeping an eye on

the research students, while she spent most of the year 1964–5 with Thomas in Ghana. His was a wise and calm presence, greatly appreciated in that team of young enthusiasts. And his insight into the possibilities of anomalous dispersion brought real dividends. He began by helping Clive Nockolds to solve another structure from the B_{12} family, Vitamin B_{12} monoacid.

> It all depends on whether you use a right- or left handed system. When I looked at Clive's work, he had made a mistake. He had already measured 6000 reflections. The moment we changed over and did a synthesis, lo and behold every atom came out beautifully. It was one of the most exciting periods of my life, seeing a huge structure coming out.[20]

The insulin group also benefited from Ramaseshan's advice. Partly influenced by discussions with him, Eleanor Dodson began to write the computer programs that would eventually, once the data were good enough, make it possible to solve the insulin structure. Ramaseshan himself noted that the friendliness and informality of the lab, so different from the more formal structures he had experienced in India, had a direct influence on its productivity.

> I don't think anywhere else in the world have I seen so much science being done in such a relaxed way – the only way you can do science. Whenever it was sunny we used to watch cricket, then go to a pub . . . From the point of view of relaxation and doing science it was one of the best periods of my life.[21]

Viswamitra, a lecturer in physics at the Indian Institute of Science in Bangalore, had the same experience when he came in the autumn of 1965. Dorothy asked him to work on an antibiotic called thiostrepton, a molecule of about 150 atoms, whose chemical formula was unknown. She told him frankly that there were problems, in particular that no one had managed to make a heavy atom derivative. Viswamitra (shortened to 'Mitra' by Dorothy) had no more luck, but he did manage to grow crystals of the native substance in a different and more tractable form. He then began to apply a combination of new mathematical methods and his own intuition in coaxing the positions of the five sulphur atoms in the molecule from the Patterson maps.

> No one thought I would get anything out of it. But Dorothy was never less than enthusiastic; she gave me complete freedom to do what I wanted, I did no more heavy atom work after that. The family visits to her home were another thing that contributed to our success. Not that we were talking about crystallography – but somehow you would come back and feel that now you could do even better.[22]

After a year Dorothy showed her confidence in Viswamitra by asking a post-doc from New Zealand, Bryan Anderson, to work with him on the problem, writing the computer programs needed to complete the analysis. The structure eventually came out after Viswamitra had gone back to India.

Viswamitra was followed by his own student, M. Vijayan, who came to join the insulin group when Margaret Adams left (see Chapter 8). Vijayan and his wife Kalyani were not the only visitors to benefit from Dorothy's deep personal concern for the well-being of all her associates. All the Bangalore crystallographers who spent time with her stress the personal kindnesses she showed them: the telegram welcoming Ramaseshan, his wife Kausalya and their children to Europe when they arrived at Naples after a long journey by ship; Dorothy's offers to babysit, dinner and loans of cots and baby baths; her invitations to Christmas dinner (and mortification when she realized afterwards that she should have offered vegetarian dishes). Happiest time of all was a second visit by Vijayan and Kalyani in the late 1970s, during which, having previously suffered two miscarriages, Kalyani found herself to be pregnant again. Dorothy personally ensured that she had the best possible care at Oxford's John Radcliffe Hospital. On 12 May, Dorothy's own birthday, a daughter was safely delivered – Devi Dorothy.

Dorothy never encouraged her overseas visitors to stay permanently (the Dodsons were an obvious exception). On the contrary, particularly with those from developing countries, she urged them to take their skills back home and stimulate scientific research there. She once asked Venkatesan why he thought another Indian researcher had settled in the United States. 'Because the facilities for research in India are poor,' he replied. 'She looked at me and said, "Look Van, the work I did under very difficult circumstances gave me the greatest satisfaction." It was very inspiring to me.'[23]

All the Indian scientists who worked with Dorothy developed new fields of research on their return to their home country, passing on their experience to students who are now setting up a further generation of new laboratories.

Dorothy made several visits to India, twice in 1979 as a visiting professor at the Indian Academy of Sciences. On the first of the two visits, in February, Thomas came with her. He was keen to make the acquaintance of E. M. S. Namboodiripad, who in 1957 had made international headlines when the Communists won the elections to the State Assembly in Kerala, and he became Chief Minister of the first Communist government to achieve power through the ballot box. Vijayan was also a Communist from Kerala, and organized the visit. While they were there Dorothy had a bad cold, and Vijayan arranged for her to have an examination at a medical centre in Trivandrum. The doctor told him that her heartbeat was irregular, that she really should not exert herself or undertake any lectures. But when a group came from the local university and asked her to speak to them, she accepted at once.

Vijayan became even more anxious when she and Thomas – who was himself not a healthy man – announced that they wanted to make the journey back to Bangalore by train rather than plane. Finding the sleeping berths all fully booked, Vijayan was almost in despair.

What to do? Night was coming on, and I could not imagine even normally Dorothy sitting up all night, and especially with this heart condition. In the end I just told people who Dorothy was, and there were lots of volunteers to give up their berths for her. Not only that, but people who were travelling with children all brought their children for Dorothy's blessings. Thomas said, 'It's all nonsense,' but Dorothy said, 'No, it is not like that.' She understood that they were simply showing respect and deference for scholarship.[24]

On their return to Bangalore Thomas himself fell seriously ill; the atmosphere of the city seemed to have aggravated his respiratory problems. For days he lay in the guest house of the Indian Institute of Science while doctors phoned his own doctor in England for advice. Ramaseshan was astonished at Dorothy's calm fortitude in the face of this crisis.

> He was seriously ill and we thought he would die. But Dorothy was scheduled to give a lecture in the Institute, and she went and gave a wonderful lecture. Absolutely calm, collected, none of them would have known that Thomas was so ill.[25]

The Bangalore doctor, having exhausted the resources of conventional medicine, took to chanting mantras and persuaded the unbelieving Ramaseshan to promise 1000 rupees to the god Lord Venkateswara if Thomas recovered. When at last he did, the doctor made Ramaseshan pay up, 'as the party of the second part had kept up his end of the contract'.[26]

In the autumn of the same year Dorothy returned to complete her visiting professorship, this time touring the north of the country. Once again, her health was a cause for concern. But despite falling sick in Darjeeling, she insisted on going ahead with a trip that Ramaseshan had promised, to see the sun rising on the Himalayas.

> At 4 a.m. we drove miles and stood on top of Tiger Hill. Before the sun rose, its rays hit the world's highest peak, Mount Everest, which stood there in solitary splendour against a dark background. In succession the lower peaks, hundreds of miles apart, all above 25,000 ft appeared one by one . . . till finally the great Kanchenjunga exposed herself in the yellow fiery light . . . When the sun was finally up Dorothy spoke. 'It was truly magnificent. I

would not have missed it for the world. Thank you, Siv, for not cancelling this visit.'[27]

In her international contacts, Dorothy made scientists from each country she visited feel that their relationship with her was in some way special. Vijayan suddenly realized this in 1986 when he went to Beijing for a meeting on small molecules. Dorothy was there, so was a delegation from the USSR Institute of Crystallography, and of course the Chinese crystallographers from the Institute of Biophysics.

> Interacting with her in China was remarkable. We often think of Dorothy as our very own, and the Chinese do exactly the same. So do the Russians. She is just the same everywhere. That came into sharp focus in China.[28]

As Dorothy collected honours and distinctions at home and abroad, she was well aware that her eminence gave her influence. And in the cause of education, science and world peace, she was prepared to use that influence wherever she could. At home in Oxford, she was one of the prime movers in an initiative to found a college to cater for graduate students, mainly from overseas, for whom there were few places in the traditional undergraduate colleges. The result was Linacre House, which became Linacre College in 1965, with its own Principal and Fellows. Dorothy was the first to be elected an Honorary Fellow of Linacre.

At the end of the 1960s she was invited to join a committee set up under the Liberal leader Jo Grimond to investigate the administration of the University of Birmingham. It gave her an insight into university structures never achieved in her years at Oxford. One of the committee's main findings was that women, who made up almost 50 per cent of the students, were very poorly represented among the staff. However, there were substantial numbers of women working part-time who had no proper contractual status, and did not show up on the books. The report, presented in 1972, recommended the introduction of flexible and part-time contracts, now standard throughout the university system. It made Dorothy realize that her own house needed putting in order in that respect, for Eleanor Dodson and her other part-time women workers.

> She came back to Oxford and immediately wrote me a
> contract. It was certainly before my last child was born,
> because it was the only time I ever had any maternity pay
> or anything like that. Up till then she had run this very
> casual system where people were paid what was in the
> coffers. She finally realized that you needed something
> more formal, and that she had been very underpinned by
> the fact that she had a proper job at Somerville from the
> '30s, and that they paid her while she was having children.[29]

In 1970 she was elected Chancellor of Bristol University, the first woman in the country other than members of the royal family to hold such a post. She could have just turned up each year to present degrees, but that was not Dorothy's style. Weighed down by a heavily gilt-embroidered gown that had been made for Winston Churchill, a previous Chancellor, she used the platform to speak out against cuts in education funding and against the move from grants to loans for student maintenance.

She made a point of meeting the students, accepting invitations from student union leaders so that she could hear their point of view. The line she took in her speeches year after year was exactly what they wanted to hear – that student numbers should be expanded, and that grants for maintenance and tuition should be increased in line with inflation. It so happened that her Chancellorship coincided with a savage round of government cuts in higher education that left Bristol having to reduce its budget by 11 per cent. Speeches were not enough. Dorothy wrote to the Minister for Education, Keith Joseph, and went to see him to make her case. At the same time she wrote to the Prime Minister, her former student Margaret Thatcher, who replied: 'Please do get in touch if you want to have a talk about the issue you are raising with Keith Joseph or indeed any other issue. I do so much value your advice and guidance.'[30] Joseph was a cerebral and urbane minister, and Dorothy found him sympathetic – so sympathetic that she thought she must have failed to make her point.

Thank you very much for seeing me. I fear in the course of our in many ways enjoyable conversation I may not have made as strong a plea as I intended for a reversal of the present cuts in student numbers in universities.

I do believe the present levels we aim at of graduate education are too low in relation to the needs of the country. Reversal of some of the cuts would be a signal of hope for the future.[31]

Dorothy's efforts did not win a reprieve for Bristol or the university system as a whole. But for the students and staff, it was immensely encouraging to know she was on their side. When the Bristol University authorities decided to close its School of Architecture in order to stay within budget, a decision taken while she was away in the Sudan with Thomas, Dorothy lent as much support as she could to the campaign to save it. As Chancellor she had no executive powers. But she exercised her right to preside at a crucial meeting of the University Court at which an appeal was to be heard, despite a warning from the Vice-Chancellor that it could get out of hand, and ensured that the protesters got a fair hearing. And she fired off letters to local businesses in an effort to raise private funds. In the event, the school was not saved, but again, Dorothy's active involvement in the issue won her warm support.

A happier project concerned the setting up of a hostel for students from overseas. Dorothy personally contributed to the fund-raising effort, and was delighted to open the building in 1986. It was named Hodgkin House in memory of Thomas, who had died in 1982. From then on she was a regular visitor, delighting as always in the mixing of young people from all over the world.

Dorothy did not seek out positions in public life, but they tended to find her. In the mid-1970s she attained her most prominent role on the international stage as President of the Pugwash Conferences on Science and World Affairs.

The Pugwash Conferences were inspired by Bertrand Russell, the British philosopher, who in 1955 issued a historic appeal against the dangers of war now that nuclear weapons were available. Russell sent the document to Albert Einstein, who signed it only days before his death. It was published with nine further signatories, but has always been known as the Russell–Einstein Manifesto. It began as follows: 'In the tragic situation which confronts humanity, we feel that scientists should assemble in conference to appraise the perils that have arisen as a result of the development of weapons of mass destruction . . .' It went on to urge readers to 'think in a new way', and to preserve the future of humanity by renouncing war as a means of settling disputes. It suggested that worldwide nuclear disarmament would be a useful first step, although it was 'not an ultimate solution'. More than forty years after the Manifesto was issued, the prospect of an end to war seems as far off as ever. But scientists did heed the call to 'assemble in conference to appraise the perils . . .' The first meeting took place in 1957 with just twenty-five participants, at the home of the industrialist Cyrus Eaton in the village of Pugwash, Nova Scotia. Most were physicists, some of whom, including Leo Szilard and Joseph Rotblat, had worked on the atom bomb project during the Second World War. There were representatives from the Soviet Union, China and Japan as well as Europe, Australia and North America. The first meeting made it a priority to gather scientific information about the nature of the nuclear threat, both used in conflict and in weapons testing.

The themes of the short- and long-term effects of nuclear explosions and the dangers of atmospheric and underground testing were developed at a succession of further conferences in other parts of the world, dubbed Pugwash Conferences after their first home. As time went on other scientific issues, such as how to verify compliance with international weapons treaties, were added to the programme.

At the time of the first meeting Dorothy did not have close connections with any of the Pugwash founders. She was, by coincidence, in Canada when it took place, and met one of the participants, Professor J. S. Foster, at a party given by her sister in Ottawa. But he gave her 'a very cynical, unsympathetic view of the whole affair'.[32] As time passed, however, she began to receive more positive reports from close friends who had become Pugwashites, including Conrad Waddington, Linus Pauling and

Kathleen Lonsdale. The first quinquennial conference was held in London in 1962, and Lonsdale arranged for Dorothy to be invited.

This was a large and impressive meeting – it was the only occasion on which I saw Bertrand Russell. I did not do much in the way of attending working sessions but spent the afternoon in a boat on the Thames visiting Greenwich in the company of Alex Rich and Igor Tamm, who spent most of the time discussing and drafting their plans for 'Black boxes' to monitor underground nuclear tests.[33]

Her eager participation particularly struck Joseph Rotblat, one of the original signatories of the Russell–Einstein Manifesto, who is still, at the age of ninety, occupied full-time with Pugwash activities as its President. 'I remember the animated way in which she talked to many people. She knew the Soviet scientists, who trusted her and knew of her scientific achievement. They had trust in her scientific integrity. This was a great asset.'[34] But Dorothy was busy with insulin and did not immediately involve herself further. She was happy to help, however, when asked to make use of her unique network of international contacts. A source of great disappointment to the Pugwash executive was that since the first meeting attended by the physicist Chou Pei Yuan, no Chinese had attended a Pugwash conference. In 1965 Dorothy received a letter from Alexander Rich, a crystallographer from MIT and former colleague of Pauling's, who was one of the principal Pugwash organizers. He asked whether she thought the Chinese could accept an invitation to a Pugwash conference if it was held in Ghana. Dorothy talked to Nkrumah himself about this, and to the Chinese ambassador to Ghana Huang Hua. Nkrumah said there would be no problem; the Chinese were more equivocal. Eventually, at Rich's suggestion, the Ghanaian Academy of Sciences issued an invitation to the Chinese Academy of Sciences to send representatives to discuss disarmament issues, with Pugwash being represented only informally. But even this compromise did not succeed. A further suggestion of Rich's, that Dorothy might help to get some Chinese to a conference on proteins in the United States, was no more successful. Nevertheless Dorothy impressed the organization with her contacts and her willingness to use them, and she was invited to the next quinquennial conference at Ronneby in Sweden.

By this time her concern for the long-term future of humanity had been overtaken by her anguish at the immediate fate of one particular section of it: the people of North Vietnam. She saw no justification whatever for US intervention in the affairs of Indochina, and was appalled to hear of the toll of civilian casualties of the bombing of North Vietnam that began in February 1965. So she was immediately receptive to approaches from a variety of organizations that sprang up in the mid-1960s with the aim of supporting the North Vietnamese and bringing the war to an end, all of whom could see the value of having a Nobel prizewinner and an OM on their letterheads.

The first of these, and the one with which she was associated for longest, was the Medical Aid Foundation for Vietnam. This organization was the creation of another remarkable woman, Joan McMichael. McMichael, herself a lifelong Communist, trained as a doctor in the 1920s and had been involved in medical relief during the Spanish Civil War. She had set up health programmes for children in deprived areas of London in the post-war years, and involved herself in local government. She was one of the delegates at an international women's conference in 1963 where she heard moving first-hand accounts of the suffering caused by the Vietnam war, at a time when American involvement was still in its early stages. Aged nearly sixty, she set up the Medical Aid Foundation for Vietnam in 1965, holding its inaugural meeting in the House of Commons with the help of the Labour MP Renée Short. Supporting victims of the battle zones in Indochina occupied the rest of her life until she died in 1989, in her office almost to the end.

She won support from a substantial group of influential people, including MPs, scientists and doctors, and by the end of her life had raised £2.5 million. After the war was over she launched the British Hospital for Vietnam appeal, enabling the hospital at Ky Anh, close to the border between north and south, to be rebuilt. Later the organization expanded its interests and became Medical and Scientific Aid for Vietnam, Laos and Kampuchea, providing journals, textbooks and scientific equipment as well as medical supplies.

Dorothy at first turned down McMichael's invitation to become President of her charity, but agreed to be a Vice-President (she took on the Presidency a few years later). As in the case of her early association with Pugwash, she did not concern herself with the day-to-day running of the organization, but tried to use her influence to help. In 1969 while in Paris, she and Thomas called on Madame Binh, the leader of the People's Revolutionary Government delegation at the peace talks. They talked about her hopes for the future.

> As the conversation suddenly flagged, Madame Binh changed the subject and asked, 'Joan McMichael is a very remarkable person, tell me why does she care so much for us? She spends all her life working for us. She seems to love us so much. How does this happen?' I could only say that her love is returned, perhaps because she found friends who stand for the same causes she cared for and themselves gave all in their power to the perfecting of the world.[35]

Dorothy invited Madame Binh to the Hodgkin family home at Crab Mill, hoping to be able to set up a meeting between North and South Vietnamese scientists there. But the death of the North Vietnamese leader Ho Chi Minh late in 1969 meant that the plan had to be shelved, and it was not revived.

In 1970 Dorothy agreed to become a member of a Commission of Inquiry into US War Crimes in Vietnam, set up by the Stockholm Conference on Vietnam and chaired by Gunnar Myrdal. This body collected evidence, in the form of harrowing photographs and eye-witness accounts from both sides, of the suffering caused by US action in Vietnam, including the bombing of schools and hospitals. It also raised awareness of the environmental destruction that was taking place through the use of defoliants and the deliberate bombing of North Vietnamese flood defences.

Dorothy lost no time in placing this information in the public eye. In March 1971 she published an article in the Saturday Review section of *The Times* in which she stated her unequivocal support for the people of North Vietnam and the People's

Revolutionary Government in the South. She praised the self-sufficiency of the Vietnamese villagers, noting the impressive levels of literacy among the young. She suggested that Madame Binh was a leader to rank with Indira Gandhi. She quoted what she had learned through the War Crimes Commission from disaffected American ground troops who were sickened by the brutality of the war. She pointed out that high-level bombing made it too easy for pilots to be unaffected by the suffering they caused. She admitted that she personally had no experience of bombs at close quarters, but added a typically personal anecdote before making a direct appeal to the readers.

> I remember Nelly, who once cooked for us and went to nurse in Birmingham during the Blitz, saying when she came back for the weekend that nothing in her nursing training had prepared her for the state of human bodies hit by high explosives . . .
>
> At night and at odd moments of the day I often find myself thinking about what is to be done about the state of the world today. The contrast between the miseries of war and poverty and the possiblity of pleasant ways of living in a world at peace is so great. But to get peace one has to restore confidence between nations and peoples . . .
>
> Ten million tons of ammunition have already been used by the United States in Indo-China. There should be no more.[36]

She was annoyed that the newspaper used a photograph of her to illustrate the piece, rather than a picture showing the injuries caused by fragmentation bombs that she had provided. The excuse, that the picture would look a bit odd next to the recipe for stuffed green peppers elsewhere on the same page, suggests that the paper had little sympathy with the views she expressed. The article provoked at least one hostile letter from a reader, chastising her for falling for Communist propaganda, and raised eyebrows at Oxford High Tables. She may not have convinced any of those not already committed to the anti-war movement, but she certainly got their attention.

Later the same year Dorothy and Thomas were invited to visit

North Vietnam as guests of the government, and to give lectures on insulin and Africa respectively. Paying their own fares, but accepting the hospitality of their hosts in the country, they went to Hanoi via Moscow in September 1971. Dorothy enjoyed meeting Vietnamese scientists, and later invited one of her hosts to send a research student to her laboratory, although this plan never came off. But much of their time during the two-week visit was spent touring the country and seeing for themselves how the North Vietnamese were coping with the US bombardment. They were enchanted by the country, and by the people they met. The most striking feature of the villages and factories they visited was that they seemed almost entirely populated by girls in their late teens and early twenties. The young men were all in the Army, while the mothers and children and older people had been sent into hideouts in the jungle.

> One was reminded often of Britain in the Blitz [wrote Thomas]. But there is a particular beautiful Vietnamese way of doing things – and more Socialist construction is going on there than we ever achieved . . .
> More impressive was the deputy herself who, at the age of 16, had organized a women's militia that built itself what our young interpreter called 'a fortress' at the edge of the village. It was really a very simple anti-aircraft site, where the girls lived and which they manned in shifts, growing rice in any time that they could spare from their military duties, and where they had shot down two American aeroplanes in 1966 and 1967. They gave us a brief demonstration of how they'd done it.[37]

They also noted factory workers singing as they worked, and the generosity of villagers in highland areas donating bamboo poles and pigs to assist their compatriots in the flood-hit lowlands. Dorothy commented on the warm friendship between the elderly Buddhist nun at a temple they visited and the young woman who was her local Communist deputy. Interviewed for Radio Hanoi, she said the most impressive thing she had seen was 'people, in spite of all they have had to endure, managing to live and look well and beautiful and happy'.[38]

With these images of smiling faces still fresh in her mind, Dorothy was appalled to hear of the renewed American aerial bombardment launched on Christmas Day 1971. She wrote immediately to Henry Kissinger to protest, and in response received an invitation from the Second Secretary at the US Embassy in London to tell him about her visit. Once again she was able to make her feelings public, this time in an article in the *New York Times*.

> It seems incredible that any civilized nation should drop
> bombs on the pleasant fields and villages we saw, on
> Christmas day, or any day. All that we learned in Vietnam
> made it clear that people were anxious to work towards
> peace . . . Time and effort and money need to be turned
> seriously from warmaking to peacemaking – and soon – if
> more beautiful countries and many intelligent people are
> to be saved from destruction.[39]

In 1973, with every encouragement from her parents, Dorothy and Thomas's daughter Elizabeth went to Hanoi to teach English and help edit English language publications. She had in fact thought of going in 1968, the year of the Tet Offensive. Dorothy had learned that the departure of Freda Cook, who had been teaching in North Vietnam and now, aged seventy, was returning to England, would leave the country with no English language specialist. Elizabeth had been teaching in Zambia for over two years and was keen to replace her. So she wrote and applied for the post, but heard nothing in reply. Instead she accepted a post in Khartoum, to teach history at the University. Five years later there was a summons, out of the blue, asking if she could come to Vietnam at once; she had got the job. She stayed until after the fall of Saigon in 1975. First Thomas and then Dorothy came out to join her for a few weeks in 1974.

Although she had in the past put her name to appeals and manifestos for causes she supported, the Vietnam War saw Dorothy using her celebrity to make personal, high-profile statements for the first time. It is doubtful that any single individual could have influenced the course of that conflict, but her uncompromising stance against US policy in Vietnam helped to put heart into the antiwar movement, and, as in the case of China, her personal approaches to the Vietnamese helped them to feel they were not without friends in the West. Was she naïve in her view of the North Vietnamese regime? Perhaps, although today most observers would agree with her condemnation of American actions. But she thought in terms of people, not regimes, and spoke as a friend on behalf of her friends in the North. It was a position she found easy to defend, as Tom Blundell remembers.

> One or two Fellows of Linacre [Blundell's college] thought they would get her down and question her and expose her. They were expecting a political analysis but they didn't understand Dorothy. She talked about the people she'd met, the people she knew, the scientists she'd met, and was therefore extremely difficult to attack, because she saw everything in terms of people. All the interactions I've known her have, China, India, Poland, Soviet Union, Ghana, she always took that approach. It was an emotional positioning, a human interaction.[40]

As long as the conflict in Vietnam continued, Dorothy had little further to do with Pugwash. When she went to the Ronneby conference in 1967 she met some of the key Pugwash scientists for the first time, including Cecil Powell from Bristol and the Russian physicist Peter Kapitza. But she spent all her time in the working group on Vietnam instead of the one to which she had been assigned.

> It was fascinating but very frustrating. The official US State Department view was so strongly pressed by certain of the Americans it was extraordinarily difficult to get any statement agreed which said what most of us wanted.[41]

In 1969 she was invited to join one of the smaller Pugwash symposia, held at Marianska Lazny in Czechoslovakia. It was less than two years since the Soviet occupation of the country, providing a test of the Pugwash principle that participants were invited as individuals, not representatives of their nations. Dorothy was lukewarm in her assessment in a private letter to

Thomas. 'The meetings were curious – mostly too repetitious with a lot of too general statements and a background of tension. But . . . the USSR delegation is here for the first time they say since the occupation . . .'

Her relationship to Pugwash underwent a dramatic change in 1974. She received a visit from Joseph Rotblat and Rudolf Peierls, another émigré and former nuclear researcher who had just retired as Oxford's Wykeham Professor of Physics. They asked her if she would take over as the organization's President when the current holder retired the following year. Rotblat remembers her reaction.

> She was hesitant – not reluctant but hesitant – because she had so much to do. We reassured her that she would only have to come to one meeting per year, but we both knew that would not be the case, because she took everything seriously and thought Pugwash was important. She also understood what she could contribute, and therefore she accepted.[42]

Why Dorothy? Rotblat admits frankly that the executive wanted to 'exploit her scientific fame'; she herself later said that her Chinese connections were an important factor, as Pugwash had still not succeeded in getting any Chinese to attend its conferences. With events in South East Asia still unsettled, Chinese participation was seen as highly desirable. Dorothy was certainly willing to be exploited in this way, but even she did not anticipate the extent to which Pugwash would take over her life. She wrote modestly to the Secretary General, Bernie Feld, towards the end of 1975: 'I do hope I may be some use to the purposes of the organization, even if my presence is rather casual and occasional.'[43]

The 25th conference was held in Madras in 1976 and Dorothy, newly appointed as President, gave the opening speech in the presence of Prime Minister Indira Gandhi. After the Madras conference Feld retired, and his place was taken by another American, the former Director of Research and Development for the World Health Organization, Martin Kaplan. Kaplan saw that there was some need to revitalize the organization. In its early days it had attracted a great deal of publicity, and could with justification claim to have made important scientific contributions to agreements limiting nuclear weapons. The Nuclear Test Ban Treaty of 1963, the Nuclear Non-Proliferation Treaty of 1968, and the first round of SALT agreements in 1972 all made use of principles that had been developed in discussions by Pugwash working groups. But by the mid-1970s Pugwash had to a certain extent lost its focus. Its membership had expanded to include not only physical and life scientists, but social and political scientists as well. Its topics for discussion now included the security implications of the economic imbalance between developed and developing countries, and it began to tackle issues which were already the concern of other special interest groups. Whereas in the early days the reports produced by Pugwash working groups contained valuable analyses of scientific information, attempts to tackle issues that were essentially political were less likely to reach a consensus. A succession of regional conflicts, including those in the Middle East and South East Asia, deflected attention from the central issue of nuclear disarmament.

In terms of its public profile, there was a limit to the extent to which Pugwash could continue to attract coverage by essentially repeating the message of the Russell–Einstein Manifesto. Yet its preferred way of working, through private meetings of private individuals who (theoretically) did not represent their governments, excluded the possibility of giving the world's media access to its deliberations, and this inevitably frustrated journalists who might otherwise have been well disposed towards the organization. Dorothy's appointment as President was a good move from a public relations point of view. The opening speeches she gave at Pugwash conferences around the world always attracted prominent coverage in the host country, and often further afield. But the underlying problems of the organization were as intractable as ever.

As Executive Secretary, Martin Kaplan struggled to find a formula that would make the organization and its conferences more effective. He certainly perceived Dorothy's role as more than that of a figurehead, as she ruefully pointed out to him before her first year as President was out. 'I find myself, and probably rightly, more drawn in than I meant to be – and certainly your

new draft suggests you want your president to attend more meetings . . . I meant to avoid more interruptions this year.'[44]

Dorothy's speeches to the annual conferences show that as time
went by she gained increasing command of the detail of disarmament issues. At first, she tended to rely on appeals to the better
nature of mankind; at Munich in 1977, for example, she quoted
Bertrand Russell expressing sentiments that she certainly shared.

> Sometimes in a vision I see a world of happy human
> beings, all vigorous, all intelligent, none of them
> oppressing, none of them oppressed, a world of human
> beings aware that their common interests outweigh those
> in which they compete, striving towards those really
> splendid possibilities that the human intellect and the
> human imagination make possible. Such a world as I was
> speaking of can exist if men choose that it should. And if it
> does exist – if it does come to exist – we shall have a world
> very much more glorious, very much more splendid, more
> happy, more full of imagination and of happy emotions
> than any world that the world has ever known before.

While her public statements never wholly lost this utopian quality, they also began to show evidence that Dorothy was
conscientious in collecting available knowledge on a variety of
topics related to the disarmament issue: the funding of defence
research, the arms trade, developments in chemical and biological weapons, verification of test bans. Compared with the leaden
prose of many Pugwash working papers, she spoke with characteristic clarity and simplicity, making global issues seem personal.
Her position as a respected Western scientist with strong Eastern
sympathies and a concern for the developing world made her
uniquely qualified to head an organization such as Pugwash.

Yet the nature of the organization itself, and the politics of the
wider world, set limits on what she could achieve. In private she
was surprisingly realistic about this. Early in her presidency she
wrote to Professor Mike Pentz of the British Pugwash Group.

> The actual piling up of armaments and the present state of
> the arms trade suggest that the scientists whether in

Pugwash or not have had no effect on disarmament or in diminishing arms manufacture. From the little I know this has not been for want of trying or for want of scientific prestige . . .

I do think Pugwash has been useful as one more way of making close contacts between leading scientists in different fields, probably in preventing worse from happening in the way of wars, probably assisting, if very imperfectly, the practice of peace.[45]

'Making close contacts between scientists' was just the way Dorothy liked to work, whether she was working for science or for peace. She quickly became involved in further efforts to gain Chinese participation, corresponding regularly with Chou Pei Yuan at the Chinese Academy of Sciences. These efforts became more urgent in 1979 after the Chinese invasion of Vietnam. But Chou refused to consider meeting to discuss long-range problems of world peace with a small group of British, Russian and American scientists because it would divert attention from 'Vietnamese aggression against Kampuchea' – the only topic the Chinese were prepared to discuss. There was no meeting. In the mid-1980s, however, once regional tensions had eased, the long courtship paid off, and Chinese delegates reappeared at Pugwash conferences for the first time since 1957.

It was a basic tenet of Pugwash that the organization should remain non-partisan with respect to any issue in international relations. It was a position that could risk alienating even substantial sections of its own membership if it appeared, however inadvertently, to condone reprehensible political actions. This was a risk that the Executive Committee took at the end of 1981 when they agreed to go ahead with plans for the 25th anniversary conference in Warsaw the next year, despite the introduction of martial law in Poland. Dorothy was not present at the committee meeting, as she was travelling in the Sudan with Thomas. But she knew of, and supported, the decision.

The American Pugwash group, however, found it impossible to remain neutral on the issue, and announced that they would boycott the meeting. After Dorothy wrote to try to persuade them otherwise, they agreed to circulate her letter to members, and to leave individual members to make up their own minds, as anything else would be 'contrary to the spirit of Pugwash'. Meanwhile a declaration circulated to all Nobel prizewinners in the natural sciences for their signatures, to be published after the conference, drew at least one vehement negative, from Rosalyn Yalow, the American medical physicist who won the Prize for Physiology or Medicine in 1977. She concluded her letter of refusal by hoping that 'the Pugwash Conference will have the courage to deal realistically with a current urgent problem of the war of a government against its own people'.[46]

The conference went ahead. It proved to be a more than usually contentious affair. Apart from the Polish situation, US–Soviet relations were at an all-time low, following the breakdown of negotiations on arms agreements and the siting of US ballistic missiles in Western Europe. The intrusion of national interests prevented any clear statements about the current position. The executive committee, including Dorothy, appeared to compound the controversy by accepting an invitation to meet the Prime Minister, General Jaruzelski. Even some of the Pugwash participants saw this as politically reckless, and in the event it looked even worse. On the day the meeting took place, 31 August 1982, a Solidarity demonstration in the streets of Warsaw was violently suppressed with tear gas and rubber bullets. The press, who once again had been invited to the conference but refused access to the working groups, were in a hostile mood. The adoption of a declaration calling for an immediate freeze on nuclear weapons by all parties, signed eventually by 111 Nobel prizewinners, was angrily reported in the American press as support for the Soviets.

Dorothy and Martin Kaplan were forced into a damage-limitation exercise, writing to the *New York Times* under the heading 'The Warsaw Pugwash Conference Did Not "Cower" to the Soviets'.

The choice of country [for Pugwash conferences] does not imply either approval of or opposition to the ideology of the government in power; otherwise, many countries would be ineligible for such meetings, given the diversity of political views among Pugwash participants . . . An

invitation for an exchange of views with the Prime
Minister, General Jaruzelski, was accepted by our Council,
as is the custom when requested by a high official in a host
country . . .Lengthy discussions were held, during which
hard-hitting questions and comments were put to the two
officials, and were answered with candour. The topics
included the suppression of Solidarity, the reported use of
brutality on prisoners and other political and economic
factors contributing to the present difficulties of Poland
and their import for European security.

. . . [They point out that papers critical of US and USSR
and Polish policy were circulated and freely discussed at
the conference.] In some Western circles we have often
been considered Soviet dupes; to them, anyone outside the
official establishment willing to sit down with the Russians
and talk of peace is suspect.

There are factions in the Soviet Union that consider
Pugwash an agent of the West . . .

We all agree that at the present time top priority must be
given to our chief objective – prevention of nuclear war.
Any other issue, however important, must take second
place in our efforts to achieve our main goal.[47]

Dorothy did not relish this kind of public conflict. But she was
soon able to put Warsaw behind her as the changing political
scene found Pugwash increasingly swimming with the tide. The
huge upsurge in support for the Campaign for Nuclear
Disarmament in Britain and similar groups in Germany, followed
eventually by Mikhail Gorbachev's recognition that the arms race
was economically disastrous for the Soviet Union, led in 1987 to
the treaty banning intermediate range nuclear forces such as
Cruise and Pershing missiles, and their eventual withdrawal
from Europe. During this period Dorothy devoted much effort to
her favoured style of intervention, a quiet word here and there
behind the scenes. She had never had the smallest hesitation
about using her contacts to achieve desired ends. An obvious
target was her former pupil Margaret Thatcher, British Prime
Minister from 1979 until 1990.

The Reaganite 'evil empire' rhetoric deployed by the

governments of Britain and the United States caused Dorothy much concern. A scrappy piece of paper in her archive headed 'Notes for Margaret' begins 'Object: to rethink relations with the Soviet Union on the basis that friendship is possible and would be to everyone's advantage – trade – science – art – the lot'. It may have been an aide-memoire before a visit she made at the Prime Minister's invitation to lunch at Chequers, her official country residence, in 1983. She continued to keep up gentle pressure through correspondence, sending, for example, a petition calling for a ban on chemical weapons in 1986. This, as with all her approaches, received a courteous and detailed personal response. Thatcher agreed that a ban was desirable, but argued that the current obstacle to its achievement was the Soviet position on verification. Dorothy delayed her reply until after she had herself made a trip to Moscow to meet fellow-Pugwashites who had taken part in a workshop on chemical weapons. By that time the Soviet side was showing a greater willingness to accept verification, and Dorothy reported her satisfaction with the situation to Thatcher.

> I like to think the change in Soviet attitudes has been helped by the experiments in progress on what international verification actually means in practice. We [Pugwash] had some investigations in a West German chemical factory two or three years ago; similar ones are likely to take place in an East German chemical works early next year. And now there is also the example of the very successful cooperation of Evgeny Velikhov and Frank van Hippel [Russian and American Pugwash scientists] on nuclear test monitoring. So I have become rather hopeful.
>
> I do hope you go to Moscow and perhaps elsewhere in the USSR – and find it enjoyable.[48]

Soon afterwards Thatcher met Gorbachev in Britain, famously calling him 'a man I can do business with', and subsquently she did indeed go to Moscow. The former Prime Minister herself, now Baroness Thatcher, denies that Dorothy's proddings had any influence in this decision. She was certainly not a lone voice – it had been Foreign Office policy for years to try to encourage the

Prime Minister to take a greater interest in East–West affairs, and the accession of Gorbachev as President made it easier for her to do so. At least it can be said that Thatcher always listened to what Dorothy had to say, even if she did not agree. 'We just took a different view and we both knew it: she couldn't dissuade me and I couldn't dissuade her. Yes, she was idealistic – but no amount of idealism could conceal the tyranny of the Soviet regime.'[49]

Thatcher's connection with Dorothy must, however, have had something to do with the fact that her 1987 Moscow visit took in the USSR Academy of Science's Institute of Crystallography. The Director at that time was Boris Vainshtein, whom Dorothy had first met in 1953, and whom she had since come to know well. His report on the Prime Minister's visit must have raised a wry smile on the face of her former tutor. 'Everybody here was fascinated by this clever and charming lady, who, despite her numerous political duties, is still very keen on science.'[50] The following year a delegation from the Institute visited England at the invitation of the Royal Society, and was received at 10 Downing Street. Ushered into the Prime Minister's study, they noticed at once a portrait of Dorothy on the wall above the desk.[51] Despite their political differences Margaret Thatcher counted herself among Dorothy's greatest admirers, and continues to do so.

The Soviet authorities did not leave any doubt that they regarded Dorothy's relentless efforts to maintain East–West dialogue as very valuable indeed: in 1987 they awarded her the Lenin Peace Prize. Joseph Rotblat recalls that she had some anxious discussion with him about whether or not she should accept it. They realized there was a possible danger of her being 'drawn into the Soviet sphere', which might compromise her position as President. However, the prize was being offered to her personally, not to Pugwash. She decided to accept the honour for herself and travelled to Moscow for the ceremony. She donated most of the prize money to Pugwash, however; the remainder she quietly gave away to individuals she regarded as deserving.

Dorothy did not live to see it, but in 1995, fifty years after the bombing of Hiroshima and Nagasaki and forty years after the Russell–Einstein Manifesto, Pugwash and its President Joseph

Rotblat were awarded the Nobel Peace Prize. The citation under-lined what perhaps had been the main role of Pugwash all along, even when its efforts seemed most futile – to give authority and respectability to the arguments for disarmament across political boundaries.

> The Conferences are based on the recognition of the responsibility of scientists for their inventions. They have underlined the catastrophic consequences of the use of the new weapons. They have brought together scientists and decision-makers to collaborate across political divides on constructive proposals for reducing the nuclear threat . . .
>
> It is the Committee's hope that the award of the Nobel Peace Prize for 1995 to Rotblat and to Pugwash will encourage world leaders to intensify their efforts to rid the world of nuclear weapons.[52]

10

'Recently everything has become more hopeful'

Retirement and after,
1977–1994

Retirement did not come easily to Dorothy. She liked to be working, and she liked the company of people who shared her interests. Beautiful as Crab Mill was, the idea of withdrawing to the country and tending her roses had little appeal. Only physical frailty eventually forced her to curtail her scientific and other activities, and even then she did everything in her power to stay in touch.

She took official retirement from the Wolfson Professorship in 1977, the latest possible date, when she was sixty-seven years old. Much of her energy in the last few years of her appointment was taken up with ensuring that her work would continue in younger hands. The insulin work, now taking the structure to ever-finer resolution and broadening out to encompass insulins from many other species, had in practice been managed by Guy Dodson for around a decade. He and his wife Eleanor quickly became indispensable to Dorothy. They were much more than colleagues: they were dear friends, they were almost family. The Dodson children regarded Dorothy as a surrogate grandmother, their own being the other side of the world. (Eleanor Dodson says that Dorothy always noticed and responded to children in a very special way, and others have said the same. Siv Ramaseshan remembers his own children, in Oxford in October 1964, exclaiming, 'Our Dorothy has won the Nobel prize!')

The question of what Guy and Eleanor were to do after Dorothy retired became increasingly urgent almost from the moment the group moved into its new lab in the Zoology/Psychology Building in 1971. They were in the same position as all Dorothy's former colleagues, in that neither had a permanent job in Oxford: Guy was still, after all those years, a post-doc paid from Dorothy's research grants, and Eleanor a part-time research assistant. Others there at the same time had either always intended to move on, or were preparing to do so. John Cutfield and Bryan Anderson were New Zealanders who expected to return home when their Fellowships were up; the same applied to Vijayan, who was going back to India. Tom Blundell left for a post at Sussex University; he later inherited Bernal's Chair in Crystallography at Birkbeck. (Later still, rather to Dorothy's disapproval, he took a senior post in scientific administration as Chief Executive of the Agriculture and Food Research Council; he is now a professor of biochemistry at Cambridge.) But for the Dodsons, and for Dorothy herself, the idea of breaking the bond that had developed between them was hard to bear.

Initially Dorothy hoped that she would be able to arrange a job for Guy in Oxford. But as the Royal Society Wolfson Professor, she found herself on the outside, without influence – as she told Eleanor, she had not sat on a committee for fifteen years. Guy had to look elsewhere. He applied for a lectureship in the Chemistry Department at the University of York, where there was already a flourishing crystallography group in physics. Dorothy put the full warmth of her appreciation of all he had done into the reference she wrote for him. So it was that in 1976 Guy and Eleanor set off north for another ancient city, with a rather less ancient university, to set up a new crystallographic laboratory. There they could continue to work on insulin and related problems in protein structure. Today Guy has a professorship in the Chemistry Department; the lab flourishes, very much in the style of Dorothy's, with a constant stream of researchers from many countries coming to learn new skills and exchange views on world affairs.

Meanwhile Dorothy applied for another two years' grant and carried on until the last possible minute, with a much smaller team, finishing up remaining projects as far as possible. It was really a matter of winding down the operation. Her last DPhil student, Sue Cutfield, had finished her thesis in 1975 (while simultaneously caring for a new baby) and gone home to join her husband. To help her Dorothy invited Vijayan and Kalyani to come to Oxford for her last year, when almost everyone else had left. Kalyani tied up some loose ends on the Vitamin B_{12} research, until she had to leave to prepare for the birth of her baby. Vijayan worked very closely with Dorothy, reconciling the results of two different refinements of the insulin structure; each would begin the day by enquiring anxiously about the health of the other's spouse.

Rather to the disappointment of the Oxford Chemical Crystallography Department, Dorothy arranged for her four-circle diffractometer, an X-ray generator and two precession cameras, which had been bought with grants for work on insulin, to be transferred to the Dodsons' lab in York. Then there was little left to do but move out. All trace of her occupation was soon obliterated by the expansion of Experimental Psychology into what had been her territory, as had been agreed before she moved in.

But Dorothy was not left without an Oxford base. As early as 1974 the Professor of Inorganic Chemistry, then about to retire himself, had offered her a room in the white-painted two-storey building at 9 Parks Road that had just been taken over by Chemical Crystallography. There she installed her index cards of references, her books, her models and her boxes of reprints, and there she continued to read, write and examine her maps for more than ten years. The Department was now run by Keith Prout, who had taken over when Tiny Powell retired. He remembers that she took a great interest in what the younger students were doing, and was always ready to stop for a chat about someone's research. But he had known her long enough not to be taken in by her frail exterior – he knew the ruthlessness with which she had pursued her scientific goals. He remembers with amusement Thomas coming in one day, before going away on a trip, and entreating him to 'take care of my dear little Dossie'. Another crystallographer remembers seeing Prout solicitously helping the arthritic Dorothy into a taxi outside the department.

The taxi driver seemed anxious. 'Will she be all right?' he asked. 'Of course she'll be all right,' was the reply. 'She's only going to Moscow.'[1]

Dorothy remained extremely busy with her outside interests. Her Chancellorship at Bristol, her Presidencies of Pugwash and of Medical and Scientific Aid for Vietnam, Laos and Kampuchea, her place on the committee of the International Union of Crystallography as Past President – none of these had any age limits, and if such a thing were possible she pursued them with even greater diligence after retiring from her Oxford post. On the scientific side, she received as many invitations as ever to speak at conferences or visit laboratories. She was fêted wherever she went. The European Crystallography Conference was held in her honour in Oxford in 1977, and in 1980 crystallographers, Linus Pauling among them, came from far and wide to celebrate her seventieth birthday with a symposium and a party in the garden at Somerville. To mark the occasion some of her closest colleagues (Guy Dodson, Jenny Glusker and David Sayre) produced a volume of reminiscences and reports in her honour, which remains one of the best sources there is on her early scientific life.[2]

By this time Dorothy had achieved the status of doyenne among crystallographers. The previous two decades had marked the passing of many members of an earlier generation, those who had laid the foundations for the subject and had provided her with the inspiration and support to sustain her own research career. As the most eminent survivor, Dorothy found herself in increasing demand as an obituarist, an obligation she carried out willingly and with some style. As early as 1964, in her Nobel speech, Dorothy remembered those who had not lived to see the award: the ebullient, enthusiastic American 'Fan' Fankuchen, who had succeeded her as Bernal's assistant; the good-humoured Bill Astbury, Bernal's contemporary under W. H. Bragg at the Royal Institution, who had led the way with crystallographic work on protein fibres in his laboratory at Leeds; and the Swedish protein chemist K. Lindestrom-Lang.

By the time of her opening speech as President of the International Union of Crystallography in Kyoto in 1972, she had to note the passing of three of the most significant contributors to the history of the subject. Kathleen Lonsdale, the tough, single-minded physicist who looked like a 'sweet, gentle, elderly grandmother', had succumbed to cancer in April 1971 aged sixty-eight. Dorothy had last seen her only a few weeks before, 'in her room at University College, to which she had, very irregularly, walked in her dressing gown from her bedroom in University College Hospital across the way, to find some papers she needed in connection with the book . . . she was writing.'[3]

In an affectionate and admiring memoir, Dorothy wrote not only of her science, but of her efforts to see science applied in a socially responsible manner. She revealed Lonsdale's hand in the first international code of practice to protect uranium miners from the effects of radiation, and related a charming anecdote about her reputation as a pacifist.

> In no country that she visited did she receive a more moving welcome than in Japan. She found when she arrived that so many flowers had been sent to her they filled every room in the small hotel in which she was staying. She discovered that it had been reported in the papers that she had gone to prison rather than work on the atomic bomb . . . She immediately had the report corrected saying that, of course, she would have gone to prison rather than work on the atomic bomb, but nobody had, in fact, asked her to do so. The result of this announcement was that more flowers came in than ever. They had to be stood in buckets all down the street.[4]

Dorothy also chose to quote, with apparent recognition, Kathleen Lonsdale's own prescription for women's success in science.

> For a woman, and especially a married woman with children, to become a first class scientist she must first of all choose, or have chosen, the right husband. He must recognize her problems and be willing to share them. If he is really domesticated, so much the better. Then she must be a good organizer and be pretty ruthless in keeping to her schedule, no matter if the heavens fall. She must be

able to do with very little sleep, because her working week will be at least twice as long as the average trade unionist's. She must go against all her early training and not care if she is regarded as a little peculiar. She must be willing to accept additional responsibility, even if she feels that she has more than enough. But above all, she must learn to concentrate in any available moment and not require ideal conditions in which to do so.[5]

Only three months after Kathleen Lonsdale died she was followed by the Grand Old Man of British crystallography, Sir Lawrence Bragg. The community had only recently celebrated his eightieth birthday with a symposium at the Royal Institution (at which Dorothy had mischievously made the 29-year-old Vijayan take her place on the programme, 'because there was no Indian among the speakers'.) Bragg was still working on an account of the development of X-ray analysis, which records for later generations the excitement of the early work he undertook with his father.[6] Although strictly speaking Dorothy traced her scientific ancestry to the elder Bragg, who had pioneered the application of X-rays to biological molecules, Lawrence Bragg had always been a benevolent presence in her life, sending warmly admiring letters to mark all her most significant achievements.

The loss of Lonsdale and Bragg was followed by an even sadder parting. On 15 September 1971, after a series of strokes beginning almost ten years before that gradually incapacitated him, John Desmond Bernal died at the age of seventy. Dorothy's obituary of him (written some time before) appeared in *The Times* the following day, before she had even heard the news. She and Thomas were in Hanoi at the time, and learned of Bernal's death from Nguyen Van Huong and Dang Vinh Thien from the State Committee for Science and Technology.

They had never met him, but thought of him as someone greatly to be loved and admired, whose death was a loss to everyone. We talked about him, what he was like, his marvellous breadth of knowledge, his intense interest in science and in people . . .[7]

It is probably not putting it too strongly to say that there was no one that Dorothy 'loved and admired' as much as Bernal. Her belief in his virtual omniscience comes out in a story she told in the first Bernal Lecture, which she gave at Birkbeck College a year before his death (at the time he was already too ill to attend).

When I was in Stockholm, taking part in a TV programme, I was asked, 'What would you do if somebody gave you a piece of the moon?', and I said, very quickly, half joking, half serious, 'Oh, I should pass it on to J. D. Bernal.' I was sure he would know more than I did about the kind of structures to expect in moon rocks and good experiments to try on them.[8]

Dorothy, the Nobel prizewinner, would always defer to her mentor in matters not directly within her arca of expertise. The last paper on which she and Bernal were co-authors came out in 1940; they did not collaborate in a formal sense thereafter. But Dorothy always kept Bernal informed of the progress of her research. She was a frequent visitor to the Birkbeck laboratories, and although many of Bernal's research interests were not directly related to hers, she kept in close touch with what his colleagues were doing, and contributed where she could. Together they shared in the achievements of others: they are captured together in photographs visiting East Berlin for the opening of Käthe Dornberger-Schiff's new research institute in 1962, or viewing with admiration David Phillips's model of lysozyme in 1965.

The nature of their relationship had certainly evolved since the early days at Cambridge, but retained, from Dorothy's perspective at least, a sense of inequality: she saw him, without qualification, as a towering figure in science and world affairs. She never understood, for example, why he was not awarded a Nobel prize, either for science or for peace, something for which she unsuccessfully lobbied once she had won her own prize. In the Bernal Lecture, she said:

[W]henever there was a serious international crisis, threatening all our lives, we could only wish that he would spend even longer than he did, working for international

cooperation and world peace. There were moments when
he seemed almost the only person who would and could
go anywhere in the world to encourage rational solutions
in all conflicts and who would be welcome whatever
country he visited, whatever its political persuasion.[9]

What of her personal feelings? The passion Bernal had inspired in
her as a young woman had matured into an undying love and
loyalty, feelings that she shared with others in his immediate
circle. This loyalty expressed itself in a determination to preserve
a view of him that admitted no doubts about the astuteness of his
political judgement, or any public admission of his human fail-
ings. Eileen Bernal, who cared for him through the last years of
his life, thought it impossible, at least in the short term, to speak
freely about his relations with people. She supervised the sorting
of his papers, to be archived in the University Library at
Cambridge, and stipulated that the box containing correspondence 'of a personal nature' should be closed for fifty years.

For her part, Dorothy undertook to write Bernal's biographical
memoir for the Royal Society, despite being already committed to
writing Katherine Lonsdale's. These long essays, which at that
time could run to as many as sixty pages, are traditionally supposed to be published within a year of the death of the Fellow in
question, a tall order for a scientist with a busy schedule. Dorothy
finished Lonsdale's in time for the 1975 volume, but Bernal's did
not appear until 1980. It was worth waiting for: she had been
characteristically thorough in her research. It was easy enough for
her to give a concise and lucid account of his scientific work; she
was also deeply familiar with his writings on science and society,
his work with the World Peace Council and the World Federation
of Scientific Workers, and his relations with the Soviet Union. To
inform herself further she went to the lengths of visiting his
childhood home, Nenagh in Ireland, where she met his brother
Kevin, and interviewing many of his friends and family. She read
exhaustively among Bernal's diaries and unpublished manu-
scripts for accounts of his life before she knew him, and drew on
a number of interviews Eileen Bernal had herself carried out with
his former colleagues.

There are, of course, silences in the work that resulted. Bernal's defence of Lysenko and its aftermath rates a single line; his ejection from the Council of the British Association for the Advancement of Science is not mentioned. Dorothy documents Bernal's meeting with Eileen Sprague and their marriage; she mentions only in passing that two of his four children had other mothers. She includes herself in the story only in a footnote, and in the occasional 'we' that reveals her to have been present on one or other occasion reported. If Bernal could be described as a flawed genius, she does her best to hide the flaws.

You would not expect, of course, to find a 'warts and all' account of the life of any scientist among the *Biographical Memoirs of Fellows of the Royal Society*. But Dorothy's memoir, partial as it is in both senses, remains for the time being the only authorized account of Bernal's life. The science writer Maurice Goldsmith published a short biography in 1980, a project from which the guardians of Bernal's memory withdrew their support before it was complete.[10] Dorothy herself wrote a highly critical review of the book in the journal *Nature*, accusing the author of relying too much on gossip. To date there is no truly comprehensive and clear-sighted account of this charismatic and complex man.

When her dear friend Max Perutz wrote an article about Bernal in the *New Scientist*, which in passing noted his support for the Soviet Union, she sat down and drafted a seven-page letter to him. (She never sent it, but the draft remains in the archive.) Its main object seems to be to correct the impression that he was blind to the horrors of Stalin's dictatorship. She lists instances she knew about (such as the case of Hermann Field and his relatives, see pp. 267–9) in which Bernal had protested at Soviet actions, or tried to intercede on behalf of people imprisoned or accused by the regime.

> From casual conversations with Sage from time to time I got the impression that he was deeply concerned with the processes in the Soviet Union reversing Stalin's terror, releasing prisoners . . . The one occasion on which he certainly protested . . . was over Hungary [the invasion of Hungary by Soviet troops in 1956]. He spoke at a protest meeting in London and then went on to the Soviet Embassy where he met Harry Pollitt [General Secretary of

the British Communist Party and a friend of Bernal's] who upbraided him. This was the occasion . . . when he wept . . . Hungary seemed so awful. He had thought that the new Soviet leadership – Khruschev – would act differently. Yet he could see their dilemma. And oddly enough, Hungary . . . has in the end done rather well in creating a liberal socialist state.[11]

Sorrow at the passing of her friends was compounded for Dorothy by concern at the condition of her husband. Thomas's health, precarious at the best of times, had taken a serious turn for the worse. For much of his life a heavy smoker, he found that his lungs had become so bad that he could not climb a flight of stairs, or walk any distance at all. Catching a cold made him seriously ill; he nearly died in Bangalore in 1979 (see Chapter 9). He became increasingly dependent on Dorothy, for care, for company, for conversation. For a brief period the two of them lived in the Master's Lodgings in Balliol College, where Thomas received daily physiotherapy, because he could not manage the stairs to the third-floor flat at 20 Bradmore Road. Most of the time they lived at Crab Mill, where Thomas's mother lived in a house just up the road until well into her nineties – she died in 1979. Ill as he was, Dorothy was happy to be able to spend more time with Thomas. For his part, being at home meant that he could field Dorothy's correspondence for her when she was away, and take any necessary action. He still had projects of his own to work on: the book on the history of Vietnam that he had begun after their visits to Hanoi during the war, and which he completed by the autumn of 1979; and his verse autobiography _Don Tomás_, planned to cover his life in twelve cantos in the style of Byron's _Don Juan_.

Winters were the worst times for Thomas, and whenever possible Dorothy took him abroad, to Greece or India for example, to avoid the damp and cold of Oxford. In December 1981 they left for a long visit to the Sudan. For three months they lived in Khartoum North with Sulafa Khaled Musa, a great friend of Elizabeth's and grand-daughter of Babikr Bedri and her husband Ahmed Bedri. Then they moved to Omdurman, to stay with Babikr Bedri's son Yusuf. Thomas spent much of the time laid up in bed. Dorothy took the opportunity to seek out people who

had known her parents, making careful notes for the autobiography she had begun to think of writing. In the warm, dry air,
Thomas seemed to improve a little.

In March they took a slow route home, stopping for a while at
the little town of Tolon in Greece, where Thomas had enjoyed a
holiday the year before. Elizabeth and her partner Peter Carter
joined them there, and 'for a time all seemed well and very
happy'. But after one expedition he suddenly seemed very tired;
and three days later, on 25 March, he collapsed and died from
heart failure in the small hotel where they were staying.

Dorothy arranged for Thomas to be buried there and then, in the
village churchyard on a hillside overlooking the sea with mountains behind. It was his own wish to be buried where he fell, first
outlined in a cheerful letter from Dakar in 1959, perhaps repeated
later as his health declined while he continued as peripatetic as
ever.

> I should like, I think, a too old-fashioned Christian burial,
> with a few jolly revolutionary hymns – like 'He Who
> Would Valiant Be' (the original version 'Hobgoblins and
> foul fiends' and all that – oh, and 'O Quanto Qualia' of
> course too!) and any others that people can think of –
> primarily because cremation has always seemed to me
> extremely depressing – and I am not scientifically minded
> enough to wish to give myself to a hospital (I'm afraid) –
> Also I would like there to be a pleasant small party
> afterwards with some rather good burgundy or claret –
> Nuits St Georges (chateau-bottled for preference)
> perhaps? – plenty of it – the kind of party that people
> would really enjoy.
> On the other hand, if I were to die in some remote place,
> I would like to be buried as near as possible where I was –
> this bringing of corpses back home always seems a
> frightful fuss. But you could have the party just the same! I
> may say, I am only sticking these ideas down while I think
> of it – after a good lunch – since it seems as well to put
> them down some time – I have no intentions of doing
> anything rash this time – and every intention, *in sha' allah*,

of being back on our wedding day – But you could file this
somewhere for future reference . . .[12]

Dorothy missed Thomas terribly, so much so that she changed
visibly in physical appearance. The radiance dimmed; her face
and body lost the motherly curves of middle age, the smiles came
less readily. Guy Dodson began to think she must be physically
ill, perhaps with cancer. Diffidently he asked if anything was
wrong. 'She knew what was in my mind at once – it was really
disconcerting how she could read your thoughts. "No, Guy," she
said, "it's just grief"'.[13]

Her grief was not lessened by the knowledge that for some
years she had enjoyed only a partial share in Thomas's affections.
Thomas's brother Edward arranged for the three completed
cantos of *Don Tomás* to be printed and privately circulated by
subscription, as Thomas had wished. And it was not until then
that some of Dorothy and Thomas's closest friends learned the
full extent of Dorothy's self-denial. Thomas dedicated the book
not to Dorothy but to Maire Gaster (née Lynd), 'Beatrice to his
Dante', as Edward Hodgkin put it in his introduction.[14] Known to
all as BJ (a contraction of her childhood pet name, 'Baby Junior'),
Maire Lynd had been Thomas's first great love. They became
engaged when he was an undergraduate, only twenty years old;
Thomas had suffered when she broke the engagement. From the
time of their marriage Dorothy knew of this past history, writing
a few months afterwards to say that she was 'strangely pleased'
to hear that in his dreams she had been 'mixed in there with B. J.'

Lynd married Jack Gaster, a fellow-Communist, and had children of her own. But she and Thomas stayed in touch. During the
early 1960s she came out to Ghana, where her daughter was
working as a governess to friends of the Hodgkins, and at about
this time she and Thomas rekindled their affair. On his return to
Britain, Thomas would make weekly visits to London to be with
BJ, and for a week each year they would go away together for a
holiday. He made no attempt at concealment. Dorothy was disapproving, but did not appeal to him to respect her feelings in the
matter – she said she thought the time he spent with BJ was distracting him from his work. But it was at just this time that she
began to take up opportunities to travel away from home, and to

throw herself into the work of national and international organizations. Elizabeth thinks that the two developments were not unconnected. 'I've always felt it was a strong factor in her giving up so much time to these engagements – it was so to speak to validate her life as her internal life became less satisfactory.'[15]

During the early 1970s Thomas considered leaving Dorothy altogether for BJ, but, unsurprisingly, found no support at all among his relatives for this idea. For her part, BJ did not want to leave her husband. Such a move, had it happened, would have greatly shocked the many friends who saw Thomas and Dorothy as a model couple. In his verse autobiography Thomas summed up a long digression on the nature of marriage with a description of his own compromise:

> *Preferring one fixed and enduring passion,*
> *Not living though exactly in that fashion.*

As Thomas became older and iller, Dorothy came to accept that it might be helpful to have someone to look after him when she was away, and BJ openly stayed with Thomas in Ilmington on these occasions. He continued to see her until the end of his life; Elizabeth remembers him phoning BJ from Greece a week before he died, looking forward to seeing her again at Crab Mill.

Dorothy never talked about how she felt at this development. Even Elizabeth, to whom she was very close, could not draw her out on the subject.

> Dorothy was not one to bare her heart; she was difficult to talk to about personal things. I remember her asking me what I thought of it, but the normal discomfort about talking of close personal things with Dorothy became worse.[16]

Yet the family view is that neither Thomas nor Dorothy saw his feelings for BJ as a betrayal. Their relationship had always allowed for the possibility of love outside marriage, and Thomas had certainly had other, briefer affairs. Late in his life, Thomas himself suggested to Elizabeth that perhaps, in the end, forty years of shared life were more important than anything else.

Dorothy's love for Thomas was undiminished, as Thomas himself recognized. The only mention of her name in the unfinished poem, anticipating a later canto that was to deal with his marriage, comes in the lines:

> *Wedding my dearest Dorothy, who sticks*
> *To me still, maugre science, sins, scrapes, snores –*

More than a year after Thomas died, Dorothy was invited to the Woman of the Year lunch in London. Guests were asked to speak on the theme 'A Woman's Best Friend'. Others may have seen it as an opportunity for frivolity; Dorothy just stood up and talked about Thomas.

In the years that followed, Dorothy often confessed to a terrible loneliness, especially when writing to friends who had been similarly bereaved. Her family were a great solace. Luke was a lecturer in mathematics at King's College London; during the 1960s he and Anna had separated, and in 1970 he had married Jean Radford. They adopted a daughter, Emily, and some years later a son, James, to add to the three grand-children by his first marriage, Dominic, Kathy and Mick. Toby, working for an international crop research organization in Rome, also parted from Judi, mother of his sons Simon and Dan; with his second wife Fay he had two daughters, Rebecca and Sarah. Dorothy took great delight in her grandchildren – and in time her great-grandchildren – and it was a family in which the generations seemed to mix easily. Just as in her laboratory everyone had called her Dorothy, children and grandchildren alike all used her childhood nickname, Dossie.

It was to Elizabeth that she most often turned. Elizabeth had been most influenced by Thomas and most closely shared his interests. When Thomas died Elizabeth had been working on a PhD (on Timbuktu and the Niger Bend in the seventeenth century), and for the next few years was able to spend time at home and help Dorothy with her still busy life. After gaining her doctorate she obtained a research post at London's School of Oriental and African Studies, which kept her away from Crab Mill during the week. And in 1989 she joined Amnesty International, working at first for the release of political prisoners in Morocco. This took her abroad regularly, and again kept her in London during the week. Dorothy would have like to see more of her, but was proud of her daughter's work, continuing the family tradition of trying to change the world. She eagerly awaited her daughter's returns home on Friday evenings, refusing to sit down to dinner until she had arrived whatever the hour.

For several more years Dorothy kept up a punishing schedule of international travel and conferences, trips to York to work with the Dodsons on insulin, and work in her Oxford office. In the course of 1987, for example, she went to the United States, Canada (twice), Austria, Romania, Poland, Greece and Russia. The following year the tally of foreign cities included Paris, Geneva, Prague, Birmingham Alabama, Trieste, Philadelphia, Montreal, Ottawa, Vienna, Lindau, Moscow and Tbilisi. But her own health was failing. Her arthritis had steadily worsened during the previous two decades, and although she never complained, those close to her knew she was often in pain. On the last few trips, she had always taken a family member along to help – Elizabeth, or more often one of her older grandchildren, by then at university themselves. Walking was slow and painful, and she found it more convenient to use a wheelchair to move between rooms at conferences, or to travel the corridors at airports.

Elizabeth decided that it was time her mother gave herself a rest. She began to persuade her to turn down at least some of her many invitations. Dorothy was not unwilling to agree (although in her letters of refusal she found it useful to blame her daughter), because she had one major project she wanted to finish: an account of her own life, commissioned by the Alfred P. Sloan Foundation for a series of scientific autobiographies. It was to feature chapters centring on each of the geographical locations that had been important in her life, beginning with Egypt and the Sudan and moving through Palestine, Oxford, Cambridge, the United States, Russia, China, Africa, India and Vietnam. Part of her reason for doing it was a recognition that there would be a demand for an account of her life story – she was asked to tell it increasingly frequently to interviewers. At the same time she found herself dissatisfied with other 'attempts on her life', as she called them.

The most substantial of these began ten years earlier, a

projected full-length biography by Frank Pagan. Pagan was a
childhood acquaintance and classmate, a son of the Beccles family
with whom the Crowfoot girls had lodged when their parents
were abroad. He had made a career in publishing, and after his
retirement wrote to ask Dorothy if he might take on the task of
recording her life. Her reply, in 1978, was hesitant.

> Thank you for your letter which I have been thinking over
> a little slowly.
>   Thomas's view is that no one should attempt to write the
> life of a living person and I have some sympathy with this,
> but also some differences. It does seem to me that unless
> between us we record something of the events in which we
> took part over the years no one may ever know about them,
> and I don't see either Thomas or myself settling down to
> write autobiographies . . . My feeling is that if you liked it
> might be possible to have a series of conversations out of
> which a kind of narrative account could grow, not one out
> of which any serious evaluation of life and achievements
> would be made – but I am not sure that such a project
> would be sufficiently interesting to you . . .[17]

The project did go ahead, and for the next two years Pagan assid-
uously collected material and began a draft. But Dorothy found it
difficult to be enthusiastic about his efforts, confessing to Betty
Murray her anxiety that 'he doesn't seem to me to care enough
about accuracy'. After his draft reached about 1939, she told him
that perhaps the rest should wait until she herself had written up
her own recollections.

She did not begin her own manuscript in earnest until 1987.
From that time on, when asked to lecture she usually offered
talks on her 'life in science'. Sadly the work also remained
unfinished: somehow there was never enough time. The early
chapters, painstakingly drafted by hand on (unnumbered!) loose
sheets of paper, tell the stories she found herself repeating time
after time to interviewers wanting to know about the origins of
her success. These have been reproduced in Volume III of her
Collected Works.[18] The later ones, just a few pages each dictated for
transcription, are more fragmentary; the planned sections on

India and Vietnam were never written at all. Throughout what remains, the style of storytelling is curiously childlike. On the one hand there is no introspection, no analysis of her own motives, very little description of her feelings; on the other, there is no recognition that the reader, perhaps not knowing anything of the people and events she mentions, might benefit from a little more background. These characteristics are not typical of Dorothy's writing, and simply betray the haste with which she was trying to finish the project before time ran out. In the numerous papers and lectures she wrote in earlier years on the history of her scientific work, she went to considerable trouble to place it in its scientific and historical context.

It was partly through the need to gain time to work on the book, and partly through recognition of her own increasing infirmity, that Dorothy finally decided to relinquish her remaining official responsibilities. In 1988 she gave her last speech to the graduating students of Bristol University, to be succeeded as Chancellor by the Governor of the Bank of England. Walking up to the podium in that heavy robe for the last time, she gave a simple address directed to the students (the graduands on this occasion included Guy and Eleanor Dodson's eldest son Richard). In it she expressed the hope that at least some of them might 'live modestly and do serious things'. At the same ceremony she derived enormous satisfaction from awarding honorary degrees to Moiseev Markov, the eighty-year-old Soviet Academician she had worked with on the Pugwash executive committee, and to Daphne Park, then Principal of Somerville.

The same year she resigned the Presidency of Pugwash in favour of Joseph Rotblat, who was two years older than she, but who, at the time of writing, still holds the post. She first proposed to step down as President of MSAVLK in 1987, but the indomitable Joan McMichael, herself four years older than Dorothy, persuaded her to withdraw her resignation. Two years later McMichael was dead, and Dorothy managed to resist the pleadings of her successor that she stay on for the sake of the morale of the organization.

Dorothy may have been withdrawing from public activity, but by this time moves had been made in a variety of quarters to ensure that she should not be forgotten. When Somerville College planned a range of new buildings to provide accommodation suitable for the vacation conference trade, it was immediately named the Dorothy Hodgkin Quadrangle. Containing within it a Margaret Thatcher Conference Centre, the development was opened in 1991 with both of the college's most illustrious graduates in attendance. In keeping with her iconic status, several organizations had commissioned portraits of her to be on permanent view. The first was the Royal Society. In the mid-1970s it occurred to Dorothy's old friend the organic chemist Sir John Cornforth that although the Royal Society had been electing female Fellows for thirty years, no portrait of one hung on its walls. To him, 'no better subject to remedy this deficiency could be imagined' than Dorothy.[19] Council raised no objection to the project as long as the funds came from elsewhere, and Cornforth circulated an appeal to members. The members responded so enthusiastically that the target was exceeded almost immediately.

The first artist commissioned was Graham Sutherland, whom Dorothy had met as he was a fellow-OM, and who had painted the Queen and Winston Churchill. Dorothy and Thomas spent a very pleasant few days with Sutherland at his country house in September 1979 while he took photographs and made a number of watercolour sketches. But the artist died that winter, and never completed the portrait. One of his watercolours now hangs in the Royal Society; another belongs to the Hodgkin family. The commission was then given to Bryan Organ, who painted a tranquil study of Dorothy sitting on a garden bench, apparently deep in conversation with someone unseen.

The third distinguished artist to take Dorothy as his subject on behalf of the Royal Society was the sculptor Henry Moore. Dorothy had met Moore soon after she returned from Cambridge as a young woman, when some of her Cambridge friends asked her to arrange a lunch in her rooms for an exhibition of young artists they were organizing. More recently, he had noted the gross deformation of Dorothy's hands when they met at a formal dinner – Moore was also an OM. Approached by Sir Rex Richards, founder of the Oxford Enzyme Group, Moore declined to produce a full portrait but agreed to draw Dorothy's hands for the Royal Society.

The best-known painting of Dorothy is the one by Maggi Hambling that hangs in the National Portrait Gallery. It shows her deeply absorbed in her work, at the cluttered table in the upstairs room at Crab Mill which she used as a study. To the delight of some viewers and the distress of others, she has four hands, two raised to hold a magnifying glass and consult a sheet of data, while the other two work on a structure diagram on the table below. She wears heavy-rimmed spectacles, and wisps of her hair rise unrestrained from her head. Models of insulin and Vitamin B_{12} are arranged in the foreground. Through the window you can see that the garden at Crab Mill is covered in snow.

Hambling completed the painting over five days which she spent at Crab Mill in early March 1985 with the Hodgkin family.

> I first went to meet Dorothy about three months before, and she received me very graciously. We walked around everywhere and she made it clear she would sit wherever I wanted her to. We went up to this room where she worked, with various of her models about, and I knew at once then that that's where I wanted to paint her. I knew that I wanted to make a painting about her and her work, as opposed to her sitting in a chair looking at me.[20]

She began work on a Monday morning, first making a charcoal drawing on paper 'to discover the composition', then moving to paint straight on canvas.

> I asked Dorothy to continue with her work as if I wasn't there. It was very important to me that she was sitting at her table with the light pouring through the window – I wanted to paint her as a kind of channel of the light, between the window and the model of insulin . . . At the end of that first Monday morning, at least three hands happened in the painting. Her hands were like busy little animals going through the papers, holding the pen, holding that magnifying glass . . . I think it does give a sense of someone entirely concentrated. I hope what comes out of it is her brain in action – something going on between the papers, her hands and her brain, and the stillness of the rest of it.[21]

They got on well together, Elizabeth remembers, because both liked a structured day. Dorothy would work while Hambling painted her in the mornings. After lunch Dorothy would rest while Hambling continued work on other parts of the picture, and they would meet for supper in the evening before retiring early for the night. Hambling noted Dorothy's intense engagement with everything that was going on around her – the progress of the snowdrops in the garden, news of people in the village, Elizabeth's daily activities – completely at odds with 'the corny image of the absent-minded professor'. She also watched her deal patiently and kindly with a very young and inexperienced local journalist, and calmly agree, in response to a telephone call one evening, to fly to Tokyo the following week on Pugwash business. It was these observations that led her to describe Dorothy as 'the closest person to a living, walking saint that I have ever met'.[22]

At Crab Mill Dorothy continued to deal with a substantial amount of correspondence, documented in the notebooks of her friend and secretary Irene Sabin. From 1987 until 1992 Sabin would come from her cottage next door and take dictation on Tuesday and Thursday mornings. She would type the letters while Dorothy rested in the afternoon, then return them for Dorothy to check and sign. The letters show that even when her travelling days were almost over, she still felt herself a participant in science and world affairs. She followed the succession of dramatic events of the late 1980s and early 1990s with close attention through television news broadcasts: someone she knew somewhere was almost bound to be affected. From some quarters the news was good. The ending of the Cold War filled her with an optimism about the prospects for nuclear disarmament that she had not felt in all her years as Pugwash President. She shared in the general rejoicing at the new freedoms in the former Iron Curtain countries, despite the evidence of the failure of the Communist experiment.

Elsewhere she had less reason for rejoicing. The violent repression by the Chinese government of pro-democracy demonstrations in Tian'anmen Square in 1989 caused her much anguish, as did the break-up of Yugoslavia, where she had made a number of scientific contacts. She wrote anxiously to Russian friends about the declining economic situation in their country. She took up the case of a former deputy science minister in Romania, Ion Ursu, whom she had met through Pugwash, now ill and imprisoned under the new regime; she wrote several letters both to Margaret Thatcher and the Romanian government on his behalf.

Foremost among her concerns was the conflict between Arab and Israeli in the Middle East. She had inherited a deep affection for the Arab world from her father. Both her trip to Jerash as a young woman and Thomas's espousal of the Palestinian cause influenced her strongly, and she made determined behind-the-scenes efforts to bring representatives of the two sides together under the Pugwash umbrella even after she was no longer President. She had contacts both at the Weizman Institute in Rehovot, where Gerhard Schmidt had been director until his early death from cancer, and at Birzeit University on the West Bank. She felt frustrated at the weakness of the Arab position, as she confessed to Thomas's brother Edward. 'I do wish I could think of something good for the Palestinians to do rather than throw stones and burn tyres. On the whole I have found the press and TV on Channel 4 usefully sympathetic.'[23]

Invited by President Mitterand of France to a conference of Nobel laureates in January 1988 on 'Facing the 21st Century – Threats and Promises', she tried strenuously to get the Arab–Israeli conflict on to the agenda. The meeting was organized and chaired by the Holocaust survivor, Zionist and winner of the Nobel Peace Prize, Elie Wiesel. He suggested that instead she might speak for some minutes on the subject during her closing address, and several participants ('including Henry Kissinger') asked her for copies of what she had said. She took as her text a verse from the *Rubáiyát of Omar Khayyám*, which in many ways encapsulates her own approach to world politics:

> *Ah love, could thou and I with fate conspire*
> *To grasp this sorry scheme of things entire*
> *Would we not shatter it to bits, and then*
> *Remould it nearer to the heart's desire?*

Despite this close engagement with world events, Dorothy confessed to her sister Diana that she was bored to be stuck out at

Crab Mill without regular contact with science and scientists. Not that she was ever left alone for long; she had many friends and neighbours in Ilmington who helped in practical ways, passed by for a chat and generally kept an eye on her. Christine Warmington and her mother Annie helped with cleaning and cooking; George Frost did the garden. Irene Sabin gradually added to her secretarial duties help with shopping and preparing meals. But none of these friends, valued as they were, could bring the sparkle back to her eyes in the way that her scientific friends did.

One of her most regular visitors was Judith Howard, today Professor of Crystallography at the University of Durham, who did her DPhil with Dorothy in the 1960s. Howard saw rather little of Dorothy as a student, partly because her supervisor was away such a lot, and partly because she herself worked with neutron diffraction rather than X-rays and so had to commute to the laboratories of the United Kingdom Atomic Energy Authority at Harwell, a few miles away from Oxford. But they became close when Howard moved to Bristol as a lecturer, and her lab provided Dorothy with a scientific bolt-hole when she had had enough of ceremonial and University politics. In 1990 the Department of Chemistry at Durham had a vacancy for a Professor of Crystallography, and Howard found that she was in the running.

> I told Dorothy that the Head of Department had said, 'Are you going to apply?' and I had said, 'No, I don't think I will.' It was a long way from home – 300 miles. And he said, 'Do you know any other women, because they're supposed to be good at that sort of thing aren't they?' Somewhat incensed, I told Dorothy this, but she said, 'Of course you must apply, don't let that sort of comment get in your way.'[24]

Howard applied and got the job. Thereafter she would travel regularly backwards and forwards from the country house she and her husband had bought near Bristol, a journey that took her past Ilmington. And she would always call to see Dorothy and bring her the latest scientific gossip.

Howard's was the principal hand behind the celebration

organized for Dorothy's eightieth birthday in May 1990, another chance for her to see her colleagues from all over the world. There was a conference and two dinners at Linacre College, arranged by Howard with help from Margaret Adams and the Dodsons. The Truebloods came from California, Jack Dunitz from Switzerland, Galina Tishchenko from Moscow; the then President of the International Union of Crystallography, Mario Nardelli, gave an after-dinner speech. The following day there was a party in the garden at Crab Mill. It was supposed to be for family members and neighbours, but in the end a substantial number of the scientists came too, together with representatives of Pugwash and the Vietnamese Ambassador. Professor Vasiliescu from Romania dubbed it the 'peasants' party', and declared it the highlight of the weekend. The celebration included the planting of three trees, cedar, birch and may, a gift from Pugwash. Dorothy insisted on being wheeled up the steep bank to the planting site, then getting out of her wheelchair so that she herself could plunge a spade into the earth.

That year, the International Congress of Crystallography was held in Bordeaux, in August. Dorothy had missed the previous meeting, which had been held in Australia in 1987, thinking it was too far to travel on top of the hectic schedule she already had that year. It was the first time since the organization's foundation that she had missed an International Congress. Bordeaux was so much closer to home that even though she had almost given up travelling, she thought it might be possible. Guy and Eleanor Dodson encouraged her, and it was settled that she should stay with them at their holiday house in nearby Bergerac. But, Eleanor remembers, they almost regretted it.

It was very hot, pushing 40, it was just awful. And Dorothy was just lapping it up . . . but after four days she was exhausted. They were having a banquet that night and she was desperate to go, but the organizer said she shouldn't; it was a buffet and would be a terrible crush. So we persuaded her to come back to Bergerac with us, where it was comfortable. The next day it was a wonderful rest day. Someone came to visit, and Guy overheard Dorothy saying to him, 'Guy thinks he's too tired to go in tomorrow, so I'm

going to miss such and such a session.' And we had just
rescued her from almost total exhaustion![25]

In November that year, a few days before she was due to leave for
Ireland to give a talk, Dorothy fell at Crab Mill and broke her hip.
She looked so frail when she came home from hospital that
Elizabeth feared she would not last until Christmas. In the new
year she made a slow recovery, although she now needed 24-
hour care; a professional nurse stayed with her during the week,
while Luke and Jean shared her nursing with Liz at weekends.
But despite the artificial hip she had received, she never walked
again, nor did she give another lecture. Her voice, always quiet,
had faded almost to a whisper. Invited to present the occasional
award, such as the Hodgkin Prize of the British Crystallographic
Association, none but the recipient could hear the few words she
offered, even with the assistance of a microphone. When she sat
in lectures she increasingly appeared to be, and often was, fast
asleep. To her friends it was wonderful that she continued to
make the effort; to those who knew her less well, such moments
could seem awkward and embarrassing.

The 1993 meeting of the International Union of Crystallography
was scheduled to take place in Beijing. (The British delegation to
an Extraordinary General Meeting late in 1989, led by Judith
Howard, had helped to defeat a move to shift the location as a
protest at Chinese actions in Tian'anmen Square. Dorothy was not
at the meeting, but her influence was apparent in the warm support of the British crystallographers for their Chinese colleagues.)
By this time Dorothy was extremely frail; it never entered
anyone's head that she would be able to go. But the previous
December, after watching a television programme that was critical of China, she suddenly told Elizabeth that she needed to
speak to Guy Dodson. Elizabeth put through the call to York, and
gave Dorothy the phone. 'Guy,' she said, 'I think I may have given
you the wrong impression, and you might think that I wasn't
intending to go to the International Union of Crystallography
Congress in September.'

This time hardly anyone supported her decision, but she was
so insistent that Elizabeth and the Dodsons went ahead with the
arrangements, not believing until the last minute that she would

really go. Her doctor refused to certify her fit to travel. The Royal Society, which was to put up some of the funds for the trip, asked the question in everyone's minds – 'What if she dies in China?' Tang Youqi and the rest of the Chinese were equally worried on this point, determined though they were to 'spare no effort to make her safe and happy'. Dorothy made it perfectly clear that she didn't mind at all if she died in China. Elizabeth noticed that as the date of the Congress drew nearer she grew more and more excited, seeming to feel a new burst of energy.

> One Monday morning I was just leaving for London, with twenty minutes to go before her nurse arrived, she said 'I think I'll just get dressed and surprise Jackie when she comes, I do it sometimes with my nurses' – which was totally untrue, she hadn't done it for years. I said 'You can't possibly do that, you can't even get out of bed.' And she said 'I think I could, I could move about crabwise holding on to the furniture.'[26]

Elizabeth stalled this particular enterprise by waking a weekend guest and getting him to sit with Dorothy until the nurse arrived. Even an attack of pleurisy three weeks before she was due to leave could not dampen her spirit. On the day of her departure Irene Sabin got her ready, dressing her in a Laura Ashley denim dress with a lace collar 'to make her look as young as possible'. She and George Frost saw her off sadly, convinced she would never survive the journey. Elizabeth and the Dodsons were all accompanying her to Beijing. Urging her to hold her head up as they wheeled her through the airport, they reached the plane without anyone questioning whether Dorothy was fit to travel. The first evening in China she was able to sit surrounded once again by her scientific friends, and despite the exhaustion of the journey she 'just perked up'. During the Congress she made Elizabeth take her to the more important lectures, especially those given by her close friends, and each evening she would 'whisper shrewd observations about them'. For most of the Congress participants, their joy at seeing her was mingled with sadness; she looked so frail, a mere shadow of her former self, and it was clear she had not long to live.

When she finally reached home, after a journey during which

Dorothy could not hide her pain and distress, Elizabeth and Irene Sabin undressed her and put her to bed. Calm at last, she lay back on the pillows, smiled beatifically and whispered, 'Thank you.'

In mid-July the following year, Dorothy fell and broke her hip again while at home at Crab Mill. She was taken to hospital, where her condition stabilized after two days, although she did not regain consciousness. Family and friends congregated at once: Elizabeth, Luke, Jean and their children from London, Toby and his family from Rome, the older grandchildren Dominic, Kathy, Mick, Simon and Dan, some of them from even further afield. They took turns to sit with Dorothy round the clock for the twelve days she remained in hospital. Friends visited too – the Dodsons, Judith Howard, a former student Sofia Candeloro de Sanctis from Rome, now also a professor. (Seeing Howard and Candeloro de Sanctis chatting quietly across Dorothy's bed, Toby asked, 'What is the collective noun for women professors of crystallography?')

Luke and Elizabeth decided to bring their mother home on Wednesday, 27 July, and the hospital supported their decision. On Thursday Dorothy's sister Diana arrived from Ottawa, and Joan came from Oxford. Through Thursday night, as Dorothy survived another crisis, the family kept their vigil, singing, reciting poems, and playing music. The following day, Friday, 29 July 1994, she died in her home with her family around her. She was buried with a simple ceremony at the local church in Ilmington.

In March the following year a service was held in Dorothy's memory at the University Church of St Mary the Virgin in Oxford. The church was packed to hear friends, former students and members of the family read from the Bible, from Shakespeare's sonnets and from Dorothy's first speech as President to the Pugwash Conference in 1976. The moving address given by Max Perutz on that occasion sums up perhaps better than anyone has ever done what made Dorothy so distinctive in her dealings with the world and the people in it.

> There was a magic about her person. She had no enemies, not even among those whose scientific theories she

demolished or whose political views she opposed. Just as her X-ray cameras bared the intrinsic beauty beneath the rough surface of things, so the warmth and gentleness of her approach to people uncovered in everyone, even the most hardened scientific crook, some hidden kernel of goodness. It was marvellous to have her drop in on you in your lab, like the Spring. Dorothy will be remembered as a great chemist, a saintly, tolerant and gentle lover of people and a devoted protagonist of peace.

Select bibliography

The following titles have provided essential background in the writing of this book.

Adams, P. (1996), *Somerville for Women*, Oxford University Press.

Dodson, G., Glusker, J., Ramaseshan, S. and Venkatesan, K. (1994), *The Collected Works of Dorothy Crowfoot Hodgkin*, vols I–III, Bangalore: Interline Publishing (referred to in the Notes as *The Collected Works*).

Dodson, G., Glusker, J. and Sayre, D. (1981) *Structural Studies on Molecules of Biological Interest*, Oxford: Oxford University Press (referred to in the Notes as Dodson et al.).

Ewald, P.P., ed (1966), *Fifty Years of X-Ray Diffraction*, Utrecht: A. Oosthoek.

Glusker, J. and Trueblood, K. (1985), *Crystal Structure Analysis: A Primer*, Oxford: Oxford University Press, 2nd edition.

Judson, H.F. (1979), *The Eighth Day of Creation*, London: Jonathan Cape; reprinted 1995 by Penguin Books.

Morrell, J. (1997) *Science at Oxford 1914–1939*, Oxford: Oxford University Press.

Werskey, G. (1988) *The Visible College: A Collective Biography of British Scientists and Socialists of the 1930s*, London: Free Association Press.

Original source material
The main source of original material on Dorothy Hodgkin's life is

the archive of her papers in Oxford's Bodleian Library (referred to in the notes as DMCH papers). This includes both the formal archive of her scientific and public activities, which is catalogued, and a collection of her private correspondence and other papers, which is not.

Extracts from Dorothy's unfinished autobiography (part of which is published in *The Collected Works*), and from her many letters to Thomas, are not given individual references in the text.

The letters home of the late Miss K. M. E. Murray provide lively first-hand, contemporary accounts of life at Somerville between 1928 and 1938. They remain in family hands. References to these in the notes are abbreviated to KMEM letters.

A copy of the manuscript of the unfinished biography of Dorothy Hodgkin by Francis Pagan is in the hands of the Hodgkin family. I have used it as a source of letters from Dorothy to her parents, the originals of which I have not been able to track down. It is abbreviated in the notes as Pagan ms.

Videotaped interviews with Dorothy Hodgkin were recorded by Professor Harry Bradford for the Archives of the Biochemical Society, and by Dr Max Blythe of the Oxford Centre for 20th Century Medical Biography at Oxford Brookes University for the Medical Sciences Video-archive of the Royal College of Physicians.

Abbreviations in the notes
DMC – Dorothy Mary Crowfoot
DMCH – Dorothy Mary Crowfoot Hodgkin
GMC – Grace Mary Crowfoot
JWC – John Winter Crowfoot
KMEM, Elisabeth Murray
TLH – Thomas Lionel Hodgkin

Notes

1 'It was a rather rackety childhood in a way: Cairo and Norfolk, 1910–1928
  1 Elisabeth Crowfoot, *Grace Mary Crowfoot, 1877–1957*, unpublished manuscript.
  2 G. M. Crowfoot (1926), 'Note on excavation in a Ligurian cave', *Man*, May issue.
  3 Unsent letter to Rev R. J. Campbell, among GMC papers, quoted in Pagan ms.
  4 John Crowfoot to Molly Hood, quoted in Pagan ms.
  5 Mary Crowfoot to Molly Hood, quoted in Pagan ms.
  6 Jimmy Collins to DMCH, DMCH papers.
  7 Katie Stevens to GMC, GMC papers, quoted in Pagan ms.
  8 Elisabeth Crowfoot, interview with the author.
  9 Pagan ms.
  10 KMEM letters.
  11 GMC to Crowfoot daughters, DMCH papers.
  12 Criss Gardner (née Deeley) to DMCH, DMCH papers.
  13 J. A. de C. Hamilton (1935), *Anglo-Egyptian Sudan from Within*, London: Faber and Faber.
  14 DMCH papers.
  15 JWC to Sir Lee Stack, Sudan Archive, quoted in Pagan ms.
  16 JWC to DMC, DMCH papers.
  17 Notes for a lecture, DMCH papers.
  18 JWC to DMC, DMCH papers.
  19 JWC to GMC, quoted in Pagan ms.
  20 Pagan ms.
  21 DMC to GMC, GMC papers, quoted in Pagan ms.
  22 DMCH papers.
  23 Transcript (translated from the French) of the 1925 League of Nations General Assembly.
  24 Bragg, W. H. (1925), *Concerning the Nature of Things*, London: G. Bell and Sons.
  25 Parsons, T. R. (1924), *Fundamentals of Biochemistry in Relation to Human Physiology*, 2nd edn, Cambridge: W. Heffer and Sons.

26 Sir John Leman School report, 1925, DMCH papers.
27 Norah Pusey to DMC, DMCH papers.
28 DMCH file, Somerville College Archives.

2 'Don't you understand, I've got to know!': Somerville and Oxford, 1928–1932

1 GMC to DMC, DMCH papers.
2 ibid.
3 GMC to Crowfoot girls, DMCH papers.
4 Crowfoot, J. W. (1931), *Churches at Jerash*, NewHaven: Yale University Press.
5 DMCH, video interview with Guy Dodson, Biochemical Society.
6 *Oxford Magazine*, 9 June 1927, p. 558.
7 Obituary of Jane Willis Kirkaldy, *Somerville College Report and Supplement*, 1931–2.
8 Merricks, L. (1996), *The World Made New: Frederick Soddy, Science Politics and Environment*, Oxford: Oxford University Press.
9 Adams, P. (1996), *Somerville for Women*, Oxford: Oxford University Press.
10 *Transactions of the Faraday Society* 1929, vol. 25, pp. 253–420.
11 DMC to GMC, quoted in Pagan ms.
12 M. Tomlinson, quoted in Williams, T. (1990), *Robert Robinson: Chemist Extraordinary*, Oxford: Oxford University Press, p. 94.
13 Bohr, N. (1913), 'On the constitution of atoms and molecules', *Philosophical Magazine*, vol. 26, p. 1.
14 DMCH papers.
15 DMC to Crowfoot parents, DMCH papers.
16 KMEM letters.
17 ibid.
18 ibid.
19 DMCH autobiography.
20 KMGM letters.
21 DMC to GMC, quoted in Pagan ms.
22 KMEM letters.
23 DMC to GMC, quoted in Pagan ms.
24 A. F. Joseph to DMC, DMCH papers.
25 DMC to GMC, quoted in Pagan ms.
26 KMEM letters.
27 ibid.
28 DMC to GMC, quoted in Pagan ms.
29 KMEM letters.
30 ibid.
31 ibid.
32 ibid.
33 ibid.
34 DMCH papers.
35 DMCH file, Somerville College Archives.
36 KMEM letters.
37 ibid.
38 DMC to GMC, quoted in Pagan ms.

39 F. Brewer to DMC, DMCH papers.
40 Powell, H. M. and Crowfoot, D. M. (1932), 'Layer-chain structures of thal-lium di-alkyl halides', *Nature*, vol. 130, pp. 131–2.
41 Powell, H. M. and Crowfoot, D. M. (1934), 'The crystal structures of dimethyl thallium halides', *Zeitschrift für Kristallographie*, vol. 87, pp. 370–78.
42 T. W. J. Taylor to J. D. Bernal, Bernal Archive.
43 T. W. J. Taylor to DMC, DMCH papers.
44 DMC to J. D. Bernal, Bernal Archive.

3   **'My years at Cambridge were rich with new discoveries': J. D. Bernal and Cambridge, 1932–1934**

1 Hodgkin, D. C. (1981), 'Microcosm: the world as seen by John Desmond Bernal', *Proceedings of the Royal Irish Academy*, vol. 81B, pp. 11–24; and DMCH papers.
2 N. Heatley, interview with the author.
3 Krebs, H. (1981), *Reminiscences and Reflections*, Oxford: Oxford University Press.
4 ibid.
5 Peter Wooster, interview with Eileen Bernal, copy in DMCH papers.
6 Arthur Lanham, interview with Eileen Bernal, copy in DMCH papers.
7 ibid.
8 H. Megaw, letter to the author.
9 Hodgkin, D. (1977), 'Structures of life', *Chemistry in Britain*, vol. 13, pp. 138–40.
10 Solicitor's letter, DMCH papers.
11 Gwen Koblenz, née Davies, quoted in Pagan ms.
12 See Blow, D. M. et al. (1997), 'Steroids, steroid binding proteins and hydrophobic binding sites', *Current Science*, vol. 72, pp. 477–82.
13 DMC to Crowfoot parents, quoted in Pagan ms.
14 Adams, P. (1996), *Somerville for Women*, Oxford: Oxford University Press.
15 DMC to Crowfoot parents, quoted in Pagan ms.
16 Bernal, J. D. and Crowfoot, D. M. (1934), 'X-ray photographs of crystalline pepsin', *Nature*, vol. 133, pp. 794–5.
17 J. D. Bernal, *Microcosm* (unpublished ms), quoted in Hodgkin, D. (1980), 'John Desmond Bernal', *Biographical Memoirs of the Fellows of the Royal Society*, vol. 26, p. 23.
18 Bernal, J. D. (1929), *The World, the Flesh and the Devil*, London: Routledge and Kegan Paul; reprinted 1970 by Jonathan Cape.
19 Werskey, G. (1988), *The Visible College*, London: Free Association Books.
20 DMC to Crowfoot parents, quoted in Pagan ms.
21 M. Fry to DMC, DMCH papers.
22 C. H. Waddington to DMC, DMCH papers.
23 ibid.
24 H. Megaw, letter to the author.

4   **'It'll serve me absolutely right if the thing is all wrong': Oxford, insulin and Thomas, 1934–1937**

1 Craig, B., in *Somerville College Report and Supplement 1994*, p. 48.

2 Interviews with Nesta Dean, Marjorie Harding, Mercy Heatley, Jean Medawar and others.
3 Transcript of seminar given by DMCH at Corpus Christi College on 3 March 1989 on 'Chemistry in Oxford 1928–1960', copy in DMCH papers.
4 DMCH autobiography.
5 See note 3.
6 ibid.
7 Dale, H. H. et al. (1926), *Lectures on Certain Aspects of Biochemistry*, London: University of London Press.
8 J. D. Bernal to DMC, DMCH papers.
9 DMC to J. D. Bernal, Bernal Archive.
10 H. Dale to DMC, DMCH papers.
11 DMC to J. D. Bernal, Bernal Archive.
12 Crowfoot, D. (1939), 'X-ray single crystal photographs of insulin', *Nature*, vol. 135, pp. 591–2.
13 R. Robinson to DMC, DMCH papers.
14 Recalled in her first speech as Chancellor of Bristol University in 1971, DMCH papers.
15 DMC to J. D. Bernal, Bernal Archive.
16 A. Beevers to DMC, DMCH papers.
17 DMC to GMC, DMCH papers.
18 Quoted by Barbara Craig from information received from K. M. E. Murray, in *Somerville College Report and Supplement 1994*.
19 Notes made by K. M. E. Murray of her memories of Dorothy.
20 See Werskey, G. (1988), *The Visible College*, London: Free Association Press.
21 DMC to JWC, quoted in Pagan ms.
22 DMC to J. D. Bernal, DMCH papers.
23 GMC to DMC, DMCH papers.
24 D. F. Hodgkin to DMC, DMCH papers.
25 DMC to J. D. Bernal, DMCH papers.
26 D. F. Hodgkin to DMC, DMCH papers.
27 DMC to GMC, quoted in Pagan ms.
28 DMC to Helen Darbishire, Somerville College Archive.
29 ibid.
30 DMCH papers; this may, as Dorothy's daughter Elizabeth thinks, have been a romantic reconstruction of events on Antonius's part.
31 Reproduced in Riley, D. (1981), 'Oxford: the early years', in Dodson et al.
32 Transcript of seminar given by DMCH at Corpus Christi College on 3 March 1989 on 'Chemistry in Oxford 1928–1960', copy in DMCH papers.
33 Riley, op. cit.
34 ibid.
35 DMC to TLH, DMCH papers.
36 DMC to J. D. Bernal, DMCH papers.
37 ibid.
38 ibid.
39 Adams, P. (1996) *Somerville for Women*, Oxford: Oxford University Press, p. 220.
40 B. Craig, *Somerville College Report and Supplement 1994*.

41 Pagan ms.
42 Notes made by K. M. E. Murray based on her letters home.

5 'Nobody could be indifferent to the search for the truth about proteins':
   Proteins and pregnancy, 1938–1939

 1 Hager, T. (1995), *Force of Nature: The Life of Linus Pauling*, New York: Simon and Schuster.
 2 For example see Abir-Am, P. (1987), 'Synergy or clash: disciplinary and marital strategies in the career of mathematical biologist Dorothy Wrinch', in Outram, D. and Abir-Am, P., *Uneasy Careers and Intimate Lives*, New Brunswick: Rutgers University Press.
 3 Hodgkin, D. (1976), Obituary of Dorothy Wrinch, *Nature*, vol. 260, p. 564.
 4 Abir-Am, P. (1987), 'The Biotheoretical Gathering', *History of Science*, vol. 25, pp. 1–71.
 5 K. Popper to DMCH, DMCH papers.
 6 See Kohler, R. (1991), *Partners in Science*, Chicago: University of Chicago Press.
 7 Wrinch, D. M. (1936), 'The Pattern of Proteins', *Nature*, vol. 137, p. 411.
 8 Letter from J. D. Bernal to D. Wrinch, Wrinch papers, Sophia Smith Collection, Smith College.
 9 Riley, D. (1981), 'Oxford: the early years', in Dodson et al.
10 DMC to D. Wrinch, Wrinch papers, Sophia Smith Collection, Smith College.
11 Crowfoot, D. (1938), 'The crystal structure of insulin I', *Proceedings of the Royal Society A*, vol. 164, pp. 580–602.
12 Hager, T. (1995), *Force of Nature: The Life of Linus Pauling*, New York: Simon and Schuster.
13 DMCH to TLH, DMCH papers.
14 DMCH to J. D. Bernal, DMCH papers.
15 Bernal, J. D. (1939), 'Vector maps and the cyclol hypothesis', *Nature*, vol. 143, p. 74.
16 Bragg, W. L. (1939), 'Patterson diagrams in crystal analysis', *Nature*, vol. 143, p. 73.
17 D. Wrinch to DMC, DMCH papers.
18 Pauling, L. and Niemann, C. (1939), 'The structure of proteins', *Journal of the American Chemical Society*, vol. 61, p. 1860.
19 DMCH to D. Wrinch, Wrinch papers, Sophia Smith Collection, Smith College.
20 ibid.
21 ibid..
22 D. Wrinch to DMCH, Wrinch papers, Sophia Smith Collection, Smith College.
23 Hodgkin, D. (1976), 'Obituary of Dorothy Wrinch', *Nature*, vol. 260, p. 564.
24 DMCH to Marjorie Seneschal, DMCH papers.
25 Adams, P. (1996), *Somerville for Women*, Oxford: Oxford University Press.
26 K. M. E. Murray to her parents, quoted in Pagan ms.
27 A. Beevers to DMC, DMCH papers.
28 GMC to DMCH, DMCH papers.
29 DMC to J. D. Bernal, DMCH papers.

30 Perutz, M., Address delivered at the memorial service for Dorothy Hodgkin in the University Church, Oxford, on 4 March 1995.

31 DMCH to J. D. Bernal, DMCH papers.

32 ibid.

33 Buckley, C. W. (1938), *Arthritis, Rheumatism and Gout*, London: H. K. Lewis and Co.

6 'All this penicillin racket you know': War and penicillin, 1939–1945

1 Bernal, J. D. (1939), *The Social Function of Science*, London: Routledge and Kegan Paul (reprinted 1967).

2 Hodgkin, D. (1980), John Desmond Bernal, *Biographical Memoirs of Fellows of the Royal Society*, vol. 26, pp. 17–84.

3 J. D. Bernal to Rockefeller Trustees, copy in DMCH papers.

4 Memo, Hodgkin file, Rockefeller Archive Center.

5 Bernal, J. D., Crowfoot, D. and Fankuchen, I. (1940), 'X-ray crystallography and the chemistry of the steroids', *Transactions of the Royal Society A*, vol. 239, pp. 135–82.

6 Carlisle, H. (1981), 'Dorothy and cholesteryl iodide', in Dodson et al.

7 ibid.

8 ibid.

9 C. H. Carlisle and D. Crowfoot (1945), 'The crystal structure of cholesteryl iodide', *Proceedings of the Royal Society A*, vol. 184, pp. 64–83.

10 Max Perutz, interview with the author.

11 Dunitz, J. (1994), 'Dorothy Crowfoot, an introduction to her work and personality', in *The Collected Works*.

12 Macfarlane, G. (1979), *Howard Florey: the Making of a Great Scientist*, Oxford: Oxford University Press.

13 W. Wardlaw to DMCH, DMCH papers.

14 B. W. Low, interview with the author.

15 B. W. Low to DMCH, DMCH papers.

16 Transcript of video interview with Edward Abraham, Biochemical Society Archive.

17 DMCH autobiography.

18 ibid.

19 E. Mellanby to DMCH, DMCH papers.

20 C. W. Bunn to DMCH, DMCH papers.

21 B. W. Low, interview with the author.

22 ibid.

23 ibid.

24 B. Low to DMCH, DMCH papers.

25 Hodgkin, D. C. (1972), 'Gerhard Schmidt's first researches in X-ray crystallography', *Israel Journal of Chemistry*, vol. 10, pp. 649–53.

26 Carlisle, H. (1981), in 'Dorothy and cholesteryl iodide', Dodson et al.

27 Crowfoot, D., Bunn, C., Rogers-Low, B. W., and Turner-Jones, A. (1949), 'The X-ray crystallographic investigation of the structure of penicillin', in Clarke, H. T., Johnson, J. R. and Robinson, R. (ed.) *The Chemistry of Penicillin*, Princeton: Princeton University Press, pp. 310–67.

28 C. Bunn to DMCH, DMCH papers.

29 ibid.
30 J. M. Robertson to DMC, DMCH papers.
31 B. Low, interview with the author.
32 DMCH papers.
33 W. Astbury to DMCH, DMCH papers.
34 Transcript in DMCH papers.
35 Letter from DMCH to Marjorie Seneschal, DMCH papers.
36 Letter in DMCH papers; extract quoted in Rose, H. (1994), *Love, Power and Knowledge*, Cambridge: Polity Press.
37 K. Lonsdale to J. D. Bernal, Bernal papers, Cambridge University Library.
38 Anon. (1945), 'Chemistry of penicillin', *Nature*, vol. 156, pp. 766–7.
39 C. Bunn to DMCH, DMCH papers.
40 Crowfoot et al. (1949), 'The X-ray crystallographic investigation of the structure of penicillin', in Clarke, Johnson and Robinson (ed.), op. cit., pp. 310–67.
41 Vincent, E. A. (1994) *Geology and Mineralogy at Oxford 1860–1986*, Oxford: Oxford University Press.
42 DMCH to J. D. Bernal, DMCH papers.
43 W. L. Bragg to Registrar, Oxford University Archives.
44 A. Beevers to DMCH, DMCH papers.
45 Morrell, J. (1997), *Science at Oxford 1914–1939*, Oxford: Oxford University Press.
46 Memorandum from H. M. Powell to the General Board of the Faculties, Oxford University Archives.
47 D. Veale to C. Hinshelwood, Oxford University Archives.
48 Flora Philpot, interview with the author.
49 ibid.
50 Hodgkin, D., certificate of election, Royal Society Archives.

7   'The molecule that appears is very beautifully composed': America, Russia and Vitamin B$_{12}$, 1946–1960

1 DMCH to Rockefeller Foundation, copy in DMCH papers.
2 G. Pomerat, diary entry, Rockefeller Archives.
3 G. Pomerat to DMCH, DMCH papers.
4 Draft autobiography, DMCH papers.
5 Medical form with Rockefeller Fellowship application, Rockefeller Archives.
6 DMCH to D. Wrinch, Sophia Smith Collection, Smith College.
7 Report to the Rockefeller Foundation, Rockefeller Archives.
8 *Somerville College Report and Supplement 1994*, p. 53.
9 Elizabeth Hodgkin, interview with the author.
10 ibid.
11 Maureen Mackay, interview with the author.
12 Dunitz, J. (1994), 'Dorothy Crowfoot Hodgkin – an introduction to her work and personality', in *The Collected Works*.
13 J. Cornforth, interview with the author.
14 J. Dunitz, interview with the author.
15 D. Sayre, interview with the author.
16 A. Sayre, interview with the author.
17 D. Sayre, interview with the author.

18 D. Sayre to DMCH, DMCH papers.
19 K. Lonsdale to DMCH, DMCH papers.
20 Oxford University Archives.
21 H. Lipson to DMCH, DMCH papers.
22 DMCH to J. Sheehan, copy in DMCH papers.
23 Rose, H. (1995) *Love, Power and Knowledge*, Cambridge: Polity Press.
24 DMCH to DSIR, copy in DMCH papers.
25 Lester Smith to DMCH, DMCH papers.
26 DMCH to Lester Smith, DMCH papers.
27 Draft autobiography, DMCH papers.
28 Lester Smith to DMCH, DMCH papers.
29 Owen, M. (1995), 'Janet Maria Vaughan', *Biographical Memoirs of Fellows of the Royal Society*, vol. 41, pp. 499–514.
30 White, J. G. (1981), 'The Princeton work on the structure of B_{12}', in Dodson et al.
31 DMCH to J. G. White, DMCH papers.
32 Richards, A. and Wolpert, L. (1988), *A Passion for Science*, Oxford: Oxford University Press.
33 J. H. Robertson, interview with the author.
34 D. Phillips, interview with the author.
35 Robertson, J. (1981), 'Memories of Dorothy Hodgkin and the B_{12} structure in 1951–54', in Dodson et al.
36 J. Glusker, interview with the author.
37 Glusker, J. (1981), 'Vitamin B_{12} – twenty-five years later', in Dodson et al.
38 G. Pomerat, diary entry 1954, Rockefeller Archives.
39 L. Smith to DMCH, DMCH papers.
40 Brink, C. et al. (1954), 'X-ray crystallographic evidence on the structure of Vitamin B_{12}', *Nature*, vol. 174, pp. 1169–71.
41 Trueblood, K. (1981), 'Structure analysis by post and cable', in Dodson et al.
42 Draft autobiography, DMCH papers.
43 Trueblood, K. (1981), 'Structure analysis by post and cable', in Dodson et al.
44 K. Trueblood, interview with the author.
45 Glusker, J. (1981), 'Vitamin B_{12} – twenty-five years later', in Dodson et al.
46 Trueblood, K.N. (1981), 'Structure analysis by post and cable', in ibid.
47 DMCH to J. White, DMCH papers.
48 J. White to DMCH, DMCH papers.
49 Hodgkin, D.C. et al (1955), 'The crystal structure of the hexacarboxylic acid derived from B_{12} and the molecular structure of the vitamin', *Nature*, vol. 176, pp. 325–8.
50 J. Glusker, interview with the author.
51 A. Todd to DMCH, DMCH papers.
52 DMCH to K. Trueblood, DMCH papers.
53 J. Glusker, interview with the author.
54 A. Todd to DMCH, DMCH papers.
55 Bragg, W. L. (1962), 'The growing power of X-ray analysis', in Ewald, P. P. (ed.) *Fifty Years of X-Ray Diffraction*, Utrecht: A. Oosthoek, p. 131.
56 L. Pauling to DMCH, DMCH papers.
57 Hager, T. (1995), *Force of Nature*, New York: Simon and Schuster.

58 Werskey, G. (1988), *The Visible College*, London: Free Association Press.
59 R. Wyckoff to DMCH, DMCH papers.
60 Werskey, G. (1988), *The Visible College*, London: Free Association Press.
61 Draft autobiography, DMCH papers.
62 ibid.
63 Werskey, op. cit.
64 Draft in DMCH papers.
65 National Archives and Records Administration, Bethesda, Maryland.
66 DMCH to B. Lipscomb, DMCH papers.
67 B. Lipscombe to US Consul-General, copy in DMCH papers.
68 Hager, op. cit.
69 Lord Dainton, interview with the author.
70 Sayre, A. (1975), *Rosalind Franklin and DNA*, New York: Norton.
71 Watson, J. D. (1968), *The Double Helix*, New York: Atheneum.
72 M. Perutz, interview with the author.
73 Kendrew, J. C. et al. (1958), 'A Three-Dimensional Model of the Myoglobin Molecule Obtained by X-Ray Analysis', *Nature*, vol. 181, pp. 662–6.
74 D. Sayre, interview with the author.
75 GMC to DMCH, DMCH papers.
76 ibid.
77 Elizabeth Hodgkin, interview with the author.
78 ibid.
79 McGrayne, S. (1993), *Nobel Prize Women in Science*, New York: Carol Publishing.
80 Elizabeth Hodgkin, interview with the author.
81 K. Lonsdale to DMCH, DMCH papers.
82 Craig, B., in *Somerville College Report and Supplement 1994*, p. 50.
83 Oxford University Archives.
84 ibid.
85 ibid.

8 'I seem to have spent much more of my life not solving structures than solving them': The Nobel prize and insulin, 1960–1969

1 GMC to DMCH, DMCH papers.
2 K. Trueblood to DMCH, DMCH papers.
3 DFH to DMCH, DMCH papers.
4 Papers of W. L. Bragg, Royal Institution.
5 Perutz, M. (1981), 'Forty years' friendship with Dorothy', in Dodson et al.
6 Draft autobiography, DMCH papers.
7 Bernal, J. D. (1964), 'Dorothy Hodgkin and the structure of natural compounds', *New Scientist*, 5 November.
8 R. Robinson to J. D. Bernal, Bernal papers, Cambridge University Library.
9 Hodgkin, D. (1965), 'The X-ray analysis of complicated molecules', *Les Prix Nobel*, pp. 157–78.
10 Draft of speech to students, DMCH papers.
11 DMCH to TLH, DMCH papers.
12 T. Blundell, interview with the author.
13 W. L. Bragg to DMCH, DMCH papers.

14 G. Pomerat, diary entry 1955, Rockefeller Archives.

15 D. C. Phillips to DMCH, DMCH papers.

16 ibid.

17 J. Kendrew to D. Phillips, Phillips papers, Bodleian Library, Oxford.

18 Lord Phillips, interview with the author.

19 J. Pringle to Sir F. Sandford, Oxford University Archives.

20 T. Blundell, interview with the author.

21 Lord Phillips, interview with the author.

22 M. Harding, interview with the author.

23 ibid.

24 ibid.

25 D. Cruickshank (1995), 'John Rollett and Chemical Crystallography', *BCA Crystallography News*, no. 53.

26 E. Dodson, interview with the author.

27 ibid.

28 ibid.

29 David Blow, interview with the author.

30 Eleanor Dodson, interview with the author.

31 Marjorie Harding, interview with the author.

32 Crowfoot, D. and Riley, D. (1939), 'X-ray measurements on wet insulin crystals', *Nature*, vol. 144, p. 1011.

33 G. Dodson, interview with the author.

34 ibid.

35 ibid.

36 M. Adams, interview with the author.

37 T. Blundell, interview with the author.

38 G. Dodson, interview with the author.

39 ibid.

40 DMCH to SRC, DMCH papers.

41 T. Blundell, interview with the author.

42 G. Dodson, interview with the author.

43 M. Vijayan, interview with the author.

44 Hodgkin, D. C. (1971), 'X-rays and the structure of insulin', *British Medical Journal*, vol. 4, pp. 447–51.

45 G. Dodson, interview with the author.

46 Perutz, M. (1981), 'Forty years friendship with Dorothy', in Dodson et al.

47 T. Blundell, interview with the author.

48 Adams, M. J. et al. (1969), 'The structure of rhombohedral 2-zinc insulin crystals', *Nature*, vol. 224, pp. 491–5).

49 S. Ramaseshan to DMCH, DMCH papers.

50 DMCH to Walter Sullivan, copy in DMCH papers.

51 G. Dodson, interview with the author.

52 T. Blundell, interview with the author.

53 ibid.

54 Blundell, T. et al. (1972), 'Insulin: The structure in the crystal and its reflection in chemistry and biology', *Advances in Protein Chemistry*, vol. 26, pp. 274–402.

55 T. Blundell, interview with the author.

56 Hodgkin, D. C. (1972), 'The structure of insulin', *Diabetes*, vol. 21, pp. 1131–50.
57 Blundell, T. et al. (1971), 'Atomic positions in rhombohedral 2-zinc insulin crystals', *Nature*, vol. 231, pp. 506–11.
58 Baker, E. et al. (1988), 'The structure of 2Zn pig insulin crystals at 1.5Å resolution', *Philosophical Transactions of the Royal Society of London B*, vol. 319, pp. 369–456.
59 G. Dodson, interview with the author.

9 **'Born not for herself but for the world': China, Africa, India, education and peace, 1959–1988**

1 Ceauşescu, E. (1983), Stereospecific Polymarisation of Isoprene, Oxford: Pergamon Press.
2 Herdan, I. (1996), *Liao Hongying – Fragments of a Life*, Dereham: Larks Press.
3 K. Lonsdale to DMCH, DMCH papers.
4 Tang, Y. Q. (1981), 'Personal recollections', in Dodson et al.
5 Tang, Y. Q., interview with the author.
6 D. Bryan, interview with the author.
7 ibid.
8 DMCH papers.
9 Tang, Y. Q., interview with the author.
10 Chinese Academy of Sciences to DMCH, DMCH papers.
11 Gu, X. C., interview with the author.
12 Liang, D. C., interview with the author.
13 Hodgkin, D. (1975), 'Chinese work on insulin', *Nature*, vol. 255, p. 103.
14 Gu, X. C., interview with the author.
15 Draft autobiography, DMCH papers.
16 ibid.
17 ibid.
18 K. Venkatesan, interview with the author.
19 ibid.
20 S. Ramaseshan, interview with the author.
21 ibid.
22 Viswamitra, interview with the author.
23 K. Venkatesan, interview with the author.
24 M. Vijayan, interview with the author.
25 S. Ramaseshan, interview with the author.
26 Ramaseshan, S. (1997), 'Dorothy Hodgkin', *Current Science*, vol. 72, pp. 423–6.
27 Ramaseshan, S. (1997), 'Dorothy Hodgkin and the Indian Connection', *Current Science*, vol. 72, pp. 457–63.
28 M.Vijayan, interview with the author.
29 E. Dodson, interview with the author.
30 M. Thatcher to DMCH, DMCH papers.
31 DMCH to K. Joseph, DMCH papers.
32 DMCH to M. Pentz, DMCH papers.
33 ibid.
34 J. Rotblat, interview with the author.

35 Hodgkin, D. (1989), 'Joan McMichael', *Guardian*, 7 August 1989.
36 Hodgkin, D. (1971), *The Times* Saturday Review, 20 March.
37 Hodgkin, T., notes for a lecture, DMCH papers.
38 ibid.
39 Hodgkin, D. (1972) *New York Times*, 7 January.
40 T. Blundell, interview with the author.
41 DMCH to M. Pentz, DMCH papers.
42 J. Rotblat, interview with the author.
43 DMCH to B. Feld, DMCH papers.
44 DMCH to M. Kaplan, DMCH papers.
45 DMCH to M. Pentz, DMCH papers.
46 R. Yalow to DMCH, DMCH papers.
47 D. Hodgkin and M. Kaplan, letter to the editor, *New York Times*, 28 September 1982.
48 D. Hodgkin to M. Thatcher, DMCH papers.
49 Baroness Thatcher, interview with the author.
50 B. Vainshtein to DMCH, DMCH papers.
51 Vainshtein, B. (1994), 'Meetings with Dorothy', in *Collected Works*, vol. 1, p. xviii.
52 Nobel Foundation.

10 'Recently everything has become more hopeful': Retirement and after, 1977–1994

1 McGrayne, S. (1993) *Nobel Prize Women in Science*, New York: Carol Publishing.
2 Dodson, G., Glusker, J. and Sayre, D. (1981), *Structural Studies on Molecules of Biological Interest*, Oxford: Oxford University Press.
3 Hodgkin, D. (1971), 'Dame Kathleen Lonsdale, FRS, 1903–1971', *Chemistry in Britain*, vol. 7, pp. 477–8.
4 Hodgkin, D. (1975), 'Kathleen Lonsdale', *Biographical Memoirs of Fellows of the Royal Society*, vol. 21, pp. 447–84.
5 ibid.
6 Bragg, W. L., Phillips, D. and Lipson, H. (1976), *The Development of X-Ray Analysis*, London: Bell.
7 Hodgkin, D. (1980), 'John Desmond Bernal 1901–1971', *Biographical Memoirs of Fellows of the Royal Society*, vol. 26, pp. 17–84.
8 Hodgkin, D. (1970), *Birkbeck, Science and History*, Birkbeck College, pp. 3–16.
9 ibid.
10 Goldsmith, M. (1980), *Sage: A life of J. D. Bernal*, London: Hutchinson.
11 DMCH to M. Perutz, draft in DMCH papers.
12 TLH to DMCH, DMCH papers.
13 G. Dodson, interview with the author.
14 Hodgkin, T. L. (1983), *Don Tomás*, privately printed.
15 Elizabeth Hodgkin, interview with the author.
16 ibid.
17 DMCH to F. Pagan, DMCH papers.
18 Dodson, G., Glusker, J., Ramaseshan, S. and Venkatesan, K. (1994), *The Collected Works of Dorothy Crowfoot Hodgkin*, Bangalore: Interline Publishing.

19 Cornforth, J. (1982), 'Portrait of Dorothy Hodgkin', OM, FRS, *Notes and Records of the Royal Society of London*, vol. 37, pp. 1–4.
20 M. Hambling, interview with the author.
21 ibid.
22 ibid.
23 D. Hodgkin to Edward Hodgkin, draft in Irene Sabin's notebooks.
24 J. Howard, interview with the author.
25 E. Dodson, interview with the author.
26 Elizabeth Hodgkin, interview with the author.

Index